MW01702938

PC Magazine®
Digital SLR Photography Solutions

PC Magazine® Digital SLR Photography Solutions

Sally Wiener Grotta and Daniel Grotta

Wiley Publishing, Inc.

PC Magazine® Digital SLR Photography Solutions

Published by
Wiley Publishing, Inc.
10475 Crosspoint Boulevard
Indianapolis, IN 46256
www.wiley.com

Published by Wiley Publishing, Inc., Indianapolis, Indiana
Published simultaneously in Canada

ISBN-13: 978-0-471-77320-7
ISBN-10: 0-471-77320-4

Manufactured in the United States of America

10 9 8 7 6 5 4 3 2 1

1K/RX/QU/QW/IN

Library of Congress Cataloging-in-Publication Data

Grotta, Sally Wiener, 1949-
PC magazine digital SLR photography solutions / Sally Wiener Grotta and Daniel Grotta.
p. cm.
Includes index.
ISBN-13: 978-0-471-77320-7 (paper/website)
ISBN-10: 0-471-77320-4 (paper/website)
1. Photography--Digital techniques. 2. Single-lens reflex cameras. I. Grotta, Daniel, 1944- II. Title.
TR267.G765 2006
775--dc22
2006003354

To Edith and Noel Wiener
Thank you for your loving support,
friendship, and ever-diligent red pencil

About the Authors

Professional photographers, as well as internationally recognized journalists and industry consultants, **Sally Wiener Grotta** and **Daniel Grotta** are known for their down-to-earth, easy-to understand approach to fun, creative photography, and image editing. They have used, tested, and/or reviewed most of the digital cameras (and related hardware and software) that have been introduced since the beginning of digital photography. However, regardless of how many cameras they have handled, the Grottas have never lost sight of the whole reason they started with all this—their fascination with how much more of the world they can see, enjoy, and capture through a camera lens. The Grottas have traveled all over the world on assignment and understand what it takes to get a great picture in all kinds of situations, from Antarctica to the Amazon rain forest, from war zones to the most difficult shot—the group family picture.

The Grottas are the authors of *PC Magazine Guide to Digital Photography* (Wiley Publishing, Inc., 2004), *Shooting for Dollars: Simple Photo Techniques for Greater eBay Profits* (Peachpit Press, 2005), and other books. They have written many hundreds of articles and reviews on digital photography, photo editing, and imaging for a wide variety of major magazines, including *PC Magazine*, where they have been contributors for more than 10 years. The Grottas are often interviewed on television and radio, and their lectures, seminars and e-seminars on digital photography and imaging are popular for the depth of their knowledge, their clarity of insight, and great accessibility. Daniel is the president and lead analyst of DigitalBenchmarks, widely recognized as a premier independent digital camera and imaging test lab. A former chapter president of the American Society of Media Photographers, Sally's photographs and digital images have appeared in various fine art exhibitions and many publications throughout the world.

Credits

EXECUTIVE EDITOR
Chris Webb

SENIOR DEVELOPMENT EDITOR
Kevin Kent

PRODUCTION EDITOR
Angela Smith

COPY EDITOR
Foxxe Editorial Services

EDITORIAL MANAGER
Mary Beth Wakefield

PRODUCTION MANAGER
Tim Tate

VICE PRESIDENT AND EXECUTIVE GROUP PUBLISHER
Richard Swadley

VICE PRESIDENT AND EXECUTIVE PUBLISHER
Joseph B. Wikert

PROJECT COORDINATOR
Kristie Rees

GRAPHICS AND PRODUCTION SPECIALISTS
Carrie A. Foster
Mary J. Gillot

QUALITY CONTROL TECHNICIAN
Charles Spencer

PROOFREADING AND INDEXING
Techbooks

Contents at a Glance

Contents

Acknowledgments

We have enjoyed writing this book, not only because it is one of our favorite subjects but also because it gave us an excuse to talk with and spend time with people whom we respect. Our thanks go to our fellow photographers and artists, who shared their insights and photographs, including Eric Brissaud, Peter Calvin, Joseph Cartright, Dan Clark, Helen Delillo, Bruce Dorn, Maura Dutra, Dr. Albert Edgar, Richard Ettinger, Kathryn LeSoine, Jay Maisel, Josh Marten, Lindsey Silverman, Philippe Tarbouriech, and Peter Treiber.

Thank you also to the numerous experts and manufacturers' representatives who were so helpful: Kate Aldinger, Nicole Andergard, Hilary Araujo, Michele Moninger Baker, Sasha Barausky, Pam Barnett, Justyna Bednarski, Shayne Bowman, Elizabeth Boukis, Michael Bourne, Richard Brill, Alicia Bucknam, Michael Bulbenko, Ned Bunnell, Charlé-John Caifiero, Melanie Carpena, Cyrille de la Chesnais, Gary Chesnutis, Matthew Chilton, Yee Choi, Jim Christensen, Tanya Chuang, Sally Smith Clemens, Geoff Coalter, Michael Conley, Kevin Connor, Michael Corrales, Christina Cu-Ito, Alex Curyea, Mark DeHaven, Lou Desiderio, Patricia Doherty, Anna Doi, Duke Doudna, Paul Ellis, Jane Fainer, Ed Fasano, Lucy Ferreira, Bonnie Fladung, Deborah Gallin, Bill Giordano, Jessica Gould, Leigh Grimm, Kenneth Hagihara, Dan Havlik, Scott Heath, Steven Blake Heiner, Catherine Hughes, John Jatinen, Amy Johnsonbaugh, Kyle Kappmeier, Monisha Khanna, John Knauer, Andy LaGuardia, Jason Ledder, Krista Lee, Brian Levey, Ryan Luckin, Chris MacAskill, Kathy Madison, Luc Marin, Andy Marken, Michelle Martin, Stephna May, Mike McCoy, Ray McGoldrick, Carla Meeker, Cheryl Meyers, Leonard Musmeci, Robert Ozankan, Alicia Pedroza, Yvonne Petro, Sara Pfaff, Liz Quinlisk, Nicole Ramirez, Steve Rosenbaum, Jan Rossee, Michael Rubin, Natalia Sandin, Joe Schorr, Gail Scibelli, Tony Severenuk, Nav Sihota, Jennifer Shanks, Greg Shore, Jon Sienkiewicz, Karen Skowronski, Patrick Smith, Perry Solomon, Andrew Staples, Michael Steavenson, Deborah Szajngarten, Michele Taylor, Karen Thomas, Steven Tiffin, Emmanuelle Trebuchet, Darren Vena, Saurabh Wahi, Betty Watkins, Chuck Westfall, Christine Wilhelmy, Mark Williford, Merrit Woodward, Ashley Wolf, Mike Wong, Josie Wrucke, Ken Yang, and Eric Zarakov.

Canon, FujiFilm, Konica Minolta, Nikon, Olympus, and Pentax loaned us cameras, lenses, and accessories and provided illustrations. All our photographs in this book were taken with their DSLRs.

The following companies generously provided hardware, software, accessories, illustrations, and/or information: Adobe Systems, ACD Systems, ADS Tech, Apple Computer, Bogen, Colorvision, Corel Corporation, DO Labs, Eastman Kodak, Delkin, Epson America, Extensis, Foveon, GretagMacbeth, Hahnemuhle USA, InferPoint, iView Multimedia, LaserSoft Imaging, LowePro, MFuel Direct, Micron Technology, Microsoft, NETGEAR, NTI, On One Software, Pantone, SanDisk, Smugmug, SnagIt, Targus, Tiffin, Wacom, and Zoran.

Models who are featured in photographs in this book include Tessa Barrett, Tiyee Champagne, Uju Christian, Todd d'Amour, Rowan Mercer, Kellie Sanchez, Heather Stuart, and Jeff Wills. And properties where we were made welcome with our cameras include Grower's Nursery (Newfoundland, Pennsylvania), Journey's End Farm (Sterling, Pennsylvania), The

French Manor (Newfoundland, Pennsylvania), The Northeast Theatre (Scranton, Pennsylvania), Pampered Pets (Canadensis, Pennsylvania), Roger and Stephanie Spots' home, The Sterling Inn (South Sterling, Pennsylvania), and Joyce Stone's home.

And, of course, we wish to express our gratitude to the folks at John Wiley & Sons, especially Kevin Kent and Chris Webb.

If we left anyone out, please forgive us. A book of this depth involves so many generous people, and we appreciate all of you.

Introduction

Back in the summer of 1991, while doing research for a book at the Maine Photographic Workshop, we passed by a beautifully restored brick building with a small but intriguing sign by its door. Kodak Center for Creative Imaging. CCI, as it quickly became known throughout the photographic industry, was Kodak's fledgling effort to evangelize the brand-new field of digital imaging. Although it wasn't scheduled to officially open for another week, we wandered in and were greeted by CCI assistant director Katrin Eismann, a recent Rochester Institute Technology graduate. She gave us a brief tour of the facility—lecture halls, camera studios, computer workstations, scanner room, exhibition print gallery—while explaining what digital imaging was and how it would shortly revolutionize photography.

We were later joined by Fred Shippey, a long-time Kodak engineer, who happened to have with him a prototype of Kodak's very first Digital Single Lens Reflex camera (DSLR), the $25,000 DCS-100. Short for Digital Camera System, the DCS-100 married an off-the-shelf Nikon F3 SLR body with Kodak's 1.3-megapixel digital back; the camera and back were tethered by cable to a 10-pound, shoulder-carried storage unit that held the power supply and a 200MB hard drive. While this huge, heavy, and cumbersome camera had no LCD viewer on its back, photographers could review their just-shot pictures on the storage unit's 4" black-and-white video screen. Quite candidly, image quality was awful—pictures were small and noisy, had a strong cyanic cast, and likely as not, blew out the highlights. But those significant shortcomings were overshadowed by the thrill of having the images available almost immediately. They could be instantly reviewed, quickly uploaded to a computer, edited with a new software program called Photoshop, and output in minutes on a microwave-sized Kodak color printer originally designed for use on nuclear submarines—all in less time than it took to process a roll of film.

Sally spent much of that weekend playing with the DCS-100, and later, we even took an intense one-week introductory course at CCI. (Kodak was very accommodating once they learned that we wrote a regular column for *Photo Pro* magazine and that we had an assignment to do a related cover story for *Popular Science*.) We became firm converts to digital photography and within the year wrote a groundbreaking best-selling book on the subject (*Digital Imaging for Visual Artists* published by McGraw-Hill). We even were appointed to the faculty of CCI, but alas, it closed for budgetary reasons before we had an opportunity to teach there.

Not long after, we owned the first practical professional DSLR, the $11,000 DCS-200. Kodak had managed to shrink the unit considerably by using the smaller Nikon N8008S body instead of the F3 body, getting rid of the separate storage unit and embedding a 60MB hard drive and rechargeable battery into the camera back. Image quality had improved, though resolution had inched up to only 1.5 megapixels. What's more, it had no LCD screen, so the only way Sally could review her pictures was to attach the camera to an Apple PowerBook. Nevertheless, Sally was the first professional photographer to shoot 100 percent digital at Comdex, which was then the world's largest computer trade show. When she managed to corral Microsoft cofounders Bill Gates and Paul Allen for a quick portrait, she mischievously asked Bill if she could take his picture without film. Not realizing what she held in her hands, Bill told her, that's okay; he would wait until she changed rolls. Paul Allen had to take Bill aside to explain that Sally was holding a digital camera. Sally got the shot, and Bill called her "the digital lady" whenever he saw her for some time afterwards. We still have that DCS-200, though it's been sitting unused in a drawer for years (where we also keep our old film Leicas, Nikons, and Hasselblads).

Not long after, Kodak unveiled its DCS-460, the first DSLR that pros could truly get excited about. It featured an off-the-shelf Nikon F4 body at the front end, and on the back end Kodak incorporated its revolutionary 6-megapixel CCD, which at the time was the highest-density image sensor in the world. What's more, the DCS-460 offered removable media in the form of a credit-card–sized memory storage device with the catchy name of a PCMCIA card. And despite its $25,000 price tag, the DCS-460 sold like hotcakes to pros who had been waiting for a digital camera that could begin to compete with film.

Although Kodak dominated professional digital photography for years, fielding at least a dozen different DCS models, camera manufacturers Nikon, Canon, Fuji, Olympus, and Minolta were all doing accelerated R&D on DSLRs and eventually introduced their own models. As Kodak's monopoly eroded, prices began falling, image quality and performance improved significantly, and all those features we have come to regard as essential—instant on, LCD screens, CompactFlash memory cards, FireWire or USB interfaces, RAW file formats—became standard. But DSLRs remained tantalizingly and elusively beyond the pocketbook of most serious photographers until Canon introduced the world's first sub-$1,000 DSLR, the Digital Rebel. In short order, Pentax, Olympus, Nikon, and other manufacturers released their own inexpensive, relatively easy-to-use DSLRs. Nowadays, you can buy a complete DSLR system for only hundreds of dollars, though more advanced pro units still run into the thousands.

Today's DSLRs handle better, shoot faster, and take far better pictures than DSLRs of only a few years ago. And although purists and traditionalists will still dispute the point, DSLRs can take as good as, or better, photographs as film-based SLRS. But they do require more knowledge and attention to details than using a consumer point-and-shoot digital camera. The purpose of this book is to help you, the photographer, to more quickly master using a DSLR.

Getting into the mindset of shooting digital requires learning new terms and techniques, as well as unlearning old habits. It won't be particularly difficult, because many of the same principles you used shooting your film-based SLR are the same with a DSLR. We'll cover those issues and details that will make your photographic experience more pleasant and productive, and—bottom line—assist you in producing high-quality images for personal pleasure or professional profit. So, read on, preferably with camera in hand. Try out the techniques and tips we suggest to see if they work for you. Take risks, try new things, and be ready to make mistakes. Only by doing can you truly learn how to get the most out of your camera, to transform it from an expensive techno-toy into a familiar friend capable of producing great photographs. Above all, have fun in your photography.

Sally Wiener Grotta and Daniel Grotta

PC Magazine®
Digital SLR Photography Solutions

Part

Assembling the Right Equipment

Chapter 1

Under the Hood of Your Digital SLR

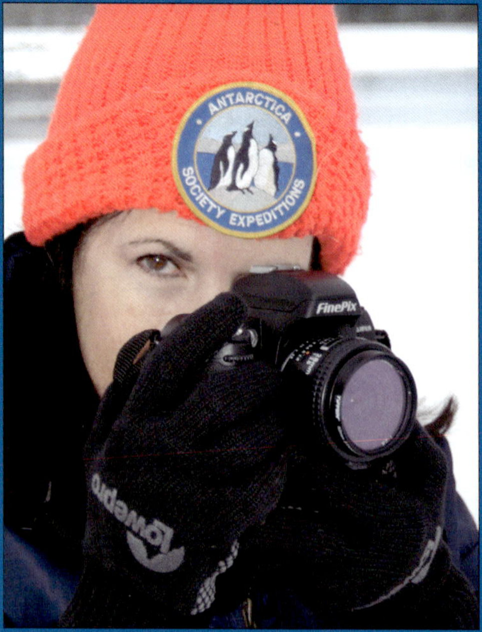

Sally using a Fujifilm S3Pro. (Photo taken with a Nikon D2x, with a 24-120mm lens set at 40mm, 1/100 at f4.2)

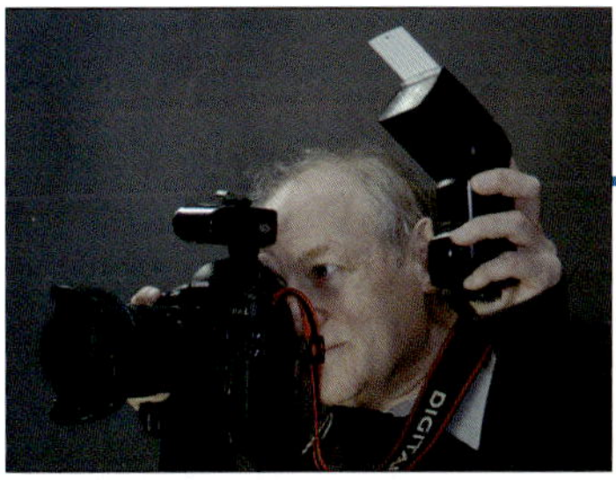

An infrared slave trigger on the camera body can wirelessly trigger the off-camera strobe. (Photo taken with a Nikon D2X, with a 24–120 lens set at 58mm, 1/30 at f5.)

Congratulations on your wisdom and good fortune in owning (or considering buying) the best type of digital camera on the market. Digital Single Lens Reflex cameras (DSLRs) are fast performers, permit the greatest degree of control and flexibility, and — bottom line — produce the highest image quality of all standalone digital cameras. You could even say that a DSLR is a digital camera on steroids. However, all this power comes at a cost — most DSLRs are complex devices that require a significantly higher degree of photographic knowledge and skill to operate properly than does your typical consumer digital camera.

This chapter:

- Describes what DSLRs are and how they differ from other types of digital cameras
- Explores the differences and distinctions among various kinds of image sensors
- Discusses how the size of your camera's image sensor affects your photography
- Explains how digital photographs are captured and created by DSLRs
- Provides guidance on selecting a DSLR that best fits your needs, shooting style, and budget

What, Exactly, Is a DSLR?

While we all recognize a Digital Single Lens Reflex camera as a digital camera with interchangeable lenses (see Figure 1-1), a DSLR also has the following basic attributes:

- An optical reflex viewing system that uses a mirror to direct light to the photographer's eye while focusing and framing, which swings out of the way to allow light to reach the shutter and image sensor during exposure
- A full range of exposure, color, and other adjustment tools that gives the photographer unparalleled choice and control over image capture
- A physically large CCD (charge-coupled device) or CMOS (complementary metal-oxide semiconductor) image sensor with larger and deeper pixel wells than most consumer digital cameras
- And, of course, a system that consists of individual components and accessories, the most important of which are true interchangeable lenses

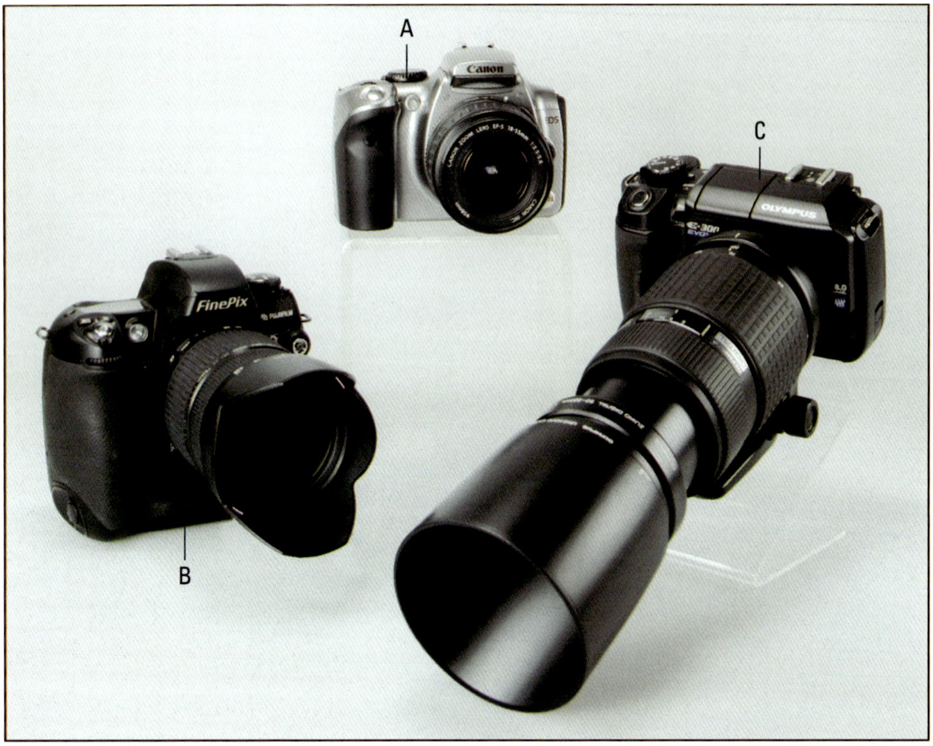

Figure 1-1: Whatever the model or manufacturer, DSLRs have certain things in common. The most obvious attribute is that they use interchangeable lenses. Pictured here are (A) the Canon EOS Digital Rebel, (B) the Fujifilm FinePix S3 Pro, and (C) the Olympus Evolt E-300. (Photograph taken with a Nikon D2X, 24–120mm lens set at 39mm, 1/10 at *f*10)

Reflex Viewing System

Every Single Lens Reflex camera (whether film or digital) has an ingenious combination of mechanical and optical components that allows the photographer to use an optical viewfinder to preview the subject through the same lens used to take the photograph. Called TTL (through-the-lens) viewing, this is a very different arrangement from the LCD screen display on most digital cameras or the eye-level electronic viewfinder in many advanced consumer and prosumer digital cameras. Why? Because an optical viewfinder is much brighter and sharper, is far more realistic, and transmits completely accurate colors directly to the photographer's eye. Not being electronic, it requires no battery power, there's no image smear or time delay, and you can view the subject anytime, even when the camera is switched off. Looking through a reflex viewing system is almost the same as glancing out a window, while looking through an LCD display or electronic viewfinder, no matter how large, is like staring at a television set. There's no comparison in quality.

DSLR-Types

One other category of cameras shares some, but not all, DSLR attributes: the so-called DSLR-type, or prosumer camera (see the sidebar figure). And that has caused some confusion in nomenclature.

Like a true DSLR, models such as Sony's Cyber-shot DSC-R1, Konica Minolta's DiMAGE A200, or Panasonic's DMC-FZ30, offer eye-level through-the-lens viewing, lots of controls and features, a more robust body, and usually, faster performance and better image quality than most consumer digital cameras. They even have something of the look and feel of true DSLRs.

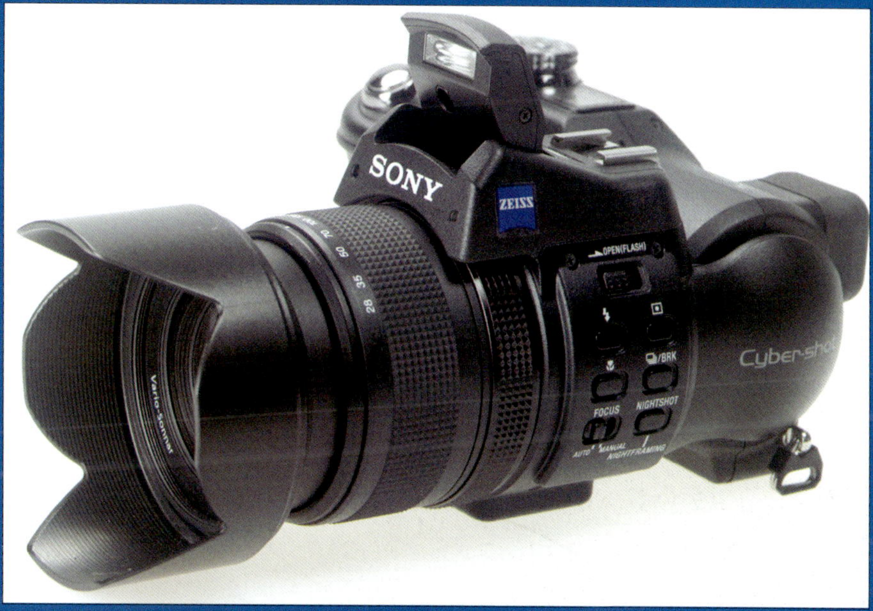

The Sony Cyber-shot F828 is a DSLR-type camera and not a true DSLR. The first hint is that you can't remove the lens from the body.

But under the hood, DSLR-type cameras are substantially different critters. You can easily recognize a DSLR-type by the following attributes:

- Unlike the true DSLR's lens interchangeability, all DSLR-types come equipped with a permanently attached, nonremovable zoom lens.
- Most, though not all, have significantly smaller image sensors than those found on true DSLRs.
- Performance and workflow aren't nearly as rapid.
- With a handful of exceptions, the eye-level viewfinder isn't an optical reflex system, like a true DSLR, but an EVF, or electronic viewfinder.

We'll explain later in this chapter why those differences make DSLRs superior to DSLR-types.

Continued

DSLR-Types *(continued)*

That's not to say that DSLR-types don't have their own attributes and appeal, especially for amateur photographers whose priorities include cost, convenience, and ease of use. DSLR-types are generally smaller, lighter, easier to operate, and less expensive than true DSLRs (if not the initial cost, then in savings for all the interchangeable lenses you won't be tempted to buy). Most also come equipped with extreme zoom lenses, and some even have built-in optical stabilization (anti-shake technology, for steadier telephoto shots or pictures taken at slower shutter speeds). And since the lens is attached, you have just the one unit — the camera — to carry around.

DSLR-types also provide a good range of controls, and if you understand how to use them, you'll get great photos. Most of the principles and suggestions we give for creative, efficient, and effective photography in this book also apply to DSLR-type cameras.

Most SLRs allow TTL viewing through the use of an optical mirror, tilted 45 degrees and positioned behind the lens, that directs the light from the lens onto a piece of ground glass or textured plastic, which is the same size and shape as the film frame or image sensor. (See Figure 1-2.) This allows the photographer to view the projected image exactly as it will register on the film or image sensor, including focus and depth of field. What makes this system work is that the mirror's position isn't fixed; it swings out of the way the instant the photographer presses the shutter button. Once the mirror flips out of the way, the light passing through the lens is directed at the image sensor or film plane. A mechanical shutter behind the mirror opens, the light exposes the image sensor or film, and the shutter closes. In most SLRs and all DSLRs, the mirror is spring-loaded, so it automatically drops down (or sideways in some cameras) after the shutter is closed, instantly restoring the through-the-lens view to the photographer.

All this happens, literally, faster than the blink of an eye.

Most SLRs/DSLRs incorporate a pentagon-shaped glass prism that sits on top of the ground glass or textured plastic, which allows the photographer to view the image at eye level rather than waist level. Also, because the through-the-lens view might be too dark for the photographer to see any detail when using a small *f*-stop (closing the diaphragm in the middle of the lens, to increase depth-of-field or to allow correct exposure in bright light), most modern SLR/DSLR lenses incorporate an automatic diaphragm that keeps the lens aperture at its largest (brightest) opening while viewing and focusing, instantly "stops" or closes down to the preselected aperture while taking the picture, and immediately springs back open after the exposure is finished. (See Chapter 5, regarding *f*-stops, aperture, and depth of field.)

Interchangeable Lenses and Other System Components

Every true DSLR features interchangeable lens capability. (See Figure 1-3.) In fact, many DSLRs are marketed and sold without a lens — you buy only the body and either purchase a lens separately or attach a compatible legacy lens you may already own. On the other hand, consumer or prosumer digital camera lenses are always permanently attached to the model you buy and cannot be changed, swapped, or removed. This great divide means that the DSLR gives photographers extensive choice over the type, speed, focal length, and other attributes of the optics they wish to use to take photographs.

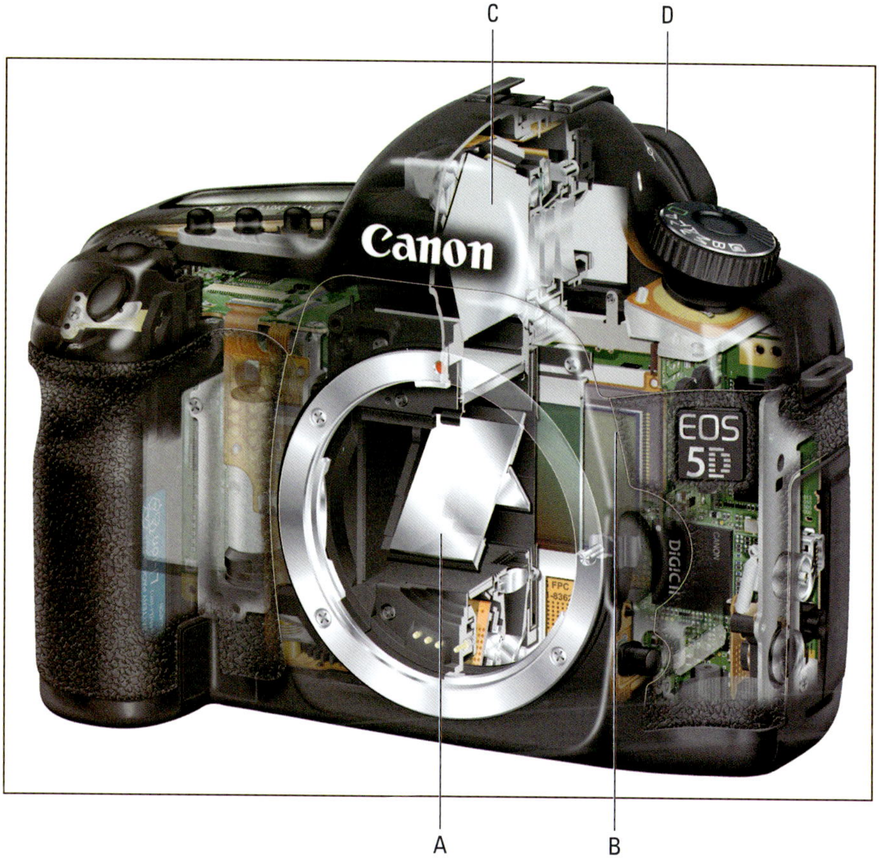

Figure 1-2: This cutaway illustration of the Canon EOS 5D shows (A) the mirror in front of (B) the image sensor. The mirror directs the light from the lens through (C) the pentaprism to (D) the optical viewfinder. (Illustration courtesy of Canon Corporation)

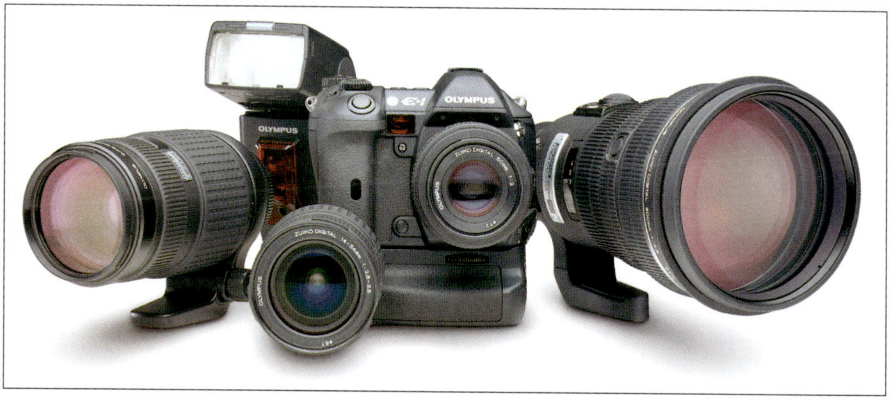

Figure 1-3: DSLRs are systems and not just cameras. You buy the body and then add lenses, strobes, and other accessories. (Photo courtesy of Olympus America)

Pentaprism or Porro-Mirror?

Most SLRs and DSLRs give the photographer an optical eye-level view by adding a pentaprism-shaped hunk of optical glass on top of the ground glass or textured plastic that displays the image reflected up from the mirror. (See Figure 1-2.) That's why most SLRs/DSLRs have that distinctive trapezoid-shaped peak on top of the camera. The purpose of a pentaprism is to use its internal reflection to right side up and reverse the image, so the view is the same as one would see with the naked eye. However, the downside to having a pentaprism is that it adds weight, size, and expense to every SLR and DSLR.

To help reduce size, weight, and cost, some manufacturers have gone back into yesteryear's technology to create a viable substitute for the pentaprism: a porro-mirror (see the sidebar figure). Instead of a single piece of glass, a porro-mirror is constructed of several fixed mirrors that bounce the light so that the image is righted for direct eye-level viewing, just like a pentaprism. Only, a porro-mirror is smaller, lighter, and less expensive to manufacture. And because it isn't shaped like a pentagon, the camera's profile can be smaller and flatter.

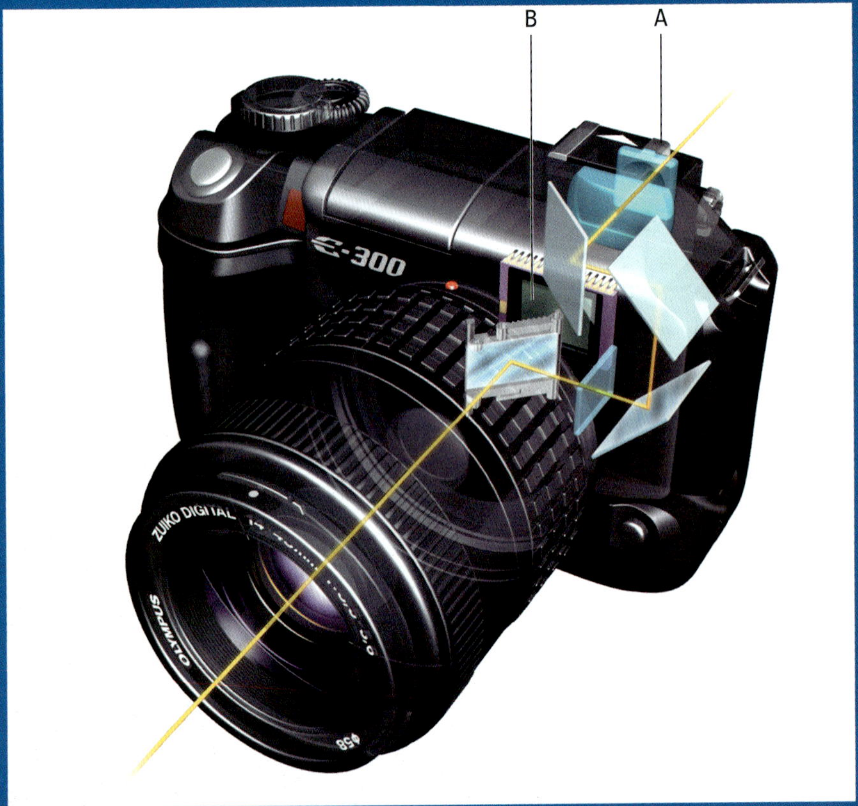

The Olympus Evolt E-300 uses the porro multiple mirror system to direct the light (indicated by the yellow line in this diagram) from the lens to (A) the optical viewfinder. When you press the shutter button, the primary mirror realigns to direct the light to (B) the image sensor. (Illustration courtesy of Olympus America)

Olympus, Nikon, and Canon have opted for porro-mirrors instead of pentaprisms on some of their DSLR models. While porro-mirrors can be potentially darker and visually less accurate, we've seen very little difference between the size and brightness of a pentaprism versus a porro-mirror system (for example, the Canon 20D as opposed to the Canon Digital Rebel XT), and in fact did not even realize that both the Nikon D70 and D70s used a porro-mirror (which Nikon called a Porroprism) system until we read the camera specs. While these Nikon and Canon DSLR models come equipped with porro-mirrors that sport the same familiar trapezoid-peaked shape as pentaprism-type DLSRs (an affectation rather than a necessity), the Olympus Evolt E-300 has a low, flat profile that many find more attractive, and certainly smaller, than traditional DSLRs.

Interchangeable lenses are a mixed blessing on digital cameras. On one hand, the ability to select and use a particular lens from among many available gives the photographer extensive creative control. What lens you use directly affects what your picture will look like. (See Chapter 2.) On the other hand, interchangeable lenses are an added expense, above and beyond the cost of the camera itself. A good lens can set you back as much (or even more) than your DSLR body. And if you want a range of lenses — zoom, fisheye, ultra-wide, high-speed normal, portrait, macro, medium telephoto, extreme-telephoto, digital-specific, perspective change, and so on — the cost can run into many thousands. What's more, you'll have to lug those extra lenses around with you in your camera bag.

But there's one other, more serious problem with interchangeable lenses that doesn't apply to consumer digital cameras: dust. Dust is one of your DSLR's worst enemies. Once dust is deposited onto your image sensor, it will diminish image quality and can be devilishly difficult to eliminate. Because the lens is removable, DSLRs are particularly vulnerable to dust, dirt, dandruff, hair, and other airborne particulates (not to mention rain and snow). True, there's some measure of protection in that a DSLR's mirror and the shutter are usually in the down and closed positions while you're changing lenses, keeping out most of the dust and dirt that could drift or blow into your camera body. However, dust can easily accumulate in that open space when you're changing lenses, so when you take pictures, thereby exposing the electrically charged image sensor, the dust trapped inside the body can be irresistibly drawn to it.

Tip

To try to minimize dust on your image sensor, protect your camera body and lens when changing lenses. Keep the lens mount of the camera body pointed downward. Don't remove the lens rear cap until you are ready to attach it to the camera. Try to stay out of the wind while changing lenses, and if that isn't possible, try to protect your camera and lens, by turning and putting your own body (or some other large object, such as a car or building) between the camera and the wind.

The Pellicle Mirror

Most, but not all, SLRs incorporate a movable optical mirror as part of their viewfinder system. That's because the movable mirror is the most practical means to enable through-the-lens viewing. However, movable mirrors are complex and prone to break down, add to construction cost, and are somewhat noisy. And even with the noise and vibration dampeners most camera manufacturers incorporate as part of their mirror reflex systems, the movable mirror introduces a small amount of vibration inside the camera that can, at least theoretically, negatively impact image sharpness and stability.

One solution is to completely do away with the movable mirror. This is accomplished by replacing the movable mirror with a special fixed mirror that simultaneously reflects light to the photographer's eye *and* passes it through to the film or image sensor. Technically, it's called a pellicle mirror, although it's more commonly known as a beamsplitter.

A pellicle mirror fixed at a 45-degree angle between the lens and the film plane/image sensor allows 90 percent of the light to pass straight through the mirror, while reflecting 10 percent up to the photographer's eye. That's usually enough light to enable the photographer to frame and focus the lens, as well as enough light to permit perfect exposure. Because the mirror is fixed, the camera is less expensive to build.

However, while pellicle mirrors work well in bright light, it becomes difficult to see through the lens in low light. No DSLR to date uses a pellicle mirror; however, they were incorporated in Olympus's groundbreaking Camedia E-10 and E-20 prosumer digital cameras (the immediate predecessors to Olympus's first true DSLR, the Camedia E-1). With the relentless pressure to reduce costs and develop workarounds, we may see its reintroduction in future generation DSLR models.

In addition to using interchangeable lenses, DSLRs are designed as camera *systems* that can be enhanced or augmented through add-ons, accessories, and other components. These include, but are not necessarily limited to:

- Electronic strobes
- Flash brackets
- Studio strobelights
- Filters and special effects glass
- Lens extenders and tubes
- Microscope and telescope adapters
- GPS receivers
- Interchangeable focus screens
- Hi-point sports or waist-level finders

- Rubber eyecups
- Wireless interfaces and remote shutter releases
- Auxiliary battery packs
- Underwater housings
- Gadget bags and cases

We cover accessories in Chapter 3 and strobes in Chapter 8.

Of course, many photographers shoot very successfully using only the bare bones basics: a camera body, a solitary lens, and perhaps the electronic flash that's built into over half the DSLR models on the market. Fact is, you don't really need anything other than a camera body and lens (plus a battery and memory card) to create or capture award-winning photographs. But system accessories can greatly expand the photographer's horizon and ability to produce pictures that are more dramatic or aesthetically interesting than those taken with only a standard lens and camera body.

Why DSLRs Are Superior to Consumer and Prosumer Digital Cameras

Now that we've described what a DSLR is, the obvious question that comes to mind for anyone considering investing anywhere from $500 to tens of thousands in a DSLR camera or system is "Why would I want a DSLR over other, less expensive types of digital cameras?" Right off the bat, here's a short list of unassailable advantages that DSLRs enjoy:

- Higher-quality images
- Faster operating speed
- Interchangeable lenses
- More accurate viewing and framing
- Better construction
- Greater versatility
- More creative control
- Longer battery life

We've already discussed the advantages and benefits of interchangeable lenses and more accurate viewing and framing, now we'll briefly touch upon the other points that give DSLRs inherent superiority over consumer and prosumer digital cameras.

Higher-Quality Images

All other things being equal (similar megapixel count, photographer's skill level, identical shooting conditions, same subject, etc.), DLSRs can produce higher-quality images than consumer and prosumer digital cameras. As we'll explain later in this chapter, DSLRs' larger image sensors and bigger, deeper photoreceptor sites (pixels) help create greater sensitivity to light, higher signal-to-noise ratios, more details in the highlights and shadows, fewer artifacts, sharper edges, and better colors. Also, DSLR lenses give photographers greater choice and control over depth-of-field (the area between the foreground and background that is in focus).

Faster Operating Speed

DSLRs are inherently faster than consumer and prosumer digital cameras, because DSLRs have the following:

- More memory buffering (temporary electronic storage for just-taken images until they can be processed)
- More and faster DSPs (digital signal processor chips, for helping sort and assemble the captured data ones into recognizable photographs)
- Image sensors whose design allows data to be moved much faster (technically called frame transfer, which is speedier and more efficient than most consumer digital cameras' inline data transfer)

The practical effect is that most state-of-the-art DSLRs are virtually instant-on devices (ready to shoot less than one second after you turn on the power), have no discernible shutter lag (that annoying shot-robbing hesitation on consumer digital cameras between the instant you press the shutter and when the camera actually takes the picture), allow for higher sustained rates of shooting (how many frames you can capture, process, and save within a certain number of seconds), and generally feature faster burst modes than available on most consumer digital cameras. Also, most DSLRs bristle with lots of analog (physical) controls on the body, for easy and rapid selecting and changing settings. Even the most common features in consumer digital cameras' controls are typically buried within the menu structure, which can be frustrating and time-consuming to find and activate. (DSLRs also have menus, which, depending on the model, tend to be for less frequently used commands and options.)

Better Construction

All DSLRs are larger and heavier devices, and being built upon a solid metal frame or chassis (usually aluminum or magnesium, but sometimes steel), they are designed to absorb shocks better than most consumer digital cameras. Most DSLRs come with molded battery grips and large surface areas covered by no-slip material, use better grade metals and plastics in construction, and have more care and attention devoted to assembly and quality control checks. Despite being more complicated instruments with more moving parts, DSLRs are generally better suited for a higher volume of use and abuse than consumer digital cameras.

However, there are major quality differences between inexpensive and more advanced DSLRs. Inexpensive models usually have a tough polycarbonate (high-impact plastic) exterior, and their lenses are not as heavy or well constructed. On the other hand, more expensive DSLRs are covered by metal, have environmental seals at exposed points to protect against dust and the weather, and their industrial strength shutters are rated for many thousands more clicks. Also, pro DSLR lenses are heavier and better built than entry-level DSLRs and come equipped with stronger mounts (the rings used to attach them to the camera body).

Greater Versatility

First, the bad news. Because a DSLR's image sensor is usually exposed only for a fraction of a second, when the mirror swings up and the shutter opens, DSLRs are missing two features that are offered on most consumer and prosumer cameras: video capture and real-time previewing on the LCD screen. (All DSLRs allow users to review the electronic image on their LCD displays within a second of being shot.)

Offsetting these two minor restrictions is a wealth of functions and features. These include (but are not necessarily limited to):

- RAW file format, in addition to JPEG and TIFF (see Chapter 4)
- A full range of exposure options (see Chapter 5)
- Total white balance (see Chapter 6)
- Versatile in-camera adjustments to image appearance (see Chapter 6)
- A wide range of ISO equivalencies to adjust the image sensor's light sensitivity (see Chapter 5)
- Different color models (see Chapters 6 and 11)
- Customizable default options, so the photographer can save and retrieve frequently used camera's settings (see Chapter 6)

Depending upon the specific model, DSLRs also may offer various special features, such as time lapse photography, built-in filters, audio annotation, wireless or wired remote control, internal anti-shake technology, ultrasonic image sensor cleaning, and so on.

More Creative Control

Creative control is the ability to precisely manage all the technical elements in a composition—exposure, perspective, lighting, focus, depth of field, tonality, and color. As we explain in Chapter 2, the choice of the lens focal length (size) will determine perspective, or whether the foreground and background are compressed and appear closer than they really are, or just the opposite effect. Also, the DSLR's larger focal length lenses permit much more latitude in using depth of field creatively (choosing what elements should be in sharp focus and what should be blurred). In addition to different focus modes, most DSLRs allow the photographer to select the point of focus in the viewfinder. (See Chapter 5 regarding depth of field and focus.) All DSLRs are enabled to sync (fire) with auxiliary strobelights or studio strobe setups, which provides more control over illumination. (See Chapter 8.) And the variety of other built-in controls gives the photographer a wide range of tools to use to express her own personal vision of the image.

Longer Battery Life

While consumer digital cameras image sensors are smaller and generally don't require as much electricity to operate, other components, such as the LCD screen and built-in flash, are heavy power drains. DSLR photographers don't use their camera's LCD display as much (because they use the optical viewfinder for framing and focus), nor are many inclined to fire their camera's built-in flash (for those DSLRs that come equipped with one), preferring instead to shoot with an auxiliary strobe having its own power supply. Plus, being bigger cameras, most DSLRs also come with larger-capacity rechargeable batteries and have various power-saving technologies. The upshot of all this is that most DSLRs give you hundreds more shots than consumer digital cameras. We've accidentally left various DSLR bodies in the On position overnight (without the automatic shutoff enabled) and still had enough power left for a day's heavy shooting. (But we don't recommend doing the same.)

Image Sensors

Most digital camera owners think of the photosensitive semiconductor image sensor chip at the heart of all digital cameras as infinitely reusable film. Actually, the two are quite different in how they work and what they do. While it's not really necessary to understand all the nitty-gritty technical details about image sensors, it's useful to become familiar with some of the basics, such as:

- The difference between CCDs and CMOS
- The importance of the physical size of the chip as well as the size, depth, and shape of each pixel
- Why image sensors fabricated for DSLRs are inherently better and faster than those inside most consumer digital cameras
- The comparative pros and cons of the various types of image sensors

Film

Let's first look at what film is and does, and then contrast it to a typical image sensor.

Film is composed of millions of tiny, irregularly shaped photosensitive silver halide crystals evenly coated onto a thin, flexible Mylar base that undergo an instant chemical reaction when and where they are struck by light passing through the camera's lens. Varying degrees of light striking the film affect the intensity of the chemical reaction. Where no light is present, the crystals remain unchanged. Later, the film is processed, using a series of chemical baths, to develop and fix (make permanent) the image that appears. Rather than being only pitch black or totally white, the image created reflects a continuous tone that may range from absolute black to complete white, but also to every shade in between (grey). If it is instant film (such as Polaroid makes for its cameras), a concentration of chemicals in a separate pack are broken open and evenly spread over exposed silver-halide-covered paper, developing and fixing the image simultaneously.

Generally, there are two different types of film: positive and negative. Positive film, also known as transparency film, is processed in such a way that the dark silver halide crystals are oxidized, or become dark, and the unexposed crystals are dissolved, letting light shine through the Mylar base. This allows the images to be viewed directly, either by holding the film up to any light source or displaying it through a projector. Negative film is just the opposite: when developed, the silver halide crystals struck by light are oxidized, or turn dark, and the unexposed crystals are dissolved, thereby reversing the light and shadows. The film is then projected through an enlarger onto photosensitive paper, where the image light and shadow are reversed once again, displaying a positive image.

Color film is a sophisticated extension of black-and-white film. Instead of one layer in which the silver halide crystals are oxidized or dissolved, there are at least three layers, each one sandwiched in between a layer of transparent red, green, and blue gelatin filters. As light passes through each filter layer onto the photosensitive layer, it absorbs the colors of the image that are identical or similar to the filter layer's color, that is, the red filter layer absorbs all the reds in the image, and none of the green and blue portions of the spectrum. (See Figure 1-4.) Then, depending upon the type color film (negative or transparency), the silver halide crystals are developed and replaced either by (negative) cyan, magenta, or yellow dye ("dye couplers"), or (transparency) red, blue, or green dye couplers. The gelatin filters dissolve during processing. When the three color layers are viewed together, they display all the colors of the visible spectrum. Of course, this is an oversimplification of a complex process—some color films have as many as 20 layers sandwiched together, and must pass through as many as a dozen different chemicals during processing.

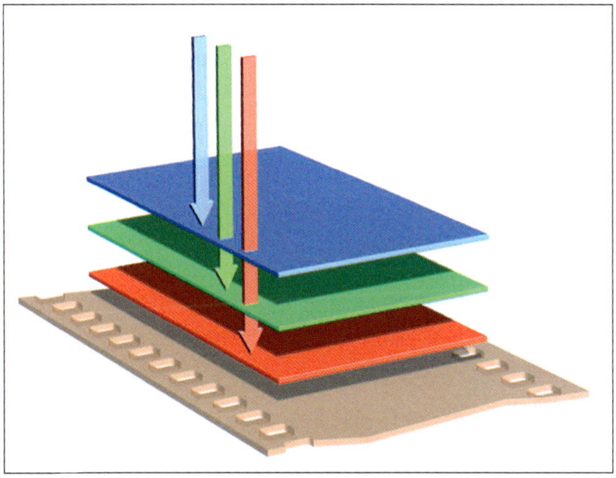

Figure 1-4: Color film uses layers of transparent color gelatin filters to register the type and amount of different color light passing through the lens. (Courtesy of Foveon)

Playing the Angles

There's one important difference between film and image sensors that can prove problematical with image sensors. Light can strike film from any angle and cause a chemical reaction. It really doesn't matter much if the light passing through the lens hits the film straight on (as it does in the middle) or at an oblique angle (as it does on the edges).

This isn't true with image sensors, however. Ideally, light should strike the image sensor's pixels straight on, not at oblique angles. Otherwise, image quality may suffer. Camera manufacturers are aware of this problem and have come up with a variety of workarounds and solutions to channel the light coming through the lens so that it hits the pixels straight on. (See Chapter 2.)

Image Sensors

An image sensor is an electronic semiconductor computer chip that has been treated so that it is photosensitive. Instead of film's use of millions of silver halide crystals, each of which produces a chemical reaction whenever and wherever light strikes it, an image sensor has millions of tiny etched, bucket-like photoreceptor sites — also called pixels (short for picture elements) or pixel wells. The pixels react electrically when struck by light (or photons), generating electrons. If there are enough electrons, an electrical charge is generated and passed on to an amplifier on the sensor. If there aren't enough photons (or light) to create electrons that pass on an electrical charge, the pixel is said to remain in a negative state, which will eventually represent a black point in the image. But if there are sufficient electrons generated, it will flip to a positive (or white) state. However, because the image sensor is an analog (not digital) device, it can also produce in between shades of grey.

Depending upon the type image sensor (described later in this chapter), the analog charge is converted to the zeroes and ones of binary data either in the image sensor itself or externally, using a companion semiconductor chip called an ADC (analog-to-digital converter). With binary, you are talking the digital language that every computer understands. And when you calculate and map the electrical state of all the millions of pixels spread over an entire image sensor, you end up with visual data that can be processed into a photograph.

Of course, this is an oversimplification of a complex process, but it pretty much describes what happens inside every digital camera image sensor. Creating color from what are essentially black-and-white pixels requires even more technological legerdemain. Most image sensors bond tiny, alternating red, blue, or green filters in front of each pixel so that only those colors with similar wavelengths pass through into each corresponding pixel well. The red, green, and blue filters resemble a checkerboard mosaic, but when all the visual data are processed and reassembled, the image will reflect all the colors of the spectrum.

Actually, the most commonly used checkerboard pattern of tiny red, green, and blue filters ("filter array") is known as a Bayer pattern, named after Kodak scientist Bryce Bayer who was head of the inventing team. Initially developed in the mid-1970s for the space program, the

Bayer pattern image sensor has found its way into the overwhelming majority of digital cameras. Interestingly, the Bayer pattern image sensor is not a symmetrical checkerboard of an equal number of red, green, and blue pixels. Rather, the number of green pixels is doubled, because the human eye sees green as sharpness. (See Figure 1-5.)

To help focus light into each pixel, microscopic lenses, or microlenses, are placed over each and every pixel. This helps reduce or eliminate technical problems, such as aliasing and blooming, which can occur when light doesn't strike each pixel head on.

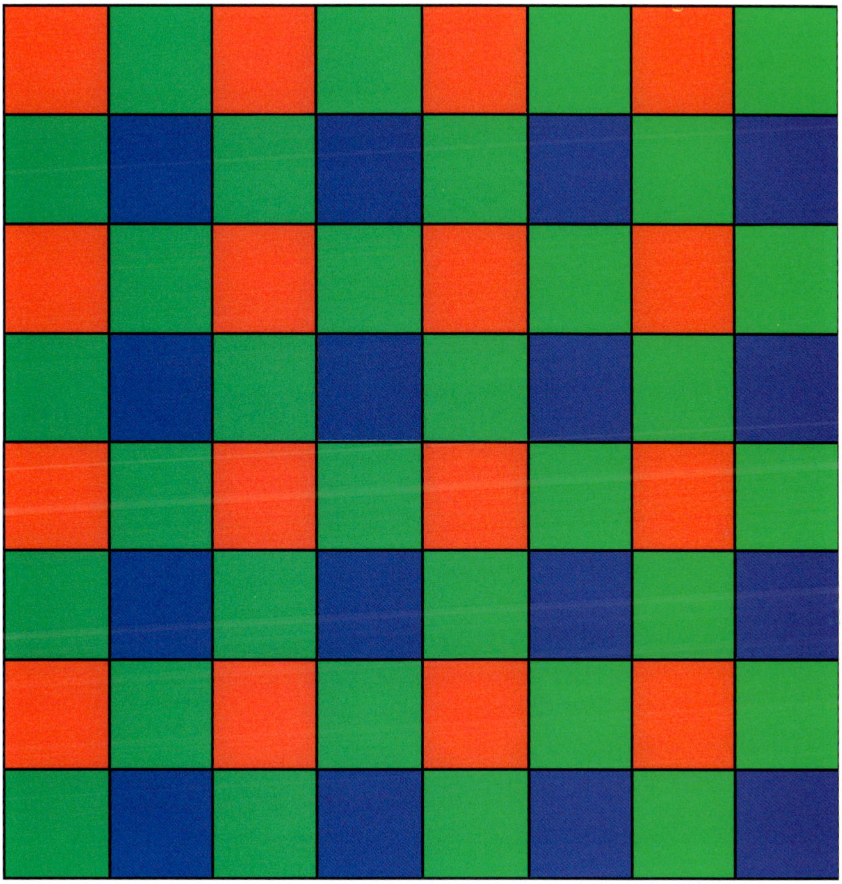

Figure 1-5: A color filter array is placed over the image sensor to enable it to capture color. The Bayer Pattern, which is the filter array most often used in digital colors, doubles the number of green pixels in its red, green, blue (RGB) checkerboard pattern. In DSLRs, the checkerboard is made up of millions of blocks of color filters — as many as there are pixels on the image sensor.

Analog versus Digital

One of the defining differences between film and digital image capture is that film is analog, while digital is, well, digital.

- Digital divides all information into two discrete (binary) states: zeroes and ones, or on and off. Put together enough of these zeroes and ones, and you can theoretically describe anything, including a photograph.
- Analog is what lives in the real world and can be touched or seen. It is a continuous ramp of information.

For photography, analog is a continuous tone with no breaks within the gradient of a color. In digital photography, the initial capture (by the image sensor) is analog — made up of continuous electrical charges — but it is converted to digital data within the camera. Digital emulates film's continuous tone by creating so many millions of points of information that it fools the human eye into seeing an unbroken gradient of color. One of the criteria for judging digital image quality is to determine just how well continuous tone is emulated by the digital data.

However, simply placing a filter array and microlenses in front of pixels doesn't yield enough information to recreate true colors. That requires some analysis of what the pixels are and where they are located so they can be assembled into an actual photograph. Information about adjacent and nearby pixels is used by the camera's intelligence to guesstimate exactly what the correct color of the pixel should be. This process is known as *interpolation*.

CCD VERSUS CMOS IMAGE SENSORS

Most digital cameras use one of two different types of image sensors: CCD and CMOS. (Other types are generally very specialized and used primarily by the military or for scientific research.) Both chips work by converting photons to electrons and then measuring or reading the number of electrons, or the electrical charge. What they do from that point on differs, but the end result is the same — data that can be translated into an image.

- **CCD** is an abbreviation for charge-coupled device, so named because each pixel's electrical charge is measured and the accumulated charge of that, plus adjacent (coupled) pixels, is transferred to the edge of the image sensor array. At this point, all the charges are analog and must be converted to digital data. This is done by a separate ADC (analog-to-digital converter) chip. All CCDs are dedicated chips used only in recording images.
- **CMOS** (complementary metal-oxide semiconductor), however, is more versatile in that it converts the analog signal to digital data within the sensor itself and does not require a separate ADC. That's possible because, in addition to photo diodes (which every CCD also has), each CMOS also incorporates transistors and logic circuits. Besides being faster, CMOS is much more power efficient than CCDs, requiring less

electricity and therefore being better on battery life. What's more, having all those capabilities within the image sensor itself means that CMOS-powered digital cameras require fewer components and are therefore simpler and less expensive to build. In addition, CMOS chips themselves are generally much less expensive to make. (A CMOS fabrication plant costs about $125 million to build, and it can also be used to crank out a wide variety of CMOS computer chips and not only image sensors. A CCD fabrication plant costs well over $1 billion to build, and its sole products are CCD digital camera image sensors.)

So what's the actual difference between the two chips, and why should you care?

We used to be able to say without any fear of contradiction that CCDs produced significantly higher-quality images than CMOS. Most early CMOS-equipped digital cameras were cheapies, with a resolution of only 2 megapixels or less. Even today, most novelty and very inexpensive, low-resolution (under 3 megapixel) digital cameras use CMOS image sensors. (A basic component kit with lens and image sensor can cost manufacturers as little as $4!) However, in recent years, CMOS technology has improved significantly, overcoming some of the initial engineering problems that contributed to poor image quality and low sensitivity to light. Today's state-of-the-art CMOS image sensors — at least in the over 6 megapixel range — can be every bit as good as comparable CCDs.

So, does it make a difference whether your DSLR camera has a CCD or CMOS image sensor? Not really, unless you want a full-frame (the same size as a piece of 35mm film) chip. Presently, the only full-framed image sensors on DSLRs are CMOS. We'll talk about the advantages (and drawbacks) to full-frame image sensors a little later in this chapter.

The Internal Imaging Chain

The process of taking and saving a picture is pretty much the same on a DSLR as any other type of digital camera: point the lens at the subject, and press the shutter. From that point on, the electronics kick in. The image sensor is exposed, and the electrons are collected in the pixel wells.

If the camera uses a CCD, the electrons are passed on to an ADC (analog-to-digital converter) to create the digital data. Then, the data are fed to one or more DSPs (digital signal processors) that mosaic and demosaic the pixels (interpolate the color). The data are organized into a recognizable picture that can be displayed on the LCD screen. At the same time, various imaging algorithms are applied to the image data, creating an RGB photo file. The image processing is one of the things that distinguishes one camera model from another, using algorithms defined by the manufacturer's proprietary image science and preferences.

If it is a CMOS, the one most significant difference is that the electrons are converted to digital data on the image sensor, and other image processing may be applied in various areas of the CMOS chip, or elsewhere within the camera.

If you are saving in RAW file format, the electrons are converted to digital data, but the image processing is bypassed completely, leaving that to the photographer to complete at a later time (see Chapter 4).

Fuji's SuperCCD and Foveon's X3 Image Sensor

While the overwhelming number of consumer digital cameras and DSLRs use standard Bayer pattern CCD and CMOS image sensors, there are two exceptions worth noting: Fuji's SuperCCD, which is used only in Fuji cameras, and Foveon's X3, which is incorporated in Sigma's SD9 and SD10 DSLRs. (At the time of this writing, there were hints that another major camera manufacturer may soon be using X3.)

- **SuperCCD** — While the SuperCCD uses the standard Bayer pattern of red, green, or blue filters in front of every pixel, each pixel has a unique octagonal or honeycomb shape (See the first figure in this sidebar). The pixels are positioned at a 45-degree angle, which means that every 9 pixels combine into a square. Each of those squares can also function as a pixel. This particular arrangement of using abutting pixels to increase resolution is called hardware interpolation. Fuji claims that its SuperCCD technology interpolation can boost effective resolution by as much as 100 percent. Thus, a SuperCCD with 6 million physical pixels may capture as much data as a conventional 12-megapixel CDD.

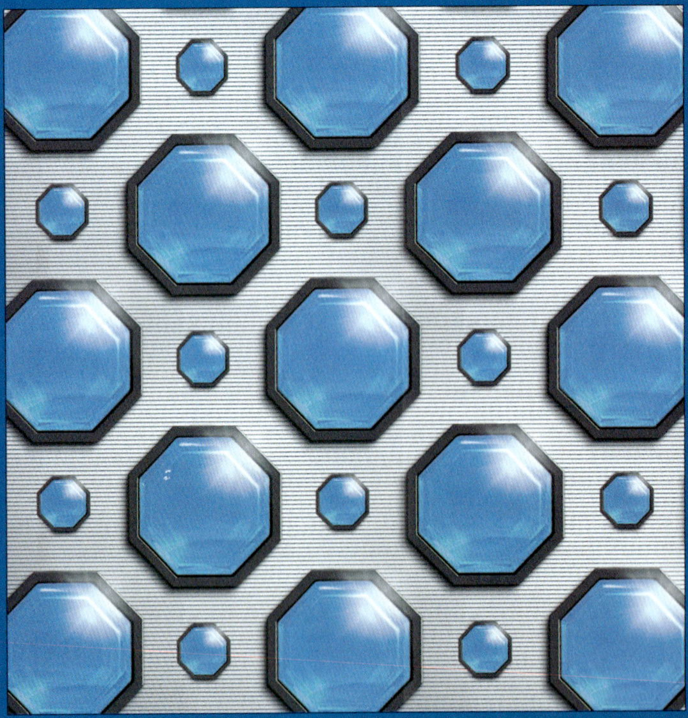

All of Fuji's SuperCCDs use octagonal rather than square or rectangle pixels. The SuperCCD SRII alternates large and small pixels to increase dynamic range. (Courtesy of Fujifilm)

Fuji's latest version, the SuperCCD SRII, alternates large pixels and small pixels. The large pixels are much more sensitive to light, which is useful in capturing more data in the dark or shadowed areas. The small pixels aren't as sensitive to light, and therefore are excellent for capturing bright highlights without blowing out. Together, they have the ability to extend the overall dynamic range, which in turn means smoother image gradation or tonality. The Fuji FinePix S3 Pro DSLR actually allows the photographer to select the desired dynamic range setting. For example, he or she might want a higher dynamic range for shooting outdoors in bright sunlight, or a narrower dynamic range for taking portraits in a studio.

The SuperCCD is a proprietary technology, fabricated exclusively by Fuji for Fuji cameras.

- **Foveon X3** — Instead of alternating red, green, and blue pixels (which has the effect of reducing overall resolution by two-thirds, since three pixels must be combined to produce one full-colored pixel), Foveon engineers designed the X3 chip to capture all three primary colors in a single pixel well. (See the second figure in this sidebar.) This it does by using the principle that each color has a different spectral wavelength. The silicon of the CMOS chip has the ability to absorb the different colors at different depths, and at each different depth is embedded a separate photodetector. Because all three primary colors are captured by each pixel, there's no need for a filter array bonded to the CMOS. And theoretically, it means that resolution is effectively tripled, since only one pixel is needed to create color, not three pixels as with Bayer pattern chips. The X3 chip also supposedly produces superior color, sharper images, and fewer artifacts.

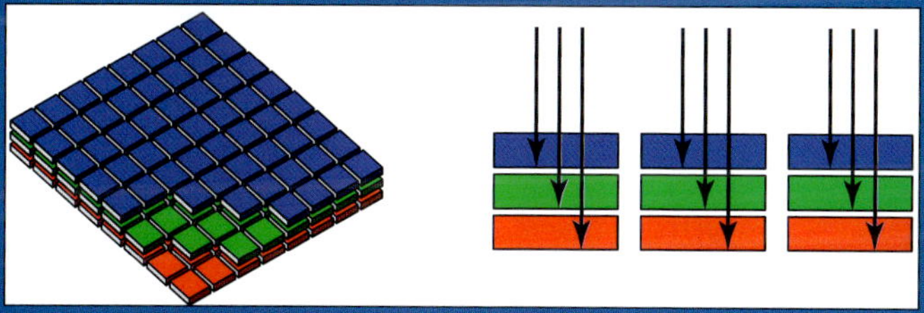

Foveon's X3 collects all three primary colors in each pixel well, instead of using a Bayer pattern checkerboard of red, green, and blue. (Courtesy of Foveon)

WHAT ABOUT MEGAPIXELS?

The best-known digital camera buzzword is *megapixels*. In the inimitable American way, manufacturer hype has made the "more is better" argument an article of faith, and many consumers have bought into the myth that the more megapixels their digital camera has, the better it must be. (More megapixels are usually more expensive, of course.)

Actually, megapixel is only a measure of size, not quality. More megapixels mean that you can produce bigger enlargements or crop small areas and blow them up without losing image definition. It has nothing to do with image quality. In fact, jamming more pixels on a small-sized image sensor can degrade image quality (see the section "Image Sensor Size" later in the chapter). On the other hand, digital cameras with larger pixel counts tend to have better optics and other higher-quality components than smaller pixel count cameras. That's because the price—and potentially, the profit—is greater, so the manufacturer can afford to stuff better grade components into their cameras. Also, mediocre image quality may not be readily apparent with a low megapixel digital camera outputting to a 4×6" snapshot-sized print, but enlarge the image, and any deficiencies become more obvious. So, to keep their customers happy, manufacturers try to ensure that digital cameras with higher megapixel counts are capable of producing better quality images.

Our advice is to choose your DSLR based upon your intended output. If you shoot primarily for the Web and know that your pictures will rarely, if ever, make it into print, you don't need a high-megapixel camera. (In fact, just about any DSLR has much more resolution than you actually need for the Internet.) Some, but not all DSLRs feature a range of resolutions that scale down to VGA (640×480), which is probably the most appropriate Web resolution. You may wish to avoid those DSLRs that don't offer such low-resolution options; otherwise, you'll end up spending lots of time resizing your pictures with image-editing software. If you are shooting portraits and the biggest enlargements you make for clients is 11×14", an 8-megapixel DSLR will probably work well for you. It's only if you plan on larger exhibition prints (16×20") or are shooting magazine ads and covers that you'll want and need the highest-resolution DSLRs (10 megapixels and higher).

IMAGE SENSOR SIZE

Size matters when talking about image sensors. Not necessarily the megapixels, but the physical dimensions. DSLRs have physically larger image sensors than most consumer digital cameras, and for good reason. That's because the size and depth of each pixel have a direct bearing on how good your picture can look. Also, the overall dimensions of the image sensor itself offer important advantages over cameras with smaller image sensors.

How much larger are DSLR image sensors over most consumer digital camera image sensors? In actual real estate, between 4 and 100 times larger. Table 1-1 looks at the size image sensors found in three DSLRs and two consumer digital cameras, all having the same density of approximately 8 megapixels.

Table 1-1 Comparing DSLR and Consumer Image Sensor Size

Camera	*Type*	*Image Sensor Size*	*Total Area*
Samsung Digimax V800	Consumer	7.18×5.32mm	38.2mm
Nikon Coolpix 8700	Consumer	8.80×6.60mm	58.1mm
Olympus E-300	DSLR	18×13.5mm	243mm
Canon Digital Rebel XT	DSLR	22.2×14.8mm	328.6mm
Canon EOS 1D Mark II	DSLR (Pro)	28.7×19.1mm	548.2mm

Consumer digital cameras with lower resolutions (that is, fewer megapixels) are even smaller than the Samsung's CCD. At the high end of the spectrum, the image sensor size on Canon's EOS 1Ds Mark II DSLR, which has an effective density of 16.6 megapixels, is 24×36mm, or a total area of 864mm. That's the same size as a frame of 35mm film. But pro studio digital backs (which we won't be covering in this book, because they cost tens of thousands of dollars and require professional skill to use properly) can come in even larger sizes.

So, why are the DSLRs larger image sensors better than other cameras' smaller ones?

Larger image sensors for the same megapixel density means that each individual pixel can be larger. While consumer digital camera pixels are between 2 and 4 microns large (it takes a very powerful microscope to see an individual photoreceptor site), on a DSLR that same pixel is between 6 and 12 microns in diameter. The DSLR pixel well is also deeper. The larger and deeper the pixel well, the more photons it can collect and the more electrons it can generate. And more electrons mean a higher sensitivity to light and greater subtlety in color gradations and tonality (also known as dynamic range).

Practically speaking, this capacity difference means that if the pixel is small and shallow rather than large and deep, it will fill up more easily and overflow, as happens in bright sunlight. That translates into blowout or lost detail. Conversely, it will collect fewer electrons in low light, so they may not register properly. Also, with small and shallow pixels, electrons can spill over from one photoreceptor site to an adjacent photoreceptor site, causing an aberration called blooming (which appears as blemishes on the photo). There are other potential problems with small pixels (such as a lower signal-to-noise ratio, smear, etc.), which camera manufacturers try to compensate for by added image processing and other technological tricks.

In addition, the actual size of the image sensor itself, apart and aside from the diameter of each pixel, is very important to serious photographers. A larger image sensor makes it possible to:

- Have much greater creative latitude in controlling depth of field
- Reduce or eliminate the so-called lens multiplication factor
- Use special and ultra-wide angle lenses to their full advantage
- Increase the signal-to-noise ratio

Total Pixels versus Effective Pixels

When you look at any digital camera's specs, you'll usually see two numbers: total pixels and effective pixels. Total pixels are the actual number of photoreceptor sites on the entire image sensor, calculated by multiplying the number of horizontal pixels by vertical pixels. Effective pixels are the number of pixels actually used to gather light. In other words, it's the camera's actual, real resolution. The reason why there is always a difference between total and effective pixels is because a certain number of pixels are dedicated for overhead tasks, such as demosaicing, defining black, buffering, or moving data. Another reason for a smaller effective pixel count is that the manufacturer may mask part of the image sensor off, to produce a specific aspect ratio (length versus height). So, which figure is important to you? Obviously, effective pixels is the number you should be concerned with.

Depth of Field

One of the laws of optics says that the smaller a lens's focal length (technically defined as the distance from the center of the lens to the film or image sensor plane when focused at infinity), the greater its depth of field (area from the foreground to the background that is in sharp focus). Creating and controlling depth of field in a photograph — deciding precisely what is or isn't in focus — is one of the shibboleths that separates an amateur from a professional photographer.

The focal length of a camera lens (film and digital) is directly related to the size of its image sensor or film frame: the smaller the image sensor, the smaller (shorter) the lens. However, cameras with larger image sensors need bigger (longer) focal length lenses, to produce an identical area of coverage. And by definition, longer lenses yield potentially smaller depth of field.

If your objective is to always capture everything in sharp focus, a bigger lens is a bad choice. Frankly, many consumer digital cameras with small lenses don't even require focusing (although most come equipped with autofocus capability, primarily to reassure its owners), because everything from about a foot to infinity will be sharp. But longer lenses on DSLRs with larger image sensors have more limited depth of field, allowing the photographer to choose which areas of the picture will be in focus and which will be soft.

Cross-Ref

We will go more into detail about lenses in Chapter 2, and *f*-stops and depth of field in Chapter 5.

Multiplication Factor

If a lens's focal length on a 35mm film camera is 50mm, it will have all the optical characteristics of a 50mm lens (area of coverage, depth of field, etc.) on a DSLR with a full-sized image sensor (that is, a sensor the size of a frame of 35mm film). But put that same lens on a DSLR with a smaller image sensor, and it suddenly yields a correspondingly smaller area of coverage, so the effective focal length is increased, or multiplied.

Reality Check: Is a Bigger Image Sensor Always Better?

We're generally in favor of large image sensors because of the greater depth of field latitude and potentially superior image quality they are capable of producing. However, simply being bigger doesn't automatically guarantee that it will be better.

First of all, it's important to remember that the image sensor is only one component of a complex process (lens, ADC chip, processing algorithms, etc.) that determines image quality. There are also variations in the design and quality control, and the superiority or inferiority of materials.

The other disadvantage of larger image sensors is that lenses for the camera also must be larger. And heavier. And more expensive. The camera body, too, will probably be larger, heavier, and more expensive.

To help explain how the multiplication factor will affect your selection of lenses, briefly take a look at Kodak's famous "four thirds" image sensor, used in Olympus DSLRs (and soon, other cameras). The four thirds chip is so named because of its aspect ratio, or proportion of width to height. It has a physical size of 18mm×13.5mm, with a diagonal of 22.5mm. In other words, its diameter is roughly half that of a full-sized image sensor or a frame of 35mm film (which is 24×36mm and a diagonal of 43.3mm). Therefore, a 50mm lens on the DSLR with the smaller four thirds image sensor will give you only half the coverage of the DSLR with the full-sized image sensor, or, an effective coverage of a 100mm lens. In other words, a four thirds–powered DSLR has a multiplication factor of 2. (The multiplication factor is sometimes also referred to as a magnification factor.)

Cross-Ref

We'll explain more about the multiplication factor and why it's an important factor when choosing the right lens for a particular shot in Chapter 2.

Wide Angle and Specialty Lenses

If a DSLR has a multiplication factor of 1.5, it would need a 24mm lens to give the same angle of coverage and perspective as a 35mm lens on a camera with a full-sized image sensor. But being a smaller focal length, it would have significantly greater depth of field, and possibly, more or different optical characteristics and distortions. The optical difference is much more pronounced with ultra-wide angle lenses. Besides, the new ultra-wide angle digital lenses designed for DSLRs having a multiplication factor of 1.3X to 2X tend to be expensive (if you can get one for your particular camera, that is).

Noise

The larger the image sensor, the higher the signal-to-noise ratio. That's good, because the more noise that any digital camera generates, the poorer the image quality will be.

You are already acquainted with what noise sounds like on a radio or a stereo — crank up the volume (which is technically known as gain), and besides increased loudness, you can also get unpleasant static and distortion. On image sensors, noise is visible rather than audible and looks like randomly scattered specks and splotches of color throughout the image. The more noise there is, the worse the image looks.

Noise is produced when the pixels are packed very tightly together, or when you boost the camera's light sensitivity, or ISO equivalency. (See Chapter 5.) Large image sensors produce less noise because the pixels are larger and deeper, and spaced further apart, allowing the photographer to increase sensitivity to a much higher level than consumer digital cameras and still maintain a minimal amount of noise. In addition, all DSLRs have some kind of internal noise suppression.

The Downside to Large Pixels

We have touted the virtues and advantages of physically large photoreceptor sites on big or full-sized image sensors, but we haven't really noted that there is one technical downside as well: *moirés*. A moiré is an unwanted textured pattern that appears when two patterns overlap, such as a high-megapixel image sensor and a subject with lots of detail. This isn't much of a problem with consumer digital camera image sensors with a small pitch (photoreceptor site or pixel), of 4, 3, or 2 microns. But it can be very pronounced with larger pitch photoreceptor sites, such as 6.5, 9, or 12 microns. To prevent or reduce moirés, most DSLR manufacturers add an anti-aliasing (blur) infrared filter in front of the image sensor and then compensate for the reduced sharpness by automatically invoking a sharpening algorithm in the firmware. The other way to get rid of moirés is to change your shooting angle, something we'll discuss in Chapter 7.

Distinguishing the Differences among DSLRs

Pick up any high-tech brochure or go online to an electronics superstore, and you will undoubtedly see over a score of DSLR bodies, ranging in price from under $600 to over $8,000. Plus, add from $99 to over $5,000 for each lens, and between $39 and $800 for an auxiliary flash. Why the big difference? How does it affect what make and model is best for your needs, shooting style, and budget?

Here are the major differences that distinguish an inexpensive entry-level DSLR from a professional model:

- The more expensive, pro bodies are always heavier, better built, more rugged, and able to shoot tens of thousands of frames without shutter fatigue.
- Often, a pro DSLR's image sensor is bigger, with larger and deeper pixels, as well as a higher megapixel count.
- Pro models generally come equipped with more memory buffering, for faster performance, and bigger rechargeable batteries, for more shots per session.
- Pro models may offer more features, such as interchangeable focusing screens, optional wireless control and wireless transmission, more bracketing options, and so on.
- The lens series designed for pro cameras also are heavier, better built, more rugged, usually one or more *f*-stops faster, and have speedier focusing. They also may offer additional features, such as built-in image stabilization. (See Chapter 2 on lenses and Chapter 5, regarding *f*-stops.)
- Generally, the more expensive the auxiliary flash, the more versatile and powerful it will be. Top-of-the-line matched strobes are designed to interact with your camera's intelligence, to produce perfect exposure. They also pump out more light, to illuminate larger spaces; have swivel heads, for controlling shadows; and may even have the ability to become slaved strobes, for wireless use with other flashes. Less expensive strobes are usually not as powerful, the head may be fixed rather than swivel and lack some of the intelligence for ensuring perfect exposure.

Tip

Even if you can get the pictures you need with a less expensive, lighter-weight, smaller megapixel DSLR, sometimes you need to use a top-of-the-line professional DSLR that looks like a pro DSLR. We've found that some finicky clients, especially equipment-oriented techies who insist on coming on the shoot, expect you to use the best, highest-resolution, most advanced DSLR, whether or not it's really needed for the assignment. They simply don't think that you are professional enough unless you look the part. If that's the case, some photographers simply rent the camera clients insist on having them use and charge it to the client. And if the client isn't on the shoot, they'll use their less expensive DSLR and not tell their clients how they got the shot. After all, the whole point is getting the photo, not the camera you used.

Of course, there are significant differences among various brands. The lenses and accessories designed for one system usually do not work with another manufacturer's system. In fact, some lenses designed for entry-level DSLRs will not even fit on the same manufacturer's pro series, and vice versa.

So, which brand do you buy?

The most obvious answer is to buy the brand you already know and use. If you have owned and used Nikon film SLRs, for example, you are already familiar with the basic design and layout of the camera — where the controls are — and the time spent learning to transit from film to digital will be minimal. Following the same analogy, you may already own Nikon lenses and other accessories (legacy equipment) that you can use on your new Nikon DSLR (or the Fuji S Pro series, since they also use Nikon bodies). The same principle applies to Canon, Konica Minolta, Olympus, and Pentax brands.

If you have no previous exposure with a film SLR, perhaps you have had a positive experience with, and have developed an affinity or loyalty to a particular brand, such as Canon's inkjet printers or Konica Minolta's X series of consumer digital cameras. That company's level of excellence and service probably carries over to their DSLRs, so you may wish to stay with what you like and buy that brand DSLR.

Another way to decide which brand or model DSLR to buy is make a list of the things you must have in your camera. Is shooting speed paramount (for sports, nature, photojournalism, etc.)? If so, you'll want to look for a DSLR that has a fast sustained burst mode. Do you shoot in a rugged environment, such as a work site or industrial plant? Check out DSLRs that are specifically ruggedized, with environmental seals on the lens mount and ports. If you plan to shoot mostly wide angle and ultra-wide angle, you'll probably be happier with a DSLR that has a full-sized image sensor, so there's no lens multiplication factor.

You should spend for only the amount of resolution you really need, and no more. If you shoot exclusively for the Web, or the largest prints you make are 8×10", you'll be happy with a 5- or 6-megapixel DSLR, rather than springing for a more expensive, higher-megapixel DSLR that you'll never really use to the max.

To give you an idea of each manufacturer's history and photographic philosophy, we've briefly profiled each DSLR company in the sections that follow.

Tip

Don't buy into manufacturer marketing hype and buy more camera than you actually need or can afford. In fact, if this is your first DSLR, you might want to check out entry-level models rather than more advanced cameras. If you like using it and later decide that you want to upgrade to a more advanced DSLR, you can use that entry-level model as a second body, a backup camera. That's the advantage of developing a camera system based upon the same manufacturer's DSLRs, lenses, and accessories.

Canon

Canon is the 800-pound gorilla of DSLRs, outselling all other makes and models combined. As a matter of fact, by sheer dollars earned, Canon is far and away the world's number one digital camera manufacturer. After World War II, Canon's high-quality 35mm rangefinders competed head to head with much more expensive Leicas and Contaxs. Although it was relatively late introducing a professional model film SLR (1971), Canon immediately became a fierce competitor to Nikon's previously unassailable F model.

Not Quite a DSLR . . . but with Interchangeable Lenses

So far, we've covered only Digital Single Reflex Cameras with through-the-lens viewing and interchangeable lenses. But before SLRs, there was a class of professional 35mm film cameras that featured interchangeable lenses, though not TTL viewing. This was called a rangefinder camera and used an optical viewing system that consisted of a glass window with a superimposed frosted frame and a split image mirror that came together when the lens was in focus. Rangefinders were extremely popular until the advent of modern SLRs, at which point they fell out of general use because, not having through-the-lens viewing, they are terrible at taking telephoto shots.

Contax, Nikon, and Canon all once made professional rangefinder cameras, but one company dominated the field — Leica. Leica — which invented the 35mm camera in 1914 — has manufactured rangefinder cameras for some 80 years. This means that there are still lots of Leica fans who own many superb Leica lenses, none of which can be readily adapted for use with a DSLR.

That's why Epson and camera manufacturer Cosina collaborated on developing a 6-megapixel rangefinder-type digital camera body, the R-D1. Its chief virtue is that the R-D1 can accommodate many Leica M-type lenses (as well as older Leica screw mount lenses with appropriate adapters). The R-D1 is a beautifully crafted (and expensive!) precision instrument that has the look, feel, and handling characteristics of a fine 35mm rangefinder film camera. However, it also comes equipped with most DSLR features and functions, including an LCD screen. If you don't happen to have any Leica M lenses, Epson/Consina sells high-quality Leica-type lenses made by Voigtlander. Most of what we write in this book about DSLRs will apply to the R-D1 and any other models Epson/Consina releases. Note, however, that while they're great for standard and wide angle use, rangefinder cameras generally cannot be used with telephoto lenses beyond 135mm.

Canon manufactures DSLR models in all categories: low-cost entry-level for beginners, moderately priced midrange for advanced amateurs, and expensive, everything-but-the-kitchen-sink models for professionals. Canon was the first camera manufacturer to crack the sub-$1,000 barrier with its groundbreaking Digital Rebel, and its famed EOS professional series offers the highest resolution currently available in a DSLR. Equally important, at least two current Canon models feature full-frame (24×36mm) image sensors, which means no multiplication factor whatever on their lenses, giving these DSLRs the ability to capture true ultra-wide angle shots. As a photographic system, Canon offers a wide variety of lenses, strobes, accessories, and peripherals for its DSLRs, and in different price categories to reflect the needs and sophistication of its customers.

You can find out more about Canon and its products at `www.usa.canon.com`.

Eastman Kodak Company

Kodak ceased manufacturing DSLRs in 2005, but it remains an important part of the industry because many thousands of its DSLRs are still in service throughout the world. What's more, Kodak fabricates the four thirds CCD image sensor used in Olympus DSLRs, and that may eventually power future DSLRs by four thirds partners Fuji Photo Film, Matsushita (Panasonic), Sanyo Electric Co., and Sigma Corp. And due to the wild popularity of its EasyShare amateur digital cameras and peripherals, Kodak seesaws between being the #1 or #2 bestselling digital camera company in the world.

Kodak produced the world's first commercial DSLR in 1991 (the 10-pound, $25,000, 1.3 megapixel DCS-100) and has subsequently released over a dozen-and-a-half models, including dedicated black-and-white and infrared versions. (It's difficult tallying an exact count because Kodak produced numerous variations with some uncertainty whether they were different enough to be called a separate model.) At first, all Kodak DSLRs used off-the-shelf Nikon SLR film bodies as the front end, wedding it to Kodak's electronics in the rear. Eventually, they offered a Canon body as well, giving pros a choice of systems. Kodak then jettisoned Nikon and Canon bodies for its last production DSLRs, the 14-megapixel DCS Pro SLR/c (Canon lens mount) and DCS Pro SLR/n (Nikon lens mount), both of which use a Sigma camera body (very similar to the Sigma SD9 and SD10 DSLRs). You can find good used Kodak DSLR bargains on eBay and other sites that sell used photographic equipment. Presently, Kodak has no plans to bring out another DSLR model, although it remains one of the world's leading providers of both amateur and professional digital camera image sensors.

Find out more about Kodak and its products at `www.kodak.com`.

Fujifilm USA

Fuji and Kodak have been archrivals for several decades, competing head to head for both amateur and professional photographer loyalty and dollars. Like Kodak, Fuji is an image sensor fabricator, although all the chips it produces are used internally on Fuji's own digital cameras. While it produces conventional CCDs for some of its consumer digital cameras, Fuji is known for its so-called SuperCCDs. (See the sidebar titled "Fuji's SuperCCD and Foveon's X3 Image Sensor" earlier in the chapter.) Fuji also produces a line of professional DSLRs, called the Fuji S Pro series — S1, S2, S3, and so on. (However, note that Fujifilm also markets a line of prosumer S Pro cameras with double digits, such as the S20 Pro, that are *not* DSLRs, but

DSLR-types.) All S Pro cameras are built on Nikon midrange bodies (which means they use Nikon lenses and accessories), and each model incorporates a SuperCCD image sensor. S Pro models are moderately priced, halfway between serious amateur and frugal pro, and designed for optimum image quality rather than fast performance (although all models have faster FireWire, instead of slower USB, connectivity).

Fuji is a member of the Four Thirds consortium, which means that they have the right to manufacture DSLRs that would incorporate Kodak's four thirds image sensor and interchangeable lenses with four thirds mounts. This would give Fuji the ability to sell more affordable DSLRs to the serious amateur market.

Read more about Fujifilm and its products at `www.fujifilm.com`.

Konica Minolta

Just before this book went to press, Konica Minolta announced that it would be leaving the photographic field and transferring its technologies and products to Sony. This is unfortunate, since both Konica and Minolta (they had merged in 2003) had been making Single Lens Reflex cameras for generations. In fact, Minolta was one of only a handful of Japanese companies that manufactured its own optics. Minolta's Maxxum Single Lens Reflex series of film cameras was a favorite with many serious amateur photographers for their light weight, strong body, reliability, ease of use, excellent lenses, and affordable prices. Konica Minolta built its Maxxum DSLRs using the same basic film camera body, so its handling characteristics were familiar to legions of Maxxum users. And while Konica Minolta manufactured a specific line of digital lenses, almost all lenses, strobes, and other accessories designed for use with Maxxum film cameras worked on Maxxum DSLRs.

One extremely attractive feature that Digital Maxxum's have (and which by extension, all future Sony DSLRs will incorporate) that no other DSLR manufacturer offers is image stabilization built right into the camera body. Unlike other DSLR manufacturers that offer anti-shake technology built into specific lenses (and at premium prices), the Maxxum's image sensor is gimbaled, allowing it to be moved by a series of tiny solenoids, to offset camera motion. This ability to neutralize motion within the camera itself allows the photographer to shoot at least two full *f*-stops slower than would be practical using a hand-held camera and lens with no anti-shake capability.

While Digital Maxxum DSLRs were targeted primarily at the amateur market, some pros preferred them to other brands. As we write this, Sony—which has never manufactured a Single Lens Reflex camera, film or digital—will take over Konica Minolta's camera division to produce Sony-branded DSLRs, which should be able to use older Minolta lenses.

Find out more about Konica Minolta at `www.konicaminolta.com`.

Leica

Leica invented the 35mm camera, and its cameras and lenses have always been considered to be the world's very finest by knowledgeable connoisseurs and photo aficionados. Alas, they are also extremely expensive, which explains why relatively few people can afford to own Leica cameras. In recent years, Leica has attempted to go more mainstream, by pairing with Fuji and then Panasonic, to produce a Leica-branded, but Japanese-manufactured line of consumer digital cameras that are only marginally more expensive (but more nicely finished) than their corresponding Japanese models. When Leica finally decided to produce its own DSLR, it partnered with the upscale Danish film Imacon (which recently merged with famed medium format camera manufacturer Hasselblad), one of the graphics industry's best-known and most respected makers of professional scanners and digital backs. The result of this collaboration is not a DSLR per se, but a hybrid 10-megapixel digital back designed to slip onto Leica's current R8 and R9 35mm film cameras. This gives Leica owners the best of both worlds: the ability to shoot film or quickly swap to an all-digital model, using the same familiar camera body and their choice of Leica's superb "R" series of lenses. But being Leica, the cost of the camera body, Imacon digital back, and a standard 50mm Leica lens can cost half again as much as a new car.

Find out more about Leica at `www.leica-camera.com`. (Select USA from the drop-down list to see the English rather than the German site.)

Nikon

Nikon is one of Japan's oldest, best-known, and most successful camera companies. In fact, it was the first manufacturer to introduce, in 1958, a professional-grade Single Lens Reflex 35mm film camera, the original Nikon F. The Nikon F was for many years the quintessential professional SLR, in fact the only SLR the company made. Eventually, it began marketing smaller, less expensive models for serious amateurs. Nikon has been improving and expanding the F series cameras for over 45 years, but unlike other companies that adopt and abandon interfaces and standards, many Nikon lenses and accessories will fit virtually any Nikon camera, including digital models. Being able to use legacy lenses and peripherals on state-of-the-art DSLRs is powerful incentive for Nikon shooters to remain loyal to Nikon as they transition from film to digital.

Nikon markets a range of DSLRs — low-end, midrange, and pro models. Most Nikon DSLR bodies are modified film bodies, and depending upon the model, may or may not come equipped with a built-in flash. Lower-end models may use porro-mirrors rather than pentaprism optical viewing systems and have polycarbonate exteriors rather than metal coatings. The pro cameras are direct descendants of the venerable Nikon F. There are generally two classes of pro models: the H series (H for high speed) and the X series (X for excellent image quality). The H series are designed primarily for photojournalists and sports photographers and are capable of shooting as fast as the fastest motor drive film cameras. The X series combine performance with image quality in built-like-a-tank bodies. Nikon is releasing an all-new digital series of lenses for its DSLRs. However, unlike archrival Canon, no Nikon DSLR presently incorporates a full-sized image sensor.

Read more about Nikon at `www.nikonusa.com`.

Olympus

Olympus is one of Japan's oldest camera and optical manufacturer and has been selling Single Lens Reflex film cameras almost as long as Nikon. It was the first manufacturer to develop and market a from-the-ground-up DSLR that hadn't been built on or around a previous film camera model. It also was the first to introduce purpose-built, all-digital lenses for its DSLRs. In other words, Olympus is the first camera company to offer an all-digital photographic system: bodies, lenses, strobes, and other accessories.

Olympus is also the first camera manufacturer to produce DSLRs that incorporate Kodak's four thirds image sensors and four thirds lens mount standards. Its lineup ranges from an inexpensive entry-level model to an industrial strength semi-pro DSLR priced slightly above what a serious amateur DSLR would cost.

Olympus has creatively tackled the problem of dust on the image sensor. Called the Supersonic Wave Filter, it's a mechanism that vibrates 35,000 times a second, literally shaking the image sensor free of dust. All Olympus DSLRs come equipped with the Supersonic Wave Filter.

For more about Olympus go to `www.olympusamerica.com`.

Panasonic

As we go to press, the multinational electronics company Mitsushita (Panasonic) has announced a strategic alliance with Olympus to develop DLSRs that incorporate Kodak's four thirds image sensor. This will result in the first Panasonic-branded DSLR. At this time, no other information about the Panasonic camera is available.

For more about Panasonic, go to `www.panasonic.com`.

Pentax

Back in 1952, Asahi Optical, Pentax's parent company, was the first Japanese company to market a 35mm Single Lens Reflex camera. Since then, Pentax has introduced a number of firsts: first with an instant return mirror, first to add a pentaprism for eye-level viewing, first to incorporate through-the-lens metering, and first to have through-the-lens aperture priority control. While it wasn't the first company to introduce a low-cost DSLR, Pentax DSLRs are among the smallest, lightest, easiest to use, and most affordable available. Designed for simplicity and targeted at novices to serious amateurs, Pentax DSLRs run on standard AA batteries and save to ubiquitous SD/MMC cards. While its DSLRs will accommodate many Pentax legacy lenses, the company markets a line of digital-specific lenses. Pentax recently announced a strategic alliance with Korean electronics giant Samsung to produce a Samsung-branded DSLR. Whether Pentax will continue to manufacturer Pentax-branded DSLRs or will be folded into Samsung's digital portfolio remains to be seen.

Read more about Pentax at `www.pentaximaging.com`.

Samsung

In the American digital camera market, Samsung has barely been a blip on the horizon. Its first attempt to produce a product that would appeal to serious amateur photographers was a prosumer DSLR-type camera with a huge zoom lens, large LCD screen, and not much else. Wanting to move into the lucrative DSLR field, but lacking the experience necessary to develop a from-the-ground-up DSLR camera system, Samsung decided to forge a strategic alliance with long-established Japanese camera manufacturer Pentax. Its first announced product, the GX-1S, is essentially a rebranded Pentax *ist DS2. We expect to see additional models that will incorporate more of Samsung's technology.

Read more about Samsung at `www.samsung.com`.

Sigma

Although Sigma is a relative newcomer to SLRs, this Japanese company has been manufacturing low-cost, high-quality third-party lenses, strobes, and other accessories for other 35mm camera for decades. It was the first company to incorporate Foveon's revolutionary X3 image sensor into a DSLR, which at least theoretically helps eliminate color aliasing while producing more accurate colors. Sigma DSLRs are large, moderately priced cameras with nonstandard analog controls and are designed primarily for serious amateurs. They have not done particularly well in the marketplace, primarily because its SD9 and SD10 models feature effective resolutions lower than comparable DSLRs, and they save images only in a proprietary RAW file format that has not been supported by many image-viewing and -editing programs.

You can find more about Sigma at `www.sigmaphoto.com`.

Sony

Sony, one of the world's biggest and best-known consumer electronics companies, has long been at the forefront of digital camera technology. Only, it never had the optical infrastructure or practical experience to produce a DSLR. So, how do you enter this intensely competitive field against long-established companies like Canon and Nikon? You acquire the camera division of a long-established Japanese camera manufacturer, that's how.

Sony forged a strategic alliance with struggling camera manufacturer Konica Minolta, ostensibly to have them produce Sony-branded DSLRs that would incorporate technology from both Sony and Konica Minolta. In January 2006, Konica Minolta decided to leave the photographic field entirely, which probably means that Sony will assume all that company's camera products, assets, experience, and technical know-how, especially in DSLR design and production. We expect to see Sony-branded DSLRs that, at least initially, will be the next generation Konica Minolta Maxxum cameras and lenses, but carrying the Sony brand. Given Sony's huge and loyal following, as well as its marketing prowess, we expect that Sony DSLRs will garner a respectable market share among Sony consumer digital camera users who want to move up to more serious photographic equipment.

Tip

Try before you buy. The choice of a DSLR is a very personal matter, and how it feels and handles is just as important as what features it offers and how much it costs. At the very least, you should get some hands-on time on the DSLR you are interested in buying before you make the purchase. What may sound great in the specs may turn out to be too heavy, too small, or ergonomically inconvenient. You definitely don't want a DSLR you won't be comfortable with, that won't adequately fit your hands. We suggest going to a full-service photo or electronics store, such as Samy's, Frye's, B&H, or the local photography store in your town, and trying out the DSLR you like. It's all the better if there's a photo expert on staff who can advise you, although that's becoming increasingly rare these days.

Summary

DSLRs are amazing devices that offer faster performance, greater versatility, and better image quality than consumer or prosumer digital cameras. Understanding what sets them apart from other digital cameras (as well as from each other) can help you choose the right one for your needs, budget, and shooting style, as well as use your DSLR more effectively.

Chapter 2

Choosing Your Lenses

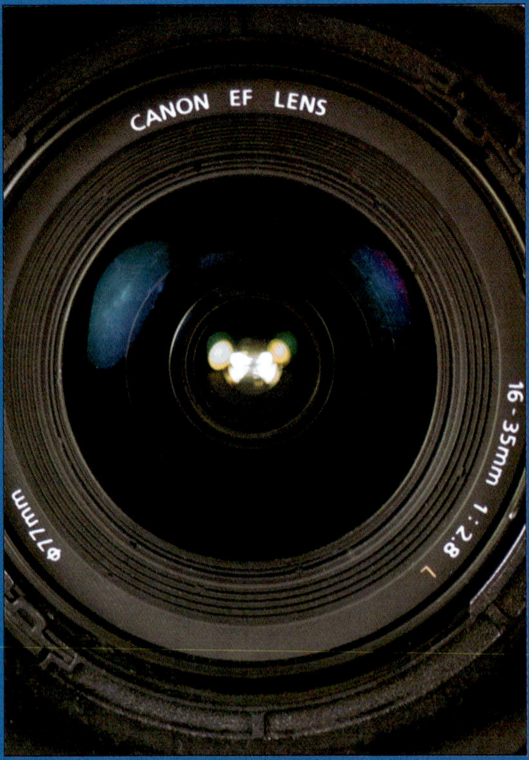

Canon digital wide angle zoom lens (Taken with a Konica Minolta Maxxum 7D, 28-100mm lens set at 60mm, 1/10 at f5.6.)

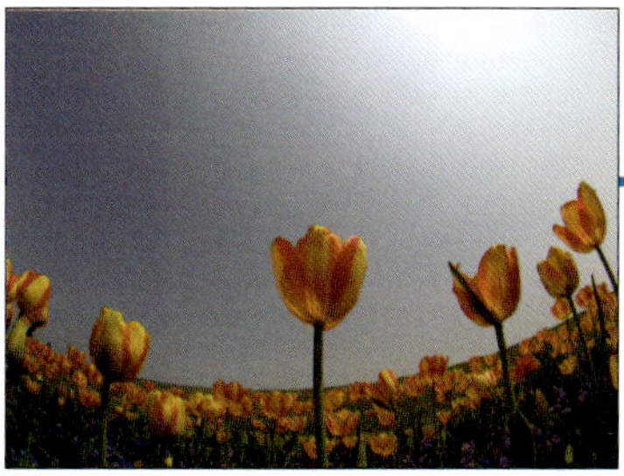

Photo taken with an 8mm fisheye lens by Hiroshi Tanaka (Courtesy Olympus Tokyo)

The ability to change lenses is one of the most important aspects of DSLR photography. This versatile option is a two-edged sword, however, because the photographer must not only carefully choose which lens to use but also spend hundreds or even thousands of dollars to buy the range of lenses needed (or simply desired!), take the time and effort to attach and detach them from the camera body, protect them, and haul them around so that they're always available to use.

In this chapter, we:

- Discuss how lenses differ in design and purpose
- Compare digital versus film lenses
- Help you understand the difference in focal lengths from film to digital cameras
- Assist you in choosing the right lens for specific applications, shooting environments, and artistic purposes
- Suggest how to make maximum use of the lens or lenses you have

Are Digital Lenses Really All That Different?

If you are like us, you may already own a bunch of interchangeable lenses that you used on your old film SLR bodies — the so-called legacy lenses. Sure, most legacy lenses will usually mount onto your new DSLR, if your new camera is the same brand as your film SLR, and probably, all the electronics will work flawlessly. (See Figure 2-1.) But manufacturers loudly and frequently proclaim that their new digital series lenses are optically superior to older film lenses. If you accept conventional wisdom (or at least advice from lens manufacturers), you're told that your older lenses are quite obsolete and that you would be foolish using them on DSLRs. The question is this, "Can you continue to use your legacy lenses on your DSLR and be reasonably assured that you will get good image quality? Or are there absolutely compelling reasons why you should switch over to the new digital lenses?"

Like so many things in photography, the answer is yes, no, and perhaps. It depends upon the DSLR and the specific lens, as well as on how high your standard of top image quality is.

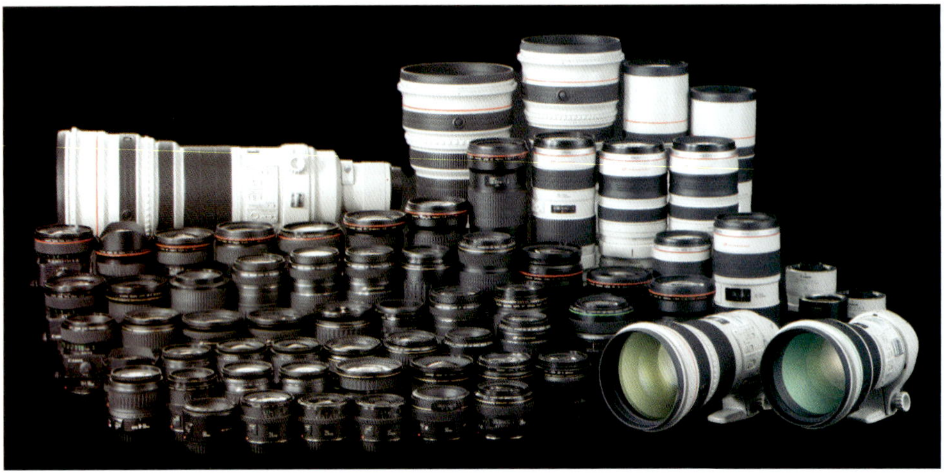

Figure 2-1: Canon has a wide array of lenses designed for both film and digital SLRs. The manufacturer of your camera will likely have a bunch of lenses from which to choose, too. Should you use the lenses you bought previously for your film camera with your digital SLR? That depends on several issues, including how picky you are about image quality and how much money you want to spend. (Photo courtesy of Canon U.S.A.)

Digital lenses are indeed optically different from film lenses. The key differences are:

- They're designed and fabricated to channel the light passing through them so that it strikes the image sensor at a more perpendicular angle than is necessary with film. (See Figure 2-2.)
- Digital lenses almost always produce a higher resolving power than comparable film lenses.

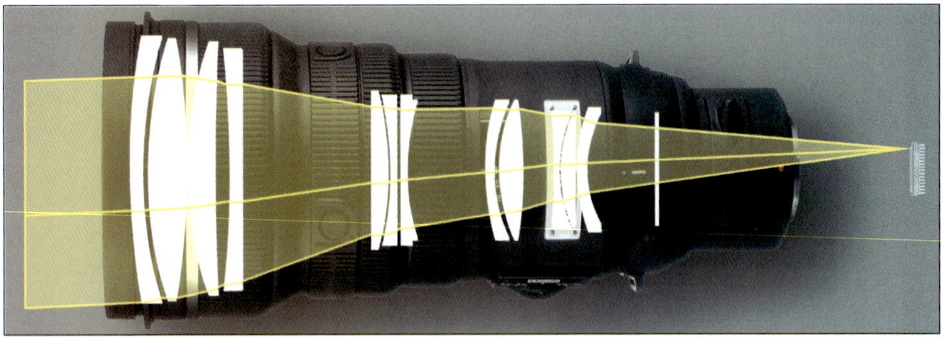

Figure 2-2: A camera lens is made up of several series of glass elements curved and engineered very precisely to control the path of light. (Photo courtesy of Olympus America)

Straightening the Light Path

Remember in Chapter 1 when we discussed pixel wells (photoreceptor sites) and microlenses we said that ideally, light should hit the pixel well perpendicular, or straight on, rather than at an angle. That's because light hitting the image sensor at oblique angles can spill over the pixel well into the adjacent pixel, which can cause blooming, color registration, and sensitivity problems that visually translate into aliasing and distortion like vignetting, and light falloff at the corners.

Film lenses will bend the light in such a way that it passes through perpendicular at the center but is sharply angled at the corners. It doesn't particularly matter at what angle the light hits the silver halide crystals of film. But nonperpendicular light is bad for image sensors. So, lenses designed specifically for digital SLRs usually straighten the light path over the entire circumference and not just in the center in the attempt to get more light to fill the pixel wells. (This is also the job of the array of microlenses placed over the image sensor.)

Greater Resolving Power

Digital lenses have to be sharper than comparable film lenses, just to keep up. The reason why is that most DSLR cameras have a slight blur filter (also called an anti-aliasing or low pass filter) in front of the image sensor to cut down on aliasing and ensure that the colors are accurate. In processing the image data, a slight sharpening algorithm is automatically added, to counteract the blur effect. Since film is chemical and not electronic, film lenses don't need a sharpening algorithm, so they don't have to have as high a resolving power as digital lenses in order to achieve the same level of image crispness. Of course, this is an oversimplification of a technically complex issue. The two other, highly technical reasons for requiring sharper lenses for image sensors than for film are something called MTF, or Modulation Transfer Function, and Nyquist frequency. We won't go into a long-winded explanation about what they are and why they are important, but, essentially, it all boils down to the fact that the highest-quality images come from those DSLRs in which the lens has twice the resolving power (sharpness) of the image sensor.

Practically Speaking, Is the Added Cost Worth It?

Because of the way they channel light into a straight path, as well as their being sharper with a higher resolving power, digital lenses will almost always give you better image quality on a DSLR than equivalent film camera lenses. That, plus the fact that they're new, they're hot, and they have lots of R&D to pay back, explains why digital lenses are almost always more expensive than comparable film lenses. One other factor is that the newer digital lenses tend to have intelligence built into them for better communication with the camera body. (See the section "Intelligent or CPU-Controlled Lenses" later in this chapter.) However, digital lenses tend to be expensive, and it does seem a pity to not use your fine legacy lenses and let them sit, gathering dust, in a dark drawer. So, to return to our original question—do you really need digital lenses to produce top-quality images?

Frankly, the advantages of digital over film lenses can be significantly diminished or even eliminated on a DSLR with an image sensor smaller than a frame of 35mm film (as the overwhelming number of models are), because of something called the multiplier or multiplication factor, as we'll explain shortly. As a rule of thumb, only the center of the lens is being used to cover the smaller image sensor. What this means in practical terms is that you probably can use your legacy lenses on any DSLR with image sensors smaller than 35mm film size without taking a significant image quality hit.

On the other hand, the edge of the lens is more critical, if you're using one of the few DSLRs equipped with a full-sized image sensor (that means it's the same size as a frame of 35mm film, or 36×24mm). Since it is the light at the edge of the film lens that tends to not follow a straight path, you will likely see a difference in the quality of your photo if you use a legacy film lens on a full-sized image sensor.

What we tend to do is use digital lenses for the focal lengths that we shoot at most frequently, and use our legacy extreme telephoto or ultra-wide angle lenses when we need them. If we find that we need to use any of the extreme focal length lenses for an important assignment (one that will pay well enough to justify the cost) that will probably be when we'll spend the money to buy a digital model.

Lens Cleaning

Dirty lenses — fingerprints, dust, dirt, lint, fibers, food or beverage bits, even rainwater droplets — can diminish image quality. And, depending upon the offending abrasiveness or chemical composition of the particulate, it can even permanently damage your expensive lens. Periodic lens cleaning should become part of your photographic routine. It needn't be an elaborate nor time-consuming process if you follow a few basic principles:

- Before applying any cloth or solvent, use a small camel's hair brush or rubber bulb to remove dirt or dust. That will keep you from inadvertently rubbing abrasive particles into the lens.
- Use only soft, lint-free tissues or cloth to touch the lens. Never apply pressure when cleaning.
- Use a rubber bulb to blow dust off the lens. Canned pressurized air projects a stream of liquid, which is so ultra-cold that it can actually crack the glass. However, you can use canned air to clean the lens barrel.
- If you wish to apply a liquid lens cleaner, use only a solvent specifically designed for a camera lens. Eyeglass solvents can be caustic and eventually damage the thin color-coated layer on the front elements of your lens. We actually prefer gently blowing our moist breath onto the lens rather than using a commercial cleaning lens solvent.
- Never apply any liquid solvent directly onto the lens. Instead, trickle a few drops onto a lint-free tissue or cloth.
- Clean in a circular motion, outward from the center of the lens to the edges.
- When not in use, store your lens in a camera bag or lens case with both the front and rear caps on.

Lastly, *don't* be obsessive/compulsive about cleaning your lenses. Overcleaning can negatively affect your lens's color coating.

When Is a 30mm Lens Not a 30mm Lens?

Before we can talk about choosing the right lens for your needs, we need to define what scale of focal length we're using. Look at the lens specifications for many consumer digital cameras, and you may see two different sets of numbers. The first range is usually much smaller, such as 6mm–18mm, while the second is significantly larger, such as 38mm–115mm. These two scales are indicative of one of the essential differences between film and digital cameras.

As we've explained, film lenses are designed to cover a full frame (36×24mm) of 35mm film from edge to edge. Put the same lens on a DSLR with an image sensor smaller than a frame of 35mm film and only the center portion of the lens — a cropped portion — is actually used. Therefore, the lens appears to increase, or multiply the size of the cropped image. (See Figures 2-3, 2-4, and 2-5)

For generations, photographers have become accustomed to distinguishing the type of lens (wide angle, normal, telephoto, etc.) being used by their focal lengths. For instance, most photographers instantly know that on a 35mm film camera, a 20mm lenses provides ultra-wide angle coverage, a 35mm lens yields a semi-wide angle field of view, 50mm is considered a normal lens, 90mm is typical of a portrait (semi-telephoto) lens, and anything above 135mm is a telephoto lens. The really long 500mm and 1000mm lenses used for Space Shuttle takeoffs and World Series photographs are ultra-or extreme-telephoto lenses. For those of us to whom such values are second nature, trying to decipher the meaning of the much smaller focal lengths of digital lenses designed for smaller image sensors is almost counterintuitive.

To resolve this confusion, manufacturers provide focal lengths both in absolute terms and as their 35mm equivalency. In fact, this practice became so universal that some manufacturers don't bother listing the actual focal lengths but use only their 35mm equivalencies.

The Multiplication Factor

Figures 2-4 and 2-5 appear to be cropped versions of Figure 2-3. Actually, the differences among the three photos are based on the concept of using the same focal length lens on different size image sensors and not cropping. This is known as the *multiplication factor*.

The multiplication factor is derived by determining how much smaller the image sensor is than a frame of 35mm film. That, in turn, tells you how much a certain focal length lens will cover. The multiplication factor has the net effect of enlarging the picture by cutting out all the visual information on the edges outside the image sensor frame and capturing the smaller area inside.

For example, all Olympus DSLRs are powered by Kodak's four thirds CCD (18×13.5mm), which is almost exactly half the size of a full frame of 35mm film. Do the math — a half-size image sensor requires only 50 percent of a film lens to provide edge-to-edge coverage, so the multiplication factor on all Olympus DSLRs is 2X. Therefore, if you put a traditional 35mm lens on an Olympus DSLR, it will give you the approximate coverage of a traditional 70mm lens. Because most Nikon DSLR sensors are somewhat larger (23.7×15.5mm) than Kodak's four thirds CCD, the multiplication factor is 1.3X. Similarly, Sigma SD9 and SD10 cameras have a smaller Foveon image sensor that measures 20.7×13.8mm, so the multiplication factor is about 1.8X.

In practical terms, the multiplication factor is useful in determining 35mm equivalency, so photographers will know the degree of coverage that their lenses will provide when mounted in front of their particular DSLR.

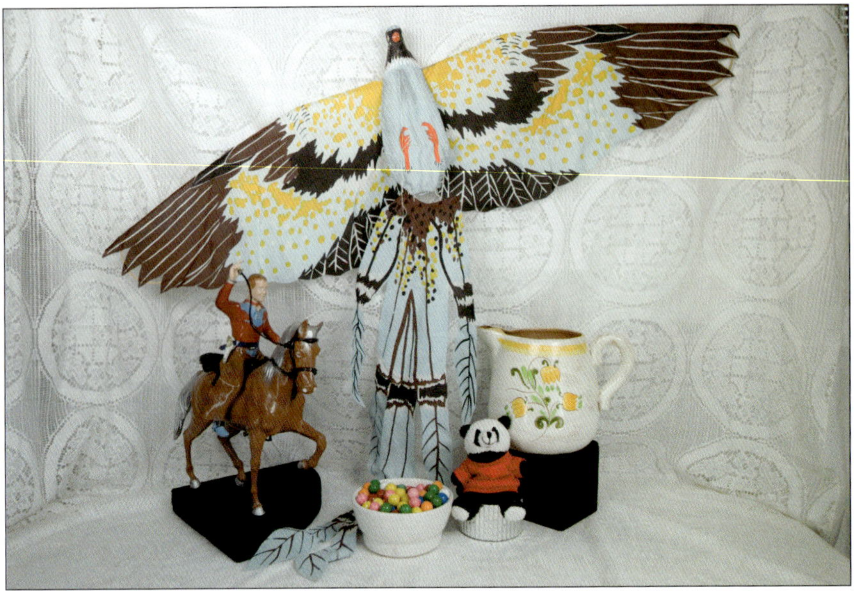

Figure 2-3: Setting a wide angle zoom lens to 30mm on a Canon EOS 1Ds Mark II, with its full-sized image sensor, gives you the same coverage as using the same or a similar lens on a 35mm film camera. (Shot at 1/100 at *f*5.6.)

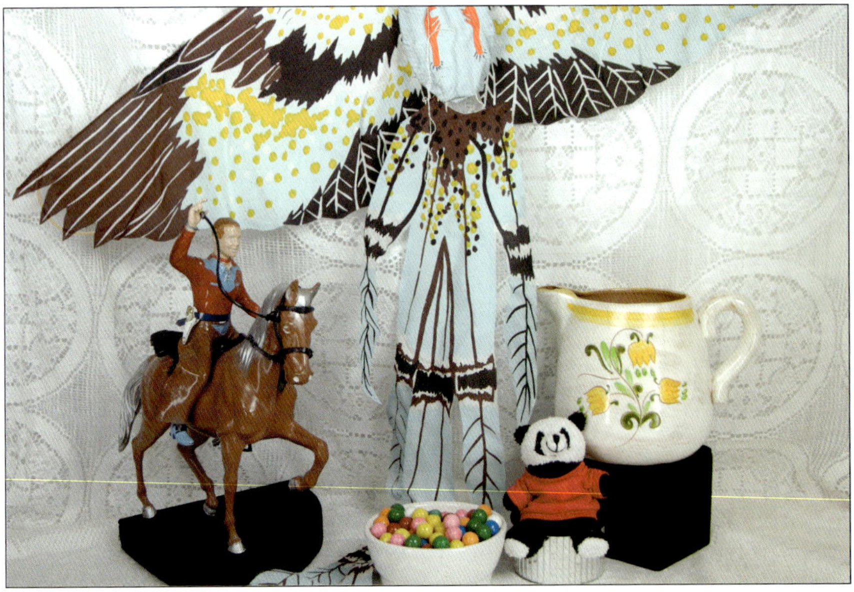

Figure 2-4: On a Nikon D2X, which has a smaller image sensor than the Canon Mark II, a 30mm lens focal length frames the same scene as Figure 2-3 more tightly, almost as though we had zoomed into it. (Shot at 1/100 at *f*4.8.)

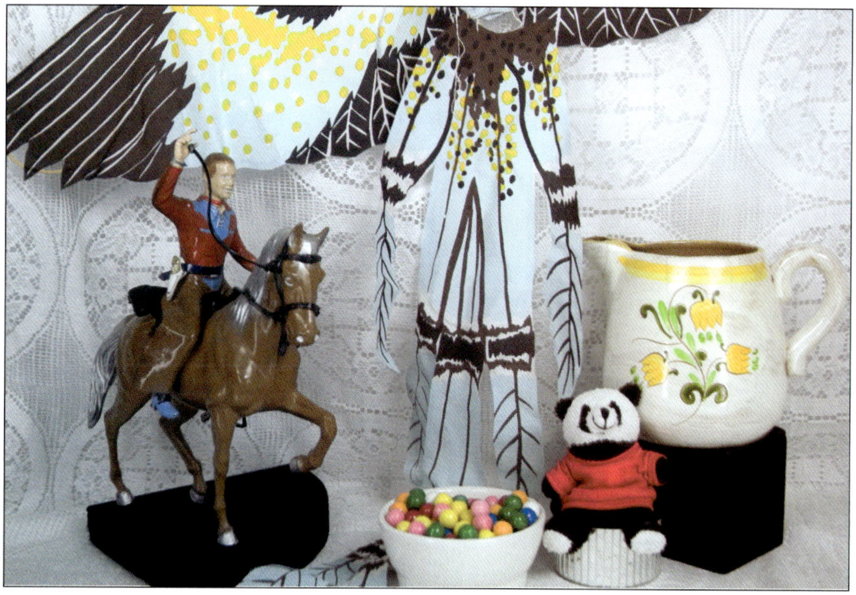

Figure 2-5: The Sigma SD10 has a smaller image sensor than the Nikon D2X, so it frames even more tightly, though this image is also shot with a 30mm lens. (Shot at 1/50 at *f*4.5.)

Depth of Field Is Another Issue

While knowing your DSLR's multiplication factor is extremely useful in selecting a lens focal length with roughly the same field of coverage as you used to get on your film SLR, calculating the effect of that lens equivalency isn't a simple or straightforward matter. That's because, although the area of coverage may be equivalent, its depth of field will not be.

Depth of field is the portion of a photo from the foreground and the background that will be in sharp focus. It can vary according to the precise point where the photographer focuses her lens, and according to the *f*-stop (aperture of the lens). Opening the aperture produces a shallower depth of field; closing or stopping the lens down has the opposite effect. (See Chapter 5.) But depth of field is also defined by the lens's focal length. Wide angle lenses produce enhanced depth of field, while telephoto lenses produce shorter depth of field.

The lens's *actual* focal length, and not its equivalency, defines its optical depth of field characteristics. Physically, the smaller the lens, the greater the depth of field. A 10mm lens is so small and shallow that, even wide open, it can capture a depth of field between 1 foot and infinity. That is true whether it is mounted on a full-sized image sensor and capturing an ultra-wide scene or is put on a camera with a 2X multiplication factor, which would then capture the equivalent of a 20mm scene. Difficulties arise when the numbers go higher. For instance, a 50mm lens captures only as much area as a 100mm telephoto on a camera with a 2X multiplication factor — but will still have the depth of field of a 50mm lens.

To achieve total creative control, a photographer shooting a DSLR with a multiplication factor must pay careful attention to the actual depth of field that lens will produce and not simply what its angle of coverage is. This won't matter much to young photographers who never used pre-electronic SLRs and lenses, since they don't have legacy knowledge that they need to rethink. But it's important information to factor in for those of us who grew up shooting film.

Distortion

All lenses are curved, and because they focus their image on a flat image sensor or film plane, there will always be some level of distortion. With many lenses, the distortion level is barely noticeable and not objectionable. However, as soon as you go to extreme wide angle or telephoto, use specific film lenses on certain digital cameras, or position your camera at certain angles, the distortion level can rise by an order of magnitude. The four pictures in this sidebar exhibit the four most common types of optical distortions associated with camera lenses.

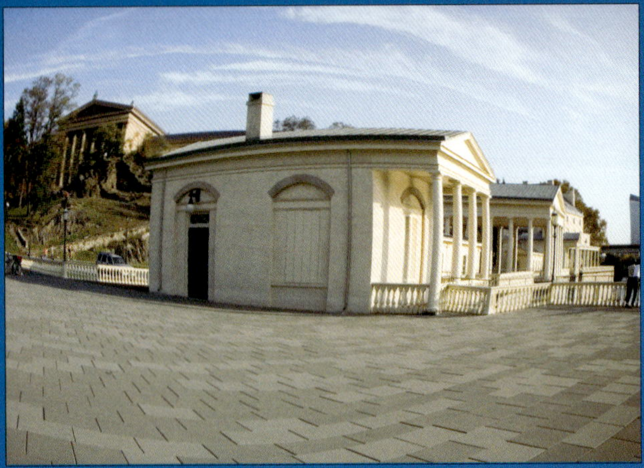

An extreme example of barrel distortion, this picture looks like a fun house effect, as though everything is bowing outward. Notice, particularly, the roof of the central building and the curved paving stones, which are physically laid out in straight lines.

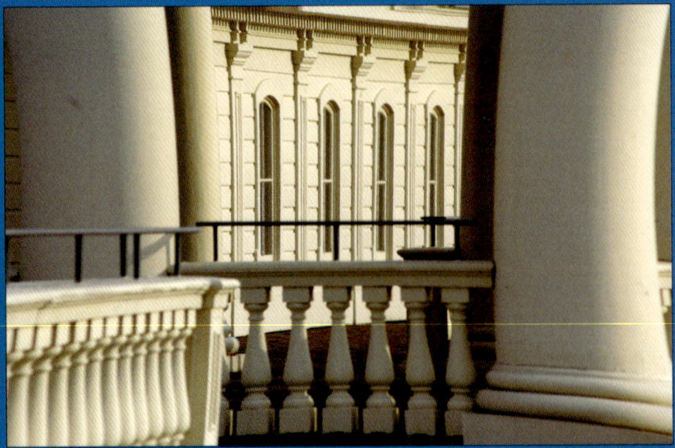

The opposite of barrel distortion, pincushioning causes the image to appear to be imploding, or falling into itself. In this scene, the large pillars are quite straight, but the distortion makes them look curved.

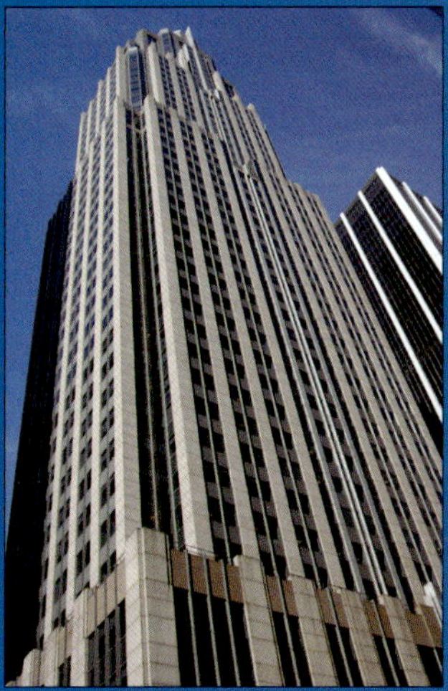

This classic example of perspective shift is caused by using a wide angle lens angled upward to photograph a skyscraper. It creates an optical illusion where straight lines seemingly bend inward and converge.

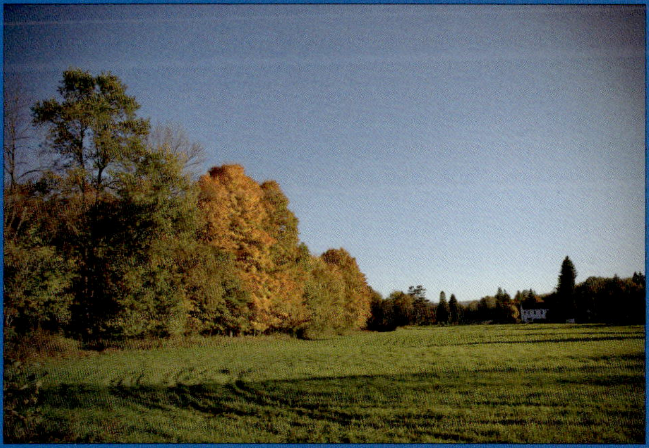

Vignetting causes a softening or darkening around the edges of the photograph. In particular, look at how much darker the sky looks in the upper corners, compared to the center of the picture.

Sometimes, distortion is good, because it becomes a creative element in your photograph. Knowing the distortion characteristics of your lenses can enable you to use them in your composition. For instance, you may like the dramatic upswing of the Dorian pillars on a museum edifice captured with an ultra-wide-angle lens. But mostly, distortion is an unwanted, uncontrollable effect that you'll want to avoid, minimize, or correct.

Tip

As we discuss in Chapter 5, the amount of light that reaches your image sensor (or film) and generates your photograph is controlled by three factors: shutter speed, aperture, and ISO setting. The aperture is the "hole" in the lens through which light travels, and it is measured in *f*-stops. The larger the aperture (the lower the *f*-stop number), the greater the amount of light you can capture, which is particularly important in low-light situations. When you hear of a lens being referred to as a fast lens that means it has the ability to open up to a larger aperture (such as *f*/1.4 or *f*/2.8) than an average lens of the same focal length (*f*/3.5 to *f*/5.6). Just like average lenses, fast lenses will close down to smaller apertures such as *f*/11, *f*/16, or *f*/22. Fast lenses are usually more expensive. If you shoot often in low-light situations, the extra cost might be worth it.

Choosing the Right Focal Length Lens

The longer your lens, the smaller angle of coverage in your photo. In other words, the greater your focal length, the closer and more tightly framed will be your image. (See Figure 2-6.)

However, there is a lot more to choosing your focal length than how close to or far away from your subject you want to get. That's because each focal length will create different perspectives, relationships, and distortions, making the choice of your lens an artistic decision. (See Figure 2-7.)

DSLR optics range all the way from a pancake-thin 7mm fisheye lens to a bazooka-sized 5000mm extreme-telephoto lens, and everything in between. What focal length lens you decide to use depends upon the picture effect you wish to achieve. Remember, the true size of the lens is relative to your camera's multiplication factor. (See the discussion of multiplication factor earlier in the chapter.) However, for the sake of simplicity, we're going to survey various focal length lenses and assume that we're shooting with a full-frame DSLR. Once you know your particular camera's multiplication factor (it will be listed in the owner's manual), you can work out the specific size lens that you need for a particular shot.

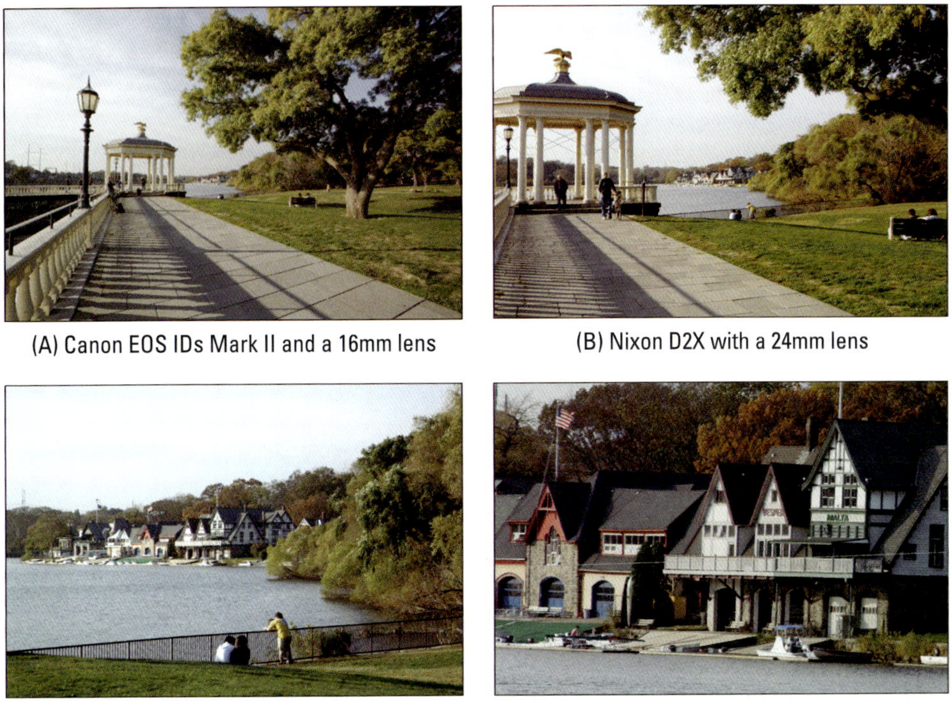

(A) Canon EOS IDs Mark II and a 16mm lens

(B) Nixon D2X with a 24mm lens

(C) Nixon D2X with 70mm lens

(D) Nixon D2X with a 300mm lens

Figure 2-6: Keeping our tripod in exactly the same spot, on the shore of Philadelphia's Schuylkill River, we changed the focal lengths of our lenses, which completely changed the photo we captured. We also changed cameras, using a Canon EOS 1Ds Mark II (with its full-sized image sensor) to get the ultra-wide view in (A). Then, changing to the Nikon D2X, which with its multiplication factor of 1.3X, took us much closer to the subject.

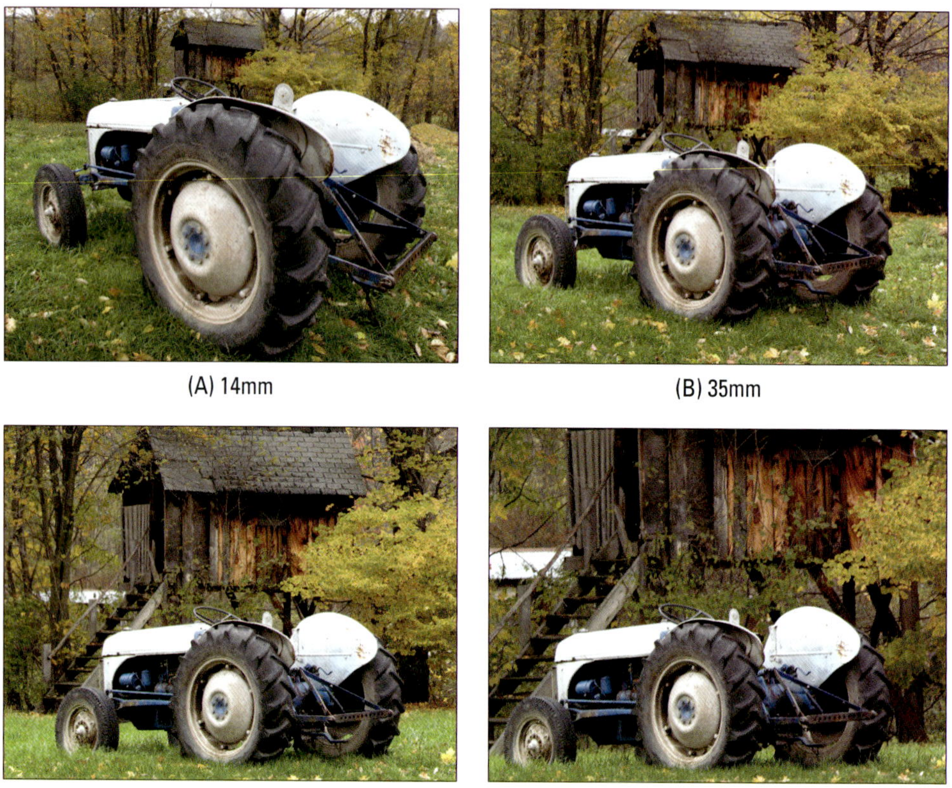

(A) 14mm

(B) 35mm

(C) 72mm

(D) 200mm

Figure 2-7: The focal length of your lens affects much more than how much of a scene is framed. In all these photos, the tractor occupies approximately the same percentage of the frame. We did this by moving farther away as we changed lenses to use greater focal lengths. But the relationship of the tractor to the other elements in the picture, as well as their relative sizes, changed dramatically with each lens. Notice in particular the size of the tree house in the background and the perspective relationships of the tree house, its stairs, and the tractor. Also, in (A), in which we were almost on top of the tractor, in order to capture the wide angle, notice how much larger the front tire seems compared to the other tires. Sally enjoys taking advantage of this kind of wide angle distortion when composing her photographs. (Photos taken with an Olympus E-1, which has a 2X multiplication factor.)

Fisheye

Many lenses between 7mm and 18mm are fisheye types, while others are conventional ultra-wide angles. You can instantly tell by looking through the viewfinder. If the picture you see looks like a funhouse mirror, with everything bowing out from the center, then it's a fisheye lens. (See the tulip photo on the first page of this chapter.) Fisheyes produce great special effects when you want something kinky or bizarre, or when you're looking for a shot in which the scene appears artificially rounded. They are particularly effective for dramatic architectural shots that give an offbeat 180-degree view of the conventional. Incidentally, you also can use a fisheye lens to capture an ultra-ultra-wide-angle view, and then apply rectilinear software to correct the perspective during image editing.

Ultra-Wide

14mm to 24mm lenses are generally considered ultra-wides, and capture between 80 and 115 degrees of coverage. For general reference, if you put a hand in front of one eye, the area of coverage you'll see with the other eye is about 90 degrees. Most modern ultra-wides are rectilinear (see the "Is Your Wide Angle Lens Rectilinear?" sidebar), with distortion coming primarily from near objects looking larger than they are and far objects appearing smaller. All digital ultra-wides are retrofocus lenses, because physically short lenses channel light obliquely rather than directly to the image sensor. (See the section on lens design later in this chapter.) Ultra-wides are great for crowd shots, landscapes, and other subjects that you want to include without having to back up to Toledo to take the shot. Conversely, they're usually not good for portraits, because they tend to distort faces and features.

Wide Angle

Generally, 24mm through 38mm is considered wide angle. Unlike ultra-wides, wide angle lenses give a relatively normal perspective. What's more, some wide angles are also high-speed lenses, good for taking available light candids. Wide angle lenses are good for shooting architecture, groups, photojournalism, and landscapes. Some photographers use a wide angle as their normal lens, because of the slightly expanded view and great depth of field it offers.

Is Your Wide Angle Lens Rectilinear?

Wide angle lenses are particularly prone to barrel distortion and extreme perspective shifts. (See the previous "Distortion" sidebar for example images.) Parallel lines, rather than remaining parallel, seem to converge or even meet somewhere in the distance. Fisheye lenses, the ultimate in ultra-wide-angle coverage (up to 180 degrees, or everything in front of the lens), warps the image so dramatically that it looks as if everything — top, bottom, sides — dramatically falls away from the center. No wonder that fisheye shots are sometimes known as the funhouse effect. Of course, some photographers want, and welcome, distortion as part of their artistic statement. To most photographers, however, such extreme optical effects are quite unwanted.

And that is why most wide angle lenses are corrected to produce a rectilinear view. (*Rectilinear* means a perspective in which parallel lines remain parallel, rather than converge at some point.) If you don't like perspective or barrel distortion, make certain that the wide angle or zoom lens you are considering buying is of a rectilinear design. You can easily tell if a lens is rectilinear or not by reading its technical specs before you buy. But if you already own a nonrectilinear lens, don't despair, because there's lots of software around, such as DxO Optics Pro (`www.dxo.com`) and Altostorm Rectilinear Panorama (`www.altostorm.com`) that can easily and automatically correct perspective and barrel distortions.

Normal

45mm to 55mm lenses are considered normal, because they feature a perspective that's roughly equivalent to the human eye. Although many photographers don't bother buying a normal lens because it provides neither an extra-wide or extra-close view, it's the one that produces the most realistic-looking perspective. In fact, it's almost the only lens that famed photojournalist Henri Cartier-Bresson used during his entire career. A normal lens is a good, all-around focal length for shooting objects and people near enough to touch or talk to, as well as landscapes and vistas. And a high-speed normal lens is excellent for candids and available light shots.

Portrait

Any lens between 65mm and 105mm is often referred to as a portrait lens because it's the ideal focal length for shooting head-and-shoulders portraits. The perspective doesn't appreciably compress or distort the image, and the depth of field can easily be adjusted to control what's in sharp focus and what's softly blurred. Besides portraiture, this focal length is also very good for close-ups, copy work, photojournalism, nature, and kids.

Medium Telephoto

135mm to 200mm is usually referred to as a medium telephoto. This focal length has limited depth of field as well as medium perspective compression, while magnifying the subject (bringing it closer) by about 2–3 times. Medium telephoto is good for some sports, children, nature, candid portraits at a distance, and capturing selected portions of distant subjects.

Extreme Telephoto

Extreme telephoto begins at 300mm and extends through 5000mm baseball-bat-sized lenses to adapters to telescopes. These lenses are designed to pull distant objects into close view, such as spectator sports, wild animals, and astronomical subjects. Image compression is extreme, which has the optical effect of making a subject appear to be very close to, or even on top of, its background. When using an extreme telephoto lens, the camera is almost always mounted on a heavy tripod and the shutter set to a high speed, because motion and blur are intensified by the long focal length.

Tip

Need more magnification? Try a lens extender. Rather than adding another expensive, heavy and bulky telephoto lens or telephoto zoom to the amount of equipment you haul around, consider buying a lens extender. Also called a lens multiplier, a *lens extender* is a short cylindrical device that fits between your lens and DSLR body and whose optics will double or triple the focal length of the lens. Lens extenders are small, light, and relatively inexpensive ($40–$100), and they don't appreciably affect focus or depth of field. The tradeoff is that you'll lose about 2 *f*-stops, and image quality won't be as sharp. Extenders are useful when you need more magnification (sports, nature, etc.), but can't afford or don't want to carry an additional telephoto.

Macro

Many DSLR fixed focal length and zoom lenses below 135mm come equipped with the ability to shoot close-ups, also called macro mode. Your lens does this either within the continuous autofocus range, or by pressing a switch on the side of the lens barrel that extends it from the normal to the macro mode. Depending upon the lens, macro can range from about 18" down to about 5". Of course, the closer you get, the more limited your depth of field will be. And when you get really close, motion shake becomes an important issue, so you'll probably have to mount the camera on a tripod to get razor-sharp shots.

But there's a problem shooting any normal lens in macro mode: they are designed for capturing three-dimensional subjects. When you shoot in macro mode, essentially reducing the world from three to two dimensions, the edges of your picture can become blurred, distorted, or darkened. That's why some optics makers produce what is called, appropriately but confusingly enough, a macro lens. A true macro lens—which can have a focal length of between 55mm and 135mm—functions normally when shooting objects and subjects at distances other than close up. However, macro lenses come equipped with extended barrels that may be able to focus down to 1" or less. And because they are optically corrected for flat field shooting, the edges remain sharp and undistorted. Macro lenses are usually more expensive than normal lenses, and also are 1–1½ *f*-stops slower. But if image quality and fidelity are critical for your close-up shots, use a true macro lens rather than simply sliding your regular lens to macro mode.

Zoom

A zoom is a lens with a variable focal length. Depending upon its configuration, a zoom can range anywhere from ultra-wide-angle to extreme-telephoto, and everything in between. The zoom range is calculated according to the lowest to the highest focal length and is expressed as a ratio (3X, 4X, 10X, etc.). The great majority of lenses sold for DSLRs and SLRs are 2X–4X zoom lenses rather than fixed focal length lenses. The reason for their popularity is fairly obvious: zoom lenses are much more versatile, giving users more optical bang for their buck. Zooms are favored by photojournalists and sports/nature photographers who can more easily track subjects, and of course, shooters who prefer adjusting the lens's focal length rather than walking closer to or further from the subject.

Zoom Lenses versus Fixed Focal Length Lenses

The $64 question is this: quality-wise, are zoom lenses as good as fixed focal length lenses? The short answer is "yes, they are," but it's slightly more complicated than a simple yes or no answer.

When zoom lenses were first introduced for 35mm film SLRs back in the early 1960s, they were quickly embraced, primarily by serious amateurs because using one zoom lens was a more convenient and somewhat less expensive option (not to mention a lot less weighty) to buying and carrying a bunch of fixed focal length lenses. The downside, however, was that zoom lenses were considered optically inferior (not as sharp or contrasty), often had to be refocused every time the focal length changed, had a slower *f*-stop and a somewhat limited zoom range, and were bigger and heavier than most fixed focal length lens. And while they generally saved money over the collective cost of a few lenses, a zoom lens was usually priced significantly higher than individual fixed focal length lenses. Nevertheless, they became a permanent part of the photographic landscape, though back then few professionals would be caught dead using a zoom lens on assignment.

Anti-Shake Lenses

For years, camcorder owners have benefited from a no-brainer technology that reduces or eliminates annoying camera shake: optical image stabilization. (Some less expensive camcorders use a method called electronic stabilization, which isn't nearly as good because it compromises image quality.) Basically, *image stabilization* is a way of counteracting, or steadying the jerky, wavering motion caused by hand-holding the camera. It accomplishes this by using tiny motors and sensors to rapidly move an internal lens element in the opposite direction from the shake. The net effect of shaky motion and image stabilization countermotion is that they cancel each other out, making for a smoother, cleaner picture.

Image stabilization proved so successful on camcorders that SLR lens manufacturers decided to build anti-shake technology into some lenses, drawing the small amount of electricity needed to operate them directly from the camera body. That way, the photographer can shoot at a slower speed, a higher *f*-stop, or both, with an assurance that the shake produced from not being able to hold the camera rock steady will be minimized or eliminated. Because of SLR and DSLR lens interchangeability and the larger focal lengths (more glass) involved, still photography lenses with built-in image stabilization tend to be heavier and cost considerably more to build than camcorder anti-shake lenses. For those reasons, until recently, most SLR and DSLR anti-shake lenses were restricted to expensive top-of-the-line telephoto and extreme-telephoto fixed focal length and zoom lenses.

Fortunately, the technology has come down considerably in price. An increasing number of digital lenses, including wide angle zooms, incorporate anti-shake technology. They still command a premium price but are only slightly more expensive than ordinary digital lenses. In fact, Konica Minolta decided to bypass the need for premium-priced anti-shake lenses and build image stabilization directly into its DSLR bodies. This allows the photographer to attach any lens and still benefit from anti-shake.

Does anti-shake work? We were somewhat skeptical until we began testing and shooting image-stabilization-equipped lenses. But after discovering that yes, we could squeeze an extra stop or two by using an anti-shake lens, we became firm believers. And because there's no image quality or performance penalty, we leave the anti-shake switch on almost all the time. The only situation in which we turn it off is during time exposures when the camera is on a tripod. We enthusiastically recommend spending the little extra it costs to buy lenses with built-in anti-shake technology. You won't be sorry.

Branded versus Generic Lenses

Every bargain-loving photographer has owned and used, or knows somebody who swears by, generic/off-brand lenses from such manufacturers as Tokina, Vivitar, Soligar, Sigma, Tamron, and the like. Such lenses almost always offer a significant price savings (in many instances, half what their branded counterparts sell for), and most even promise that optically they are as good as or even better than branded lenses. How do they stack up against better-known, more expensive company brands? More to the point, can you capture award-winning, high-quality images using generic/off-brand lenses? Like so many other things in photography, the answer is yes and no.

There was a short time, years ago, when our photographs were personal or used primarily to illustrate our articles, we did own and use a variety of generic/off-brand lenses for our Nikon film SLRs. (We use only factory brand lenses on our Hasselblads because there are no generics available for these medium-format cameras, and no Leica owner in his right mind, including us, would ever shoot with a non-Leica lens.) Buying generics/off-brands saved us significant money, and the lenses generally performed well. However, we quickly stopped using generics when we started shooting professionally, and we have never looked back. That's because the lens mounts on generic lenses tend to be less robust, and with frequent use, the focusing or zoom collars would occasionally become a little loose, sloppy. Equally important, our experience was that generic lens generally didn't deliver quite as fine image quality as their major brand's top-of-the-line counterparts. However, it wasn't a difference one would notice except under great magnification, and only when viewed by an expert.

Our advice is buy generic lenses if price is a make-or-break issue, but spring for the more expensive company brands if you're shooting professionally, are rough on equipment, or plan on making exhibition prints.

Obviously, zoom lenses got better over the years. On most zooms, image quality is almost the equal of fixed focal length lenses. Most retain sharp focus at any zoom setting and don't have to be manually tweaked every time you change the focal length. Today's zoom lenses tend to be shorter and lighter, the variable focal lengths often are more extensive, plus they are much more affordable. It's the rare pro who eschews zoom lenses these days in favor of a gadget bag full of fixed focal length lenses.

Tip

Okay, you know that any zoom lens you buy is going to be 1 or 2 *f*-stops slower than a high-speed, fixed focal length lens. This may not matter much when you're shooting in bright sunlight or using a flash, but it can be critical when shooting in available light. To minimize camera shake in low light, thereby increasing the sharpness of your picture, shoot at the lowest possible *f*-stop and at the zoom lens's widest angle. If there's still not enough light to achieve correct exposure or eliminate camera shake, try upping the ISO equivalency. (See Chapter 5.) True, the image will tend to be noisy, but you will have gotten the shot.

Tip

Under the right conditions, all lenses may produce some degree of flare (internal reflections that produce light streaks on an image). There are two tried-and-true remedies to reducing or eliminating lens flare. The first is to always use a lens hood or shade on your lens. The second way is to change your shooting position, especially if your subject is backlit. Lastly, if all else fails, you may be able to reduce or eliminate the flare from your photos by using a software clone tool in your computer. (See Chapter 10.)

But zoom lenses also have disadvantages and tradeoffs that prevent serious photographers from discarding their fixed focal length lenses. For one thing, zooms still are heavier and larger than fixed focal length lenses (though a single zoom almost always weighs less than the 2–4 fixed focal length lenses that it replaces). Zoom lenses are generally 1 or 2 *f*-stops slower than fixed focal length lenses and may even be slower yet when extended to full telephoto. Also, because they usually have more glass elements that can produce internal reflections, zooms are more prone to flare.

Because of their convenience, we use zoom lenses for most of our photography. When we're shooting in reduced available light and need the extra *f*-stop or two, we switch to a high-speed, fixed focal length lens. One fixed focal length lens that we will almost always choose over a zoom is our 65mm flat field macro lens. (See the sidebar "Macro" earlier in the chapter.)

Tip

Frankly, a lot of our film photographic equipment, including lenses, was purchased used. We bought from fellow photographers upgrading or changing their systems, and from dealers at full-service photo stores or camera shows who warranted what they sold. The advantage of purchasing them in person is that we could try out the merchandise before buying, usually by shooting a roll or two of film and examining the results. We never bought used lenses sight unseen, even from reputable firms offering money-back guarantees. If you want to save a few bucks buying used, we strongly suggest passing up those irresistible bargains on eBay or other online stores. Trek down to a full service photo store so that you can try the lens out on your own camera body. Don't buy it straight away. Take a bunch of shots and then view them on your computer monitor or output them on your desktop printer. You should buy only after you are satisfied with the results.

Why Should You Care about Lens Design?

Read any advertisement for a camera lens, and you'll be barraged with lots of technobabble touting the natural superiority of the product. "*It's a high-speed retrolinear lens made of low-dispersion ED glass with three aspherical lenses grouped into five elements, designed to reduce vignetting, chromatic aberrations, and both barrel and pincushion distortion.*" Even if you happen to know what all these terms mean, you can be like a deer caught in the headlights as you gaze at the features and specs and try to make some sort of sense out of them. As much as we hate technobabble, this stuff can be important in assessing how good and how appropriate the lens is, and how well it will perform in helping you capture the photographs you want. So, let's briefly unravel this gobbledygook into something closer to the English language.

Intelligent or CPU-Controlled Lenses

Most state-of-the-art, digital-specific lenses come equipped with a built-in computer chip or CPU, designed to automatically communicate with the camera body and react to exposure and focus information. In fact, many do not even have any mechanical means of setting the diaphragm externally—it's done in the camera control panel, not on the lens. Nor can you mechanically focus many state-of-the-art lenses simply by turning a collar on the barrel, because it's done internally, using electric motors—what is referred to as focus-by-wire.

Actually, if your lens has a built-in intelligence or a CPU, it requires that you do nothing, either to activate or disable its functions. It simply connects to and draws its power from the camera and immediately begins exchanging data.

On some DSLR systems, it is possible to use older, non-CPU lenses, as long as the lens can be physically attached to the camera. (Note that some lens series have different mounting hardware, to prevent them from being used with newer, incompatible bodies.) However, the older lens may not react correctly, rapidly enough, or at all with the DSLR's intelligence. In addition, if you use a TTL strobe, it may not fully communicate with the older design lenses. (See Chapter 8.) With some lenses, the automatic diaphragm that keeps the lens open while viewing and stops down during exposure may not work. If this is the case, you must use the lens in manual mode only.

Low-Dispersion Glass, Aspherical Lenses, and Chromatic Aberration

Most camera lenses are made of optical glass, although some also incorporate quartz, and some early and inexpensive models actually use all- or part-plastic lenses. Optical glass may consist of many different elements and compounds, such as silicon, ash, barium, fluorite, sodium, magnesium, and even lead. Low-dispersion glass (sometimes called ED, or extra-low dispersion glass) adds special components ("secret sauce") to the glass formula in an attempt to reduce or eliminate several optical defects, notably chromatic aberration.

Chromatic aberration, also called color aliasing, occurs when the red, green, and blue colors passing through the lens are focused separately on the image sensor. (See Figures 2-8 through 2-10.) Remember in high school physics, holding a prism up to the light and being rewarded with a delightful rainbow of colors spread on a table or piece of paper? That's what you *don't* want to happen with your lens, because it would cause the colors of your photo to not line up precisely. Chromatic aberrations look like thin red, green, or blue lines along edges that don't quite meet, or areas that display prismatic-like colors where only solid colors should be. So, all other things being equal, buy lenses that incorporate ED glass.

Another approach to reducing chromatic aberrations is to incorporate an aspherical element or elements (pieces of glass) into a lens. In fact, chances are that the new lens you just bought has one or more aspherical (or asymmetrical) elements, and, if price has anything to do with quality, the more aspherical elements your lens has, the better it supposedly is. Adding aspherical elements to a lens helps reduce not only chromatic aberration but also another related optical defect, spherical aberration.

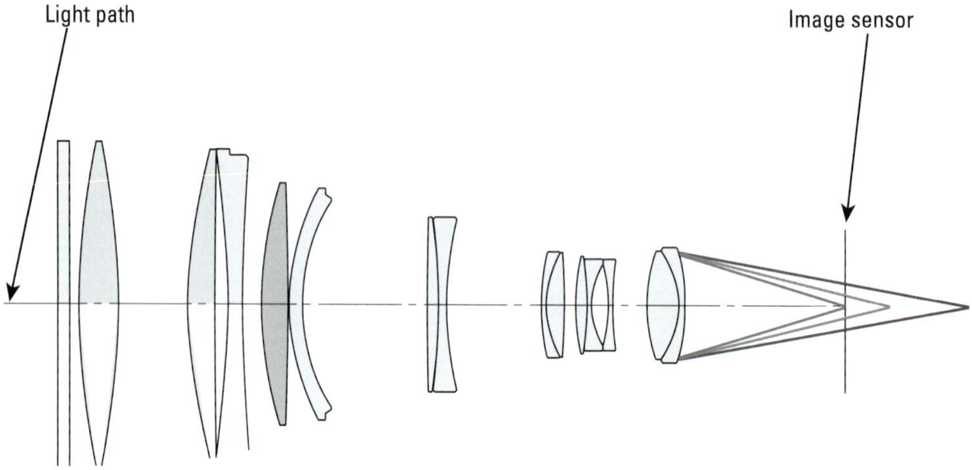

Figure 2-8: Chromatic aberration occurs when the red, green, and blue wavelengths of the light don't focus evenly on the image sensor. (Graphic courtesy of Canon USA)

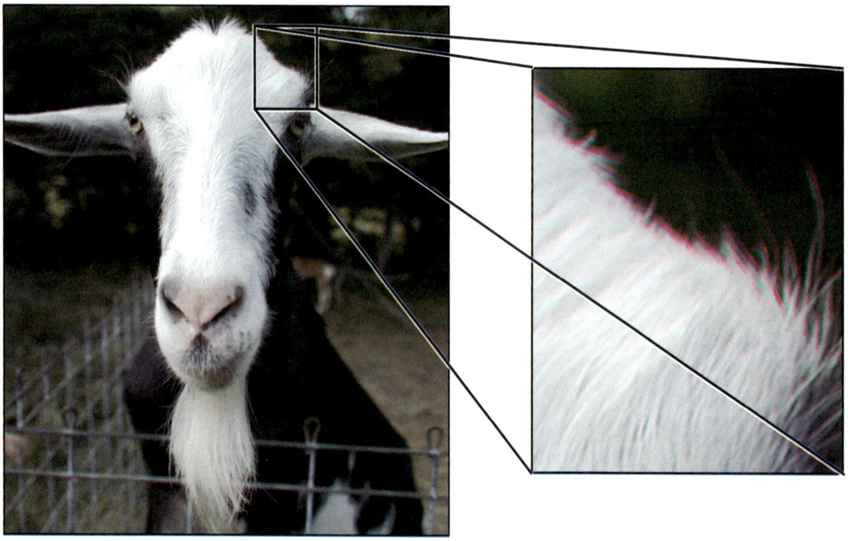

Figure 2-9: When a photo is printed small, you might not notice the image quality degradation of chromatic aberration (the photo on the left). But when printed larger, or using more precise technology, such as for an exhibition print or a glossy magazine ad, the effect of chromatic aberration is that the three primary colors do not line up correctly and the photo displays separate colored lines and artifacts. This is particularly noticeable along edges in the image, such as where the white fur in this photo appears against the dark background. But if you look closely, you can also see displaced colors throughout the white fur (the photo on the right).

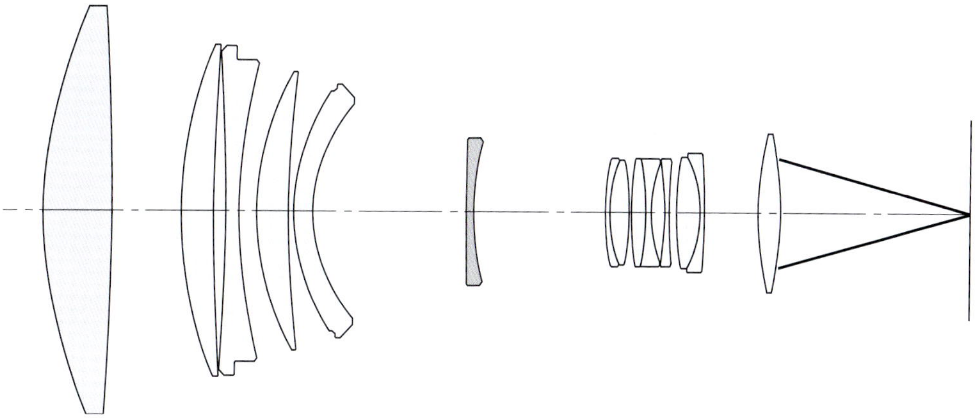

Figure 2-10: By using ED glass and/or incorporating aspherical elements in the lens design, manufacturers are able to reduce or even eliminate chromatic aberrations. (Graphic courtesy of Canon USA)

Incidentally, there's another type of chromatic aberration common to digital cameras, called *purple fringing*. It is generally caused not by a lens design or makeup defect, but by the interaction of the microlenses on the image sensor and an internal defect known as blooming (see Chapter 1 on the role of microlenses).

As its name implies, purple fringing looks like a thin fizzy purple line around the edges of a subject, especially when the subject is backlit or you are shooting with a wide angle lens. Here are some suggestions for getting rid of purple fringing:

- Change camera angles when shooting.
- Stop down the lens.
- Increase the color saturation.
- Process your photos through a utility like DxO Lab's Optics Pro or PhotoFixLens (see Chapter 3 on Accessories).

Some cameras and lenses are much more prone to purple fringing than others, so it's a good idea to read a few reviews of a particular product before you buy, to see if purple fringing might be a problem.

Retrofocus and Front Focus Lenses

According to the physics of optics, a lens's focal length is the distance between the center of the lens and the film plane or image sensor when focused at infinity. Longer lenses magnify, so they're used for telephoto shots. Shorter lenses collect a larger field of view, so they're used for wide angle photos. But there's a problem when the wide angle lens is so short that the rear element almost touches or even extends past the DSLR's mirror (which used to be why some SLRs had mirror lockup, or the ability to raise and hold the mirror out of the film plane). Or, sometimes, the telephoto lens is so large that it's too big and heavy to shoot without mounting it and the camera on a tripod.

Is Your Image Sensor Too Good for Your Lens?

One subject that digital camera and lens manufacturers are reluctant to discuss is a somewhat obscure technical issue called the Nyquist frequency (also known as the Nyquist theorem). When applied to digital photography, Nyquist frequency means that when a lens's resolving power (the ability to distinguish fine detail and render black lines black and not simply dark) is less than twice the resolution of an image sensor, visual aliasing can occur (usually in the form of moiré patterns). This wasn't an issue when megapixel counts were relatively low, because most lenses were far sharper than image sensor density requirements.

With the advent of DSLRs came higher megapixel image sensors coupled with larger photoreceptor sites, which require either a blur filter to reduce aliasing, significantly better lenses, or both. Blur filter and sharpening algorithms help improve image definition, but only up to a point. That's when superior optics make a significant image quality difference. However, although the newest, state-of-the-art digital lenses may match image sensor resolution, more megapixels do not necessarily produce sharper images or greater detail and may even reduce overall image sharpness. It's a conundrum that lens designers and image sensor fabricators are trying to deal with in a number of ways, such as by not placing microlenses in front of the image sensor or by coating the front elements of lenses so that they are fully apochromatic (color-corrected for all primary colors).

The only way that you, the photographer, can know whether a lens you are considering buying has a correspondingly higher resolving power than your DSLR's image sensor is to study technical reviews of the lens on such Web sites as `www.dpreview.com`.

That's when lens designers get creative, finding ways to produce lenses that are physically longer (or shorter) than their actual focal lengths. For wide angle, it means adding glass elements to the lens itself so that the distance from the center of the lens at infinity is greater than its actual focal length. This makes the lens practical to use, especially since, being further away, it can better direct the light straight on rather than at an oblique angle. As we explained in Chapter 1, DSLRs produce better pictures when light is focused directly into the image sensor's pixels.

When a wide angle lens is physically longer than its stated focal length (area of coverage), it is said to be a *retrofocus lens*. Sometimes, it's also called a reverse or inverted telephoto lens.

The opposite is true with telephoto lenses. The trick is to make telephoto lenses shorter than their stated focal lengths, so they will be small, light, and affordable.

Technically, a telephoto lens that is shorter than its stated focal length is called a *front focus lens*, and sometimes, simply a long lens.

Incidentally, most zoom lenses are a combination of retrofocus and front focus lenses.

The problem with both retrofocus and front focus lenses is they are prone to chromatic aberrations, especially with contrasty, backlit subjects. They also tend to be less sharp. The best way to avoid these two potential problems is to purchase a high-quality lens from a reputable manufacturer. All other things being equal, if a particular camera company offers a wide angle lens at a certain price (especially ultra-wides) and an almost identical model but at a significantly higher cost, you can be reasonably certain that the latter lens is optically superior. That's because high-quality retrofocus lenses are expensive and difficult to design and make. The same holds true to zooms and front focus telephoto lenses.

Summary

As a DSLR owner, you will quite naturally want to buy and use an assortment of interchangeable lenses. Choose those that give you the focal length and optical characteristics that you want and need. Be prepared to pay more money if you want higher-quality optics and more robust, durable lens mounts. And remember — the more lenses you have, the heavier your camera bag and credit card balance.

Chapter 3

Accessories

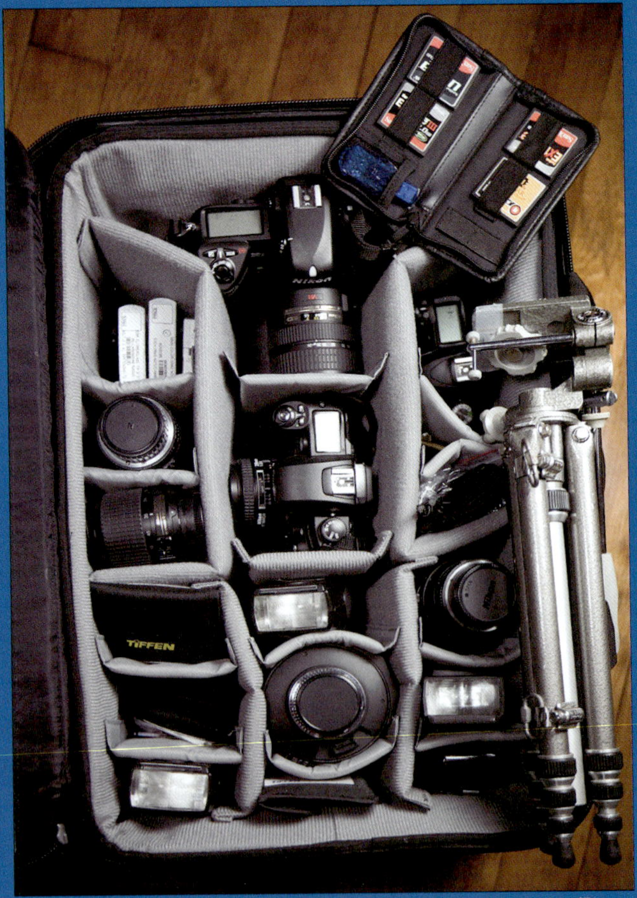

A photographer's typical bag of tricks filled with equipment and accessories. (Photo taken with a Canon EOS 1Ds Mark II, 16–35mm lens set at 30mm, 1/25 at f2.8)

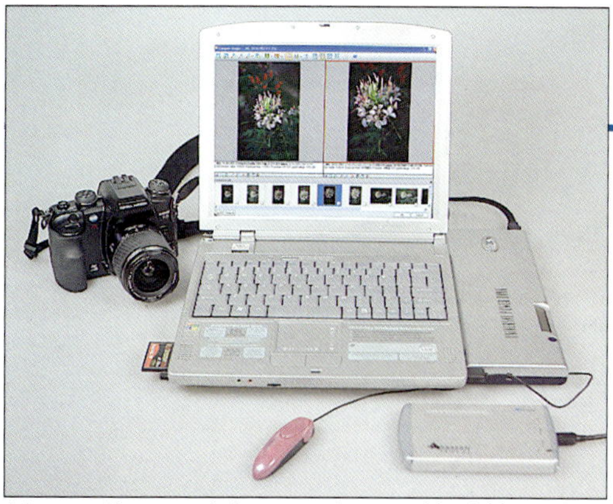

A laptop with an extended power pack, external hard drive, and Slimouse are important accessories when shooting on location. (Photo taken with a Fujifilm S3 Pro, 28mm lens, 1/60 at f4)

Unlike consumer digital cameras, most of which come equipped with almost everything you need to start shooting immediately, it's the rare DSLR that shoots right out of the box. That's because DSLRs are *systems* that consist of various components — body, lens, battery, memory card, flash, and so on — which are interchangeable and often sold separately This difference means that DSLR owners are both needful of and enthusiastic about accessorizing their cameras with a wide variety of add-ons and peripherals that increase and enhance productivity, make shooting more convenient and fun, expand creativity, and provide an extra margin of safety. What you buy, and how much you spend, depends upon your needs, budget — plus the size of your camera bag and how much weight you can shoulder in it.

In this chapter, we cover:

- Peripherals that are necessary for DSLR photography
- Accessories that will make your photography easier, more comfortable, and/or more creative
- Goodies that you may want, but that aren't strictly necessary

Necessities

There are four basic components that every DSLR system must have:

- Camera body
- Lens
- Battery (plus charger)
- Memory card

Many DSLR manufacturers market their cameras as a kit consisting of body, starter lens, and battery. Other items usually bundled with either the body or kit are:

- A CD (software allowing you to view and possibly edit RAW files)
- Shoulder strap
- Lens and body caps

- Cables (video, USB and/or FireWire)
- Instruction manual and warranty card(s)

If you plan to operate your DSLR as a tethered studio camera, you may also want an AC adapter to provide continuous power. It's usually optional and extra, since only a handful of manufacturers bundle one with the camera body.

Because of the added expense, no manufacturer currently bundles a memory card with either a camera body or kit. So, the first thing you'll need is a memory card. Actually, memory cards, because one is never enough.

Tip

Most DSLRs save images to Type I/II CompactFlash (CF) memory cards. A handful save to SD/MMC or SD cards, and a couple models can save to either Type I/II CF, SD, SD/MMC cards, or both. Several DSLRs can save either to a Type I/II CF card or an xD Picture card, or both. Unless you already have an inventory of high-capacity, high-performance cards that you want to use, it doesn't make sense to choose your camera based on the type of memory card it uses.

Memory Cards

Choosing the right memory card for your photography involves a lot more than knowing what kind of card your camera takes. (See Figure 3-1.) Other important considerations are:

- Capacity
- Speed
- Ruggedness

MEMORY CARD CAPACITY

Memory cards are one of the major limiting factors in digital photography, especially with DSLRs. The files that DSLRs generate can be quite large, so unless you want to change cards every few shots or minutes, you'll definitely want to use high-capacity memory cards of 1 gigabyte or larger. Unlike many consumer digital cameras, which can save directly only to cards of 2GB or less, every current DSLR can directly save to any size memory card. The largest capacity currently available are an 8GB CF card, a 4GB SD card, and a 2GB xD Picture card, though several manufacturers have announced even higher density cards.

Buying large-capacity memory cards isn't the same as getting a bargain-priced giant economy size item. The larger the card, the more you'll pay per gigabyte. While you can currently score a 1GB CF card for as little as $75, an 8GB CF card with comparable performance will set you back an average of $830.

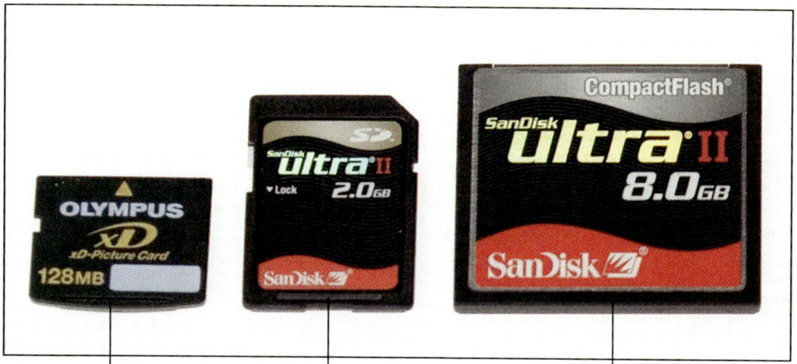

(A) (B) (C)

Figure 3-1: (A) An xD Picture card. (B) An SD card. (C) A CompactFlash card. The type of card you need is determined by your camera's requirements and compatibilities. However, there are other differences you need to consider when shopping for a memory card. By the way, the physical size of the memory card has nothing to do with its capacity. (Photo taken with an Olympus E-1, 14-55mm lens set at 54mm, 1/125 at *f*3.5.)

Tip

If your memory card becomes unreadable for some reason, don't despair. Put it aside and make sure you don't use it for saving anything that might overwrite the files that are hidden on it. Then, try one of the file recovery programs, such as ImageRecall. If you purchased a brand-name high-performance card, you might have received such software in the bundle.

MEMORY CARD SPEED

Another major advantage DSLRs have over most consumer digital cameras is that they are optimized to take advantage of high-speed memory cards. The faster the card, the quicker the camera is ready to shoot again. Card performance used to be expressed relative to a baseline, which was generally (but not universally) defined as a read/write speed of 150 kilobits per second. As card performance increased (advanced designs, faster NAND chips, better controllers, etc.), this boost was often expressed by manufacturers as how many times faster it was than first generation cards: 8X, 40X, 80X, 133X, 150X, and so on. Theoretically, a 60X card reads and writes (transfers) data 60 times faster than the original memory cards. However, because there's no universal standard, and since read and write times sometimes vary (it's often slightly faster to read an image file than it is to write one), posting this sort of speed rating can be quite misleading and confusing. Worse yet are manufacturers' descriptive but meaningless names for their high-performance cards, such as Platinum, High Speed, Professional, Ultra, Extreme, Elite Pro, and so on.

Why a Fast Memory Card Is Best

Yes, the speed of your memory card *does* make a major difference in sustained shooting situations. Your DSLR may be capable of shooting 3–8 or more frames per second, regardless of whether you use normal or high-performance memory cards, but it's the *sustained* speed that really matters when you're holding down the shutter button and clicking away. While some DSLRs have a set sustained rate of so many frames before the camera has to stop for processing and saving images, other DSLRs shoot and process simultaneously — the faster the images can be saved to the memory card, the more frames you can shoot without stopping. Also, once the buffer is full and your camera stops to process the images, you can shave precious seconds off the recovery time by using a high-performance card.

The best way to determine whether a memory card is fast is to peruse the manufacturer's technical specifications. For example, all SanDisk's Ultra II cards have a write speed of at least 9MB/sec and a read speed of 10MB/sec, and its top-of-the-line Extreme III cards clock in at 20MB/sec for both reading and writing data. You can check the Web sites of the major manufacturers (`www.sandisk.com`, `www.lexar.com`, `www.delkin.com`, `www.kingston.com`, `www.pretec.com`) for actual read/write speeds. Only, make certain that they are *sustained* and not peak speeds.

MEMORY CARD RUGGEDNESS

Do you shoot under environmental extremes, such as blistering desert heat or bone-chilling arctic cold? If so, you'll need cards designed to operate within a wide range of temperatures. Similarly, do you shoot in war zones or take your camera on mountain climbing expeditions? That's when you should be prepared to pay extra for impact-resistant, industrial-strength cards designed to take lots of physical abuse.

Incidentally, premium cards often come with important extras that help justify the higher cost. For instance, both Lexar Media and SanDisk bundle image file recovery software and a lifetime warranty with their top-of-the-line cards. SanDisk even provides a travel case for safely stowing your memory cards while on location.

Tip

Buy brand-name cards. There certainly are memory card bargains out there, and the lowest prices are usually for obscure brands that you've never heard of. Our advice (alas, told from experience) is stick with brand-name cards, even though they cost more. Often, you can't be certain that the speed or performance rating on no-name cards is accurate and honest, nor can you be assured that the card won't suddenly lose its formatting or simply die on you. And should it produce errors or stop working altogether, you may find it difficult or impossible tracking down the manufacturer for warranty replacement.

Caring for Your Memory Cards

While memory cards are quite durable (we've heard of cards that have been in floods and explosions, run over and dropped from hundreds of feet, and still survived with images intact), they are not impervious to damage or destruction. In fact, carelessly dropping an SD/MMC or xD Picture card into your pants pocket with a key chain or pocket knife can short out and destroy a card in seconds. So can simply holding one while touching any surface that generates a static electrical charge. Better safe than sorry, here are a few ways you can protect your memory cards and the images on them:

- Always store your cards in either the hard plastic shell they came in or a card wallet (they're sold at camera and electronics stores).
- Cards are valuable, so put your name, email address, and telephone number on them. We use those mailing stickers that charities regularly send to us as incentives to contribute, and trim them so that they physically fit onto the card without blocking any of the contacts.
- Once you've filled a card with important images, flick the tiny Write Protect switch on the side, so that you don't accidentally reformat the card.
- Never remove or insert a memory card into a camera while the camera is still turned on. It can scramble the memory card either temporarily or permanently.
- Periodically reformat your memory cards (always in the camera, never in the computer). This helps refresh the card, so it's less likely to lose data.
- Gently rub a pencil eraser against the gold contacts to clean SD/MMC and xD Picture cards. Then lightly brush the rubber pieces away with a camel's hair brush.
- Dedicate a place and a holder for all your memory cards when they're not in your camera or gadget bag. Because they're small and very easy to misplace, we always immediately return them to our dedicated drawer.

Battery

Most DSLRs come bundled with either a lithium ion (LiON) or nickel-metal-hydride (NiMH) battery (or batteries) and some sort of recharger. Although DSLRs are very energy efficient and can take many hundreds of frames on a single charge, fact is, when you're out of juice, you're finished shooting. The best way to avoid running out of power at critical moments is to *always* have a fully charged spare on hand. Most of the chargers that ship with DSLRs are designed to recharge the battery or batteries in 7–10 hours. Depending upon the battery, you may be able to buy a rapid charger that accelerates the process, anywhere from 15 minutes (for AA size NiMHs) to about an hour for lithium ions.

If your camera takes a dedicated LiON battery, you have a choice of buying a spare from the manufacturer or from a third-party provider. We strongly suggest passing up bargain batteries and buying the manufacturer's brand. Generally, third-party batteries are more likely to overheat, explode, die, or lose the ability to accept a full charge than manufacturers' batteries. And while that third-party battery may be warranted against damage, the warranty may not cover your camera if the battery damages it.

What about Microdrives?

Most memory cards are solid state devices with no moving parts, and, as we explained, the higher the density, the more the cost per gigabyte. But there is a less expensive alternative to high-density solid state CompactFlash cards: the microdrive. A microdrive is a tiny quarter-sized hard drive encased inside a Type II CompactFlash card format that spins at 3,600 rpms, which gives it a read/write time equal to high-performance solid state CF cards. Depending upon the brand and model, it may have a density of between 1GB and 6GB, but its price tag will be roughly half that of a comparable solid state card.

As attractive as the lower price and high performance are, there is an important downside to microdrives that inhibits most pros from using them: they can crash, just like a computer hard drive. Drop a solid state card on a cement sidewalk, and all you have to do is dust it off. A particularly hard knock or accidental drop can instantly render a microdrive card permanently useless (and the data unrecoverable). And while a solid state card can work flawlessly for years, microdrives, having moving parts, will eventually wear out and crash. So, if you are tempted to try a microdrive, we suggest using it in your studio rather than location, and be very careful handling it.

Rather than mix or match whatever happens to be available, always use a set of the same brand, age, and power rated NiMH AA batteries in your DSLR at any one time. The higher the capacity — 2200 to 2600mAh — the better.

Always store your battery (batteries) safely when it's not inside the camera, preferably in the container it came in or a small bag or wallet. That's because the contacts can get dirty and intermittently fail, or more importantly, can be shorted out by a key or other piece of metal. Shorting the battery can reverse its polarity, making it useless, or worse yet, generating enough heat to start a fire. It used to be that rechargeable batteries had memory and would gradually lose their ability to hold a charge if they weren't periodically deep discharged. Fortunately, that isn't much of an issue with modern rechargeables, especially those that come with "intelligent" chargers that automatically stop charging when the battery is at peak capacity.

CONSIDER BUYING AN AUXILIARY BATTERY PACK FOR YOUR DSLR

A number of DSLRs are designed to accommodate an auxiliary battery pack that doubles the amount of operating time. Approximately one-third as large as the DSLR body, the auxiliary battery pack usually screws into the bottom of the camera — it can be attached or removed in seconds — and has twin compartments for two identical rechargeable batteries. (See Figure 3-2.)

Besides the extra electrical power, most auxiliary battery packs double as ergonomically sculpted grips that feature a vertical shutter release, so you don't have to cramp or contort your hand to shoot the camera in the portrait mode. The grip also adds weight and stability to the camera.

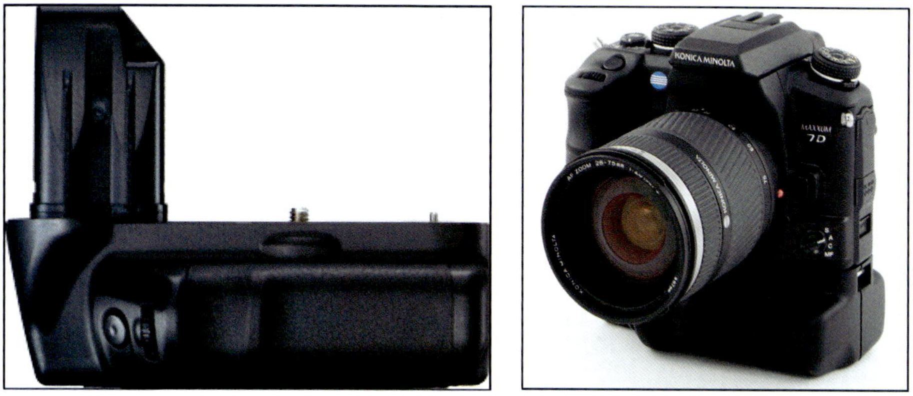

Figure 3-2: (Left) An auxiliary battery grip for the Konica Minolta Maxxum 7 considerably increases the length of time you can go on shooting without having to change or charge batteries. (Right) When attached to the Maxxum, the auxiliary battery increases the size of the camera by at least a ¼ more weight and size. It also adds a better, more substantial grip with a vertical shutter button. (Photos courtesy of Konica Minolta)

Computer System

Of course, you will need some sort of computer system to transfer, process, edit, and store the thousands or tens of thousands of images you'll be shooting with your DSLR. Initially, you probably can use whatever system you have, but eventually, you'll want a high-powered box with enough speed, memory, and storage capacity to handle your image files without bogging down. The first decision you'll have to make is like choosing Hertz or Avis, McDonald's or Burger King: will you be working on a PC or a Mac? Your choice of systems is a very personal decision, and whichever you decide will be fine. As a general rule of thumb, PCs are less expensive than Macs, but Macs are more elegant and less finicky to use than PCs. It's your call.

Mac or PC, here's a short list of what you'll probably want inside:

- Fast CPU or processor
- At least 1GB of random access memory (RAM)
- 200GB or larger hard drive
- DVD burner
- USB 2.0 and/or FireWire ports
- 17" or larger color monitor and matching graphics board with at least 128MB RAM

Some Thoughts on Selecting and Setting Up a Monitor

Choose your monitor carefully, because you'll be spending a lot of time looking at your pictures on it. Erik Willey, senior product manager for ViewSonic, a major LCD and CRT display manufacturer, advises that for optimum display and performance photographers should search out a manufacturer's advanced graphics or pro series of monitors. Unlike consumer, business, and gamer monitors, which are optimized for economy or speed, pro monitors are designed for greater color fidelity and accuracy. Typically, a graphics monitor will sell for 30–50 percent more than a normal monitor. And for better images, choose one that features digital (DVI) as well as VGA (analog) input.

Other things Willey suggests looking for in a monitor are to ensure that it has at least 100 percent EBU (European Broadcast Union) saturation, has a true color bit depth of 8-bits per color channel (most monitors are really 6-bits dithered to 8-bits), and comes with an ICC color profile. An ICC color profile "communicates to your editing program what the display's capabilities are. It acts like a translation medium, so that the images that come from the camera and are shown on the monitor and are finally output on the printer will have some correlation." For basic out-of-the-box setup, set the monitor to its native (highest) resolution, the color temperature to 6500K, and the Gamma to 2.2. Almost any graphics card will work fine, as long as it has at least 128MB RAM on board. (See Chapter 11 for more information on ICC profiles, color management, and calibrating your monitor.)

All other things being equal, consider buying a card that supports dual monitors and features twin DVI (digital) ports instead of VGA (analog) ports. That allows you to set up two monitors on the desktop, one to display your image across the full screen and the other to hold all your software's tools.

Applying the more-is-better principle, get a PC/Mac loaded with the fastest processor, the biggest hard drive, and as much RAM as you can afford. You'll also want to spring for a large LCD monitor specifically designed for graphics, rather than a general business-type monitor (See the sidebar "Some Thoughts on Selecting and Setting Up a Monitor" for more on this.)

If you don't want a full-blown desktop computer, look for a laptop that features at least 512MB RAM, 15" LCD screen, 60GB hard drive, and built-in memory card slots.

Tip

If you will be using your laptop for location shooting, you'll want to be sure to have an auxiliary battery for it, so you won't lose power. We use MFuel's Universal Power Pack, which adds hours of usability to our laptop regardless of how far we are from an electrical outlet (`www.mfueldirect.com`).

Back Up Early and Often

One of the most overlooked and neglected areas of computing is regularly backing up all your data files. (And yes, we're also guilty of forgetting to back up early and often.) Burning DVDs of your pictures is a good start, but they won't help you restore your operating system, programs, and device drivers should your hard drive crash or get wiped out by a malevolent worm or virus. For a partial or total restore, you need to institute a backup plan.

The problem is choosing, setting up, and maintaining an affordable, reliable, easy-to-use backup system. Businesses typically use tape drives for backup, but while reliable, they are expensive and slow. Also, tapes are great for archiving and storing versions of your hard drive as it was yesterday, last week, last month, or last year. That way, you can go to an earlier version if you inadvertently wiped out something important and saved that change on a recent backup. An external hard drive with backup software is affordable, simple to set up, and easy to use. It's great for daily automatic backups, since it saves every time you add or change any file. Unfortunately, it can't give you incremental, archival backups for finding and restoring old files that had been changed or deleted sometime in the past.

Despite some limitations, we use a 200GB Mirra Personal Server (`www.mirra.com`) on our network to backup those programs, directories, and files we consider important. It's not nearly large enough to back up all the drives on our network (we have about 2 terabytes total storage space), but we did set it up to automatically save every important file to the Mirra drive. For even better protection, it automatically transfers copies of those same files to Mirra's Web site for offsite storage. Maxtor (`www.maxtor.com`), LaCie (`www.lacie.com`), and other manufacturers offer similar external hard drive/software package backup solutions. Iomega (`www.iomega.com`) sells an elegant device, called the REV drive, that uses 30GB hard drive cartridges instead of tape. While the REV is a fast, practical backup solution for single users, its high cost and relatively small cartridge capacity make it impractical for network backup, especially for photographers with large image libraries.

Important Accessories

There are lots of items in our camera bag and studio that we think of as essential and indispensable, but as much as we would never want to do without them, they are not really vital for taking photographs. These are devices, gizmos, peripherals, accessories, and other miscellany designed to enhance or assist your picture-taking experience (as well as to make your wallet or purse lighter). Some may improve your pictures, while others help secure your shots against accidental deletion or corruption. Still others can save you time and energy, or make things easier or more convenient. Here's an overview of what's out there and how to choose the specific type of product for your needs, shooting style, and budget.

Card Readers

All DSLRs have the ability to directly connect to a computer. While some stalwarts and budget-minded owners use the USB or FireWire cable that came with their camera, by far the best, fastest way to transfer images to your PC or laptop is via a card reader.

Card readers turn your memory cards into drives that PCs and Macs automatically recognize, allowing you to use your operating system's drop-and-drag copy command to transfer images to the drive and folder that you designate. Or, you can use a wizard to set up an automatic transfer whenever you insert a memory card into your card reader. Depending upon how you configure it, inserting the card into a card reader can automatically open up an image-editing or image viewer program, and transfer and save all your images to a preselected folder.

Most memory card readers cost between $20 and $50 and attach via a USB port. Because it's many times faster, make certain that your card reader (and computer port) is equipped for USB 2.0 and not the much slower 1.1. If you use only one type of memory card (such as CompactFlash), you can probably save a few bucks buying a dedicated card reader that accommodates only one type card. But if you have other devices (consumer digital camera, PDA, camera phone, MP3 player, laptop, etc.), you'll probably want an all-in-one reader that has slots for all the most popular types of memory card. (See Figure 3-3.)

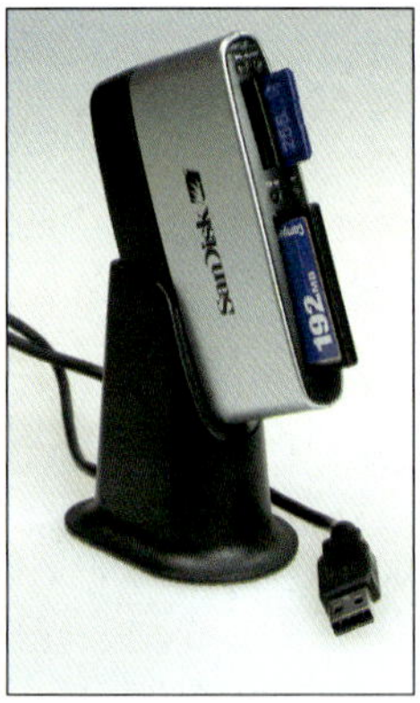

Figure 3-3: Memory card readers turn your memory cards into drives that your computer will automatically recognize. This is a SanDisk all-in-one reader that can accommodate a full range of memory cards, including CompactFlash, SD, xD Picture Card, MemoryStick, and so forth.

Tip

While most card readers are USB types, Lexar Media (`www.lexar.com`), Addonics (`www.addonics.com`), and a few other companies sell a FireWire (IEEE 1294) version. USB 2.0's peak speeds are fast, but FireWire's sustained speed is even more rapid. A FireWire card reader can shave valuable seconds off your transfer time, especially if you're moving data over from high-density cards. Of course, your computer or laptop has to have a FireWire port for it to work.

Two (or Three or Four) Strobes Are Better Than One

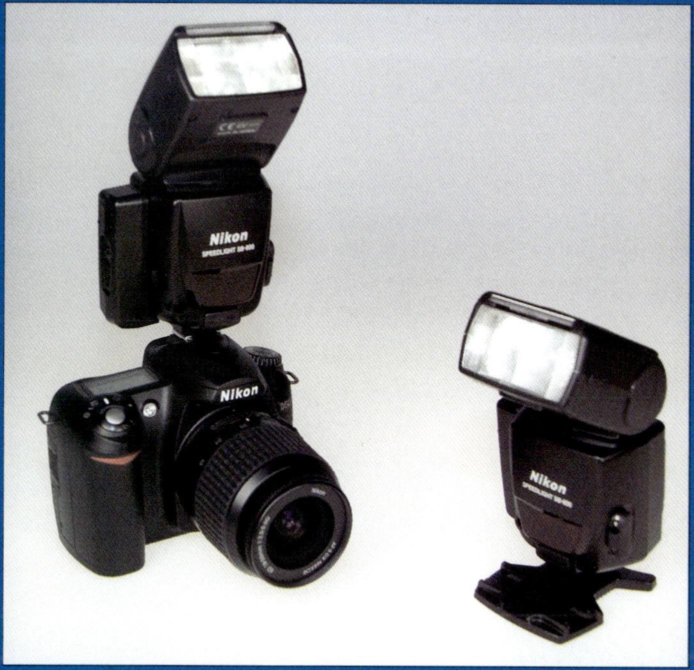

Some auxiliary strobes, like Nikon's SB-600 and SB-800, are designed to function together as multi-light setups. Each unit is set up either as a master or slave (remote units triggered wirelessly via a built-in photoelectric eye) and can easily be positioned anywhere within range. Such systems are so sophisticated that their wireless communication capability even allows the user to adjust flash intensity of its slaves remotely from the master strobe mounted on a Nikon DSLR. What's more, in an environment where other flashes might be going off and could inadvertently trigger the slaves prematurely (such as at a wedding), the user can usually avoid that possibility simply by assigning specific channels to individual strobes. Strobe accessories can include filters, diffusers, and brackets.

Auxiliary Flash

Most, but certainly not all DSLRs come equipped with a built-in flash. Pop-up strobes are handy for fill flash or quick-and-dirty indoor shots, but they're neither designed for nor capable of producing even, pleasing illumination, or operating beyond relatively short distances. For that you will need an auxiliary strobe.

All DSLRs incorporate an intelligent *hot shoe* on top of the camera's pentaprism or porromirror; better cameras also have a small round *pc connector* (that's been the name of the port for decades) for plugging in a flash cord. The hot shoe connector is usually for attaching a matched auxiliary strobe on top of the camera, while the pc connector is to sync the camera with professional studio lights. Attaching a flash to the top of your camera has an added advantage — its extended height helps eliminate or reduce red eye. (For still better illumination and red eye reduction, consider buying and using a flash bracket that will give your strobe even greater distance between the lens and the flash tube.)

There are two types of auxiliary strobes: dumb and intelligent.

- **Dumb strobes** have a single contact that the camera uses to trigger the flash. Depending upon the brand, model, and the photographer's preference, exposure is either set manually or automatically. Manual exposure is achieved by dividing the power of the strobe — expressed in a standard Guide Number — by the distance, which gives the user the proper *f*-stop to set. The primary virtue dumb strobes offer is their low price.
- As we discuss in Chapter 8, **intelligent strobes** interact with the camera body and lens CPUs to assure perfect exposure and illumination. When the strobe is fired, a built-in sensor measures the amount of light reflected back from the subject to the camera and turns the flash tube off when it thinks the exposure is right. Also called TTL (through-the-lens) strobes, you can readily identify them by the multiple contacts on their hot shoes. (See Figure 3-4.) Depending upon the make and model, intelligent strobes can also be used as wired or wireless slaves for high-speed stop-action photography, rear and front curtain sync, and so on. (For more information on TTL lighting, see Chapter 8.)

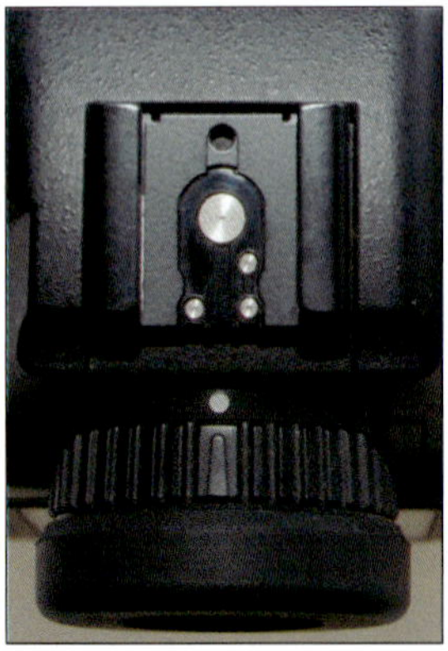

Figure 3-4: The Olympus E-10's hot shoe has the multiple contacts needed for intelligent communications between a TTL flash and the camera's sensor. A dumb hot shoe would have only one contact. (Photo taken with a Nikon D50, 18 to 55mm lens set at 55mm, 1/60 at *f*11.)

A word of advice in selecting an intelligent strobe: pass up the temptation to purchase a much less expensive generic brand and opt only for the brand and models that match your DSLR. Third-party and generic strobes are fine for straightforward photography, but to take advantage of all the special features your camera may be capable of, you'll need the power and versatility of a matched strobe.

Portable Viewers

One of most important and useful advantages that digital cameras, including DSLRs, give photographers is the ability to instantly review just-shot pictures on an LCD screen. While the LCD screen built into almost every camera is great for quick reviews, it's usually too small and not bright or detailed enough to provide the accurate visual feedback needed to properly view and evaluate your pictures. Of course, you can transfer the image to your laptop, but schlepping around a large, heavy portable may not always be convenient, especially if all you want is a quick view and fast save. That's why you may want a portable viewer, preferably one with a built-in hard drive for instant backup. (See Figure 3-5.)

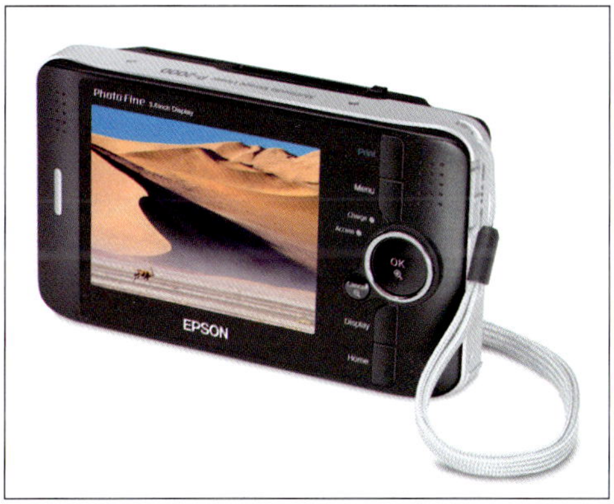

Figure 3-5: The Epson P2000 portable multimedia storage viewer. Like many similar viewers, it comes equipped with different memory card slots, a built-in battery-powered hard drive, and a large LCD screen for viewing your just-shot images. But it has the added advantage of allowing users to view images shot in many different RAW file formats. (Photo courtesy of Epson America)

Portable viewers range in size from an iPod to a paperback book. Typically, they feature an LCD screen, one or more memory card slots, a USB 2.0 or FireWire connector, rechargeable batteries, and an outlet for an AC adapter. Most also come equipped with a built-in hard drive whose density may range from 10GB to 80GB. And no, you don't need a computer or a laptop to transfer files and view your images. Some hybrid models feature a CD/DVD drive instead of a hard disk, and while they're capable of displaying still images, they're designed primarily for watching movies. Other models may also play and record MP3s. The LCD screen on a portable viewer is usually larger than the one on your camera (3" to 10", depending upon the model) and displays in a higher resolution. With pan and zoom capability, a user can look at any portion of a photograph in great detail. Some units even allow you to do some basic editing and organizing of your pictures (though we don't generally recommend using these devices for editing). More important, you can back up an entire high-density memory card in only seconds, and easily transfer them to your PC or laptop at a later time.

While there are dozens of different devices available (including iPod add-ons), costing between $200 and $700, get one that can display your RAW file images. Some models show JPEG files only, so you're out of luck if you want to view RAW images. Another decision you'll have to make is size versus capacity versus battery life. Tiny units are extremely portable and versatile, but the tradeoff for miniaturization is that they probably will have a smaller hard drive and more limited battery life. Large units have bigger screens and larger hard drives but may be too heavy or bulky to take into the field. And a unit that comes equipped with a single memory slot may be fine if you have one camera but may require an optional adapter or may not work at all with other cameras or devices that use different-sized memory cards.

CD/DVD Burners and Portable Hard Drives

A secure archival backup strategy is absolutely essential to every photographer wishing to protect and preserve her valuable pictures. While portable viewers are excellent for fast views and in-the-field backups, they are rather pricey. Nor can most of them give you the ultra-protection of burning a CD or DVD.

Most external CD/DVD burners lack the large screen of a portable viewer (though a few models have tiny LCD screens for navigating through command menus rather than image inspection), and most are not battery powered (though it's available as an option on some models). What they do is allow the photographer to insert a memory card and burn a CD or DVD without requiring a computer. (See Figure 3-6.)

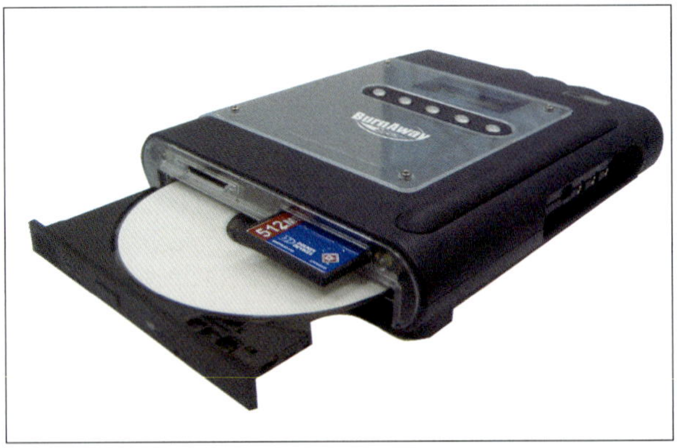

Figure 3-6: Delkin's BurnAway takes files from various types of memory cards and burns them to DVD. (Photo courtesy of Delkin)

Because of the limited capacity (660MB) of most CD burners, they do not have sufficient storage capacity for digital photographers (though they're great for general backup and music MP3s). It's simply too time-consuming and inconvenient burning multiple discs to back up a single high-capacity memory card.

DVD burners are more expensive than CD burners, but with a 4.7GB capacity, they'll back up all but the largest memory cards onto a single disc. We have found that DVD burners are useful on assignment because they assure us that we won't accidentally overwrite our valuable photo files. In addition, we can hook them up to the hotel TV for watching DVD movies. (By the way, look for a new generation of even higher-capacity DVD burners that will be hitting the market shortly.)

Most external portable hard drives range in size between 10GB and 100GB and are powered directly by your computer's USB or FireWire port. Most require a PC or laptop to operate, though some models, like Eastgear's PD series (`www.compactdrive.com`) and MediaGear's Flash-HD to Go drives (`www.mymediagear.com`) come equipped with memory card slots and can copy directly from your camera's card. Ten minutes' backup work in between photo sessions or during coffee breaks can help protect the images of even the most slapdash and insecure photographers.

Tip

Belkin (`www.belkin.com`) markets a neat, inexpensive ($40) battery-powered device, called USB Anywhere, that can connect your DSLR with a portable battery-powered hard drive, another digital camera, second memory card via a card reader, and so on, without requiring a computer. Its sheer simplicity makes backup almost effortless. Simply plug the source or digital camera in one side, the target or destination drive in the other, and press the Copy button. However, while it works fine recording to portable external hard drives and other memory cards, it can only play CD/DVD burners and not record to them.

Tripods and Other Camera Stabilizing Devices

Close-ups, extreme-telephoto shots, and low-light exposures all require using a tripod. So do scenes and subjects that demand razor-sharp pictures, time lapse and time interval photos, remote control photography, and many other shooting situations. While inexpensive, lightweight tripods are fine for most consumer digital cameras, DSLRs require somewhat heavier, more stable, and sophisticated (that is, more expensive) tripods.

There are two basic kinds of tripods: for still cameras and for video cameras. Still camera tripods have heads that move horizontally, move vertically, or tilt to any point in between. Video tripods usually traverse horizontally and vertically only, and the heads are designed for smooth panning rather than being locked down in a specific position. Of course, the best kind of device for DSLRs is a tripod specifically designed for still photography. Costs vary considerably, but a rough rule of thumb is that more expensive units will have better and smoother heads, stronger but lighter-weight composite legs, a geared center brace, an ability to accommodate heavier cameras, plus a variety of extras, like built-in spirit levels and a quick release system.

We own and use a variety of tripods, ranging from small compacts designed for travel, to large, heavy units suitable for studio photography. We usually keep a medium-sized tripod in the trunk of our car and a small tabletop unit inside our regular camera bag. We sometimes even use a small bean bag called The Pod (`www.bogen.com`) that attaches to the camera and can placed almost anywhere — on a table, alongside a light pole, across a tree branch, and so on.

Tip

Often, a tripod is too slow or inconvenient to use, but you still need some sort of stability to offset camera motion, especially when shooting with a big telephoto lens. That's when we attach a monopod to our camera and plant it firmly into the ground. A monopod is, in effect, a single-legged tripod that provides half the stability, and your holding the camera steady provides the other half. It can be set up very quickly and moved about instantly, which is why almost all pro sports photographers and photojournalists carry them on assignment. And while it doesn't really work for long exposures (1/10 of a second or slower), a monopod will often make the critical difference between getting a soft or a sharp shot.

Tip

An important drawback to using a tripod or monopod is the time and effort it takes to attach or remove a camera. To make this task both easier and faster, we attach Bogen quick release plates (`www.bogen.com`) to all our cameras and corresponding, compatible quick release clamps to the heads of all our tripods and monopods. That cuts our attach/release time to seconds.

Filters

Given that you can add an almost endless variety of special effects to almost any photograph with any high-powered image-editing program like Photoshop, what incentive would you have to buy and use filters? Or, as professional photographer Helene DiLillo puts it, "Why in the world would I ever want to screw a $30 piece of glass in front of my $1,500 lens?" While purists may object to potentially reducing overall image quality with filters, and Photoshop mavens wonder why physical filters are necessary or desirable, there's a considerable body of photographers who use, and swear by, their glass filters.

Our rule of thumb regarding glass filters is that we will use those that give us control over exposure, especially in those conditions in which we need to cut down on reflections or light. In other words, we use filters to get the best picture we can, controlling the light and exposure in ways that are difficult, if not impossible, to correct in photo-editing software.

Here's our short list of filters that we usually carry:

- Several neutral density (ND) filters of varying strengths
- At least one polarizing filter

- Ultraviolet filter
- Infrared filter

Neutral density filters are probably the most important ones for digital photographers to use, because image sensors tend to blow out highlight details. When shooting in bright sunlight, even at your DSLR's slowest ISO equivalency and fastest shutter speed, you may not be able to control depth of field properly because you might need a high *f*-stop for proper exposure. Depending upon its strength, a neutral density filter can cut the amount of light coming through the lens by one to 8 *f*-stops but leaves the colors unchanged.

An interesting variation on the neutral density filters are the ND gradient filters, in which half the glass will cut down on the light, while the other half is clear. This is great for landscapes with a bright sky or other situations in which a portion of the scene is too bright in comparison to the rest. The one drawback is that such filters are designed for half-and-half shooting, which means that you must frame your photo with the horizon (or other dividing line) very close to the center of the picture. (See Figure 3-7.)

Polarizing filters can be used to change or reduce the amount of light or reflection emanating from glass, water, and the like. They are also handy for controlling the amount of blue in a sky and can also serve as a neutral density filter under some circumstances. (See Figure 3-8.)

Ultraviolet filters help cut the amount of blue, or ultraviolet, that can creep into your pictures shot under certain lighting conditions, such as a sunlit beach or mountain scene. (Image sensors are particularly susceptible to ultraviolet light.) They also can add slight warmth to your pictures.

If you want to try your hand at infrared photography, you'll need to use a dark red filter that blocks out the entire spectrum except for infrared light.

Should You Always Have an Ultraviolet Filter on All Your Lenses?

Like many photographers, we once religiously screwed an ultraviolet filter on the front of every one of our lenses. (An ultraviolet filter cuts some of the blue out of sunny outdoor scenes but otherwise leaves the image unaffected.) Why? Because, we reasoned, if an accident occurred that would throw the lens in contact with a sharp corner or any similar hard object, it would always be cheaper to replace the filter than the lens's front element. One day a few years ago, when comparing notes with a number of our fellow photographers, most of whom also placed ultraviolet filters on all their lenses, we asked if anyone had actually scratched or cracked a filter, thereby saving the lens itself from damage or destruction. No one ever had, or personally knew of any photographer whose filter had actually protected a lens. We're not going to argue one way or another about the degree of protection that ultraviolet filters will give your lens's front elements, but personally, we now only use them for what they were originally intended — shooting in the mountains, the seashore, and other places where ultraviolet light will create a significant blue cast in the sky. For physical protection (and to minimize flare), we always use a lens shade on our lenses.

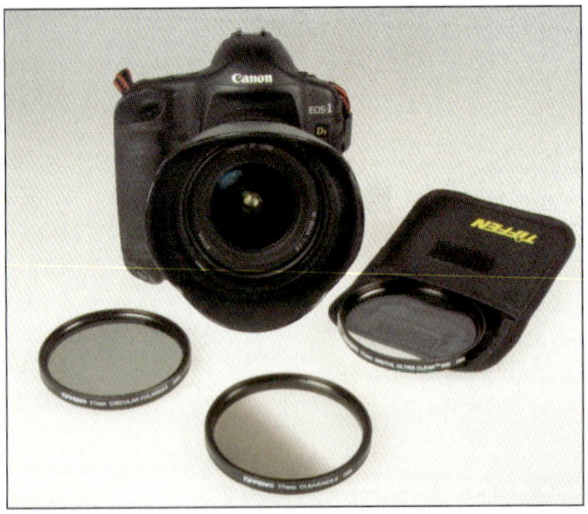

Figure 3-7: A selection of Tiffen brand filters. On the left is a polarizer, in the center is a neutral density gradient, and in the pouch is an ultra clear. (Photo taken with a Canon EOS 20D, 17-85mm lens set at 26mm, 1/10 at *f*22.)

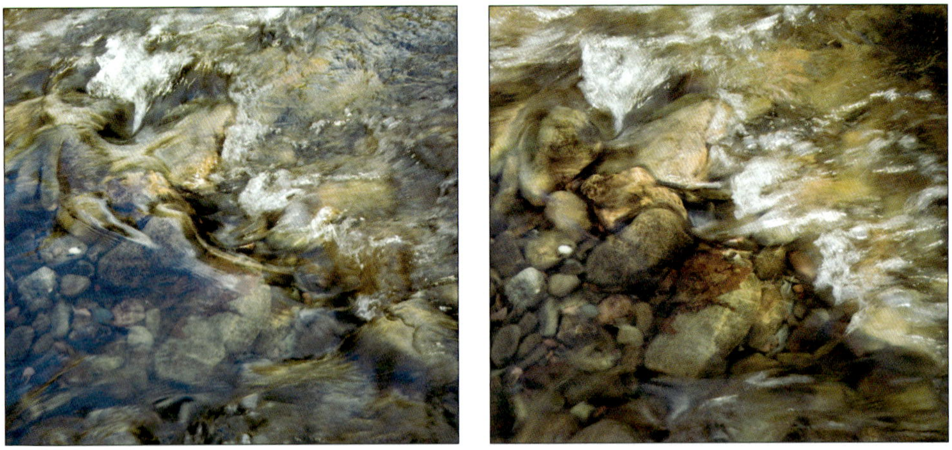

Figure 3-8: (Left) The reflections on the surface of this water are detracting, making this photo rather boring and pedestrian. (Photo taken with a Nikon D2X, 24-120mm lens set at 52mm, 1/30 at *f*4.8.) (Right) Using a polarizing filter, we were able to cut down on the reflections, which meant we could capture the textures and colors of the underwater rocks. It also reduced the overall amount of light, which meant we had to reduce the shutter speed. That, in turn, blurred the water more, lending a sense of motion to the photo. (Photo taken with a Nikon D2X, 24-120mm lens set at 52mm, 1/15 at *f*4.8.)

The neutral density, polarizing, ultraviolet, and infrared filters are truly necessary in certain situations. Others are interesting, useful, convenient, or fun. For instance, some photographers like soft focus filters, for creating moods and making a picture dreamier and more ethereal. And, then, there are the special effects, like turning any bright light source into starry highlights. Whether you want to use glass filters for special effects and other purposes than controlling light and exposure depends on your personality, time constraints, and comfort level with editing in the computer. It's certainly faster to shoot a picture as you envision it rather than "Photoshop" it. But software filters almost always give you more latitude and control.

For further information on what filters are, what they do, and how to use them, read Joseph Meehan's book, *Complete Guide to Filters for Digital Photography* (Lark Books, 2004).

Tip

Glass filters are matched to the diameter of the lens onto which they will be screwed. So, for instance, if you want a polarizer for every lens, you may need to purchase several for your camera bag. You can save money by purchasing only one of each type of filter large enough to screw onto the front of your largest diameter lens. Then get a step-down adapter ring for each of your other lenses. That will allow you to purchase only one filter of each type you want and use it on all your lenses, regardless of their size.

Bags

Now that you've accumulated lots of lenses and accessories for your DSLR, you'll need something to carry them all. This isn't a problem with most consumer digital cameras, which are small, lightweight, and have so few moving parts that you can carry them safely in anything from a purse to a backpack. But DSLRs are larger, heavier, and can be damaged or even destroyed through rough handling. For that reason, we strongly suggest eschewing informal carrying cases and opting for one or more purpose-built camera case. Camera cases are generally strongly built, well padded, and come with movable partitions that allow the photographer to create custom configurations for their equipment.

The first thing you should realize is that no single bag will ever suit all your equipment needs. We own a variety of camera bags and select the one we'll take on a shoot or assignment according to what equipment we'll be using. (See Figure 3-9.) We have big bags that can accommodate several bodies, lots of lenses, and several strobes, as well as tiny bags good for only a single body, lens, and flash. Our large bags all have wheels, for easy toting. One even has backpack-like shoulder straps for those times when we have to walk distances and still remain hands free, ready for instant shooting. Most have side or back straps for attaching a tripod or monopod, or both, and all have pockets for small accessories, like memory cards, spare batteries, and so on. One thing we always make certain of is that all our bags are water-resistant, or come equipped with a rubber or plastic hood that can be quickly pulled over to cover the outer shell. The other thing we must have are bags that can be easily opened and closed, for quick access to our equipment.

Selecting a camera bag is as personal a choice as choosing your DSLR. It should be large enough to carry the equipment you need, light enough that it won't be a physical drain, and secure enough that you won't get your equipment wet or drop items while opening. (See Figure 3-10.)

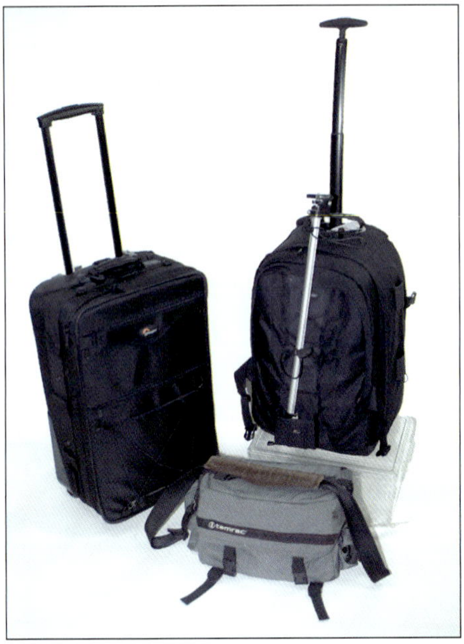

Figure 3-9: These are only three of the approximately dozen camera bags we have and use. Our large bags are all on wheels to save our backs. (Photo taken with a Konica Minolta Maxxum 7D, 28-100mm set at 28mm, 1/60 at *f*4)

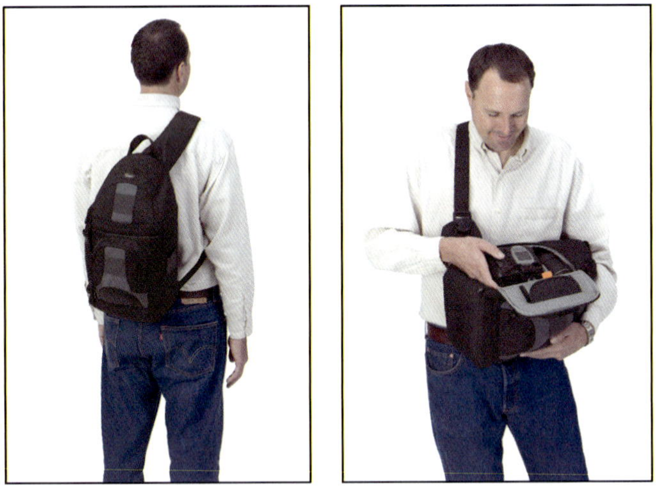

(A) (B)

Figure 3-10: This Lowepro Slingshot bag is one of our favorites for when we don't have to carry lots of equipment. It is well organized, has room for a body, a couple of lenses, two strobes, and other accessories, balances nicely on our back (A), and when we bring it around to the front to grab our camera or a lens, it is configured for easy, safe access to our equipment (B). (Photos courtesy of Lowepro)

Eyecups, Focus Screens, and Shades

All DSLRs feature optical-type eye-level through-the-lens viewing. While this makes for superior viewing (brighter image, greater detail, more accurate color, and so on), light can stream in sideways, between your eye and the eyepiece, making it harder to see the subject. You can block that extraneous light by slipping or screwing in a rubber eyecup over your DSLR's eyepiece. Not only will you see better, the increased soft contact will make your cheek and eyebrow feel better. Some DSLRs come with rubber eyepieces, but it's an extra on others ($15 to $25, depending upon the model) and usually available only from the camera manufacturer for that specific model.

In bright sunlight, it's often difficult to review your shots or navigate through menus on your camera's LCD screen. That's true, even on those models whose screens have an anti-glare coating. A shroud or hood is a relatively inexpensive ($20–$50) useful device for allowing you to see your images and menus better. Made of cloth, plastic, or metal, the shroud attaches to your LCD screen's bezel (usually by adhesive) and places small black foldout panels around the LCD screen. Because each camera back is different, you must buy a hood that's specifically designed for your particular model. You can buy hoods from a variety of companies, such as Hoodman's FlipUp LCD Cap (`www.hoodmanusa.com/flip_up.asp`).

Every DSLR comes equipped with a ground glass or plastic focusing screen that's positioned between the camera's flip-up mirror and pentaprism (or porro-mirror). That's where the optical image passing through the lens is projected for viewing. On most DSLRs, the ground glass focusing screen is fixed and not interchangeable, but on a few models, it's possible to install other types of focusing screens. Depending upon the make and model, a focusing screen may incorporate a center microprism for more precise focusing, grid lines for better display of architectural perspectives, or etched frames that show where the spot meter takes its readings. Most photographers are perfectly satisfied with the ground glass that ships with their camera, but it's nice to know that others are available should you have a specific need in mind. Check your camera manufacturer's Web site to see if your particular model can accommodate interchangeable screens, and if so, peruse a short list of the types available.

Drawing Tablets

A mouse is great for navigating around your computer monitor, but it's terrible for precise drawing. That's why photographers and serious graphics artists use a drawing tablet, which replaces the hand-guided mouse with a tool that you hold and use like a pen, pencil, or paintbrush. (See Figure 3-11.) The tablet itself—which can be anywhere from a postcard to LCD monitor in size—is lined with an electromagnetic mesh that picks up the X/Y coordinates as the pen passes over them and instantly relays that information to the screen. This allows you to draw, sketch, paint, trace, or manipulate the cursor very precisely.

Most drawing tablets are connected to the computer via a USB port. They cost from under $100 to several thousand dollars, depending upon their size and sophistication. We have Wacom (`www.wacom.com`) tablets attached to every one of our imaging stations. We especially like using the Wacom with Adobe Photoshop and Corel Painter, because the stylus is pressure sensitive, so that the on-screen brushes react to our hands, almost like real brushes. But we also have a mouse attached to the same computers, because mice are much faster and more convenient for non-graphics tasks, like navigating the Internet or scrolling through a word processing program.

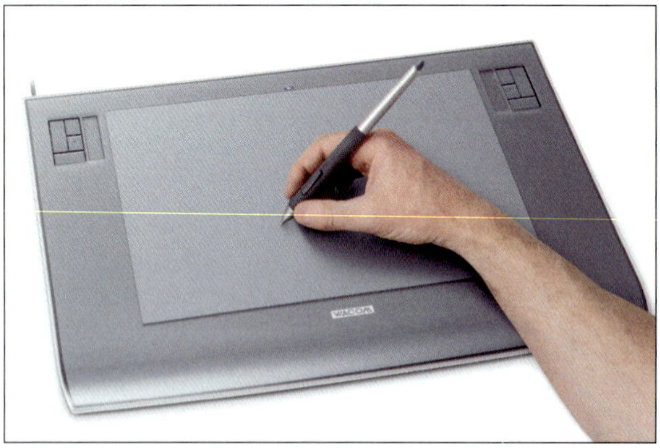

Figure 3-11: Pressure-sensitive drawing tablets give you more precise and creative control over your cursor and on-screen brushes, when working in programs such as Adobe Photoshop and Corel Painter. (Photo of a Wacom Intuos tablet courtesy of Wacom Technology Corporation)

Electronic Shutter Release

Before digital photography, you could shoot standing a distance from your camera by pushing a mechanical cable release that would trigger the shutter. Cable releases — which came in lengths from 6" to 10' — were cheap, extremely easy to use, and with a handful of exceptions, worked with almost every camera. Unfortunately, no mechanical cable release will work with any digital camera. To shoot off-camera, you'll need some sort of electronic cable release.

Depending upon the make and model, the camera manufacturer may sell a wired electronic shutter release. If you're lucky, the company makes different lengths, so you'll have a choice of buying a short or long one. Alas, each electronic release interface is nonstandard and therefore different, so what works on one model may not work on another, even from the same manufacturer. Wired shutter releases are significantly more expensive than mechanical cables but are very useful accessories for portrait, studio, and nature photographers who often shoot off-camera.

A somewhat more expensive — though much more versatile — solution is a wireless shutter release. Depending upon the make and model, they may be radio or infrared controlled and can be used at distances from 25 to 1000 feet. Wireless units must be matched to specific makes and models, though on third-party units not sold by camera manufacturers, adapters may be available that will allow you to use the same unit on different cameras.

GPS

With state-of-the-art technology, it's possible to know *exactly* where you are in the world with accuracy down to 3 feet. A Global Positioning Satellite device — GPS for short — can help you navigate a car, ship, or airplane. For photographers who need accurate reference points for identification purposes (law enforcement, military, forensics, engineering, and so on), it can insert a geographical reference point into the EXIF metadata automatically associated with every image file.

GPS units are available that integrate into specific DSLRs, or as add-on devices that link to your camera via software. For further information about the latter, check out www.geospatialexperts.com.

Summary

After purchasing the body and lens, most DSLR owners will buy and use a wide range of accessories and peripherals. Because there are so many different items available, it's easy to lose sight of the purpose of building your camera system — to enhance the photographic experience and help you get better pictures. Don't go overboard, be selective in what you need and want, and spend only what you can safely afford.

Part II

Taking Control of Your Digital Photography

Chapter 4

Mastering File Size and Structure

Chapter 5

Making Exposure Work for You

Chapter 6

Camera Controls for Better, More Efficient Photography

Chapter 4

Mastering File Structure and Size

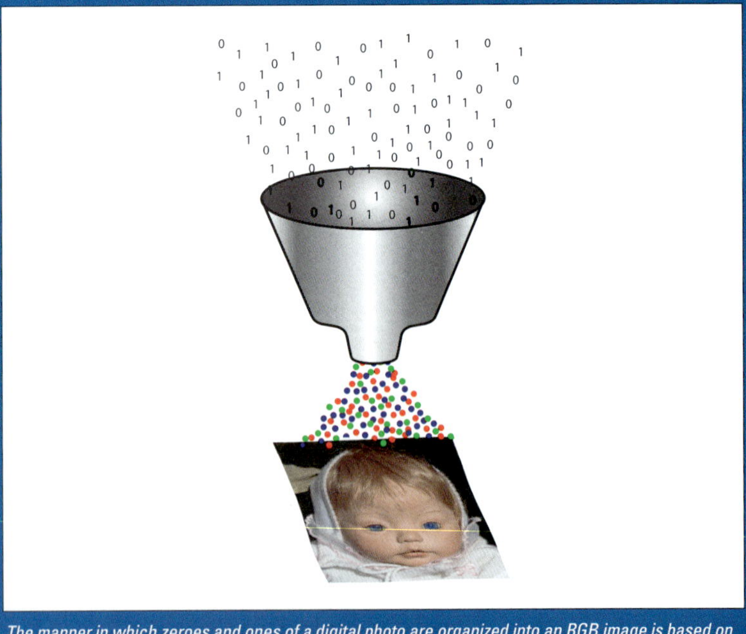

The manner in which zeroes and ones of a digital photo are organized into an RGB image is based on its file format.

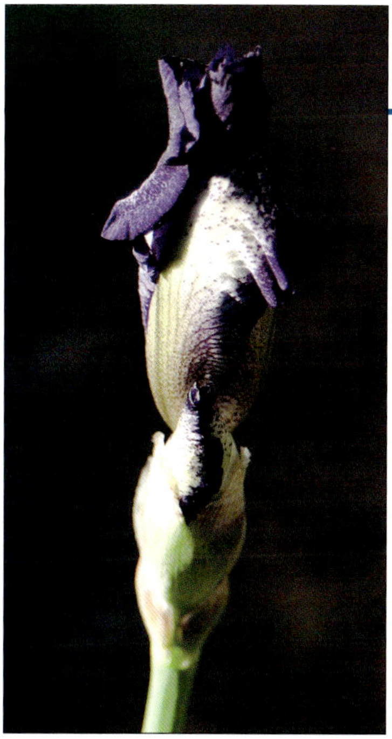

Shooting in Konica Minolta's RAW format brings out the details of the shadows and highlights of this delicate iris bud. (Photo shot with the Konica Minolta Maxxum 7D, 28–100mm lens set at 70mm, 1/250 at f5.6)

Unlike film negatives and slides, digital photo files aren't actually pictures in the traditional sense of the word. They are nothing more than a bunch of digital data (zeroes and ones, to be precise) organized in such a manner that computers and printers can recognize the information contained in the file and reconstruct your photo on a monitor, on-screen, or in print.

File formats, such as JPEG, TIFF, RAW, DNG, PSD, and so forth, define how your digital photos are structured and maintained. Depending on the file format (or formats) you choose to capture, save and/or share your photos, the method and style of the data organization will vary greatly. That, in turn, can have a significant impact on the quality, versatility, and usability of your picture files.

In this chapter, we:

- Explain the differences among the various photo file formats available to DSLR photographers
- Help you decide which file format to use and when
- Discuss converting RAW files effectively, efficiently, and creatively
- Provide guidance on understanding file sizes

Understanding the Differences among File Formats

Acronyms are the bane of our modern life. All those initials and abbreviations seem to exist only to make those who know what they mean feel superior to the rest of us. These self-styled know-it-alls seem to think that, just because they have command over the secret language it makes them members of the insider crowd. Being natural egalitarians, we try to avoid using acronyms when possible.

Unfortunately, we can't talk about file formats without using acronyms. That's because the abbreviations have become their de facto names, which we need to use and recognize whenever we are handing digital photo files.

Pixel by Pixel: Measuring a Photo's Size

You will notice in this chapter that when we talk about the physical dimensions — the width and height — of a digital photo, we use pixels as the unit of measure. The form of such measurements is 1200×1500 or 3072×2048, in which the first figure (such as 1200 or 3072) refers to the width of the photo in pixels and the second is the height. This is the definitive, unambiguous way to describe the size of a digital photo. (Incidentally, multiplying out these dimension pixels will result in millions of pixels, or megapixels. That's also how digital camera manufacturers come up with their megapixel ratings for their cameras. The one difference is when manufacturers mention megapixels, they are usually talking about the total pixel density of their image sensors. However, we're talking here about the size of the actual photograph, not the image sensor.)

The other units of measure we use in this chapter are megabytes (MB) and kilobytes (K). They refer only to the size of the photo file when it is taking up space on a memory card, your hard drive, a CD or some other storage device.

Please note that we never use inches, ppi (pixels per inch), or dpi (dots per inch) in this chapter. That's because those units of measure refer to the display size of a photo — how the pixels are determined by a scanner or will be spread out on a screen or by a printer. To know how large your photo will be when it is finally output, just divide the pixel dimensions by the number of pixels or dots per inch, and you get the inches it will display or print. For instance, take a 1200×1500 pixel photo. If it is being output on a 300 dpi desktop printer, then it would print as 4×6 inches (1200/300 = 4 and 1500/300 = 6). We'll go further into this when we cover sizing your photos according to your purpose in Chapter 12.

The following formats are used extensively in digital photography:

- JPEG
- TIFF
- RAW
- DNG
- PSD and other software-specific formats

Before we discuss how and when to use these various file formats, let's look at what they are.

JPEG

JPEG (which stands for Joint Photographic Experts Group) is the most universally recognized photo file format. Just about any computer, printer, Web site, or display device can read and use JPEG. (As a file extension, it's written as `.jpg`). That generally makes it the preferred file format for sharing pictures, especially via email. In addition, JPEG files tend to be smaller (sometimes much smaller) than the other formats, which makes sharing, using, and storing them easier, putting less strain on computer resources and hard drive space (see the sidebar on JPEG size and Table 4-1 later in the chapter).

However, JPEG does have a downside. To create those smaller files, it compresses your photos. *Compression* involves literally throwing away some of the data that defines your picture. JPEG compression works by analyzing a picture and determining what data might be considered redundant.

Suppose that you have a solid red toy block in the foreground of your photo, and each side of the block is made up of identical color values. The software creating the JPEG file may decide that it doesn't need to save the color values for every single one of those identical pixels, as long as it knows where they are supposed to be. So, JPEG throws away some, or even many of the red pixels (in the case of the toy block). Then, when the photo file is opened up, it reconstitutes the photo — much in the same way that adding water will reconstitute orange juice concentrate. This kind of compression is called *lossy compression,* because it destroys and then reinvents original photo information.

Figure 4-1 was saved as a JPEG file, with minimum compression. On the other hand, Figure 4-2 was saved with a great amount of compression. At the size they are reproduced in this book, most people can't really tell the difference between the two photos. Only when you zoom in at a high magnification (or when you print the photo at a larger size or on art quality paper, using more a precise technology) can you see just how destructive the higher compression setting is.

In other words, depending on the final output of your photo, a small or, even, a significant amount of compression may or may not matter.

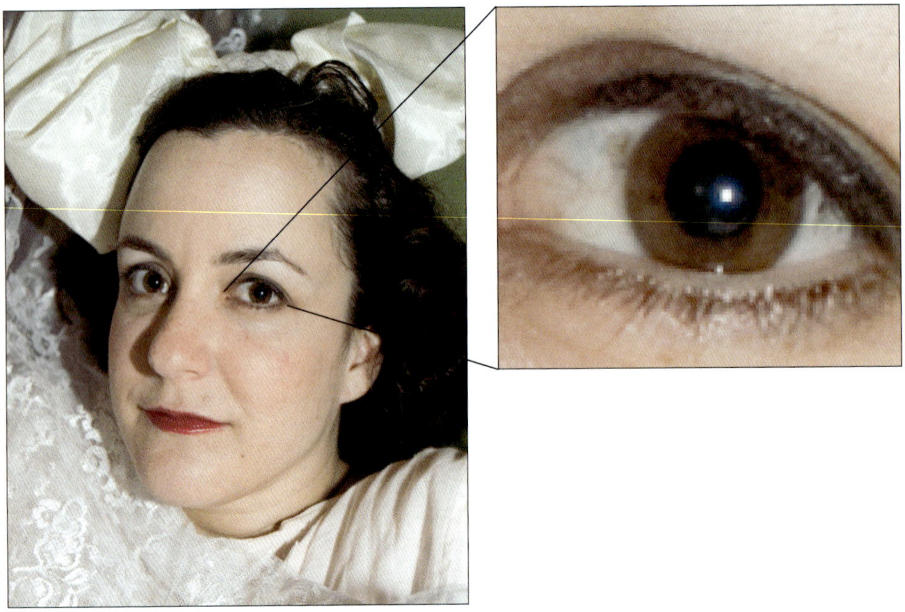

Figure 4-1: This portrait of the actress Heather Stuart (the photo on the left) was saved in Photoshop with JPEG compression set to maximum quality (minimum compression). (Series of photos taken with a Canon EOS 1Ds Mark II.) When you zoom the portrait to 500 percent magnification (the photo on the right), you can see a representation of the tiny square pixels that make up the photo. The smaller the size of these blocks, the smoother the transitions between colors and shades and the higher the quality of the photo.

Table 4-1 File Sizes of a Specific 4992×3328 Pixel Photo Saved in Various File Formats

File format	*Settings*	*File size*
CR2 (Canon RAW)	16-bit	11.5MB
TIFF	16-bit	97MB
TIFF	8-bit	48.7MB
JPEG	Maximum quality, lowest compression	6.7MB
JPEG	Lowest quality, highest compression	256K
DNG	Lossless compression, embed original file, medium JPEG preview	20.9MB
PSD	16-bit	97MB
PSD	8-bit	48MB

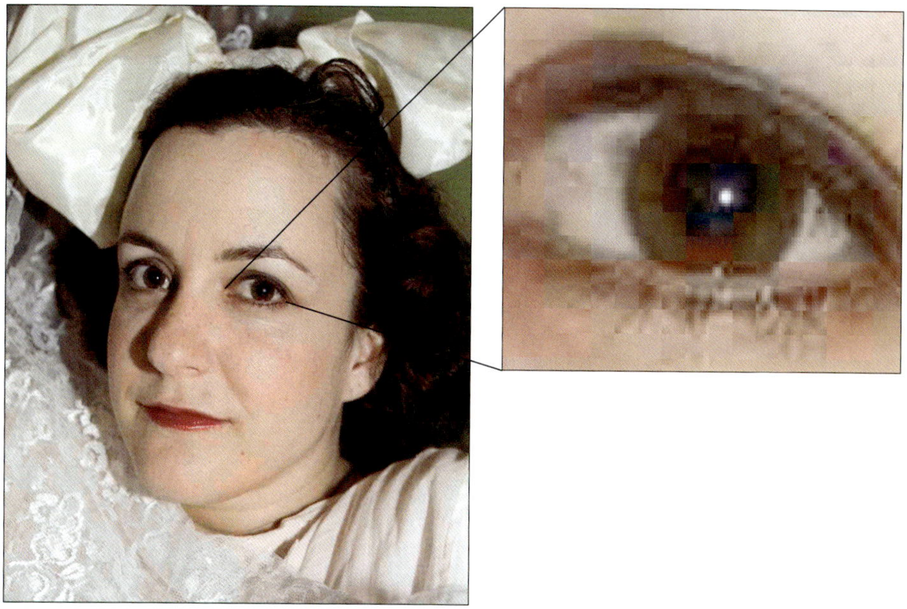

Figure 4-2: When the same portrait is saved using the lowest-quality compression setting, it looks fine reproduced at this small size (photo on the left). However, when you zoom in to 500 percent magnification this time, you can see how large the blocks are and how the transitions between colors are now abrupt and uneven. This becomes significant when you are reproducing the photo for a larger print or when the small details in the photo are important.

JPEG Size

As we said, saving a picture in JPEG will create a smaller size file than the other file formats. However, the size of the JPEG file is dependent not only on the original amount of data and the level of compression but also on the subject and composition of the photo.

For example, Figure 4-1 is a portrait of 1200×1500 pixels. When it was saved as a JPEG at the maximum quality compression (lowest amount of compression), it generated a file 975 kilobytes in size (975K). When we created another image 1200×1500 pixels, but made it only one color (red, to be precise), the maximum quality JPEG setting saved a file of only 147K. Another 1200×1500 pixel photo filled with a 256-step gradient of shades from red to white saved as a maximum quality JPEG of 320K.

In other words, the more colors and transitions a photo has (that is, the more complex a photo is) the larger the JPEG file will be. The figure in this sidebar is exactly the same size as Figure 4-1 — 1200×1500 pixels. (The fact that it has a *landscape orientation* rather than a *portrait orientation* has no effect on image size.) When we saved the sidebar figure as JPEG with maximum quality compression, we ended up with a file size of 1.1 megabytes (MB).

Continued

JPEG Size *(continued)*

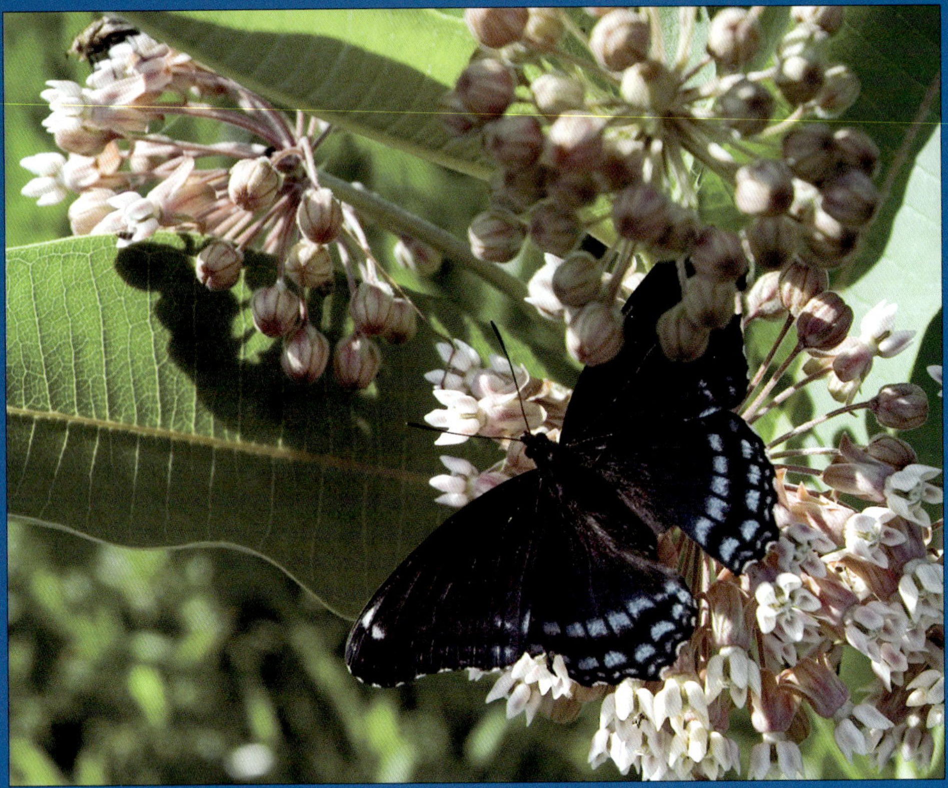

This photograph of a butterfly on a plant has many more transitions and details than Figure 4-1. Although it is exactly the same size as Figure 4-1, when we saved it using the same JPEG settings, we ended up with a larger file than Figure 4-1.

To understand why this is true, consider how JPEG works. JPEG analyzes a photo and throws away the data that it considers redundant. So only those pixels that match (or closely match) the color and exposure of adjacent points of data are considered candidates for compression. In a photo that has large areas of uniform color and light, JPEG applies its compression algorithms to a greater number of pixels. In a photo that has more transitions and small details, fewer pixels are likely candidates, which means that less data will be compressed.

Comparative File Sizes

In order to talk about the comparative sizes of various file formats, we need to define what the specific photo is, its physical size, and the settings for each save. In Table 4-1, we are referring to the original photo of Heather Stuart (Figure 4-1), which was taken with a Canon EOS 1Ds Mark II at 4992×3328 pixels.

We explain these various settings shown in Table 4-1 and their relative significance throughout this chapter.

TIFF

TIFF (Tagged Image File Format) is the highest-quality universal digital image format. (As a file extension, it's written as `.tif`.) In other words, TIFF (like JPEG) can be read by most photo-related software, output by all printers, and understood on any computer that can open photo files. (This is true only with 8-bit TIFFs, not 16-bit TIFFs. See the next section.) The biggest difference between JPEG and TIFF is that TIFF (at least the standard version of the format) doesn't throw away any of your image data. Of course, this means that TIFF files are large.

For example, the 1200×1500 pixel portrait of Heather when saved as a TIFF creates a file approximately 5.3 megabytes large. The same photo saved as a JPEG with minimum compression, maximum quality (Figure 4-1) is only 975 kilobytes, while a JPEG at highest compression, lowest quality (Figure 4-2) is a mere 88 kilobytes.

When you save a TIFF in software, some programs may give you the option to compress using what is called LZW compression. We strongly recommend against using LZW for color photos. If you must use compression to shrink a file size, save a separate JPEG version. Reserve your use of TIFFs for maintaining top quality regardless of file size, in a format that anyone and any device can read.

8-BIT AND 16-BIT TIFF

TIFF images can be saved as 8-bit or 16-bit files. This refers to the amount of data used to define your photo. To understand what this means, we'll briefly review how a digital photo is structured. (See Chapter 1 for more information about how an image sensor captures a photo.)

A digital photo is made up of *color channels*. The photos captured by digital cameras (when opened up in your computer) are RGB, which means that it has red, green, and blue channels. (See Figures 4-3 and 4-4.) These channels contain the values of the primary colors (red, green, and blue) that, when combined, make up all the colors in a photograph. (We provide a much more in-depth discussion of how photographic color is created and reproduced in Chapter 11.)

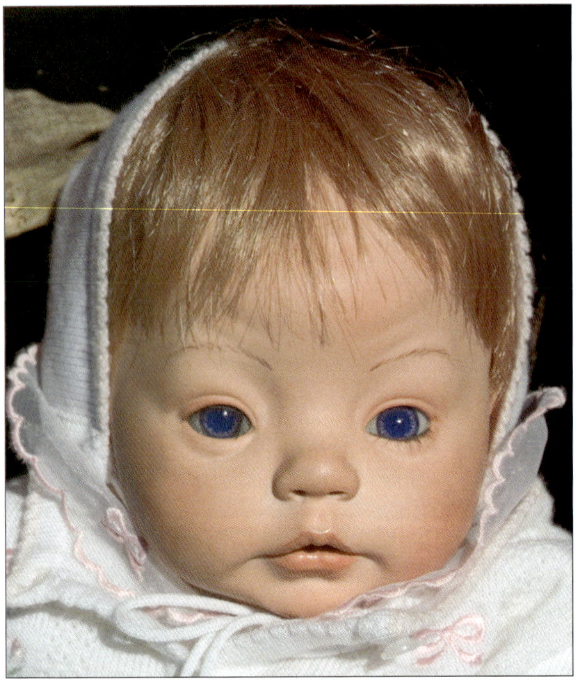

Figure 4-3: This 8-bit RGB digital photo is made up of red, green, and blue channels. (Photo taken with an Olympus Evolt E300)

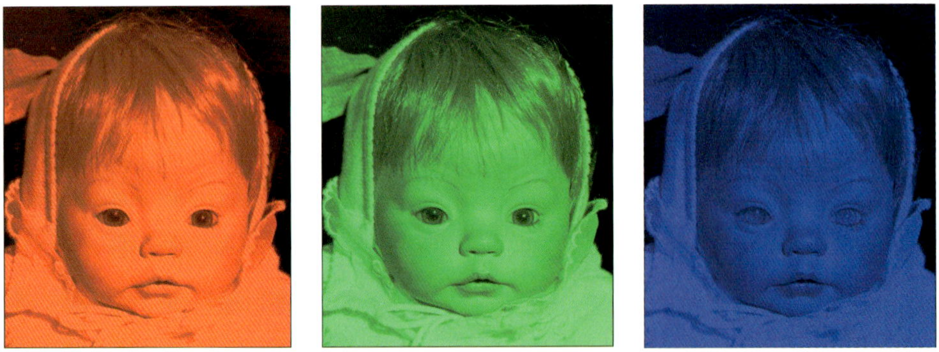

Figure 4-4: Each component color channel contains 8 bits of data about that primary color within the full image.

The vast majority of digital photos are 8 bit. That means each color channel can contain 256 discrete shades of the specific primary color (red, green, or blue). When you combine the three channels, you end up with 256 × 256 × 256 colors, or 16.7 million colors that can be used to create the details of a photo. That isn't to say that all digital photos (or even any) have all 16.7 million colors, but that each picture can be created from a palette of that many colors. The human eye can discern approximately 12 million different colors (if the person isn't color blind or color challenged), which is why 8-bit color is also called photo-realistic or true color.

16-bit TIFFs contain twice the amount of image data in each channel, which adds up to billions of possible colors. Theoretically, that means that a photo saved as a 16-bit TIFF could provide that much more the detail, including smoother transitions between colors and shades. It also results in a much larger file. For example, when we saved the 1200×1500 pixel portrait of Heather (see Figure 4-1) as a 16-bit TIFF, we ended up with a file size of over 10MB. That is double that of the 8-bit TIFF file of about 5MB. When we're working with exhibition-size photos, our 16-bit TIFFs can easily mushroom to over 100MB.

But the unwieldy size of 16-bit TIFFs isn't their primary drawback. The biggest problem is that most programs and output devices don't support 16-bit TIFF files. However, we find them invaluable when we want to maintain as much image data as possible while we're editing our photos. Later in the chapter, we'll discuss how and when to use 8-bit versus 16-bit TIFFs.

RAW

Unlike the names of the other file formats, RAW isn't an acronym. It refers to the raw, unprocessed data captured by your camera's image sensor. To understand what this means, let's review what happens when you take a photograph with a digital camera.

Going from 12-bit Capture to an 8-Bit or 16-Bit Photo

Most DSLRs are actually 12-bit devices. That means when the analog-to-digital converter (ADC) chip translates the analog data captured by the image sensor into digital data, it creates a file that has 12 bits for each of the primary color channels. However, photo-editing software and output devices don't support 12-bit image data. Therefore, the picture must be converted to 8-bit or 16-bit.

When the data is processed to create the photo file in the camera, it is *sampled* down to 8 bits, with the device or program choosing what it thinks is the best 8-bit set (such as favoring data towards the shadows or the highlights). When a RAW file is converted and saved to a TIFF photo in a RAW conversion program, you have the choice between having it sampled down to 8 bits or *interpolated* up to 16 bits. By the way, another source of 16-bit TIFFs are high-end scanners.

When light (photons) enters the camera through the lens, it strikes the image sensor, which then produces electrons. The electrons are then converted into the zeroes and ones of digital data by a chip called the ADC. If your camera is set to save your photos to JPEG or TIFF, the digital data that define your photo are then massaged and manipulated by a variety of processes within the camera. These processes allow only a small amount of user control over the decisions of how the data will be translated into a photo.

If you want to take full creative control over your photos, rather than let an anonymous team of engineers make your decisions for you, you can bypass the camera's internal processing by shooting in RAW. The file delivered to your computer won't be a true image file, but it contains all the potential of the unprocessed data as originally captured by your camera. To become a usable RGB photo file, it needs to go through special software — a RAW conversion utility. It is within the conversion software that the photographer can, if she wishes, take precise control over exposure, color, and other details that define the photo.

Tip

If you are working with a persnickety client, you may want to shoot RAW, not only for the reassurance of being able to edit the original data but also to give your work the appearance of greater professionalism. Some clients are simply more comfortable seeing their photographers using top-of-the-line equipment and the most precise procedures, even though it's the photographer and not the technology that creates a great photo.

Many experts use an old film analogy to compare shooting in RAW to JPEG or TIFF. RAW is like going back into the darkroom and making your own prints from negatives rather than dropping your film off at the photofinisher. That analogy holds true down to the amount of time you can spend tweaking and processing each and every RAW photo. That's because you have control over, and can make decisions about, settings for your photo's shadows, highlights, midtones, and color temperature. You can adjust the overall exposure, degree of sharpness, specific areas of the dynamic range, or each individual color channel. Some RAW processing utilities even provide correction tools for lens aberrations and distortions. In other words, shooting in RAW is a commitment to your photography that extends beyond taking a picture. However, it does require a certain level of expertise (and did we mention time?) to take full advantage of RAW's potential to produce superior-quality photos.

To make matters even more complex, there is no single RAW format. Every digital camera manufacturer has its own proprietary RAW format; some actually have more than one (depending on the camera model). Nikon has NEF, Minolta's is MRW, Canon's are CR2 and CRW, and so forth.

However, if you don't have the time, patience, or skills to successfully process individual RAW files, don't despair. There are RAW utilities that batch process image files (that is, they automatically process all the RAW files on a memory card). The software automatically determines what it thinks is the best way to squeeze out maximum image quality, and processes each RAW file using those settings. Generally, automatic RAW processing works, giving the photographer better quality images than he would have captured using JPEG or TIFF. But they probably won't be quite as good as manually tweaking each individual file. We use an automatic RAW processing program only when we're on a tight deadline and image quality is secondary to speed.

Despite its demands of time and expertise, like most other professional photographers, we shoot almost exclusively in RAW these days. (Actually, we shoot in RAW + JPEG. See the sidebar later in the chapter.) It gives us the creative and technical control that we used to have when we would spend all those hours in a darkroom processing and printing a single roll of film. Specifically, we find we can pull a lot more detail out of the highlights and shadows with RAW. (See Figures 4-5 and 4-6.)

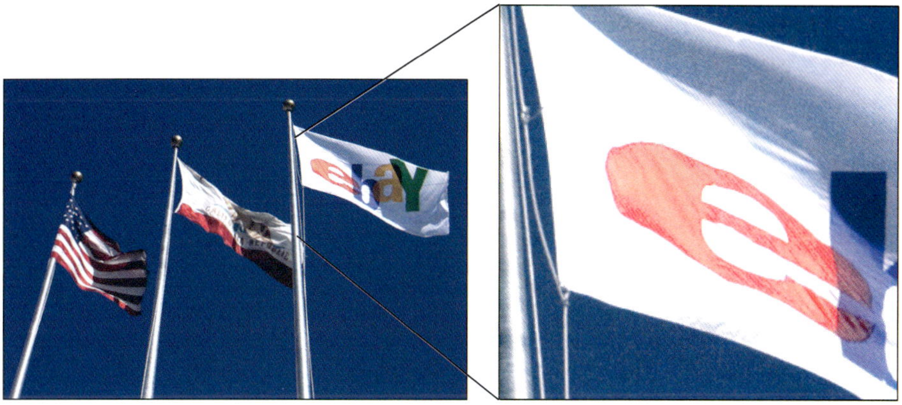

Figure 4-5: This 8-bit TIFF photograph (left) was created from a RAW file with no processing in the RAW software. Instead, we did all the exposure and color correction in Photoshop. (Photo taken with a Canon EOS 1Ds Mark II.) Looking more closely at the Photoshop-processed image (right), notice how the details in the highlights (the white of the flag, in particular) are blown out, and that the transitions within the colors are abrupt and *posterized*.

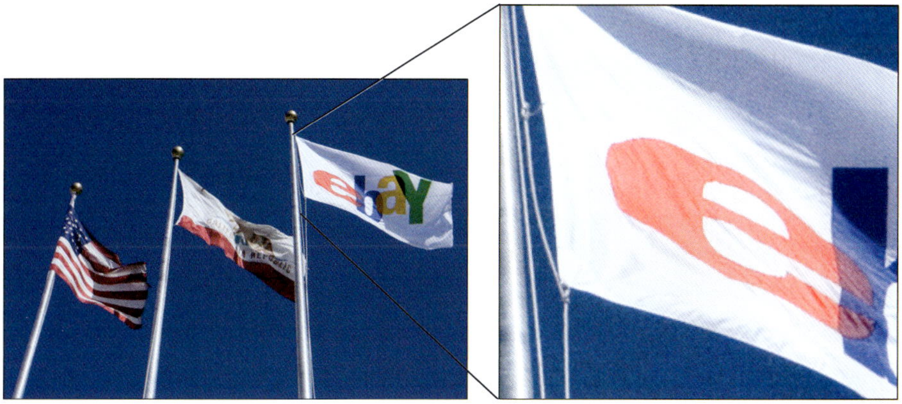

Figure 4-6: This version of the same photo (left) was edited in Adobe Camera RAW, before being converted from Canon's CR2 RAW format to an 8-bit TIFF. Looking more closely at the picture that was preprocessed in the RAW utility (right), you can see the details in the highlights are preserved (notice the wrinkles in the white area of the flag), and the transitions are smoother and more photo-realistic.

RAW + JPEG

One hybrid file format option that we use extensively is to set our camera to simultaneously create a JPEG and a RAW file of each photo we shoot. This combination gives you the best of both worlds: RAW's potential for superior-quality photos plus JPEG's universality and ease of use.

RAW + JPEG was critical back when digital asset management software (image databases) and other programs couldn't display RAW. In other words, we were blind when trying to transfer, sort, and organize RAW files on our network. The solution to this problem was to shoot RAW + JPEG. Then, we could use the thumbnails of the JPEG versions of our RAW files to decide which pictures to save or delete, where each one belonged on our network, what keywords to assign, how to rate our photos, and so on. Nowadays, all the digital asset management programs we recommend can read most RAW files. (Please see Chapter 9 for information about image databases.) However, we continue to shoot RAW + JPEG.

Originally, the JPEG duplicates were only tiny thumbnails suitable for quick viewing in image databases, but now they tend to be full-sized. That has greatly increased their usefulness. Depending on what we plan to do with our photos, using RAW + JPEG has the following advantages:

- To use when on the road. The JPEGs are great for quick viewing of what we've just shot in hand-held devices and other image viewers. (Most can't display RAW files).
- To use the photos right away (without any processing) on the Web, in documents, in email. This is especially useful if collaborators, clients, or associates are at a remote location.
- To have the option of not bothering to go through time-consuming RAW processing when the photo is exactly what we want and need.
- To see what the camera can do with the image data in terms of color and exposure, as a point of reference, while we're editing our own RAW version.

Not all DSLRs give you the option of shooting RAW + JPEG. This may seem to be a critical factor in selecting your next DSLR, but frankly, as the various RAW formats become more commonly supported, we expect that the RAW + JPEG option will become less important.

One problem with saving simultaneously to two different formats is storage space. Saving RAW + JPEG increases the amount of space each photo takes up on our memory cards and on our computers. Despite the added storage overhead, we will likely continue to use this double format because the camera's firmware can be quite smart (and getting smarter with each new model). That means the JPEG image may be exactly what we envision and need, without all the fuss of processing the RAW image.

If you've been scanning for a while, you're probably familiar with an important key to why RAW photos tend to be superior. Any editing (or *preprocessing*) you do in a scanner driver or in your RAW conversion software, establishes the attributes of the pixels that will define your photo. Any editing (or *postprocessing*) you do after the photo has been created by the scanner or by your RAW software can actually destroy the pixels defining your photo. What's more, when working in RAW, you have a larger amount of data from which to choose the pixels you want.

Of course, if the photos you shoot are always perfect and never need any editing, then you probably won't want to be bothered with shooting and processing RAW files. But if you plan to edit your photos in the computer (which means you're already committed to spending post-shoot time on them), you may as well use the tools that can produce better quality in the end.

AN IMPORTANT DOWNSIDE OF RAW

With so many different RAW file formats, each owned and controlled by the various DSLR manufacturers, you are dealing with a digital Tower of Babel. You remember the Biblical story of how everyone in the world once spoke the same language. But when people tried to build a tower to reach to the heavens, God punished their hubris by forcing them to speak such a wide diversity of languages that they couldn't understand each other's babblings. Similarly, none of these wonderful (shall we say "heavenly"?) cameras can speak each other's language.

What's important to realize is that this anarchy of proprietary formats in which we are all saving and archiving our precious photos may represent a long-term time bomb. As Paul Ellis of ACD Systems told us, "A lot of photographers don't recognize the dangers of RAW." He explained that the software you must use today to view and edit your RAW files may not work on the computers you'll be using 20 years from now.

We feel such incompatibility could happen much sooner than 20 years. In our "closet of dead technology," we hold onto old computers, operating systems, and drives, simply to be sure that we can read all our DAT tapes, SyQuest cartridges, and other ancient (from the 1980s and 1990s) archival media. Will we need to maintain 2006 computers and operating systems long after they have become outmoded and obsolete, scrounging for parts when things start to break down, just so we can continue to read and use the original RAW photographs we're shooting today?

We hope that every camera company will scrupulously keep their RAW conversion software up to date and maintain backward compatibility so that they can read all our photo files, past *and* present. Of course, not even Microsoft keeps their programs backward compatible with older file formats, and they have much greater resources than the camera companies. Then, there is that other problem that no one really wants to talk about too loudly — will all the camera companies be in business in a few years? You might say you can't imagine a world in which any of the major camera cameras would go out of business. But then, did you ever think you would see a time when IBM stopped manufacturing desktop computers? And what about Polaroid, whose instant film had given it top billing among successful photo corporations until the digital revolution of the 1990s?

Recently, third-party programs have expanded to support the most popular RAW formats for digital cameras like Canon, Fuji, Nikon, Olympus, Konica Minolta, and Pentax. Most of these programs, however, are from comparatively small, niche companies that may or may not be around 20 years from now.

The best answer would be for the photo industry to agree on a standard RAW format. But getting camera manufacturers to agree on a single standard is quite difficult — akin to herding cats. Each one believes that its own RAW format is, if not superior to the others, at least one of the things that sets it apart from its competitors.

It takes an 800-pound gorilla to herd cats. Enter Adobe with its DNG format.

Think Before You Shoot

Jon Sienkiewicz, photo industry consultant and the former vice president of marketing at Konica Minolta, has an interesting perspective on shooting RAW. "The biggest benefit of RAW," he told us, "is that it causes us to be deliberate. Digital became so easy that I didn't have to think so much when I'm shooting. Had I been shooting film, I would have given some thought and carefully considered each image, because each roll has a limited number of exposures. RAW adds a similar level of deliberateness in every step because we pay the price in speed and file size with every shot. Therefore, I'm much more conscientious when I shoot RAW."

DNG

DNG is Adobe's open standard RAW format, which it introduced in 2005. (DNG stands for Digital Negative format, taking the G from the middle of the word Negative. Unfortunately, the acronym DNF was already taken by a format unrelated to photography.)

Adobe, with its heavy-duty clout as the world's premier graphics software company, is probably one of only a handful of organizations that can force a standard on the digital camera industry. Alas, even with all of Adobe's clout, the camera companies aren't stampeding to jump on the DNG bandwagon. Whether they do or not, DNG looks as though it might be at least a good interim (if not long-term) solution.

DNG can save all your original captured RAW data, embedded within a format that Adobe claims it will continue to support through all future iterations of Photoshop. Therefore, DNG might be useful for archiving your photos now, rather than waiting for a better format to come along.

Of course, we have yet to see how this will play out. The only way to be sure that your current archives will be readable 20 years from now is to upgrade your archives to new technologies as they evolve. That, in itself, is a major undertaking, which we have found to be easier to recommend than to do. In a nutshell, that is why we maintain that closet of dead technology we mentioned earlier.

Tip

Anytime you convert from less to more, whether it is increasing the number of colors, the resolution, or the image size of your photo, you are forcing the technology to invent data. When you go from more to less, you are simply reducing the amount of data that already exists. That's why we almost always shoot at the highest level of color gamut, optical resolution, and image size.

PSD and Other Software-Specific Formats

Photoshop has its PSD format; CorelPaint has CPT; Illustrator's is AI. Nearly every major program that a serious photographer or graphics artist might use offers a proprietary file format for saving the photos and images edited or created within that program. Of course, you can, if

Choosing Your Color Model

DSLRs typically offer at least two shooting options regarding what color model they will use for defining your photos — sRGB or Adobe RGB. sRGB is the model used for display on computer monitors, including on the Web. Adobe RGB has a wider *gamut* (number of feasible colors) and is more suitable for print. We usually shoot everything in Adobe RGB because it's always possible to reduce it to sRGB. But conversion in the other direction tends not to be as good.

When working in RAW conversion software, you may have the option of other color models, such as CIE RGB, ColorMatch RGB, ProPhoto RGB, Wide Gamut RGB, and others. If we are working with a client who has a preference based on the intended output, or if we have a specific printing output chosen, then we will select the color model that matches those specifications. Otherwise, we always choose either ProPhoto or Wide Gamut RGB, both of which are wider gamut than sRGB or Adobe RGB.

For more information about color models, please see Chapter 11.

you wish, save to TIFF, JPEG, and other common standard formats in these programs. But we recommend, if you edit your photos, that you save at least one version in the program's own proprietary format.

To understand what sets the software proprietary file formats apart, we'll describe how we used to work. Back in the early 1990s, Sally was preparing a collection of her images for a one-woman art exhibit, the very first all-digital show at the Apple Market Center in midtown Manhattan. For many months, she worked hard on perfecting her images. Every time she changed a color, added some text, applied a filter, tweaked the exposure, or combined more than one image into a collage, the new portion of the picture was merged immediately into the original pixels of the picture. That made re-editing difficult if not impossible. So, she saved new versions of every single image after every significant edit. You can imagine how taxing that was on the limited computers of the time (when a 1-gigabyte hard drive could cost $2,000 and 16 megabytes of RAM topped $500).

Since then, software has matured considerably, including:

- Layers that keep elements you've added to an image separate rather than merging them into the background pixels.
- Effects and Adjustment layers that maintain the settings of your exposure, color, or special effects edits separately, so you can change or remove them without affecting anything else you've done to the picture.
- Vector text that can be re-edited at any time, including correcting spelling; changing the font, size, or position; adjusting alignment; and so on.

If you save your image in JPEG, traditional TIFF, or any other common file format, all this information is fixed and unchangeable. (Your software may or may not be able to save layers in TIFF, as Photoshop does.) But if you save one version of your photo in the program's proprietary format, you will be able to re-edit to your heart's content at any time in the future. (See Figure 4-7.)

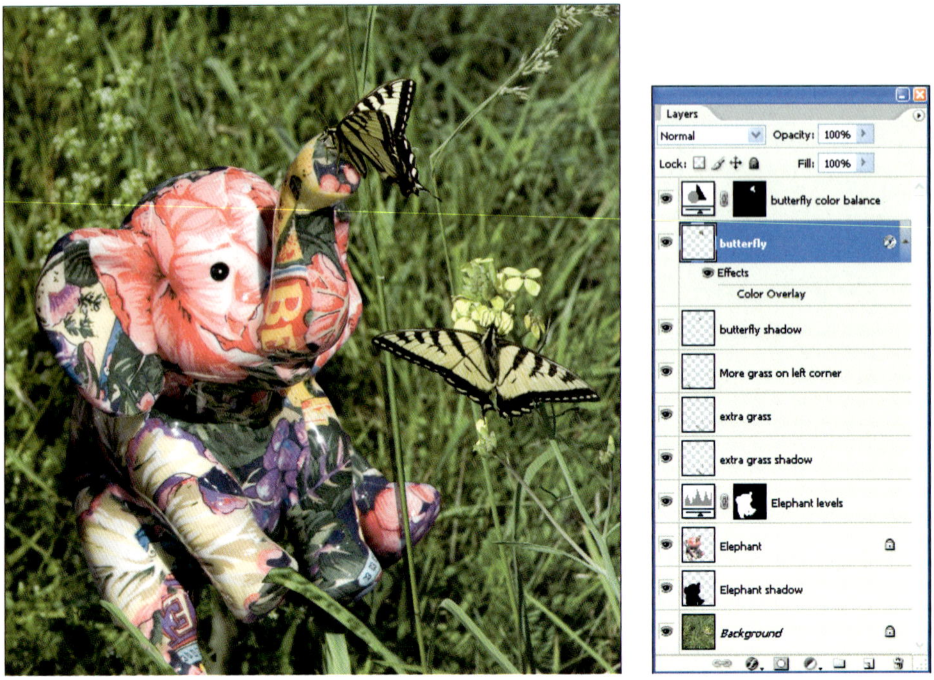

Figure 4-7: This image (left) was created from three photographs — of the elephant, the butterfly that Sally pasted on the elephant's trunk, and the background picture of the other butterfly in a field of wildflowers. This layers palette from Photoshop (on the right) shows all of the elements that went into creating the image. This includes edits to the color balance of one of the butterflies, an exposure edit (using a levels command) to the elephant, several shadows, cloned pieces of grass, and so on. What is important is that each of these edits is maintained as a separate and re-editable layer, as long as the image is saved in Photoshop's proprietary PSD file format (or a layered TIFF). Even if you don't plan on assembling these kinds of collages from your photos, the ability to save the settings of your color and exposure edits so that they can be adjusted at a future time is invaluable. (Screen capture courtesy of Adobe Systems)

While it is true that you can always add another edit to any picture, the ability to go back to the original image data and change an edit is a far superior option. Remember, unless you are working on a RAW file, every time you edit a picture, you are actually destroying original pixels. (When you work on the RAW file, you are defining the original pixels.) In photography, as in life, trying to correct a previous correction almost always compounds your problems. As with film photography, when you could always go back to the original negative, digital photography also allows you to go back to the beginning and try again — as long as you save and protect your original files and use layers whenever possible in your edited versions. (See below and Chapter 9 for discussions on protecting and archiving your original files.)

Developing an Intelligent File Format Workflow

An important key to maintaining control over your photography is to choose the right file format for the task at hand. Within the typical photography workflow, you will have to choose your format four different times:

- When taking your photographs
- When editing your photographs
- When outputting and sharing your photographs
- When archiving your photographs

While we have our own personal methodologies, no single answer is correct for everyone or for every shoot. You must determine what makes sense for you in various circumstances. All we can do is provide information about how your choices will affect your photography, your productivity, and your schedule.

First, Get the Photo

Choosing your shooting format is one of the first decisions you will need to make when setting up your camera for a shoot. Many DSLRs offer four format options:

- RAW
- RAW + JPEG
- JPEG
- TIFF

Please note that some DSLRs don't have the RAW + JPEG option, while others cannot save TIFF files. For shooting, the pros and cons of each format are rather straightforward. (See Table 4-2.)

Table 4-2 The Pros and Cons of File Formats for Shooting

File Format	*Pros*	*Cons*
RAW	Full control over how the image sensor data is converted to a photo. Ability to correct exposure and color before the RGB photo is created. Potentially, the highest-quality photos.	Time-consuming, requires skill. Larger files than JPEG.

Continued

Table 4-2 The Pros and Cons of File Formats for Shooting *(continued)*

File Format	***Pros***	***Cons***
RAW + JPEG	Same full control and quality as RAW, plus the universality and immediate usability of JPEG. The duplicate JPEG file may save you time in editing.	Double file structure takes up extra storage space and may require more time to save. Requires remembering to keep the two files together when copying, moving, and archiving the photos. Not available in all DSLRs.
JPEG	Smallest files, take up less space on memory cards, hard drives, and other storage media. Readable and usable by more devices and programs (and clients) than any other photo format. Saves faster than RAW or TIFF.	Uses lossy compression, which may diminish the quality of your photo.
TIFF	Highest-quality universal photo format.	Many DSLRs no longer save TIFF. Large files. Doesn't have the flexibility of RAW. TIFF files take the longest time to process and save, which can slow down your shooting.

As we have mentioned, we tend to shoot in RAW or RAW + JPEG. This is a conscious choice based on the following:

- Nearly every photo we take is potentially something we might want to use for an exhibition print, prepare for publication in a high-quality glossy magazine or book, or use in a fine art imaging collage.
- We don't trust technology and like having the second chance that RAW offers to correct or fine-tune exposure and color.
- We are more than willing to take the hit in productivity, speed, and added storage overhead that RAW represents (it helps that our computers have large networked hard drives and lots of RAM).
- We are seldom on a very tight deadline, since our photos are usually for our lectures, books, and exhibits. Those clients we accept all understand that we will take our time in creating the right picture. If they need the photo right away, we refer them to other photographers.

To decide which file format you want to use for your shoot, you need to think your choice through in a similar manner. Specifically, ask yourself the following questions:

- What are the shooting conditions and subject?
  - If you have full control over the lighting and exposure and have no doubt about what you're going to get, TIFF and JPEG may work just fine.
  - If the scene has deep shadows and/or lots of bright light, you can usually pull more and better detail out of them if you shoot in RAW. But remember, it will take time and skill to tweak your images using conversion software.
  - If the scene has a limited dynamic range (with most detail in the midtones), you may see less of an advantage with RAW and may be very satisfied with JPEG or TIFF.
  - If you are using a lens that tends to introduce chromatic or other aberrations, you may be able to obtain higher-quality corrections in RAW.
- What do you want to do with your photos once you've shot them?
  - If your photos won't be printed larger than, say, 8"×10" or you want to quickly deliver images without editing them, you might find TIFF or JPEG quite adequate for your needs.
  - If you expect the photo to be displayed or printed larger than 8"×10", or if details and precision are important to you (or your client), then you may be better off with RAW.
  - If all your work will be displayed on typical computer screens, as a slide show, on a Web site, and so on, then JPEG will probably be quite good for the purpose.
- How imperative is having the very top quality?
  - RAW definitely provides the opportunity for the very highest quality if you know how to take advantage of it.
  - TIFF is the highest-quality universal format, but it may slow down your shooting.
  - JPEG quality is dependent on the size of the image and the amount of compression used.
- How pressed for time are you?
  - If the shoot is a rush job and/or in an environment in which you will have few resources, JPEG will get the photos out more quickly.
  - If you can take as much time as you want or need, you might want to spend some of it in tweaking the highest quality possible out of RAW files. (Or you might prefer to use the time working in other areas of the workflow chain, such as color management.)

JPEG: The Dissenting View

Dr. Albert Edgar is not only a very fine wedding photographer, he is also one of the great geniuses in imaging science. He holds innumerable patents (200 and counting!) and was the scientist behind Digital Ice (the scanning firmware for removing scratches from film emulsion), Digital ROC (the Photoshop plug-in for the recovery of color in faded photos), Digital GEM (a utility for taming film emulsion grain patterns in scanning), and many other impressive innovations in our industry. Applied Science Fiction was the appropriate name of his company, until it was purchased by Kodak in 2004 (`www.asf.com`).

Not surprisingly, Dr. Al is one of our favorite experts on photography and imaging. When we asked him how he handles his RAW files (assuming, because he is quite a perfectionist, that he would use RAW for all his photography), he surprised us by revealing that he always uses JPEG.

"I don't use RAW," Dr. Al explains. "I'm not a rich guy and can't afford all the chips and post-storage with 4,000 images per wedding. And I am really concerned about the archivability of RAW files; some of the new encryption battles are going to ensure that RAW files can not be practically read 25 years from now." However, he predicts, "There is so much of the world stored on JPEG, there should be legacy JPEG decoders around for centuries."

Now, the fact is that Dr. Al is incredibly savvy about processing images — probably the most knowledgeable person we know on the subject. He plays with the underlying code of digital photographs the way we might click through the TV remote control. So, he is able to pull a lot of detail from a JPEG image that would be hidden from the rest of us. (His Digital SHO Photoshop plug-in gives us some of that control, enabling us to retrieve a high degree of details from shadows and highlights, even in JPEGs. Try the trial version download. It can deliver impressive results.)

Still, he is correct about one thing — high-quality (low-compression) JPEG can be indistinguishable from TIFF or RAW in many circumstances. Look at the three figures in this sidebar and before reading the caption, try to determine what format we used to shoot each — RAW, JPEG, or TIFF.

Stereo experts have told us that only a tiny percentage of people (something like 1 percent) can tell the difference in the quality of the sound between a $500 and a $50,000 stereo system. The same can be said about image quality. While we are all for precision and excellence in photography, be sure that the time you are devoting to that extra bit of quality is something that is perceptible and will affect the overall visual value of your image.

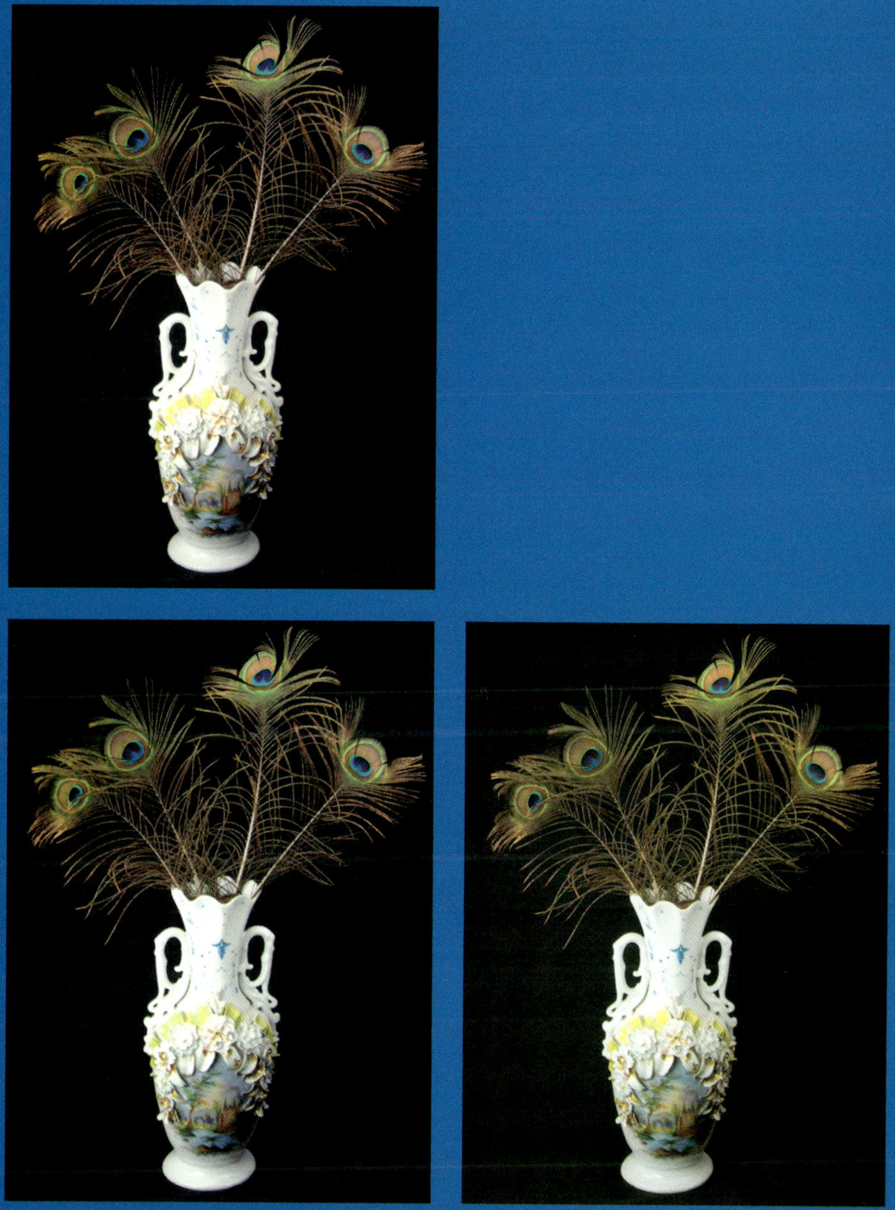

At this size and printed in mass-production for this book, the differences among these three photos are barely perceptible to most people. The figure on top was originally shot as a JPEG, using fine quality/low compression. The figure to the left was originally taken as a TIFF. The figure on the right was shot in RAW, then processed and converted to TIFF in Adobe Camera RAW software. (Depending on how these photos end up being printed, you may see a slight difference in the white details of the neck of the vase.)

- How sure are you about your exposure and color?
  - If you are in your studio or any other environment in which you are absolutely sure your shots will be bang-on accurate, JPEG or TIFF may be more efficient choices than RAW.
  - If you have any doubts or concerns about exposure or color, RAW will give you a second chance to get it right.
- Do you want to spend time on the computer, working on your photos?
  - If you want your responsibility to end with transferring your pictures to your computer and choosing the ones to use and/or deliver, then definitely shoot JPEG or TIFF.
  - If you plan to edit your photos using a program like Photoshop, shooting RAW would mean simply starting the editing process earlier, in a RAW utility. It will probably take no more time than you had anticipated, and could result in higher quality.
- What is your level of skill in computer photo editing?
  - Photo editing is definitely a skill that must be developed. Just because you're a good photographer doesn't mean you are naturally as good at using photo-editing software.
  - If you aren't comfortable with photo editing, you may hate working with RAW files — just as you may dislike manipulating JPEGs or TIFFs.
  - If you aren't intimated by computers and enjoy the learning process, you might want to develop your skills at editing to give you greater creative control over your photos. In that case, you might enjoy the challenge inherent in handling RAW files.

What Resolution Should I Shoot?

Most digital cameras offer a range of resolutions. And, yet, we never shoot anything but the top resolution, which produces the largest files. It may be true that the series of photos we're taking are destined only for the Web, and choosing a low resolution that would create the small size file appropriate for the Web limits our options. But what if one of the photos in the shoot is a beauty — one we might want to print for an exhibition?

You can always down sample a photo, reducing its resolution and, therefore, its file size. But interpolating a photo, to increase its resolution will never give you as fine quality as shooting it at the higher resolution from the start.

We used a lot of conditional verbs (may, could, might) in the preceding discussion. As we stated earlier, we can't give you one definitive answer on what is the very best file format for everyone, in every situation, shooting every subject. We have given you, instead, guidelines and perspectives that we hope will help you find the right answers for your wants and needs.

TIP

If you are running out of space on your memory card and you forgot to bring another one with you on the shoot, it is often better to shoot a lower resolution than a higher compression to fit more pictures onto the card. However, memory cards are so inexpensive these days that you can easily keep extra cards in all your camera bags and even in your wallet. Sally has cards in all her everyday purses, just in case. That's how we can have our cake and eat it, too — shooting at the highest possible resolution and best quality (or no) compression every time.

Setting JPEG Compression in Your Digital Camera

Just as we always shoot at the highest resolution, we almost never use anything but the highest-quality, lowest-level compression, when we're shooting in JPEG. Not only does JPEG use a lossy compression that can negatively impact on image quality, but also the effect of the compression on quality is cumulative. Every time you save a photo in JPEG, even more data will be thrown away. Therefore, when shooting in JPEG, we like to start out with the finest quality possible.

One way that digital camera manufacturers distinguish themselves from their competition is to use nonstandard nomenclature, icons, and switches for common tasks. Therefore, we cannot tell you exactly how to set the JPEG compression level in your specific digital camera.

The following are the typical descriptions or symbols used to refer to the various levels of compression:

- Fine (or High), Normal, Standard
- Best, Better, Good
- ★★★ ★★ ★, in which three stars are the highest quality, lowest compression, while one star is the lowest quality, highest compression.

Unfortunately, all the above are also used by some digital cameras to indicate resolution levels instead of compression. So, you're going to have to check your camera's manual to learn just where and how to set the JPEG compression on your particular camera.

Preparing Your RAW Files for Photo Editing

If you use RAW to shoot your pictures, the first step in any photo editing is to process your files in a RAW conversion utility. Once you've finished with all your settings in the RAW conversion software, then you must choose what file format you want to use to save the newly defined RGB photo. At that point, you're dealing with the same issues and choices that you must make with all photos you plan to edit. So, please read the section after our discussions of your RAW software choices for guidance on choosing among the formats for photo editing.

Tip

After you have transferred your photos from your memory card or camera to your computer, make copies of them immediately. That will protect your original photos, while you edit the copies. For guidance on developing easy workflows to protect your originals, see Chapter 9.

Converting Your RAW Files to RGB Photos

RAW data are just that — information that has been captured by your digital camera's image sensor and turned into digital data by its ADC chip. For the file to be read by a computer or printer as a photograph, the data must be massaged and manipulated, either by your camera or by you, and then converted into an RGB photo. If you shoot your pictures using your camera's RAW file format, you are taking responsibility for handling and converting the data on your own, with no help from your camera.

As a rule, the tools you'll have for working on your RAW files may be quite sophisticated and precise. (See Figure 4-8.)

Tip

The trick to learning RAW conversion controls is the same as learning any photo-editing software: check out each dialog and its settings by actually using them. Don't make your choices simply by reading the documentation (which tends to be flimsy). Try each option at a variety of settings and see how they affect your picture. To do this, save the different versions of your photo (created using various settings) under different names, and compare the results on your monitor and by printing them out. After all, isn't that really the way you learned photography in the first place — by trial and error?

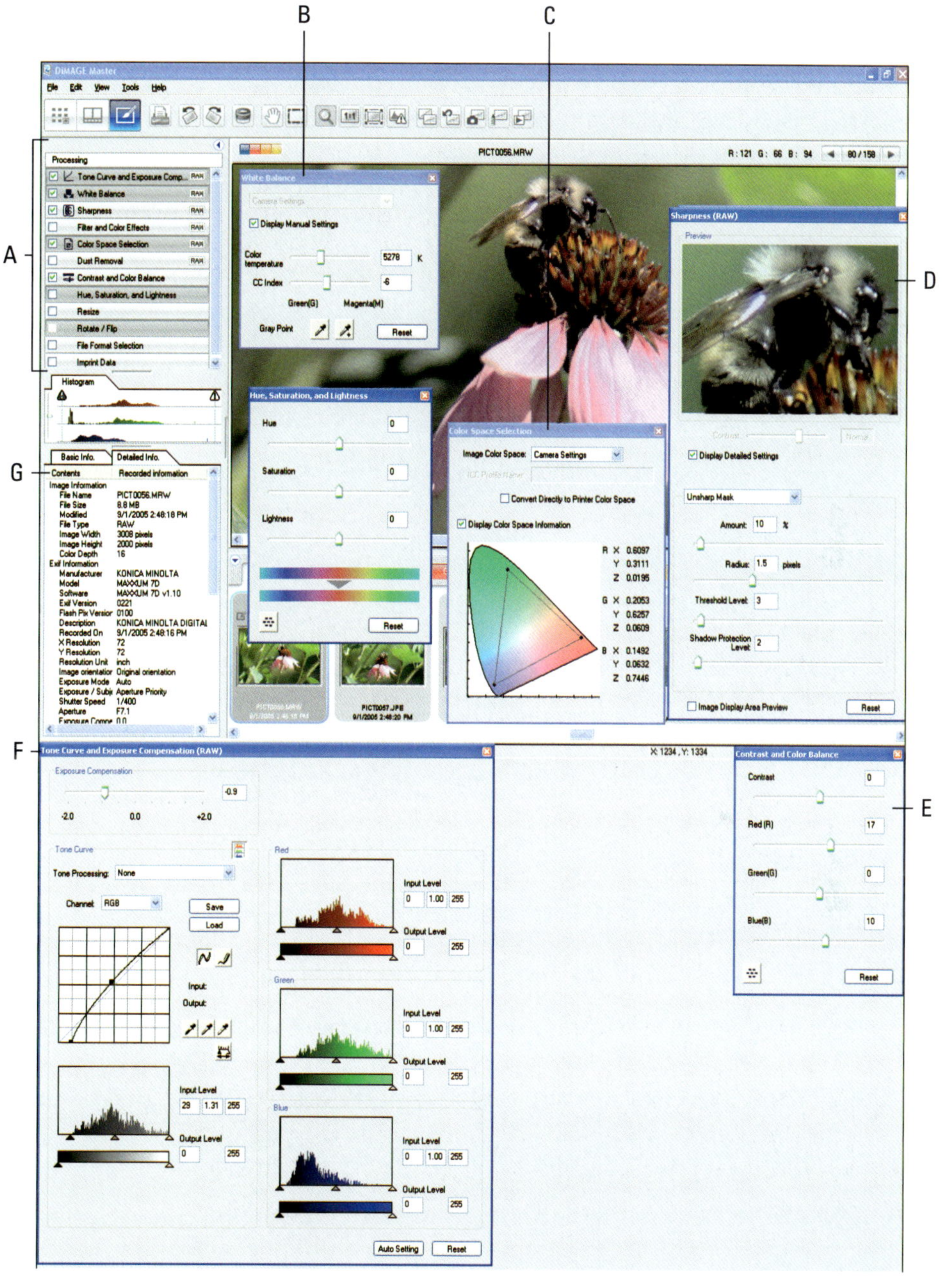

Figure 4-8: This screen capture from Konica Minolta's DiMage Master displays that RAW utility's options for editing photos taken with a Konica Minolta DSLR. (A) This list indicates the variety of controls DiMage Master offers for editing and manipulating the RAW data. Not all camera manufacturers' RAW utilities have as many options or as high a degree of precision. (B) Whatever white balance you set in your camera, you can change it once you have the photo in the RAW utility. Here, you can set color

(continued)

temperature, choose from a variety of presets (such as daylight, tungsten, fluorescent, and so on), use an eyedropper to establish a neutral grey point, or even create a grey average by clicking on several points within the photo. (The CC index is the Color Compensate scale that applies photo filter type color adjustments.) (C) As we mentioned in the Color Model sidebar earlier in this chapter, RAW utilities offer a choice of what color space (or color model) you use to define the colors in your photo. See Chapter 11 for more information about color models. (D) Adjusting the sharpness of your photo a little can do wonders, but not even a great RAW utility can compensate for an out-of-focus picture. (E) Linear sliders like these for contrast and color balance are good beginning points for editing, as preparation for more precise adjustment using other controls. (F) But the heart of all RAW utilities are these kinds of exposure and color controls, which include exposure compensation, and tone curves and histograms (for editing the relationship of highlights, shadows, and midtones), including controls for adjusting the exposure of the individual red, green, and blue color channels. Like white balance, it doesn't really matter what exposure settings you use when you shoot, since you can change them in a RAW utility. However, keep in mind that your choice of *f*-stop will affect depth-of-field, and the speed of the shutter will determine stop action. (For information on how to use histograms and exposure compensation, see Chapter 5. For information on tone curves, see Chapter 10. (G) As you can see, from the Detailed Information (taken from the metadata embedded in the file), this photo was taken with a Konica Minolta Maxxum 7D. The metadata also provide all kinds of shooting information regarding the original exposure and color settings, time and date the photo was taken, lens used, and so on. (Screen capture of DiMage Master interface courtesy of Konica Minolta)

Tip

We recommend taking advantage of two tools available in most RAW utilities to save you lots of time and effort. The first is the ability to save your settings for future use on similar photos. The second is batch processing. Both work on the principle that we all tend to take more than one photo under the same conditions whenever we shoot a subject or scene. Therefore, the settings you would use on one photo would probably apply just as well to several, if not dozens or scores, of other, similar photos.

Using Metadata

The metadata attached to your photo by the camera is a treasure trove of information and feedback. Among other things, it tells you what camera took the picture, when (time and date), at what shutter speed, aperture, and ISO settings, whether you used exposure compensation and how much, any strobe settings, the metering mode, the color model, and so forth. All this data provides great feedback to help you evaluate the shoot.

What's more, you can use the metadata to determine which photos were shot under the same conditions as others. That's invaluable for batch processing and other automated processes, because it helps you group pictures that require similar editing and adjustments.

Selecting Your RAW Conversion Utility

Quite frankly, RAW conversion utilities that are bundled with DSLRs vary widely among camera manufacturers in terms of ease of use, precision and variety of controls, speed, convenience, and quality. Such programs have two advantages:

- Your camera manufacturer's software should understand what your camera is trying to say and do.
- In most cases, the program is included with the purchase of your camera. (However, that isn't always true. Nikon has two RAW utilities: the one that is bundled with its cameras and its pro quality software, which is an added accessory and requires an additional investment.)

The fact is that camera manufacturers are not always the best sources for RAW utility software, even for programs designed specifically for their own cameras. As Jon Sienkiewicz told us, "Camera manufacturers are great at making cameras and at creating firmware, but not the best at software. Most of their software is subcontracted. On the other hand, Adobe are experts who can write circles around any Japanese [company's] software. If the manufacturers are smart, they will let Adobe and other third-party companies handle the processing of RAW."

The question is — what software should you use for the conversion?

We suggest starting out with the RAW conversion utility that came with your camera. You may be satisfied with it, and not need to look any further.

If you decide you want to try another program, download a free trial version from the Web and test it out on an actual shoot before you plunk down your hard earned cash. If you use several different converters on the same photo files, you will notice small to significant differences among the various programs' interpretations of the photographs, in terms of contrast, brightness, color response, and so forth. When checking out a converter, don't just view the photos on a computer monitor, but also print them out as you would for a typical job. This will give you a realistic view of the kind of results you can expect. A good program is like a good pair of shoes — it should fit your personality, requirements, and preferences. Don't rely on recommendations, either by us or other photographers you know and trust. That is because what fits us or others may not be the best for your needs and the way you like to work.

We use the following third-party utilities, all of which do a good job, and have different advantages:

- Adobe Camera RAW
- DxO Optics Pro
- SilverFast Digital Camera Suite

ADOBE CAMERA RAW

The initial advantage of Adobe Camera RAW (see Figures 4-9 through Figure 4-14) is that it is part of Photoshop (`www.photoshop.com`). So, if you are already using a recent version of Photoshop (CS, CS2, etc.), you won't have to pay anything extra for the RAW utility. (However, we highly recommend that you download updates on a regular basis from the Adobe Web site.) What's more, Adobe RAW is well integrated into Photoshop, making the conversion and processing a seamless part of the Adobe workflow. And, as Jon Sienkiewicz said, Adobe's engineers are superlative experts at writing code for image editing.

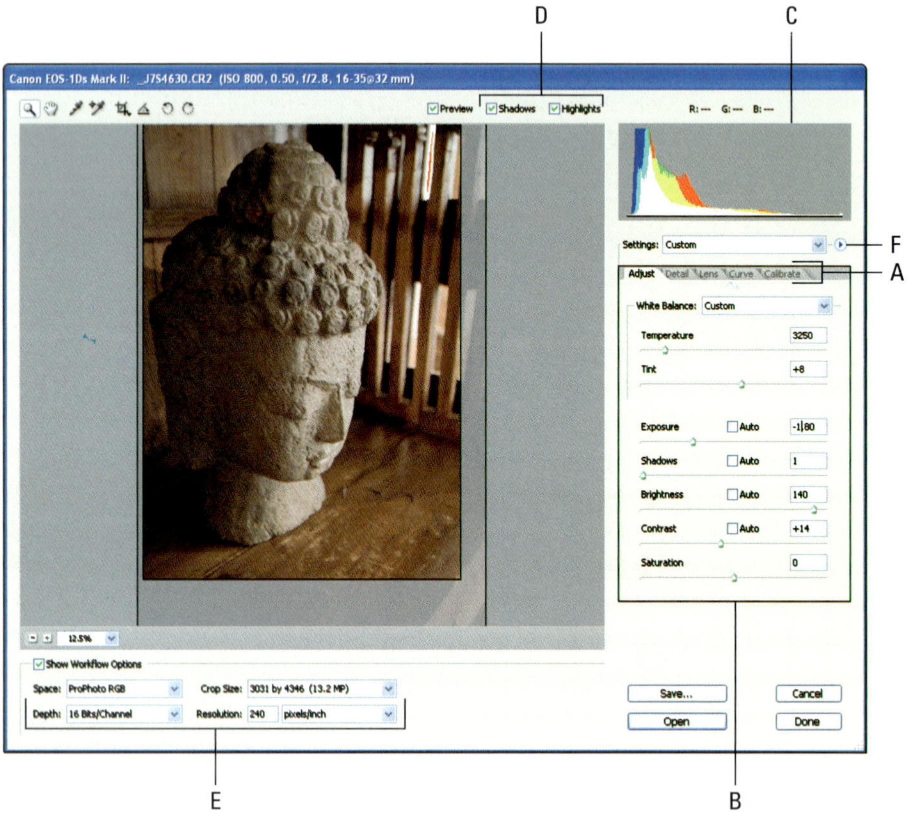

Figure 4-9: Adobe Camera RAW's main interface. (A) Click on the individual tabs to access the other commands (see Figures 4-11 through 4-14). (B) The Adjust tab provides slider controls for various exposure and color controls. (C) As the various controls on the Adjust (and other tabs) are modified, the histogram changes to provide feedback on how they are affecting the data that defines the photo. (For more information about histograms see Chapter 5.) (D) If you have the shadows and highlights options checked, the preview image will mark areas of highlights (with red) and shadows (with blue) that may be too extreme to be printable (*out of gamut*). (E) RAW provides control, not only over how a photo will be defined but also over how it will be saved and output. (F) Whenever you see an arrow of this sort, click on it to view other options. This one opens up the dialog in Figure 4-10. (Screen captures courtesy of Adobe Systems. Photo taken with a Canon EOS 1Ds Mark II)

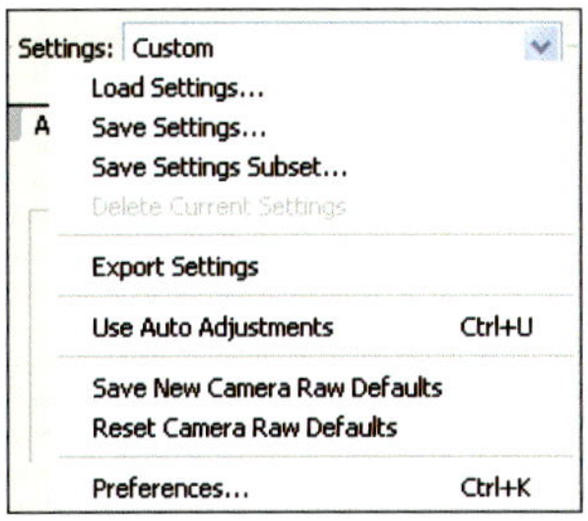

Figure 4-10: All RAW utilities allow you to save and reload any settings you create. This is an invaluable ability, given that you will probably use the same camera, lens, lights, and so on, for shooting other photos. This dialog is available for all the tabbed dialogs in Camera RAW. (See Figures 4-9, 4-11, 4-12, 4-13, and 4-14.)

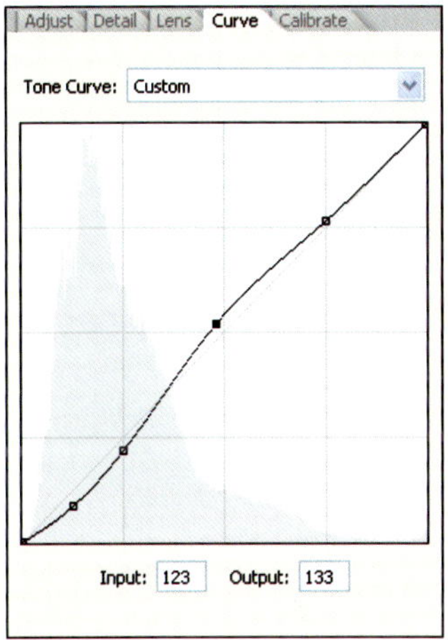

Figure 4-11: Under the Camera RAW's Curve tab is a classic gamma (tone) curve, which can give you very precise control over highlights, shadows, and all midtones in between (but doesn't act on individual color channels). For more information on using a gamma curve, see Chapter 10.

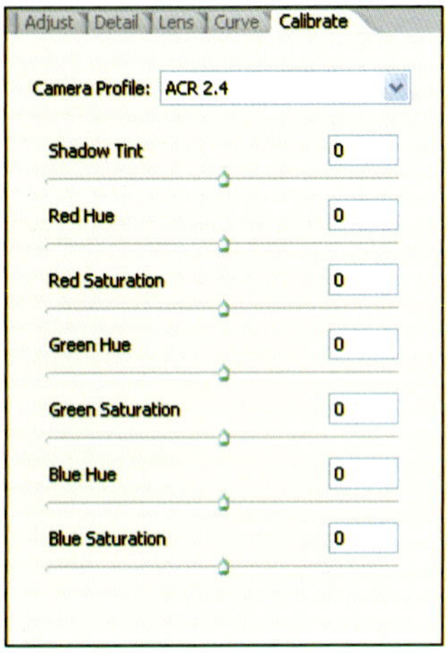

Figure 4-12: Whether you're shooting with film or digital technology, color shifts are quite common. The white balance defined by your digital camera may or may not be perfectly clean (correct), and/or may or may not be accurately interpreted by the RAW utility. That's why Camera RAW has a Calibrate tab, which allows you to tweak the colors, to remove (or introduce) any color shift.

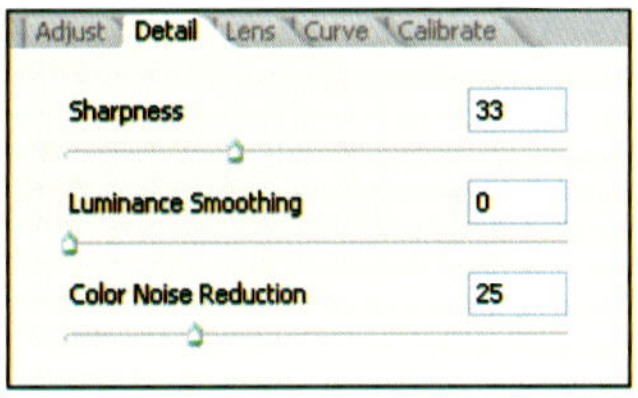

Figure 4-13: The Detail tab provides controls over the overall clarity of your photo. When working with this interface and the Lens controls in Figure 4-14, be sure to zoom in and out frequently. This allows you to see the effects of these powerful and potentially difficult tools on both the details and on the overall picture.

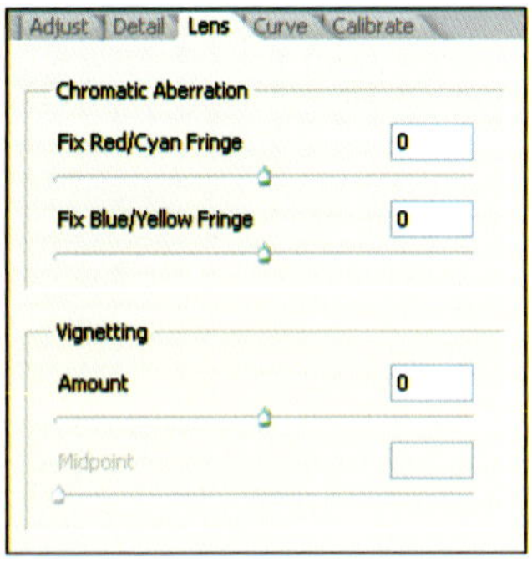

Figure 4-14: The Lens tab helps correct lens aberrations. Be sure to save these settings, because you will certainly use the same lens over and over again.

Tip

While we strongly encourage you to read everything about the controls of your RAW software that you can get your hands on, don't take anyone's word for what a setting does or the best way to use it. Instead, learn by experimentation and experience, seeing what each option does to your own photos.

We use Photoshop Creative Suite daily, which includes keeping track of the various versions of a single photo file through its Version Cue utility. So, the integrated Adobe Camera RAW is the conversion software that we turn to most frequently. It's essentially a question of convenience for us.

DXO OPTICS PRO

Photographers who use DxO Optics Pro (`www.dxo.com`) swear by it for the brilliant way it corrects lens aberrations and distortions, and for its ability to pull highlight and shadow details. As you can see from Figure 4-15, it has many more controls options than Camera RAW or most other conversion utilities. We have been impressed with the image quality we've gotten from it, even by just leaving most settings at Auto and simply tweaking those areas we want to work. However, batch processing can be time-consuming. When we have leisure time to work on our photos, or the need for that extra boost of precision and perfection (such as for Sally's exhibition prints), we turn to DxO Optics Pro. (See Figure 4-15.) By the way, DxO Optics Pro will also correct TIFF and JPEG images.

SILVERFAST DCPRO

Our favorite scanning software is LaserSoft Imaging's SilverFast, which we first discovered years ago when Epson began bundling a light version with their Photo Perfection scanners. LaserSoft now has a digital camera version of the import utility that works with RAW files — SilverFast DCPro (`www.Silverfast.com`). Like the scanning program, it can be used as a standalone program or as an Import plug-in from within Photoshop or other photo-editing programs.

SilverFast DCPro has two major advantages:

- With the purchase of an industry-standard digital camera target from LaserSoft, you can use it to calibrate your digital camera. That's invaluable in a properly color managed photography workflow. (See Chapter 11.)
- If you have been using SilverFast for scanning and are familiar with the way the interface works, your experience will put you that much further ahead in mastering the digital camera interface. (See Figure 4-16.)

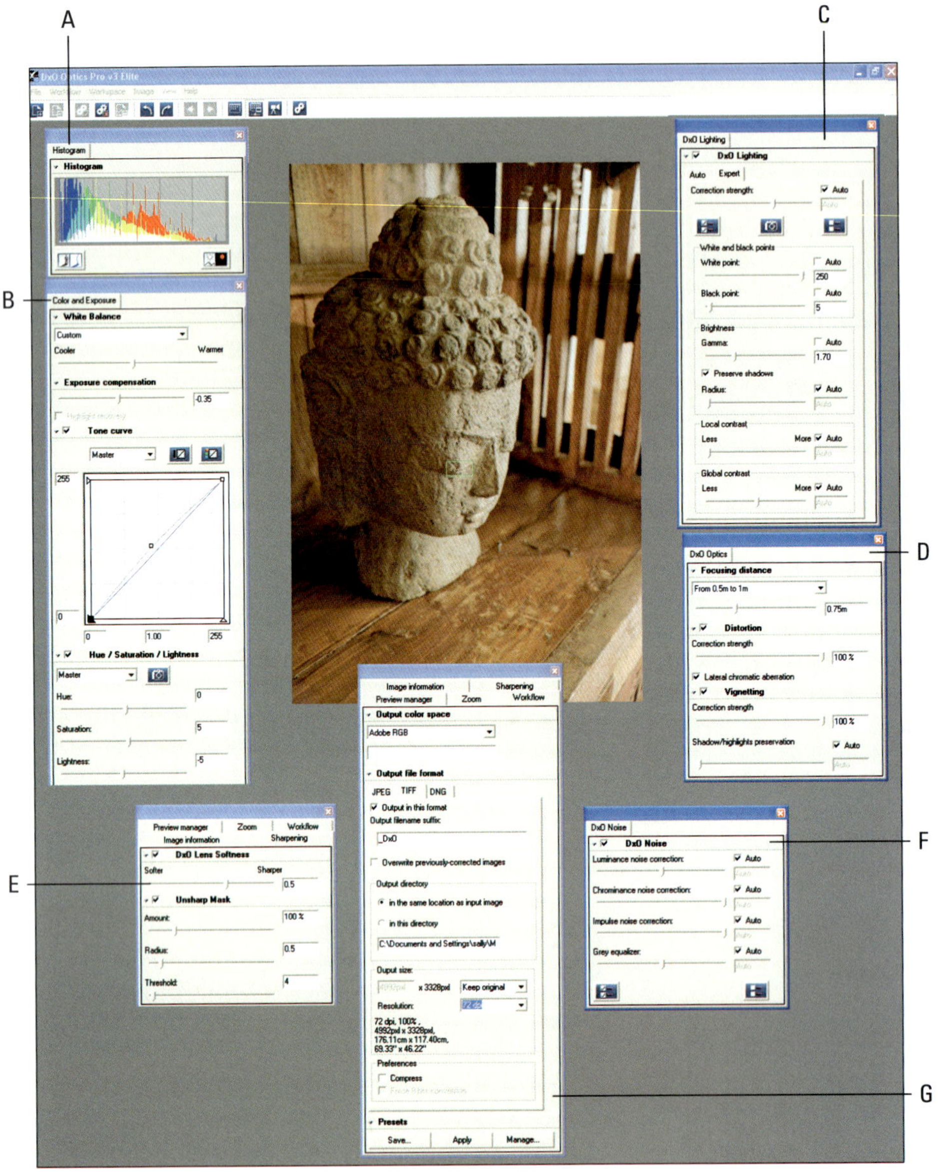

Figure 4-15: While DxO Optics Pro uses a tabbed interface like Adobe Camera RAW, each of DxO's tabbed dialogs may be pulled out and displayed concurrently. That creates a smoother and more interactive workflow. In this screen capture, we have pulled out only some of DxO's tabbed dialogs: (A) The histogram has buttons for displaying clipped areas of highlights and shadows, temporarily replacing the current preview window. (B) The color and exposure controls include a gamma curve that can work on individual color channels, as well as a hue, saturation, and lightness interface that can be set to focus on specific hues. (C) The DxO Lighting dialog is one of the program's strong suits, giving the photographer precise control over how exposure adjustments will affect shadows, highlights, and midtones. (D) At the heart of DxO Optics Pro are, of course, the optical corrections. In this photo, the

(continued)

slight barrel distortion wasn't that obvious, until compared to the version corrected by the program's Auto settings. (E) DxO's analyses of individual lenses also provide excellent control over each lens's sharpness or softness characteristics. What's more, it's intelligent, applying less sharpness to areas of greater noise. (F) Similarly, noise characteristics are tailored specifically to the camera model. (G) Controls for defining how and where your files will be saved. (Screen capture courtesy of DxO Labs)

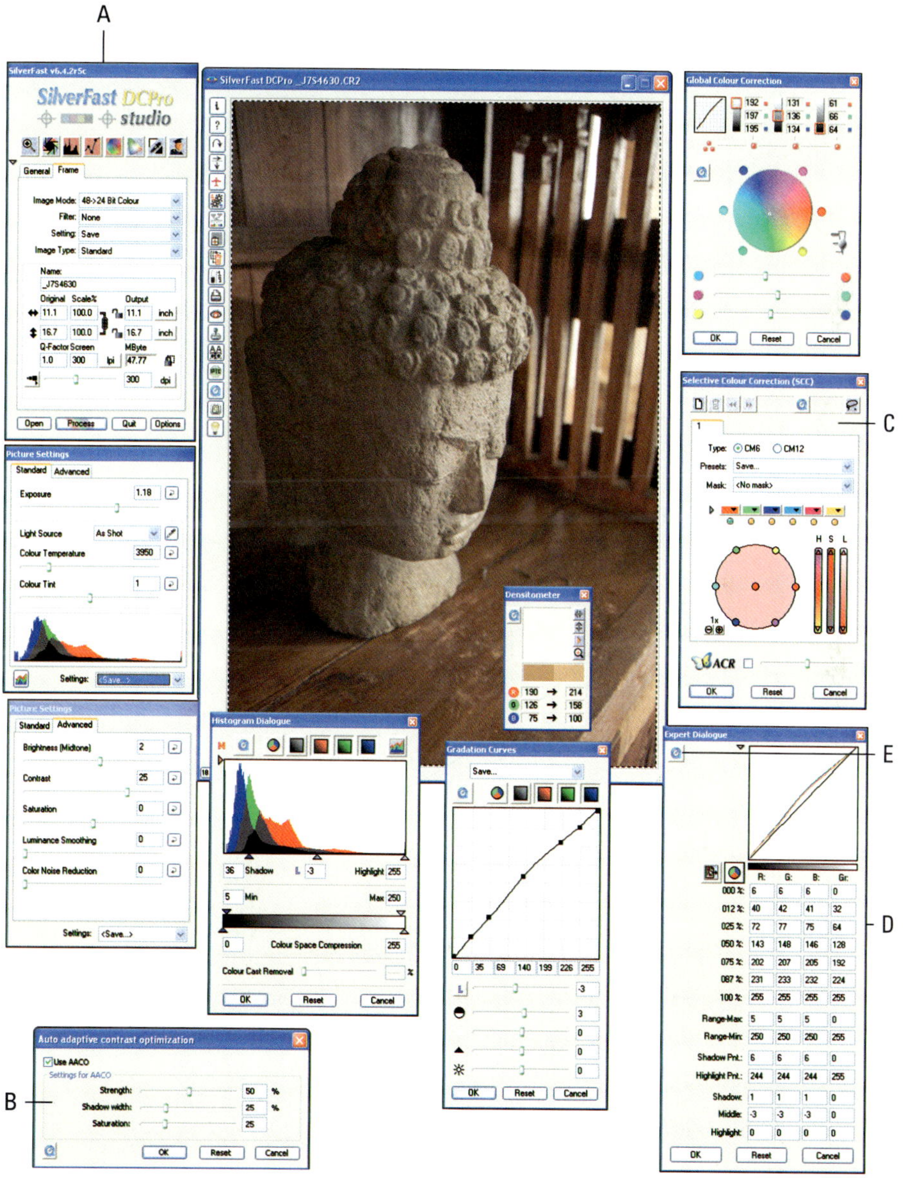

Figure 4-16: As you can see, SilverFast DCPro has many controls that are similar to those we've noted in the Konica Minolta, Adobe Camera RAW, and DxO Optics Pro interfaces. Most of SilverFast's dialogs

(continued)

are toggled on and off by clicking on an icon and, like the tabbed dialogs in Adobe Camera RAW, can be displayed only one at a time. Therefore, you'll never see all these options on your screen simultaneously. The following are some of the items that we feel set SilverFast DCPro apart: (A) If you use SilverFast scanning software, the initial screen will look very familiar to you. (B) The Auto Adaptive Contrast Optimization is another method for lightening or darkening shadows without affecting the rest of the photo's dynamic range. (C) In addition to the global color correction tools, SilverFast has one of the best selective correction tools we've seen in a conversion utility. (D) Quite frankly, the Expert Dialog is an intimidating interface appropriate primarily for those who prefer fiddling with numbers. However, we have obtained some interesting and appealing results simply by experimenting and just inputting various numbers in different slots. (E) These QuickTime movie icons will play tutorials on the individual dialogs and how they work. Some of the tutorials are great. Others, like the one for the Expert Dialog, just skim the surface, but nevertheless gave us enough nerve to play with the numbers to see what would happen. (Screen capture courtesy of LaserSoft Imaging)

In addition, SilverFast DCPro's selective color correction is one of the best we've seen in a preconversion program. Its job manager is a logical, familiar tool for batch processing. And it has a variety of photo-editing tools, such as a cloner that gives you the ability to make common corrections and even artistic choices before the data are converted to an RGB photo. (Remember: any edits before conversion create the pixels that define a photo; postedits can destroy photo pixels.)

SilverFast DC has a Virtual Light Table view, in which you can sort and organize photos, as well as create virtual albums and printed contact sheets. It also allows you to pull several photos from various sources on the network into one bin. However, the Virtual Light Table is not a full image database. (Please see Chapter 9 regarding image databases.)

Saving Your Work before Moving On

After you have made all your selections among the various exposure, color, sharpening, and other controls in your RAW conversion utility, the final decision you must make is how all your hard work will be saved. This actually involves three sets of decisions:

1. Do you want to save the RAW file with your new settings embedded?

   We prefer creating a new RAW file rather than overwriting our original, usually with the same root name having a suffix recognizable to us. That way, we can always go back to the default original at some future date, if we wish.

2. Do you want to save the settings (or recipe) that you used on this photo (or series of photos) so you can use them on future batches of pictures?

   As you develop your own personal workflows, you will find yourself using the same kinds of edits ("recipes") over and over again, especially with specific camera bodies, lenses, and lighting and exposure combinations/scenarios. It makes good sense to save such groups of settings, using descriptive names that will be immediately recognizable to you and relevant to what the recipe will do to your pictures.

3. What file format do you want to use to save the RGB photo file that will be created from the original RAW file by the conversion utility?

We almost always use 16-bit TIFF to save any RGB photo created from a RAW file. This is a personal choice based on our preference to maintain as much image data as far down the line of our editing as we can. The downside to this preference is that our image files tend to be very large, which is why we have several terabytes of storage capacity on our network.

However, we know other photographers who prefer to do the conversion to 8-bit TIFFs in their RAW utilities to save time, space, and extra steps further along. If you are working on lots of photos, and do the vast majority of your edits in your RAW conversion utility, it may make sense for you to save to 8-bit TIFF.

If your primary objective is to share your photos (especially over the Web, via email, or as part of a slideshow) and you do not wish to put them through any other kind of manipulation after the conversion from RAW, you may want to consider saving the files to JPEG.

In some workflow scenarios, it might make sense for you to create three different files of the same photo from the one RAW file, saving one each in 16-bit TIFF, 8-bit TIFF, and JPEG. Many RAW utilities allow you to automate multiple save batch options.

Naming Files

We can't emphasize enough the great value of not editing and overwriting your original photo files. We use Version Cue in Photoshop to help us organize all the versions we create of individual photographs, but simply using identical root names can help, too. For instance, we used the following names for several versions of the same photo:

- Buddha head 1 original RAW.CR2 (The original, renamed file as captured by the Canon Mark II)
- Buddha head 1 edited in CameraRAW.CR2 (The RAW file with Adobe Camera RAW edits embedded)
- Buddha head 1 16-bit edited in CameraRAW.TIF (The TIFF file created by our edits in CameraRAW)
- Buddha head 1 8-bit edited in CameraRAW.TIF
- Buddha head 1 ready for upload.JPG (The JPEG file resized and optimized for display on the Web)

Actually, we have many more versions of that Buddha head photo, but they are all saved using the same kind of descriptive, unambiguous names. That makes it much easier for us to quickly identify exactly what a file contains, regardless of the program we are using to view the files on our computers or network. It should also come as no surprise that we have nearly 2 terabytes of stored image files. Please see Chapter 9 to see how we organize all those photos for easy retrieval and archiving.

Tip

In SilverFast DCPro (and a few other programs) the setting for converting the RAW file to a 16-bit TIFF is called 48-bit color. That's because 16-bit TIFFs have 16 bits for each of the three primary color channels (red, blue, and green), and 3 times 16 equals 48.

Choosing the Right Format(s) for Your Photo Editing

Even if you do all your photo corrections and editing in a RAW conversion utility, chances are you will use a photo-editing program at one point or another. If nothing else, you will probably want to resize your photos for output. But more than that, photo-editing programs have a wide range of creative and productivity tools that have become integral to digital photography. Few serious photographers bypass photo-editing programs completely, regardless of what file format they use to capture their pictures.

Selecting the file formats to use for your photo editing can be complex, because different formats may be appropriate at various times on the same picture. In other words, choosing your file format while editing should be as free-flowing and ever-changing as your editing needs to be — dependent on the task at hand and its purpose. At the bare minimum, you will want to carefully consider your format choices at the following points of the editing process:

- When you open the image in your photo-editing software
- When you save your work-in-progress (interim saves)
- When you save your final version (or at least the version you currently believe will be final)

Your options are the following:

- JPEG
- TIFF (8-bit or 16-bit)
- PSD or other software-specific format

Essentially, we make our decisions based on how the structure of the file format will affect the amount, quality, and type of data that will be saved. The following is how we work and the thinking behind our choices.

Tip

We tend to be belt-and-suspenders types. In other words, we believe in redundant systems for protecting our photo files. Perhaps, it comes from having started with digital photography so early, when the hardware and software were more finicky and less reliable. We've also had our share of accidentally overwritten files, crashed hard drives, and lost image files. Whatever the reason, you will notice that we usually save many more versions of a single photo (and to more than one storage device) than is absolutely necessary. But, then, if this overcaution keeps us from losing a single photo (or an entire project), the cost in time and storage space is worth it.

At the Start

When we open a picture in any photo-editing program for the first time, we immediately save it with a new name that makes sense to us regarding what we are planning to do with it. At the same time, we convert any JPEG photo into an 8-bit TIFF.

The conversion of JPEGs to TIFFs is a necessary precaution, because JPEG compression is cumulative. In other words, as you edit your photo, every time you save your work in progress, JPEG will throw out more image data. That means a JPEG saved at highest-quality, lowest-compression setting, but saved several times, will end up a lower-quality image. Therefore, we almost never edit JPEGs without converting them. (We have learned to never say never without the qualifier "almost." But when we do edit JPEGs, it is nearly always because, regrettably, we have forgotten to do the conversion to TIFF first.)

Tip

Control-S (on PCs) and Command-S (on Macs) are the shortcuts for saving the current document or photo in just about every current program. Our fingers are so used to holding down the Control or Command key and hitting S that it has become an automatic, intuitive, almost knee-jerk reaction to any significant (or, sometimes, insignificant) edit we do. This excellent habit has protected us from all kinds of technical glitches that would have otherwise lost us time and work.

Saving Works-in-Progress

Our next step is deciding whether to use TIFFs (8-bit or 16-bit) or the software's proprietary format (such as Photoshop's PSD) while editing our photos.

The choice between 8-bit and 16-bit TIFFs is an easy one for us. If the photo is already 16-bit, we try to keep it at that density of data as long as possible. However, some photo-editing commands and features aren't accessible in 16-mode. So, we do what we can in 16-bit. Then, we save a new version of the 16-bit TIFF, before converting it to 8-bit TIFF to continue our edits. With some photo projects, we never need to convert to 8-bit until we are finished and ready for output.

If the photo is an 8-bit TIFF, we don't convert it to 16-bit in the photo-editing program. That would simply be asking the software to invent new data that would not improve the quality of the picture. The one exception is when we are combining elements from various photos of different bit depth into a single digital image. Then, we may convert the smaller pieces of the composition into the bit depth of the larger, base image. In such scenarios, we have occasionally converted 8-bit elements to 16-bit to get them into the collage.

Choosing between TIFFs and the program's proprietary format is not as straightforward. Generally, if we plan to use layers or masks of any kind, we will save the file in the program's proprietary format. Photoshop actually saves layers and masks in TIFF files. However, having the `.psd` extension at the end of the name tells us exactly which files have that additional structure, without having to open them up in Photoshop. In addition, we use more than one photo-editing program on many of our imaging projects. If we open a layered TIFF in a program that doesn't support the various types of Photoshop layers and masks in TIFF, and then save it within that other program, we can lose all the Photoshop-specific information.

The "Final" Version

Okay, we admit it. We often go back to tweak a photo that we had declared finished a long time ago — especially our fine art and personal photographs. And then, there are those pictures that we repurpose, having published them previously in a book and then using them as visual examples for one of our seminar PowerPoint presentations or printing them for an exhibition.

But at some point, we do finalize a photo — at least temporarily — deciding that we have done everything we need and want to achieve the current purpose. That's when we must choose how to save the completed picture.

- If the image has remained a 16-bit TIFF all along, we save a 16-bit version, plus an 8-bit version.
- If the image is a 16-bit picture with layers and masks, we save a 16-bit PSD with layers and masks intact, plus a 16- bit TIFF and an 8-bit TIFF (both nonlayered).
- If the image is an 8-bit picture with layers and masks, we save an 8-bit layered PSD and an 8-bit nonlayered TIFF.
- If the image is a flat (unlayered and unmasked) 8-bit TIFF, then we leave it at that.

As you see, we tend to have lots of different versions of our photos, even before we get to the versions needed for sharing and outputting. (See the next section.) It's that belt-and-suspenders mentality of ours. Once you have been the victim of technology glitches and accidental file erasures, you'll be just as careful as we are. But the fact is that all this caution doesn't require much extra work or effort. That's because we have automated the processes, using Photoshop's Actions. (Other programs call them *macros*.) But it does require establishing and maintaining a good filing system and organization, to keep track of the files. (Please see Chapter 10 to learn more about macros and Chapter 9 to see some of our solutions for intelligent file organization and maintenance.)

Formats for Sharing and Output

Photography exists to be shared and shown. In digital photography, you have a wide array of choices:

- Printing
- Electronic collaboration
- Posting photos on the Web
- Emailing
- Insertion into documents

The two file formats most suited for the preceding purposes are JPEG and 8-bit TIFF, with JPEG being the preferred format in all but printing. In fact, if you try to upload anything other than JPEG onto most Web sites, the host program may not even recognize the photo files.

The next sections look at each of the preceding forms of sharing and output in terms of which format is best suited and why.

PRINTING

Traditional prints are still among the most satisfying ways of viewing and displaying a good photograph.

Whether you are outputting to a desktop printer, a wide-format studio printer or using a service bureau to print your images, it is likely that the printer software can handle converting 16-bit TIFFs or PSDs to 8-bit TIFFs on the fly. However, we recommend doing the conversion from 16-bit to 8-bit TIFFs yourself in your photo-editing program before sending the file to the printer or service bureau. We usually have an aversion to allowing software or some nameless technician to automatically choose what data should be thrown away and what kept.

We usually don't use JPEGs for printing, unless it's for output that is less than 8"×10" of photos that are already JPEGs.

If you are working with a service bureau, ask them what file format they prefer. If you are working at home or in your studio, test the various formats to see if you can discern a difference.

Of course, good printing is a much larger issue that also involves good color management and appropriate file sizes. Please see Chapter 11 and Chapter 12 for more in-depth discussions on both issues.

Tip

This chapter focuses on choosing the best file formats for various purposes. For guidance on preparing, optimizing, and sizing files for sharing and output, please turn to Chapter 12.

ELECTRONIC COLLABORATION

While writing this book, all our photo illustrations were saved as 8-bit TIFFs, which is what our publisher, Wiley Publishing, Inc., requires for their production process. They don't want JPEGs because of the potential for loss of quality. (We agree with them.)

In other projects, our clients might (though rarely) prefer 16-bit TIFFs to give them a higher density of data for whatever further manipulation they might need to do to them.

We don't do actual imaging collaboration, but if we did, we would discuss with our associates the responsibilities each of us would take, which would determine what file formats would be appropriate. For instance, if we were sending photo components for a collage to an associate who would then edit them to make them visually fit together and combine them into a single picture, then we would recommend that we deliver 16-bit TIFFs. But if we were sending a completed image that our associate would be resizing and placing into a document, we would probably send 8-bit TIFFs. However, depending on the document and the level of sophistication of our collaborator and her computer, JPEGs might be more appropriate. (Please see the section later in the chapter about inserting photos into documents.)

The rule is to always deliver in whatever format and form is wanted and needed. We discuss delivery methods, such as uploading to our Web site in Chapter 12 and burning to a CD or DVD in Chapter 9.

POSTING PHOTOS ON THE WEB

Almost every photo-sharing site we know (including the premium, fee-based ones that we use) recognizes only JPEGs. If your photo is saved as a TIFF, the uploading software probably won't even see it. Therefore, we convert any photo that we want to post to JPEG.

Similarly, JPEGs are the preferred photo-realistic file format for any Web design program, such as Dreamweaver, GoLive, or FrontPage. (Yes, GIFs, which we haven't even mentioned before, are also popular, but the GIF file format isn't as good as JPEG for photo-quality images. Therefore, we usually don't recommend GIFs for photos.)

EMAILING

Photos shared via email are almost always JPEGs. They are smaller files than TIFFs, which means that they won't bog down the recipient's system. What's more, many servers won't allow large attached files through. In addition, JPEGs are the most universal file format and are readable even by systems that have no photo software.

INSERTING PHOTOS INTO DOCUMENTS

The appropriate format for photos that will be placed in documents depends on the kind of document, how it will be used, and how large the image will be within it.

For electronic documents, such as PowerPoint presentations, Adobe Acrobat files, or others that will be viewed only on a computer monitor, we have had very satisfactory results with JPEGs and use them extensively. JPEGs take up less room than TIFFs in the final file, which makes it easier to share, transport, display, or post the electronic documents.

For desktop-published documents, such as newsletters, brochures, or greeting cards, in which the photo is going to be only a small portion of a page, JPEGs are still quite good for the purpose.

Only in those photos that will be either a full page or printed professionally (such as a glossy magazine or this book), do we feel that 8-bit TIFFs may give an edge in terms of image quality.

Tip

Current Macs and PCs make it very easy to copy files to a CD or DVD. Simply drag and drop the files you want burned to the disc into the CD/DVD folder on your computer and use the operating system's command for writing the files to the CD (or DVD). However, the whole purpose of storing anything is to be able to retrieve it easily when you want or need it in the future. That's why we recommend burning your archive discs from within your image database, which will then keep track of precisely where all your files are. Please see Chapter 9 for more information on using image databases.

Which Format(s) Should You Archive?

By now, you've probably gotten the accurate impression that we don't entirely trust technology. We know it too well and have been burnt too often. That's why we save so many different versions of our photos, in a variety of formats, and to more than one storage device. You will need to make your own decisions about how much storage space and file management any individual picture or group of photos are worth.

But what about archiving our pictures for the future?

At the barest minimum, you'll want to archive two versions of your photo:

- The original, as it was shot. In fact, for an important shoot, we immediately burn a DVD directly from our memory card, before we even transfer the photos to our computer.
- Your final version, after any editing or preparation.

However, we strongly recommend that you archive additional versions, not simply to be safe but also to save you time, effort, and problems with potential format incompatibilities in the future.

If your originals were shot in the camera's proprietary RAW format, you might consider archiving the following versions:

- The 16-bit TIFF that is saved from your RAW conversion utility, before any edits.
- Adobe DNG versions of your original RAW files. A batch conversion utility is downloadable from `www.adobe.com`. Be sure to set the options to embed the original RAW data, use lossless compression, and include a JPEG preview.

Regardless of what format you use for your initial photo capture, we suggest that you also save interim versions of any photos you edit. This is especially valuable if the photos are ones that you might want to tweak further or otherwise adjust. It's much easier to go back to an intermediate step in the editing process than start all over at the very beginning. For that reason, we usually archive any key files that we saved separate from the final version, including:

- The edited 16-bit TIFF before we converted it to 8-bit for any further edits or resizing
- The layered PSD version, with all its masks, edits, and text kept separate and re-editable
- Edited files saved just before any down sampling to a smaller size or conversions to another color space. (See the discussion earlier in the chapter and Chapter 11 on color models.)

In other words, the purpose of archiving is to be able to pick up where you left off and use your photos again. So, burn any versions that will make it easier to repeat, adjust, or reverse any of the edits you have done.

Summary

A digital photo is nothing more than digital data that can be interpreted by computers, printers, and other devices, which, in turn, will display or output a picture constituted from that data. Among the various formats you can choose in various stages of your photography, each one has its purpose. However, since file formats differ in the way they organize and handle that data, understanding the differences among them will help you maintain control over image quality and usability.

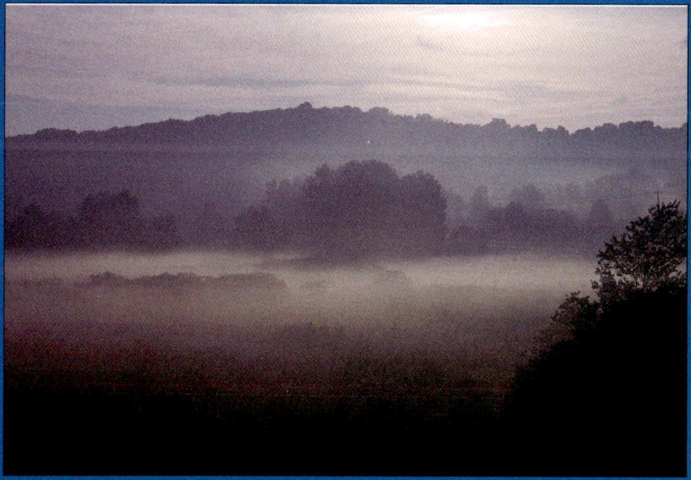

*In situations in which you have no control over the light and other conditions, shooting in RAW gives you latitude to experiment with pushing exposure. (Photo shot with Pentax *istD, 50mm lens, 1/750 at f13)*

Chapter 5

Making Exposure Work for You

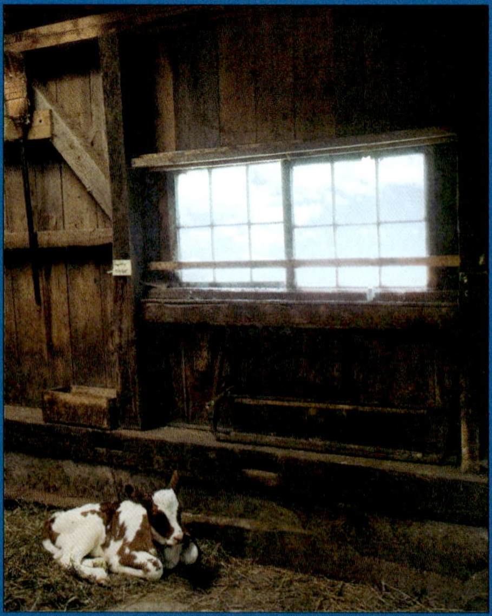

Gaining control over exposure will allow you to get even difficult photos such as of this newborn calf in a darkened barn under a bright window. (Photo taken with an Olympus E-1, 14-54mm lens set at 28mm, 1/30 at f3.2 and ISO 800.)

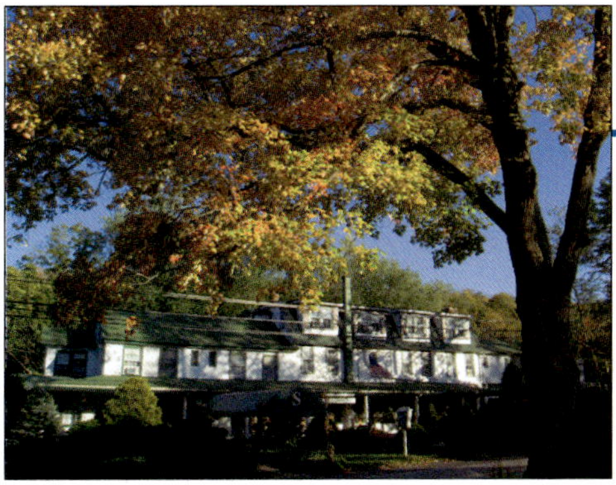

A bright autumn day at Sterling Inn. Retaining the details in the shadows without making the white details too bright requires using the right metering to help select your exposure settings. (Photo taken with a Nikon D2X, 18-55mm lens set at 18mm, 1/20 at f18.)

Light is the essence of photography. How well you control and manipulate the capture of light is key to the quality, power, and beauty of your photographs. This is true regardless of the type camera you use. But one of the things that gives shooting digital SLRs an unassailable edge over other types of cameras is the creative combination of traditional exposure tools with new digital features and functions.

In this chapter, we start with a brief review of exposure basics — principles that apply to every camera, film or digital. Then, we cover various ways you can control exposure with your DSLR, including:

- Using *f*-stops with flexible focusing to define and delineate your composition
- Choosing the right metering mode for your picture
- Understanding program modes
- Using exposure compensation and bracketing effectively and efficiently
- Deciphering and using histograms
- Making sure that your exposure is correct for your intended output

Digital or Film: The Basics Still Rule

If you're shooting a digital SRL, most likely you are already an experienced photographer. However, it's always useful to review the basics before proceeding with discussions of how to tweak or even ignore established rules of photography.

Tip

Rules are meant to be broken. Some of our best photographs have been those that our camera's built-in intelligence told us wouldn't be feasible. But that's one of the major advantages of digital. If you want to try something that your camera (or your own knowledge) says won't work, go ahead and shoot anyway. The worst that will happen is that you'll delete the picture, because it wasn't satisfactory, and then you'll try something else. Or, you could possibly end up with a wonderfully artistic expression of the scene that is uniquely yours.

Ever since the beginning of photography, exposure has been controlled by three elements:

- The size of the hole (or aperture) through which light enters the camera lens.
- The length of time that the photosensitive element (film or image sensor) is exposed to the light.
- The degree of sensitivity to light of the photosensitive element.

The next sections look at each of these factors individually, and then how they work together.

Aperture

Since the late nineteenth century, up to and including our modern digital devices, the aperture has been measured by *f*-stops. (The *f* stands for factorable, for arcane reasons that are just too boring to discuss here.)

f-stops are specific logarithmic numbers such as 1.4, 2, 2.8, 4, 5.6, 8, 11, 16, 22, 32, 45. However, on digital cameras, you will sometimes get oddball figures (in-between stops), such as 4.2, 6.7, or 9.5. Don't worry about the specific numbers. More important is what the relative values represent in terms of how they affect your photograph.

The smaller the *f*-stop number, the larger the aperture is. Therefore, lots more light gets through to the image sensor at a setting of *f*2.8 than one of *f*11.

Tip

Experiment with your camera, taking the same photograph at various *f*-stops. Every lens will have a particular *f*-stop, called the hyperfocus, at which your photos will be sharpest—typically, at a medium point, such as *f*5.6 or *f*8.

APERTURE AND DEPTH-OF-FIELD

Your *f*-stop also controls the depth-of-field of your photograph. Therefore, choosing your aperture settings becomes an important creative decision and a determining factor of your composition. The smaller the aperture (the higher the *f*-stop number), the greater amount of your picture from the foreground to the background will be in focus. When you want to soften the background, giving more visual emphasis to the central subject of your image, use a larger aperture (smaller *f*-stop number). (See Figures 5-1 and 5-2.)

Tip

The blurred background of a shallow depth-of-field is best achieved with telephoto (rather than wide angle) lenses, and with the main subject much closer to the camera than the background. When doing macro (close-up) photography, depth-of-field tends to be very shallow.

When you want everything in the photo to be in sharp, crisp focus, use a smaller aperture (larger *f*-stop number). You also may wish to set your zoom lens to wide angle rather than telephoto. (See Figures 5-3 and 5-4.)

Tip

While narrow depth-of-field (lower *f*-stop number) is often used for portraits, to blur the background and center attention on the subject of the photo, we often use a deep depth-of-field (higher *f*-stop number) to put our subject within context of the environment and things that define who the person is and/or what he does.

Depth-of-field has a direct relationship not only to the size of the aperture, but also to the size of the lens (focal length) itself. The smaller the lens, the greater its depth-of-field. In fact, in consumer digital cameras, whose lenses have very small focal lengths (compared to DSLRs), it is difficult, if not impossible, to capture a photo with a shallow depth-of-field. Similarly, when shooting wide angle with your DSLRs, or using a normal lens on a bright sunny day, you might find that your depth-of-field is *too* good, and that it's difficult to blur the background. Later in this chapter, we discuss how to handle some of the depth-of-field challenges you might encounter while shooting DSLRs.

Note

Photographers (like any group of people) have their own slang. Here are two phrases you'll hear often. To ":stop down the lens" or "close down the lens" refers to the process of reducing the size of the aperture by increasing the *f*-stop number. To "open up the lens" is the opposite, increasing the size of the aperture by choosing a smaller *f*-stop number.

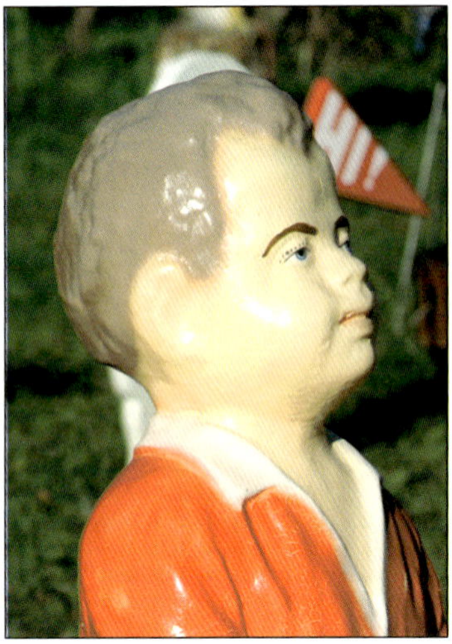

Figure 5-1: Shot at *f*11, the background elements (especially the "HI!" banner) are too clear, distracting from the portrait of this lawn ornament. (Photo taken with a Konica Minolta Maxxum 7D, 28–100mm lens set at 100mm, 1/160 at *f*11.)

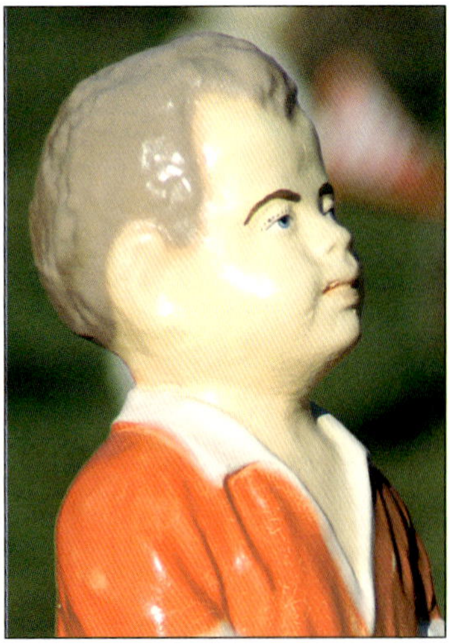

Figure 5-2: By setting the lens aperture at *f*2.8, we drastically reduced the depth-of-field, significantly softening the distracting background elements, making the composition of the photo focus on the central figure and nothing else. (Photo taken with a Konica Minolta Maxxum 7D, 28–100mm lens set at 100mm, 1/4000 at *f*2.8.)

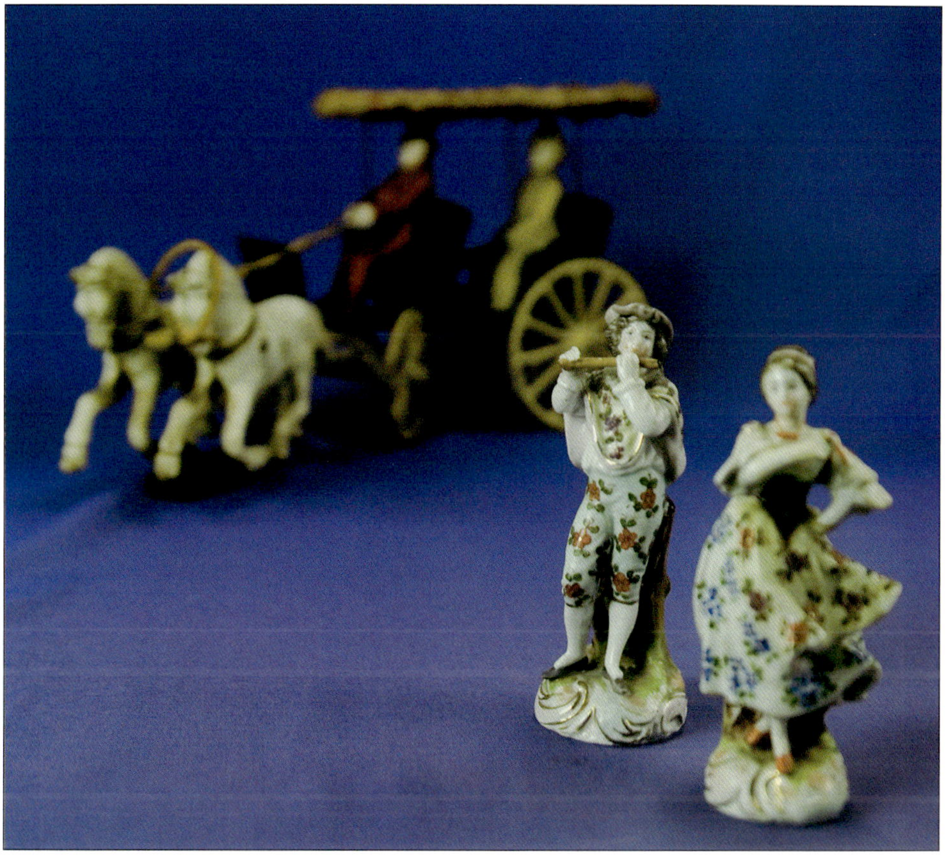

Figure 5-3: At *f*2.8, the depth-of-field of this photo is so narrow that only the figure of the flutist is in focus. (Photo taken with a Fujifilm FinePix S3Pro, 24–120mm lens set at 42mm, 1/180 at *f*2.8.)

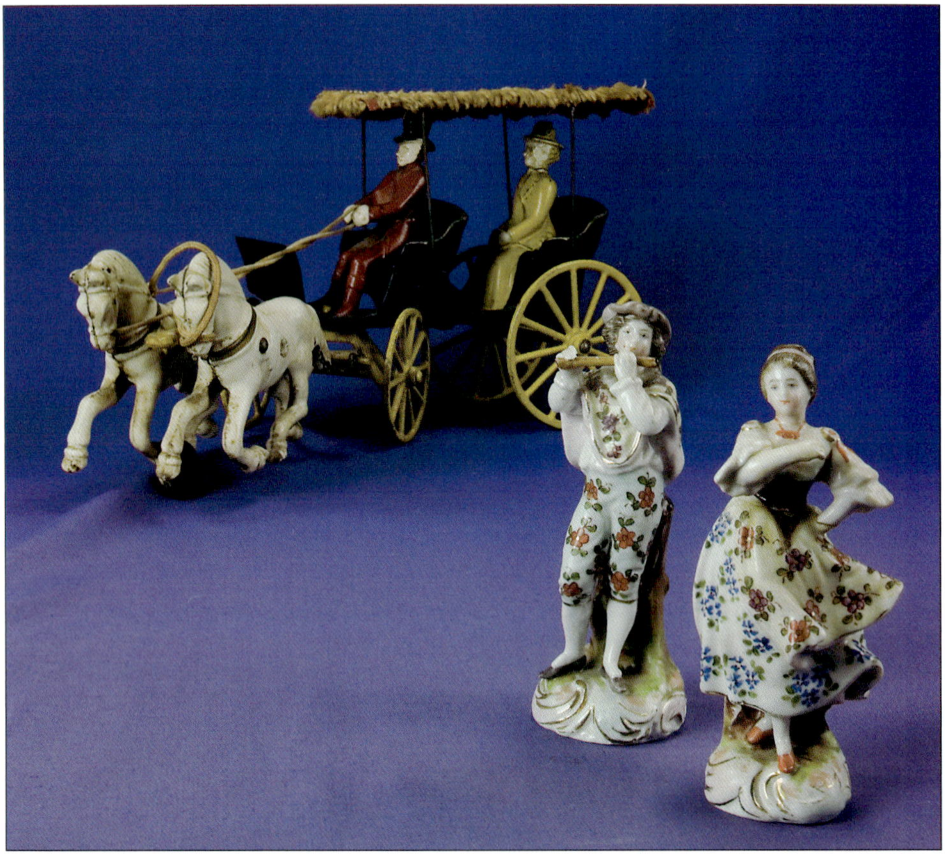

Figure 5-4: For this composition, we want all the elements to be in focus, so we reshot at *f*22 for a much greater depth-of-field. (Photo taken with a Fujifilm FinePix S3Pro, 24–120mm lens set at 42mm, 1/3 at *f*22.)

DEPTH-OF-FIELD AND FLEXIBLE FOCUS

Since your *f*-stop establishes the area of your picture that will be in focus, the center point of that area becomes an important factor in defining and delineating your photograph's composition. In other words, if you use *f*-stops and focus creatively, you can select exactly what area you want to be in focus, thereby enabling others to see the scene as you envision it. (See Figures 5-5 through 5-7.)

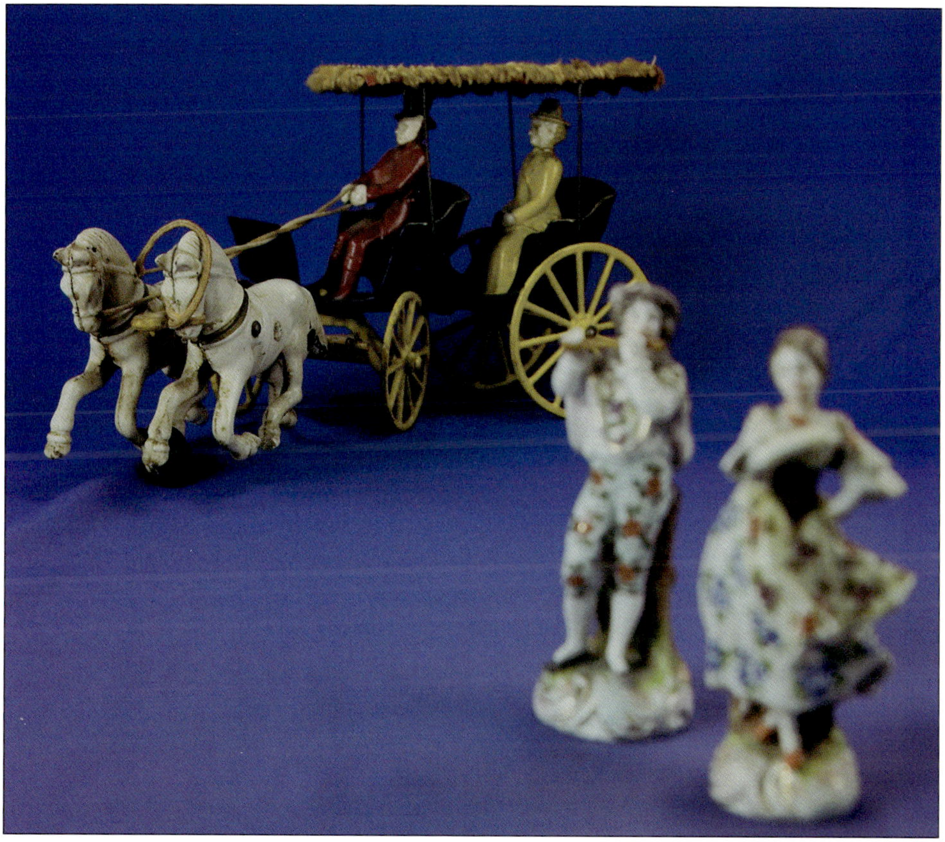

Figure 5-5: By centering our focus on the front wheel of the carriage and setting our aperture to *f*5.8, we created a photo in which the entire carriage was in focus, but the figurines in front of it are blurred. (Photo taken with a Fujifilm FinePix S3Pro, 24–120mm lens set at 42mm, 1/45 at *f*5.8.)

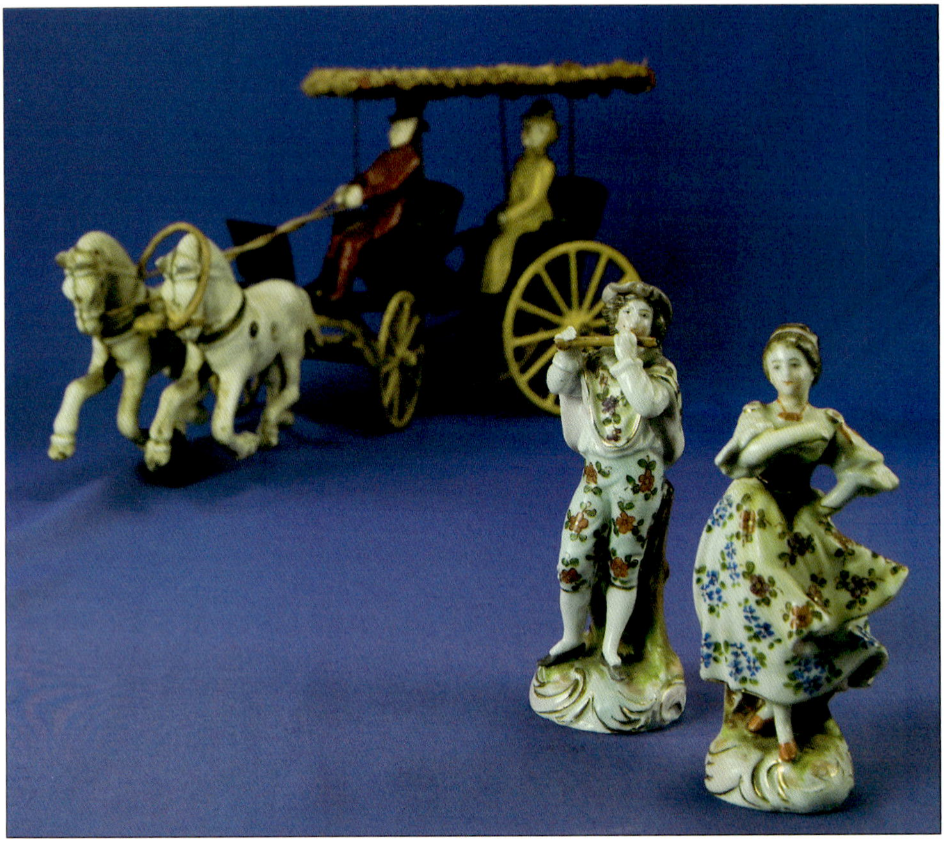

Figure 5-6: Focusing on the male figurine with the flute (as we did in Figure 5-3), but increasing our *f*-stop to *f*8 (as opposed to the *f*2.8 in Figure 5-3), we have both figures in focus, but the carriage is blurred. (Photo taken with a Fujifilm FinePix S3Pro, 24–120mm lens set at 42mm, 1/20 at *f*8.)

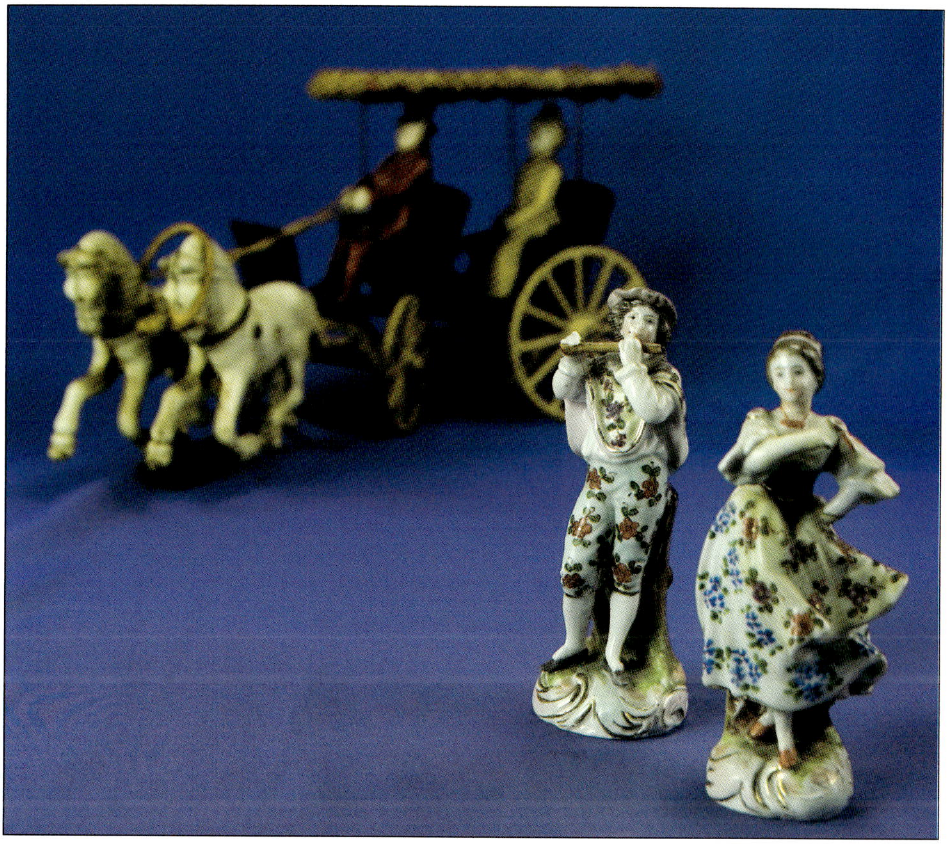

Figure 5-7: We created a subtly different picture than Figure 5-3 by focusing on the male flutist and setting the aperture to *f*4.8. The resulting photo has the flutist in focus, while the carriage and dancing female figurine are both blurred (as in Figure 5-3). But in this picture, the female is not as blurred as the carriage, giving more weight to her presence in the composition, but providing the subliminal message that the picture's main subject is the flutist. (Photo taken with a Fujifilm FinePix S3Pro, 24–120mm lens set at 42mm, 1/60 at *f*4.8.)

If the point of focus that you want to use is too uniform in color and lacking contrast for you to get a focus lock on it, either put your camera on manual focus or put a tiny piece of contrasting paper into the composition, as we did in Figure 5-8. You can then clone it out in your photo-editing software. (See Chapter 10.)

We cover focus modes, including variable (or flexible) focus controls in Chapter 6.

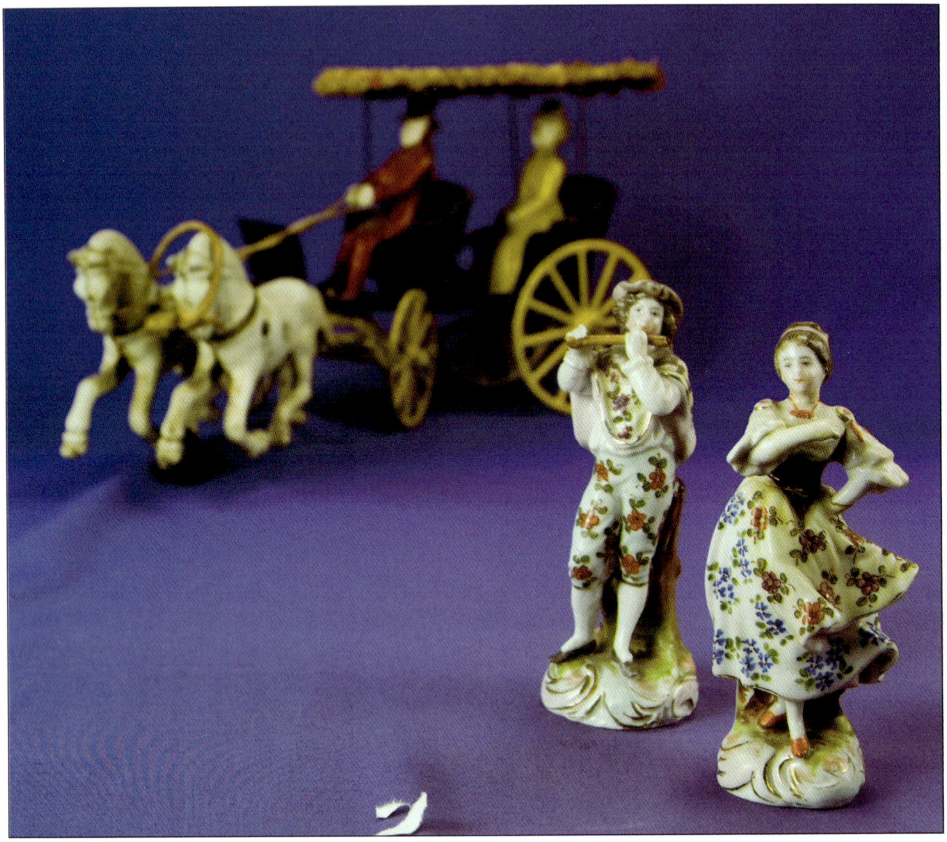

Figure 5-8: For this version of the photograph, we wanted our focus point to be in the very front of the scene. However, the uniformity of color and light at that point made it impossible for the camera to autofocus correctly. We could have put the camera on manual focus. Instead, we simply placed tiny torn pieces of paper at the focus point and let the camera's autofocus concentrate on them. Later, in Photoshop, we can clone the paper out of the picture, making it appear that it never existed. (See Chapter 10.) (Photo taken with a Fujifilm FinePix S3Pro, 24–120mm lens set at 42mm, 1/20 at *f*6.7.)

Tip

Traditionally, SLRs have had a button somewhere on the body, usually to the side of the lens, for previewing depth-of-field. Many, though not all, digital SLRs also offer depth-of-field previewing. Press it, and the lens will stop down so that you can see how much of your picture will be in focus, and what areas will be blurred. It takes the guesswork out of choosing your *f*-stop. However, it will darken the subject, anywhere from a little to a lot, so you may have to look at the scene for a few seconds until your eye gets accustomed to the reduced light.

Shutter

Shutters (whether inside the lens, in front of the lens or, as with modern SLRs and DSLRs, behind the lens) control the duration of an exposure. Shutter speeds are measured in fractions of seconds (or full seconds for long exposures). In film, shutter speeds were always specific numbers such as 1/60, 1/125, 1/250, 1/500, and so forth. But digital cameras may display very precise, in-between numbers, creating very nonstandard shutter speeds such as 1/47 or 1/323.

Tip

Digital cameras generally no longer display shutter speeds in fractions. Instead, they use whole numbers, assuming that you know they mean fractions. Therefore, 1/60 of a second is displayed simply as 60.

Like the aperture, the shutter speed you choose doesn't affect only the amount of light reaching the image sensor. It also defines how motion or action will be handled visually.

For fast motion, such as shooting sporting events, birds in flight or very active children, use a fast shutter speed. That will stop the action, at a very crisp instant in time. If you want to blur the motion, use a slow shutter speed. (See Figures 5-9 and 5-10.) Of course, the timing of when you press the shutter button is also a factor.

Use a Tripod at Slower Shutter Speeds

At slower shutter speeds, even young, strong people with remarkably steady hands will find that using a tripod gives their photographs that extra edge of crisp clarity. Just the act of breathing can introduce slight to significant motion blur to a picture.

Generally speaking, most people shouldn't try to handhold a camera when the shutter speed is less than 1/60. However, when using telephoto lenses, motion blur becomes even more critical. (If you've tried to follow a bird in flight through binoculars and seen how jerky even the slightest motion can be, you'll understand why telephoto lenses are more difficult to handhold than wide angle.) The rule-of-thumb is don't handhold below the 35mm lens equivalent you're using. For instance, if your zoom lens is set to 135mm equivalency, then your slowest shutter speed without a tripod should be 1/135. (See Chapter 2, regarding 35mm equivalencies.)

Later in the day, when you're tired, when you aren't feeling well, or as you get older, it's best to set your handhold limit to even faster speeds.

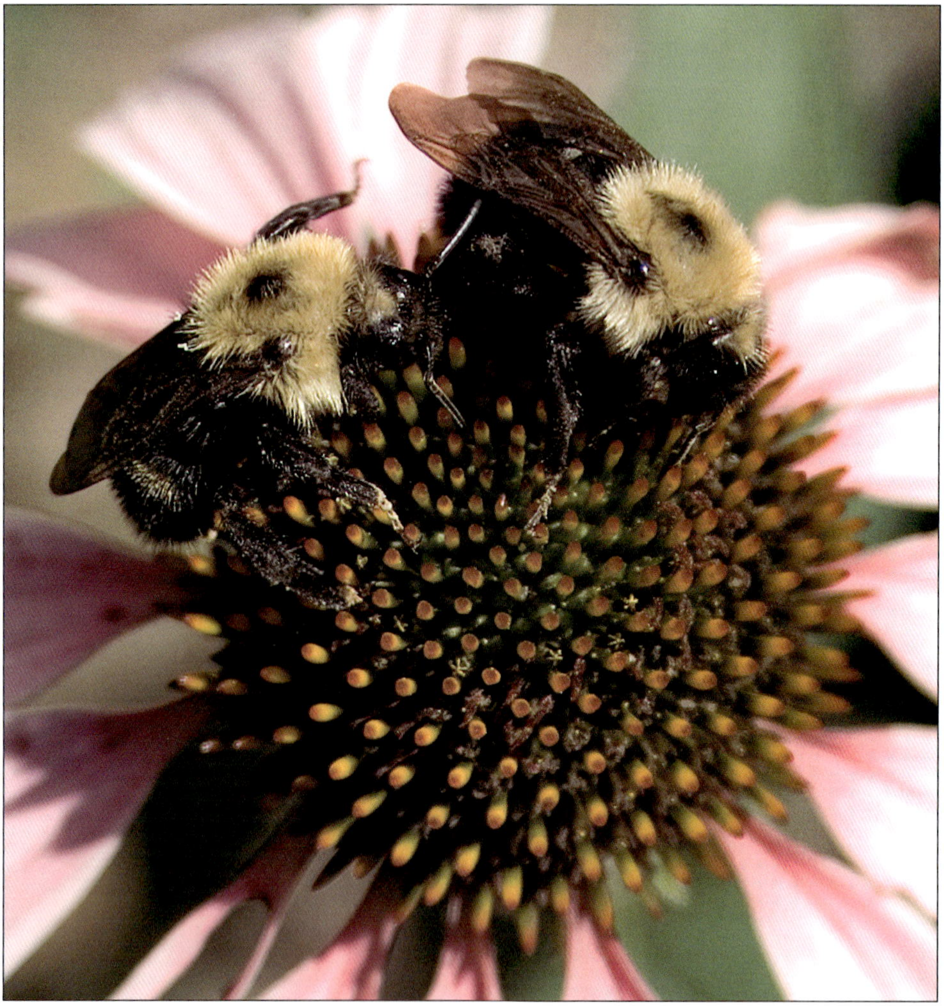

Figure 5-9: When Sally saw these bees among the cone flowers, the sun was shining brightly, which meant that she was able to shoot at 1/500th shutter speed at *f*7.1. That allowed her to stop the action of the bees' constant movement while maintaining a relatively good depth-of-field for a macro shot. (Photo taken with a Konica Minolta Maxxum 7D, 135mm lens, 1/5000 at *f*7.1.)

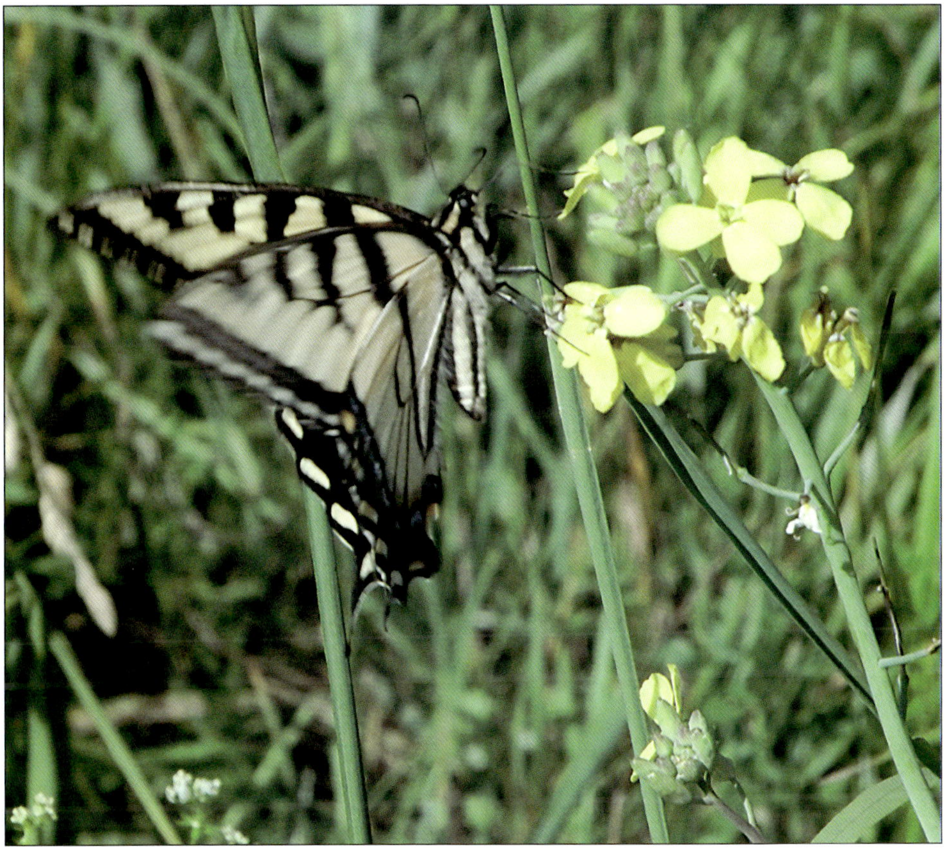

Figure 5-10: A slower shutter speed can provide an effective way to illustrate the sensation of speed and action. The bit of motion blur in this picture captures the dynamic movement of this butterfly's wings. (Photo taken with a Nikon D70, 24–120mm lens set at 97mm, 1/250 at *f*9.1.)

Light Sensitivity

While shutter speed and aperture determine how much light will enter the camera, the ISO setting establishes how sensitive the image sensor will be to the light.

The term comes from the film world, in which the ISO rating (International Organization for Standardization) measures the light sensitivity of film. You've seen the numbers on film packages — 100, 400, 800, and so on. The higher the number, the more sensitive the film is to light. The lower the number, the finer (smoother) the grain. Therefore, if we were doing a shoot in a sunny meadow, we might choose 64 or 100 ISO film. But if we were working inside, with no or limited auxiliary lighting, we might select a 400 or 800 ISO film. The rating is based on the chemical composition and silver halide grain size of the film itself.

Since it is such a familiar term to photographers, digital camera manufacturers have adopted the acronym ISO to designate the adjustable light sensitivity of their cameras' image sensors. However, technically, ISO in a digital camera isn't the same thing as the ISO of film. (That's why purists will use the term ISO-equivalency instead of simply ISO when talking about digital cameras.) When you adjust the ISO in a digital camera, what you are doing is "upping the volume," so to speak. That is, you are increasing or amplifying the electrical gain (as you might in a stereo sound system).

One of the big differences between film and digital cameras is that once you load a roll of film and set your ISO, you have to stick with that level of light sensitivity for the entire roll. Therefore, if you go from a sunny day to a dark office, the only answer is either to change film (to one with a higher ISO) or to bring lots of lights into the office.

With digital cameras, you can change your ISO setting with each and every picture, if you wish. Therefore, if you happen to be at a surprise birthday party, you can up the ISO to 800 while you wait in the semi-dark, and then set it to 200 for when all the lights go on to catch the birthday boy's look of surprise.

Of course, there's no such thing as a free lunch. Just as higher ISO films tend to be grainier, image sensors' increased light sensitivity comes with a price—noise. (See Figures 5-11 through 5-18.)

Having the ability to instantly switch to a higher ISO in changing light conditions situations is invaluable. (See the following section for a further discussion of using ISO.) But it's important to understand how any setting you use will affect your final image. As you increase ISO, you'll be introducing noise. How much noise will vary with each camera model. The impact of the noise will also vary, depending on the method and size of reproduction or display of the photograph. The key is to know your own camera's capabilities and limitations. Therefore, we recommend that you shoot a series of identical photos at each of your camera's ISO settings (as we did in Figures 5-13 through 5-17). Study them on your computer monitor and print them out, using the various methods and devices you typically employ. This will provide you with useful guidelines as to just how much noise you are prepared to accept and its impact when you increase light sensitivity.

Can't I Just Fix Exposure in RAW?

Shooting in the RAW file format (see Chapter 4) gives you great latitude, because it delivers all the data of your captured image before it is assembled into a final photo file. Therefore, yes, you can fix exposure when working in your RAW conversion utility, but with certain limitations:

- Depth-of-field, motion blur, and action freeze are controlled optically, before the light even reaches the image sensor. Therefore, they cannot be changed in the RAW utility.
- Overexposure and underexposure can result in data not being captured. In the case of overexposure, details in bright areas might be blown out, so they become one solid blob of white. Similarly, underexposure can lose details in the shadows. There's nothing you can do in a computer to reveal details that were never captured (other than paint them in).
- If a picture is severely underexposed, even if the details are there in the shadows, it's likely that they will be noisy when lightened in the computer. (Noise is those ugly pointillistic-like dots that look like colored acne on your photo. See Figure 5-17.)

Getting the exposure right when you're shooting is much easier and less time-consuming than trying to fix it in the computer.

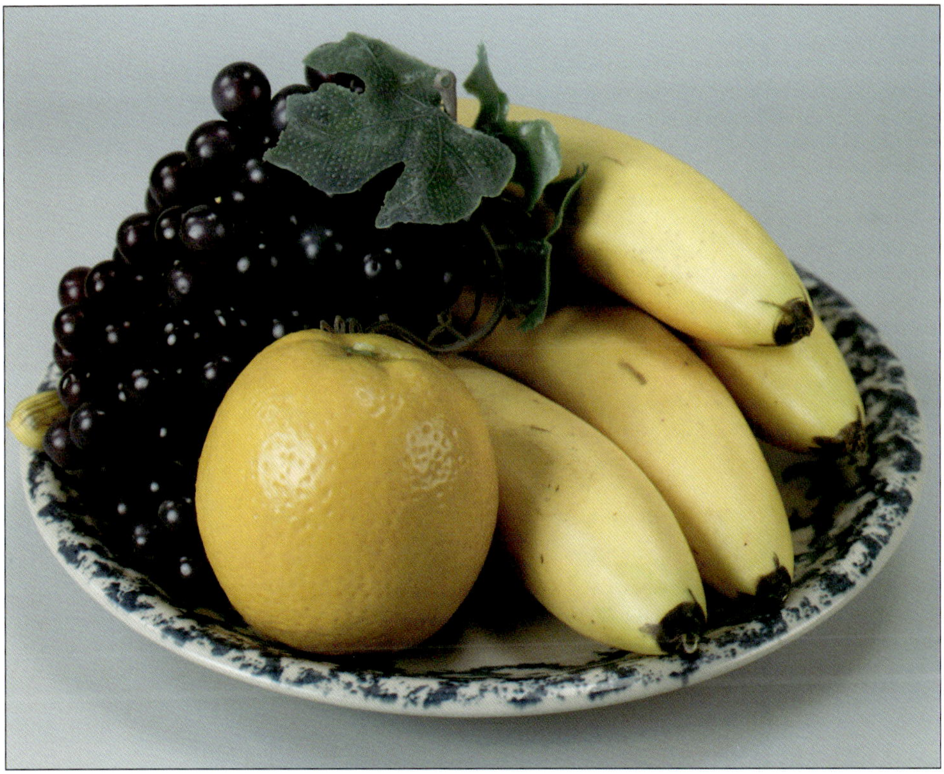

Figure 5-11: We took six identical photos of this small fruit arrangement, each at a different ISO setting. Then, we zoomed into each one (at 200 percent) to explore the ISO-to-noise relationship. (See Figures 5-12 to 5-17.) This picture was taken at ISO 100. (Photos taken with an Olympus E-1, 14-54mm lens set at 38mm. The exposure settings changed relative to the increase in the ISOs.)

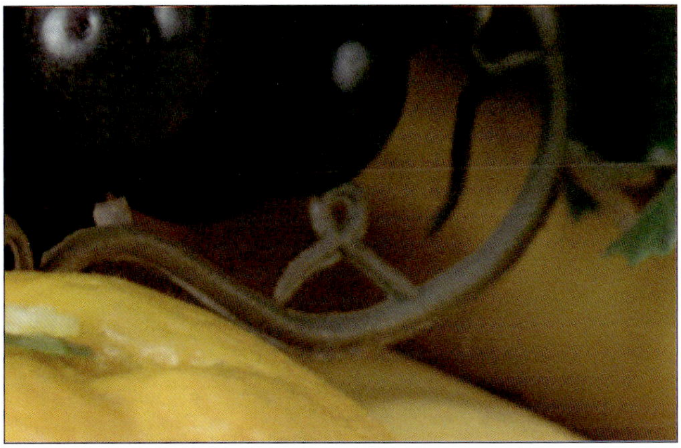

Figure 5-12: ISO 100 (1/180 at *f*4.5)

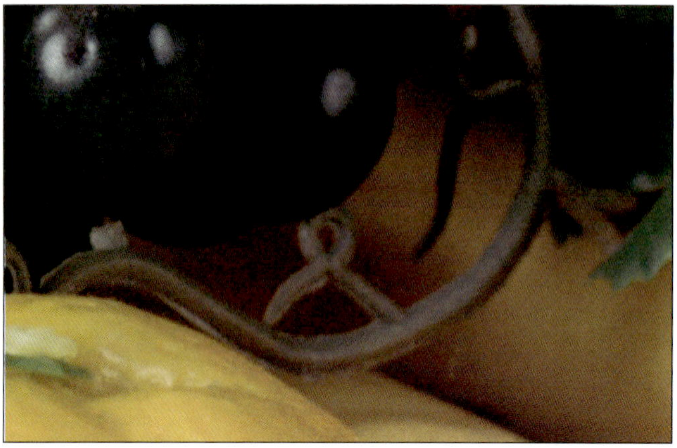

Figure 5-13: ISO 200 (1/160 at *f*4.5)

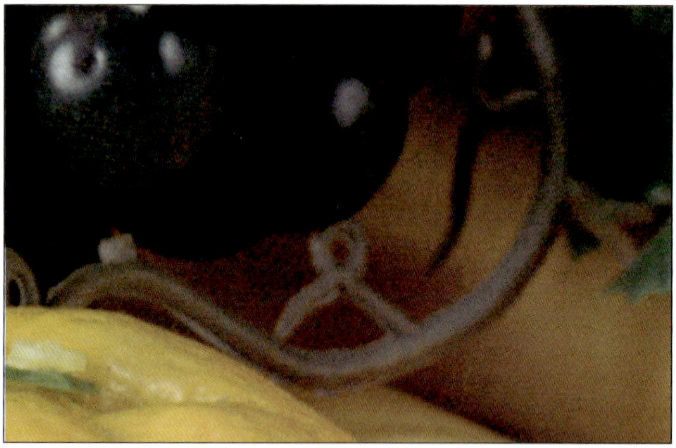

Figure 5-14: ISO 400 (1/320 at *f*4.5)

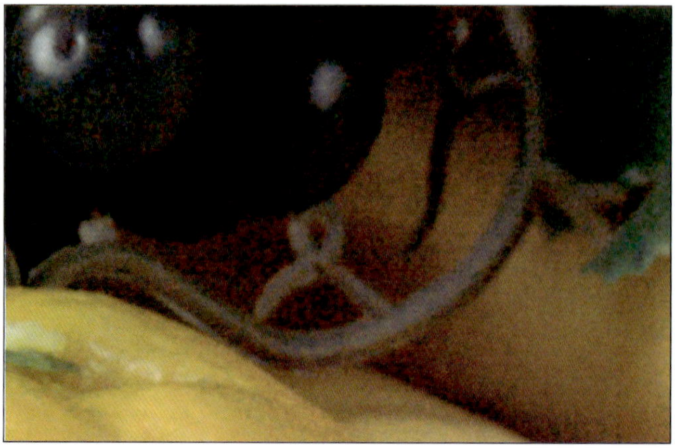

Figure 5-15: ISO 800 (1/640 at *f*4.5)

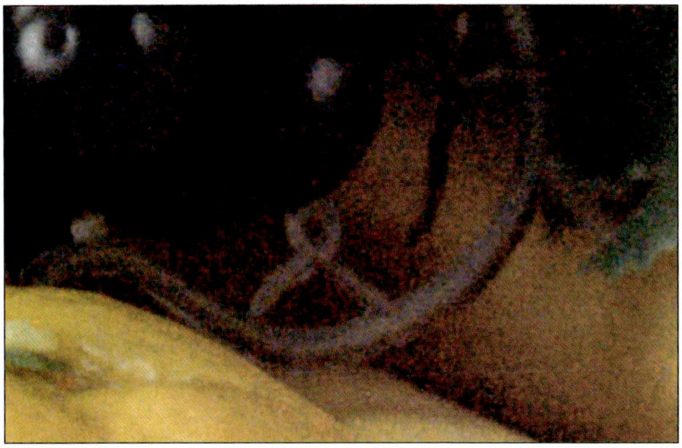

Figure 5-16: ISO 1600 (1/1000 at *f*4.5)

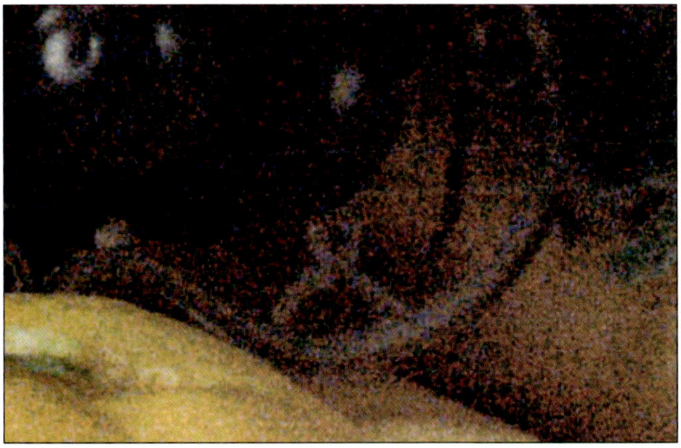

Figure 5-17: ISO 3200 (1/2000 at *f*4.5)

Incidentally, we seldom shoot as high as ISO 800, and we can count on two hands the number of times we've gone as high as 1600 (other than to demonstrate how noisy it can be).

Tip

Typically, the factory default setting for digital camera's ISO is Auto. That means the camera's built-in intelligence will analyze the scene and adjust the ISO to what it thinks is best. Automation can be great, but you can end up with pictures taken at higher, noisy ISOs without your prior approval. We recommend taking control over ISO (and its potential for increased noise) by taking it off Auto. We set the default of all our digital cameras at the lowest ISO (which is usually 100, though some go down only to 200). That ensures that most of our photos are shot at the highest-quality light sensitivity. The only time our camera boosts the ISO is when we make a conscious choice to do so.

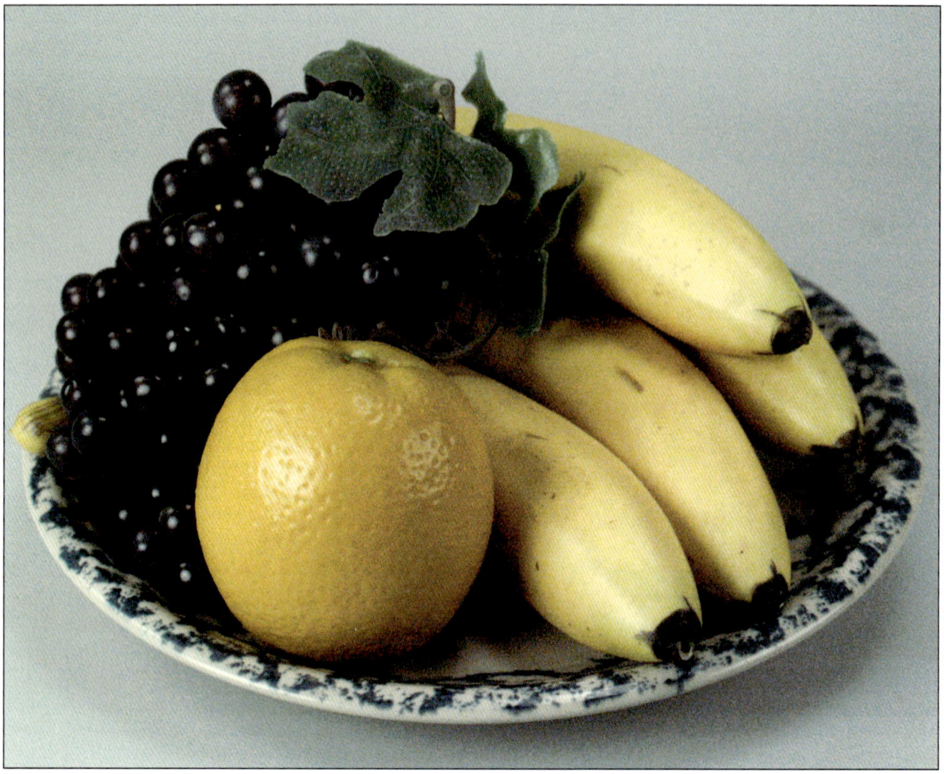

Figure 5-18: Printing this ISO 3200 version of the photo at this comparatively small size, the difference in quality between this picture and the ISO 100 version in Figure 5-12 may not be as dramatic as the zoomed-in view in Figure 5-17 would seem to indicate. But when reproduced at a larger size, or using more precise printing, the loss of detail and smooth transitions would be a visibly significant detriment to quality.

Exposure: A Careful Balancing Act

The three variables we discussed previously — aperture, shutter speed, and ISO — determine the exposure of your picture. Each has its own pros and cons for creative, effective photography:

- Aperture controls the depth-of-field.
  - When you open up the aperture (decrease the *f*-stop number) to get more light into the camera, less of your picture will be in focus.
  - When you close it down (increasing the *f*-stop), to reduce the light, more of the picture will be in focus.
- Shutter speed determines how motion is captured.
  - When you shoot at a slower shutter speed, to get more light into the photo, action will tend to be blurred.

  - When you use a high shutter speed, you're cutting down on the light, but freezing the action.
- ISO sets the light sensitivity of the image sensor.
  - If you put your ISO at a high number, to increase the sensor's sensitivity and capture more light, you may increase the amount of visible noise in your photo.
  - If you reduce your ISO to a low number, the image sensor may not capture as much light, but there will be less noise and smoother transitions between colors.

None of these options work in a vacuum. Each choice that you make regarding your aperture, shutter speed, or ISO affects the choices you have for your settings of the other two variables. And that, in turn, directly changes just what you will capture in your photograph.

The logic of the relationship between these variables is quite commonsensical. The primary purpose of all three is to get the right amount of light into the camera — that is, a good exposure. If you adjust one variable in such a way that you reduce the amount of light that particular variable allows through, you'll need to increase the light by adjusting one or both of the other variables, and vice versa.

Now, consider the relationships between these three variables.

The first step is deciding how you envision your photograph. Is one aspect more important to your composition than the others: a narrow or deep depth-of-field, or stopping or slowing motion? Do you need both a wide depth-of-field and the ability to freeze action? Or do you want to blur the background and the action? The answers to these questions determine how you will balance the relationships of *f*-stop, shutter speed, and ISO. For example:

- If your primary goal is to freeze the action, you'll increase your shutter speed, which reduces the length of time light gets through to the image sensor. Therefore, you'll want to increase the amount of light by opening up your lens (decreasing the *f*-stop number). If at all possible, you'll want to keep your ISO at the camera's lowest setting for highest quality.
- If the shutter speed still isn't fast enough for the photograph you're trying to get, even with the aperture wide open, you'll need to increase the ISO, recognizing that will increase the potential for noise.
- If you want to blur the action, you'll decrease the shutter speed, which will increase the duration of time the light streams through the lens. So, you'll want to close down the lens, and/or decrease the ISO. (We always try to opt for the latter if it will get us the photo we want, preferring a low ISO for the quality.)
- If you need a wide depth-of-field, you'll set your aperture to a high *f*-stop number. Again, that will reduce the amount of light. To balance that, you'll need to either increase the duration of the light (slow down the shutter speed) or decrease the ISO, or both.
- In subdued light, even if you open up the aperture all the way and slow down the shutter speed to the point of needing a tripod, the scene might be too dark to capture. That's when you need to up the ISO.

- There may be so much light streaming into your camera that you can have both a fast shutter speed and a small aperture. That will give you a wide depth-of-field and the ability to stop action. But if you want to soften the background, you might need to use a few other tricks to reduce the amount of light entering the camera. One tried-and-true tactic is to use a neutral density filter (1X, 2X, or 4X) or a polarizing filter on your lens. (See Chapter 3, regarding filters.) If you don't have a neutral density filter, shoot in RAW, using negative exposure compensation, and then increase the brightness in the RAW conversion utility. (See Chapter 4 regarding RAW and later in this chapter for a discussion of exposure compensation.)

In the next section, we discuss how to use various metering and exposure modes to achieve this kind of control over shutter speeds, *f*-stops, and ISO.

Tip

Attached to the file of every photograph you take with a digital camera are the metadata — information about the conditions under which the picture was shot. This includes the settings for shutter speed, aperture, ISO, flash, white balance, and so forth. It's often interesting and quite educational to study the metadata of a particularly good (or disappointing) image, to learn how it was made and why it looks the way it does. You can often access the metadata in the playback mode of your camera, as well as in your image database and photo-editing programs. (See Chapter 9.)

Tools for Getting Bang-On Exposure

One of the defining aspects of good photography is the control that the photographer has over exposure. DSLRs have powerful traditional and digital tools to help you, including:

A variety of exposure modes

Flexible metering modes

Exposure compensation

Manual and auto-bracketing

Histograms

Understanding the Various Exposure Modes

Depending on how long you have been a photographer, or, for the younger crowd, if you ever worked in a professional studio, you may remember using a handheld meter to measure the light of a scene. It was a separate device from the camera. The way you would use it would be to set the meter to the ISO of your film, point the photosensitive probe or sensor at the scene (or at the studio lights), push a button, and read the various displayed *f*-stop/shutter speed combinations that would be appropriate for that shot.

For instance, we just stepped outside our studio where the midday sun is shining brightly. Pointing a meter at the green grass, which is glistening with raindrops from a late morning storm, it suggested the following combinations to get the exposure correct for that scene:

*f*16 at 1/60

*f*11 at 1/125

*f*8 at 1/250

*f*5.6 at 1/500

*f*4 at 1/1000

*f*2.8 at 1/2000

The preceding list is just a sampling of the combinations that a typical light meter displays, all of which would deliver the same amount of light to the image sensor or film. You choose the combination that will provide the depth-of-field and the amount of action freeze or blur that you want for your photograph.

If the scene were one stop darker than the glistening grass we read, then all the numbers in the preceding list would shift by one *f*-stop to open up the aperture. In other words, instead of a reading of *f*16 at 1/60, it would have a reading of *f*8 at 1/60 (with all the other combinations adjusted in a similar manner).

By the way, the subject you are photographing is as important as the light conditions for determining the right exposure. The grass outside was brighter than it had been the day before at the same time, because today it was covered with raindrops.

Modern SLRs (both film and digital) have a light meter, usually called a light sensor, built into the camera, but it functions essentially the same way as a handheld meter. First, set the ISO. Point the lens at the scene, press the shutter button down halfway, and the camera's viewfinder will display one suggested combination of *f*-stop and shutter speed. Generally, changing that single suggested combination to another involves turning a dial on the camera. But how the specific numbers are changed depends on the shooting mode you are using.

Choosing the Right Shooting Mode for Your Photo

All DSLRs have at least four exposure modes:

- Programmed auto
- Aperture priority
- Shutter priority
- Full manual

In addition, many also have the following automated or semi-automated modes that combine focus and exposure options:

- Full auto
- Program modes

Typically, DSLRs change modes in one of two ways:

- Turn a large analog dial on the top of the body until the desired icon lines up with an indicator line or notch. (See Figures 5-19 and 5-20.)
- While looking at the control panel or through the viewfinder, press a mode button or option, and then turn a small ratcheted dial ("subdial") until you see the symbol for the mode you want.

DSLR manufacturers have almost standardized on mode icons. At least, they tend to use similar, if not identical, symbols.

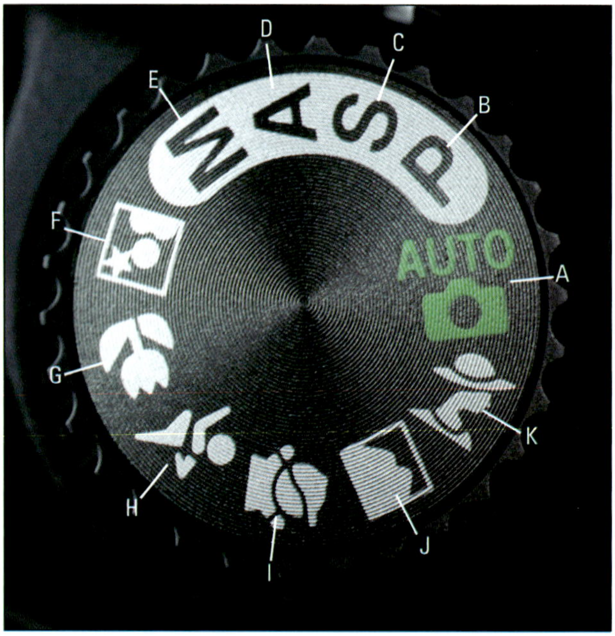

Figure 5-19: Nikon D50's mode dial. (A) Full auto, (B) Programmed auto mode, (C) Shutter priority, (D) Aperture priority, (E) Full manual, (F) Night portrait, (G) Macro, (H) Sports, (I) Child portrait, (J) Landscape, (K) Portrait. (Photo taken with a Konica Minolta Maxxum 7D, 28–100mm lens set at 100mm,1/30 at *f*4.5.)

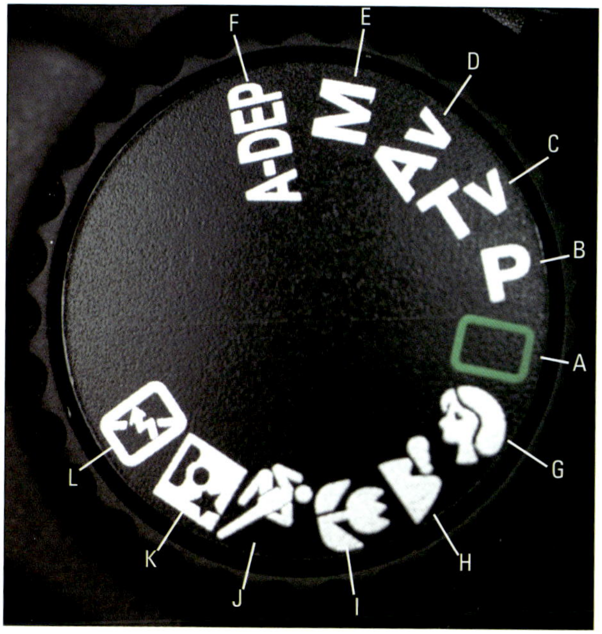

Figure 5-20: Canon EOS 20D's mode dial. (A) Full auto, (B) Programmed auto, (C) Shutter priority, (D) Aperture priority, (E) Full manual, (F) Auto Depth of Field, (G) Portrait, (H) Landscape, (I) Macro, (J) Sports, (K) Night portrait, (L) Flash off. (Photo taken with a Konica Minolta Maxxum 7D, 28–100mm lens set at 100mm, 1/80 at *f*4.5.)

The next sections look at each mode to understand when and how to best use it.

FULL AUTO

Full auto is the "point-and-shoot" mode in which the camera's internal computer makes all decisions for you. You simply aim your lens at the subject, and the camera will focus, analyze what it sees, and select the aperture and shutter speed it believes is best for the scene. Depending upon the camera, Auto also may pop up the built-in flash and trigger it, if it decides it needs additional illumination.

While Auto can be useful from time to time, it is mostly used by folks who haven't bothered to learn their cameras. If you have been shooting exclusively on auto (often a small green rectangle or green icon in the shape of a camera), now is the time to just turn the dial and take your camera off auto. You'll be amazed at how easy it is to take control over your photography and express your own personal vision, rather than that of some anonymous engineering team that designed your camera.

PROGRAMMED AUTO

Similar in many respects to full auto, programmed auto gives you much more flexibility. The camera will focus on the object(s) it thinks is the subject and then select a specific *f*-stop and shutter speed combination for what it considers the optimum exposure. However, you can change the focus point and choose a different *f*-stop and shutter speed combination.

To alter the *f*-stop, shutter speed combination, you usually just turn the subdial. How you alter the focus point will be dependent on the current focus mode. (Please see Chapter 6 regarding focus.)

Using Program Modes

Program modes are preprogrammed settings designed for specific types of photographs or shooting situations. They often encompass both exposure and focus options, plus they may adjust colors to fit the subject. Here are a few common program modes:

- **Landscape** — The camera will likely choose a small aperture for a deep depth-of-field, while focusing on the nearest item, as well as heighten the colors and contrast. It will also disable any attached flash.
- **Portrait** — In addition to setting a large aperture for shallow depth-of-field, the camera will likely balance the colors for skin tones and soften the contrast.
- **Sport** — Using a very fast shutter speed to stop action, the camera will probably also switch to continuous focus, so you can track the players and be sure to be in focus anytime you snap the shutter. Typically, any attached flash will be disabled.
- **Night portrait** — Intended for taking portraits against a nighttime background, this mode usually focuses on the closest subject, triggers the flash early, and then continues to expose (after the flash fires) to balance the background exposure.

Not all DSLRs have program modes, while others have additional, nonstandard ones. For example, the Canon 20D's Auto Depth of Field (icon shown in Figure 5-20) analyzes the position of several subjects and chooses an *f*-stop that keeps all of them in focus (great for group portraits).

While we aren't big fans of reading camera documentation, this is one situation where we recommend reading yours, to find out exactly what your camera's program modes do. Keep in mind, however, that simply because the manual says a certain mode is for, say, photographing kids, it doesn't mean you should let yourself be straightjacketed into using that mode only for kids and nothing else. Try the program modes on all kinds of scenes and subjects, even ones that are very different from the intended purpose. You'll either end up with a photo that you will want to delete, or, very possibly, discover a new creative technique.

An interesting exercise is to shoot using a program mode and then look at the metadata of the photo (either in the camera's playback or after you've uploaded the picture to the computer) to see what settings were used to take it. If you like the way the photo came out, you might want to try similar settings on your own.

Programmed auto is a great compromise for when you don't want to take the time or make an effort to do more than point and shoot, but still want to have some say about the depth-of-field and shutter speed of your photo.

APERTURE PRIORITY

For those times when you know that the depth-of-field of your photograph takes precedence over how fast the shutter speed is use aperture priority. As you select the aperture that you want to use, the camera will automatically adjust the shutter speed for what its internal light sensor perceives as the correct exposure for the scene.

SHUTTER PRIORITY

Shutter priority is the exact opposite of aperture priority. If a specific shutter speed (slow to show motion blur, fast to stop action) is more important than depth-of-field, set the mode to shutter priority, choose the shutter speed you want, and the camera will automatically adjust the *f*-stop to create the correct exposure, according to the camera's internal light sensor.

MANUAL EXPOSURE

Use manual exposure when you want to break ranks with the camera's internal light sensor. It uncouples the *f*-stops and shutter speeds so that you can set each individually. However, you won't be entirely on your own. In the viewfinder, most DSLRs display an indicator (a scale or numbers), showing how far under- or overexposed your settings are compared to what the sensor suggests.

Tip

If you are shooting a subject and the frame includes something with a highly reflective surface, such as a shiny metal or water, it may significantly throw your exposure off. If that's the case, or if it leaves a glaring hot spot in your photograph (you'll immediately see if it's overexposed or has a hot spot by looking at the camera's LCD screen in playback mode), use a polarizing filter to tone it down. (See Chapter 3 on filters.)

Metering Modes

Getting the right exposure for your photograph hinges upon having a good and appropriate light sensor reading of the scene. Two factors influence what constitutes an appropriate reading:

- What is the composition?
  - A key subject surrounded by other items (or people) of less interest or by itself against a background.
  - A key subject surrounded by other items (or people) that are of interest, but not as important.

  - A key subject that fills most or the entire frame.
  - Everything in the frame is of equal (or near equal) importance.
- What kind of lighting do you have?
  - Relatively even light throughout the scene, with only some slight variations.
  - Dramatic shadows and/or bright light in different areas, creating a wide difference among various areas.
  - Key subject in a shadow or backlit, so it is darker than the rest of the picture.

DSLRs have different kinds of metering modes, so they can handle all the preceding conditions. The three basic metering modes in most DSLRs are:

- Matrix
- Center-weighted
- Spot

Several DSLRs have other kinds of metering modes. If you understand these three modes, you'll find it easy to follow the instructions for any other metering methods your camera has.

When the Spot You Want to Meter Isn't in the Center

When the key subject isn't in the center of the frame (for instance, it might be to the side), and you want to use spot metering, do what pros have done for years, even before the digital age.

1. Point the camera lens at the key subject so that it is in the center of the frame.
2. Press the shutter button down halfway, which freezes in the exposure (and focus).
3. While still holding the shutter button down halfway, reframe the scene (which may displace that key subject out of the center of the scene).
4. Press the shutter button all the way, to capture the scene.

For those cameras that have flexible spot focus (see Chapter 6), in step #1, position the key subject so that it is in the selected focus point, rather than in the center of the frame.

Most DSLRs have two useful buttons, called AE-L (auto exposure lock) and AF-L (autofocus lock). Instead of holding the shutter button down halfway to lock in the focus and/or exposure, press the AF-L or AE-L button instead.

MATRIX METERING

While not all digital camera manufacturers call it matrix metering, most tend to have matrix metering (regardless of the name they use) as the default setting on their cameras. Essentially, it takes sampling readings from the center, the corners and, sometimes, various other points within the frame, and then it averages them. (That's why matrix metering is sometimes called average metering.)

Matrix metering works best either when the scene tends to be relatively uniform or when any areas that are extraordinarily bright or dark are small and/or peripheral to the composition. (See Figure 5-21.)

CENTER-WEIGHTED METERING

When you have a key subject or area that fills much (but not all) of the frame, with a background or corners that are either brighter or darker, center-weighted metering works well. It's a great mode for portraits.

Center-weighted reads the same sensor points as matrix metering (center, corners, and, sometimes, other areas), but when it averages the exposure values, it gives more weight (50 percent) to the center. (See Figure 5-22.)

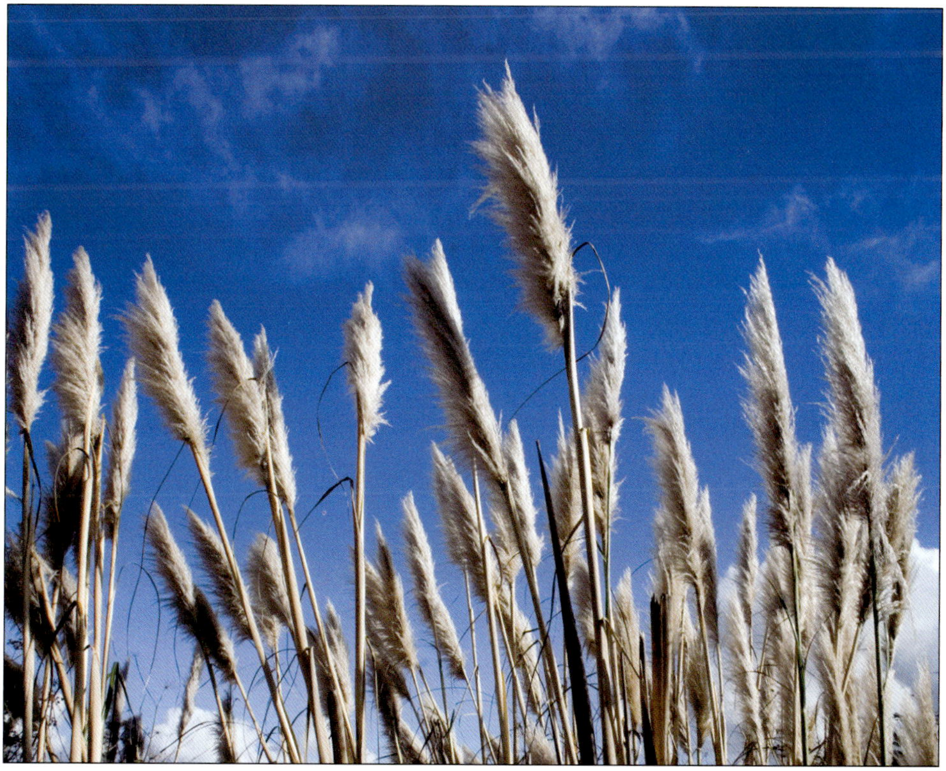

Figure 5-21: This photo was a perfect candidate for matrix metering because the entire picture is relatively uniform in lighting. (Photo taken with a Canon EOS Digital Rebel, 18–55mm lens set at 20mm, 1/100 at *f*22.)

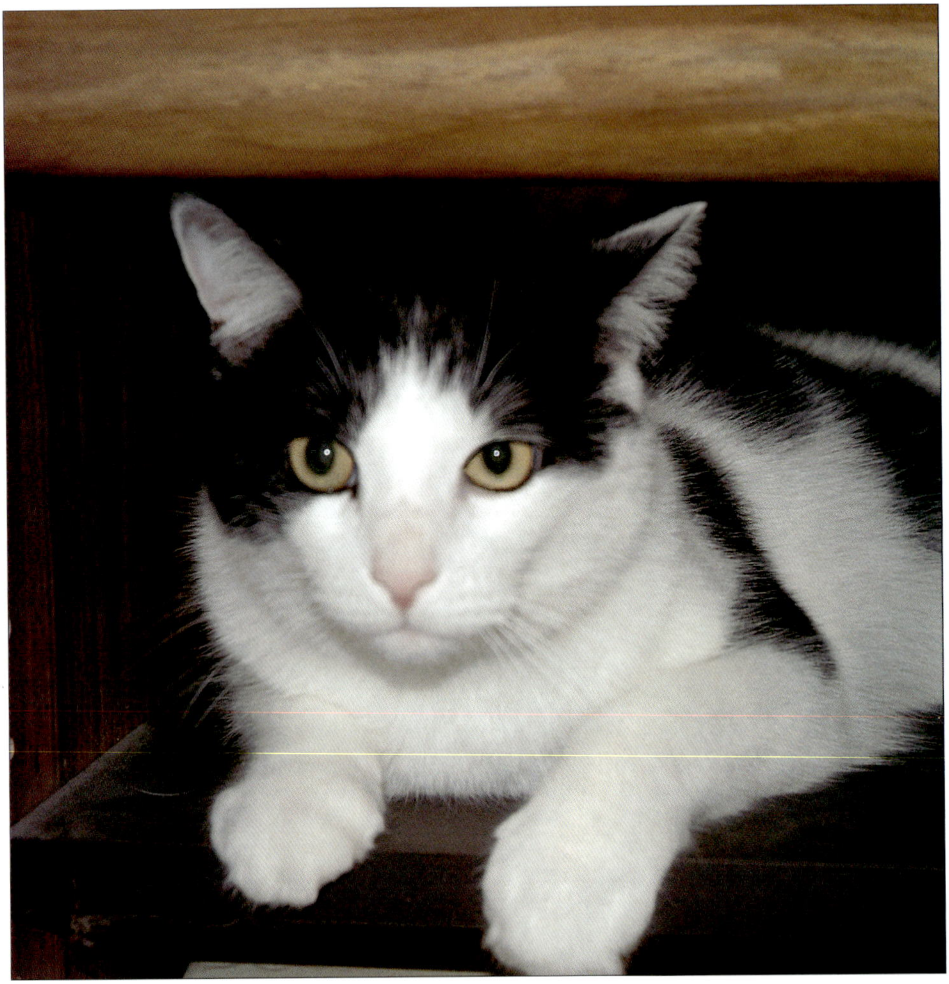

Figure 5-22: Center-weighted metering works for photos like this one of our cat Rascal, who likes to climb into dark, small cubbyholes. That's because, when averaging the exposure readings, center-weighted puts more emphasis on the central subject (Rascal) than it does the dark corners. If we had used matrix metering, the camera would have exposed to lighten up the corners a bit more. That, in turn, would have made Rascal's white fur too white, losing details in his face, paws and body. (Photo taken with a Nikon D70, 50mm lens, 1/60 at *f*4.5.)

SPOT METERING

When you have one small, but very critical area of your scene that may be darker or lighter than the surrounding areas and objects, spot metering is the best choice. It takes its reading on a small circular area (usually 5 percent or less of the total frame) in the center, ignoring the rest of the picture. (See Figure 5-23.)

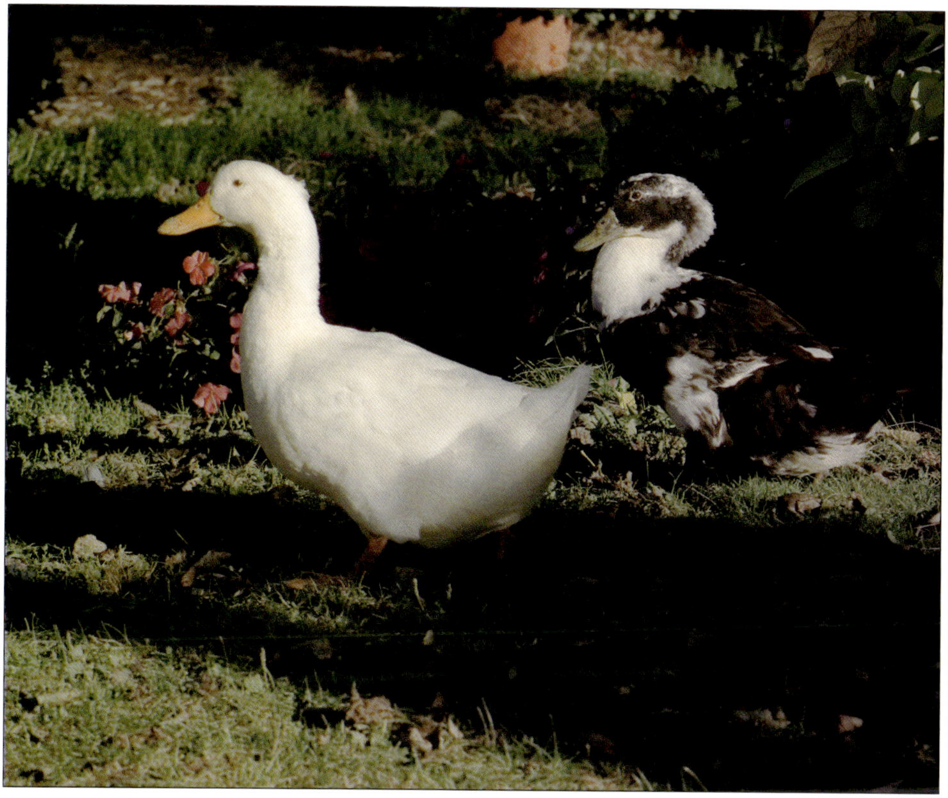

Figure 5-23: The white duck is so much whiter than the rest of this picture that if we had metered using matrix or center-weighted mode, we would have lost a great number of the details in his body. They would have been a glob of bright white highlights. By using spot metering, we made certain that the exposure was balanced to capture the soft feathery details, even in the brightest areas of the duck's body. (Photo taken with a Konica Minolta Maxxum 7D, 28–100mm lens set at 100mm, 1/1600 at *f*5.)

OTHER METERING OPTIONS

The computers inside many DSLRs are quite sophisticated. Some can analyze a scene, pick out the likely subject, and take their meter reading (and focus) from that point within the frame. Others have the ability to do some interesting weighted calculations based on the perceived colors and contrasts. Check your owner's manual to see if your DSLR features any such metering modes, and if so, by all means, try them out.

Tip

As we have said before, the best way to learn what any command on your camera does is to experiment with it. Take a series of photos, using every metering mode your camera offers. Then study them in your computer to see what affect each mode had on your pictures.

Exposure Compensation and Bracketing

Photography is an art, not a science. With all the internal computers and sensors, buttons, and controls that modern DSLRs have, they still aren't infallible. What's more, they don't possess human imagination or creative vision. Therefore, when a sensor or light meter suggests a certain exposure for a specific scene, it's nothing more than a suggestion. The truly perfect exposure might be a bit darker or lighter.

Be aware that there's one other problem with trusting technology. With film photography, we never really knew whether we had gotten the right exposure (or focus, framing, color, or anything about the picture), until we processed the roll. Conventional wisdom tells us that such uncertainty ended with the immediate feedback that modern digital cameras provide. After all, the LCD screen on the back of our cameras gives us an instant review of exactly what we just shot. Right? Wrong. The LCD is not only inaccurate, it can downright lie. That's because the screens on many cameras automatically lighten the image displayed to make it easier to see. What's more, LCD screens, no matter how large (some are 2.5"), are all relatively low-resolution representations of the image, so you can't really see small details (even when you use the playback zoom tool on your camera).

Exposure compensation is a tool that photographers have been using since the film era that continues to be invaluable for assuring that you get the photo you want. Also called exposure value (or EV), *exposure compensation* allows you to apply a negative or minus value to your exposure settings, increasing or decreasing the amount of light actually allowed to pass through the lens to the image sensor.

Typically, EV is represented by a +/- icon (see Figure 5-24) and is displayed either as a scale (see Figure 5-25) or as positive and negative numbers (such as -1.3 or +2.0).

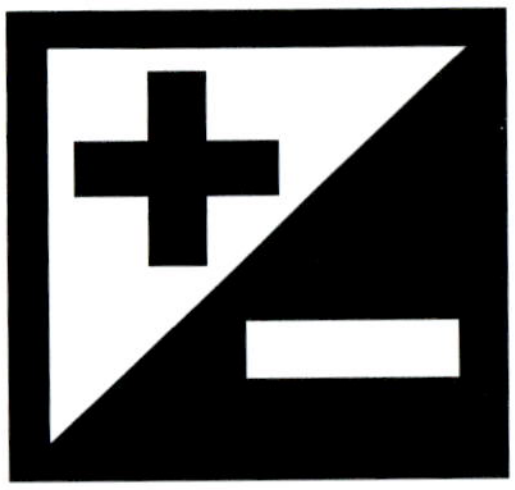

Figure 5-24: This icon on a button or in a menu option represents exposure compensation (EV). Typically, if it is a button, you hold it down while turning a subdial to set EV. If it is a menu option, you'll usually use the jog buttons or other menu controls to set it. By the way, in those instances where this icon isn't used, the command or button may be identified simply as EV.

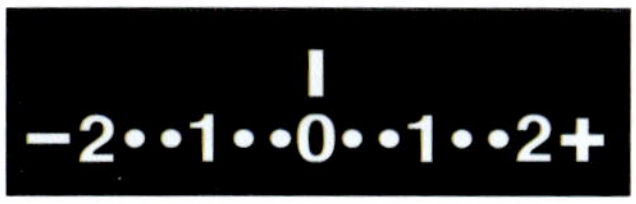

Figure 5-25: Exposure compensation is often represented as a scale like this one from the Konica Minolta Maxxum 7D. If you look through your viewfinder while adjusting EV, the marker on the scale will move up or down correspondingly. In some cameras' viewfinders, you'll see the EV numbers without the scale.

Exposure compensation numbers and increments will vary, depending on your camera model. Some go up to +/-2.0 *f*-stops, but in more expensive cameras can go to +/-3.0 or higher. Increments may be in thirds or halves of *f*-stops. When displaying EV as numbers rather than on the scale, they are shown as decimals, rounded off to the nearest tenth, rather than fractions.

You can use exposure compensation one of two ways:

- If you know that the photos you've been taking under certain lights or in a specific environment tend to shoot dark or light, you can set an EV to lighten or darken your exposures. In this case, once you've established the correct exposure value for that shoot, you may want to simply leave it at that setting.
- If you are uncertain whether or not the exposure settings suggested by your camera's sensor are correct, then you might want to bracket. Bracketing involves taking at least three shots for every one that you want. The first photo would be at EV 0, the second would be, say, EV -1, and the third at EV +1. (See Figure 5-26.) You could also use fractional increments. Depending on how finicky you are, and how important precise exposure is for the particular scene, you can bracket with three, five, seven, or more photos taken in increasing increments along the EV scale.

Tip

Be careful not to go overboard with bracketing. Remember, every photo you take represents time you'll have to spend processing. Each and every image must be uploaded to your computer, viewed, analyzed, and then either deleted or organized, processed, and stored.

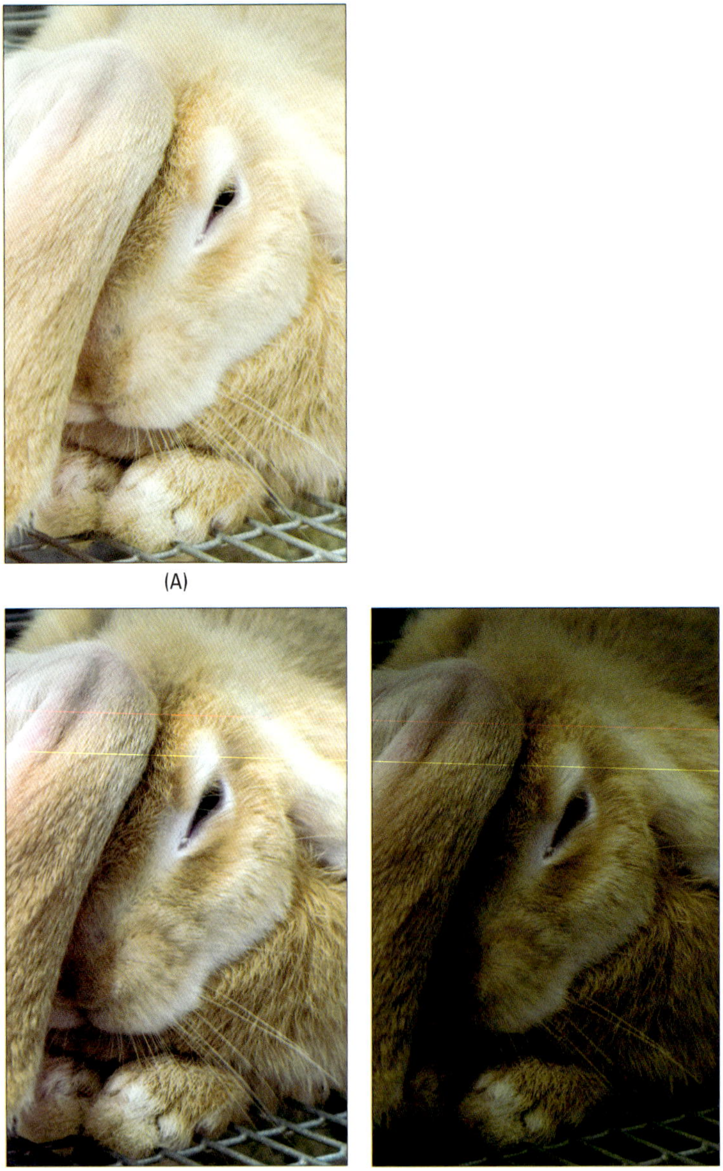

(A) (B) (C)

Figure 5-26: These three photos of a long-eared rabbit were taken in quick succession, each with a different exposure compensation value: (A) EV +1.0, (B) EV 0, and (C) EV -1.0. For this series of pictures, the camera's meter was correct, and it didn't need any exposure compensation. However, we have found that in many situations a slight EV adjustment, sometimes as little as 1/3 stop in either direction, will nail the exposure. (Photos taken with an Olympus E-300, 14–54mm lens set at 35mm, 1/10 at *f*5.)

Tip

After you are finished with any shoot in which you used exposure compensation, be sure to return EV to 0 before turning off your camera. Otherwise, you'll end up with inaccurate exposures in your next shoot, and you may not be sure why.

AUTO-BRACKETING

Until the advent of more advanced film SLRs, we used to bracket by using exposure compensation manually, or simply moving the aperture ring on the lens up or down one or two *f*-stops. The routine was snap the first picture, change the EV, snap another, change the EV again, snap a third, and so on. Not only was it slow and tiresome, it also wasted time or often meant losing a great shot.

Most DSLRs have a mode called auto-bracketing, in which you set how many stops you want to bracket on either side of the scale and how many shots you want to take up and down the scale. Then, depending on your camera model, one of two things will happen:

- Each time you take a photograph, the camera will automatically adjust the exposure according to your auto-bracketing settings. Therefore, if you set auto-bracketing to take five shots at increments of 0.3, the first time you would press the shutter button it would take a photo at EV 0. The next press of the shutter would take a shot at EV -0.3, the next at +0.3, then -0.6, and finally +0.6.
- Or, when you press the shutter button once, the camera will automatically take a series of photos rather than one shot, applying different exposure compensations according to your settings to each picture.

In either case, auto-bracketing is certainly faster than manually resetting exposure compensation with each shot. When photographing live subjects, such as our long-eared rabbit (see Figure 5-26), that immediacy and speed of shooting can make a difference in how similar each photo in the series is to the others. (Actually, the rabbit was motionless, which is why we could use such a slow shutter speed.)

As with any exposure compensation settings, be sure to disable auto-bracketing before you turn off your camera. Otherwise, you could end up with the right exposure in only one of every few pictures the next time you shoot.

Tip

If your DSLR offers auto-bracketing for white balance and other settings, try them out. Auto-bracketing is a great tool for assuring you get the photo you envision, as well as an interesting creativity tool. (See Chapter 6 regarding white balance.)

Histograms

Since you can't trust the LCD screen on the back of your camera to give you an accurate representation of the photo you just shot, DSLRs have borrowed an important tool from photo-editing software: the histogram. A histogram reveals vital visual information about your photo's highlights, midtones, and shadows. In other words, it's a statistical analysis of the light values of the pixels in your photograph. That sounds much more intimidating than it really is. Figure 5-27 looks at some histograms of various photographs, to demonstrate just how intuitive, powerful, and useful this tool can be.

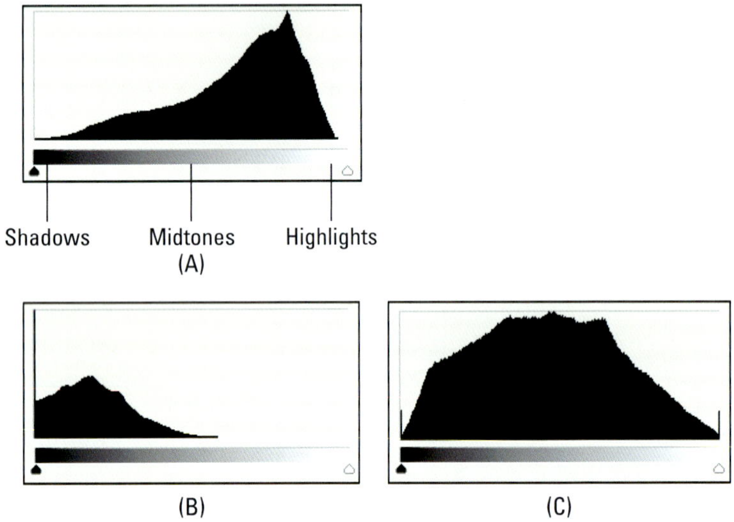

Figure 5-27: These three histograms are of the three different exposures of the long-eared rabbit in Figures 5-26. First, look at the greyscale bar under the histogram graphs. You'll notice that shadows are on the left area, midtones in the middle, and highlights on the right. The histogram in Figure (A) represents the overexposed photograph (Figure 5-26 A). Therefore, the graph shows that the majority of the pixels are in the midtones to highlight areas, with practically none in the shadows. Figure (B) corresponds to the underexposed photo (Figure 5-26 C). Notice how all the pixels are bunched to the left, in the shadows, with almost none in the midtones and zero in the highlights. But like Goldilocks and the Three Bears' oatmeal, the histogram in Figure (C) is just right, as is the well-exposed photo it represents (Figure 5-26 B). (Screen captures of histograms courtesy of Adobe Photoshop CS2)

While Figure 5-27 (C) shows a nearly perfect bell curve, of the kind that is often used to show perfect exposure, it is important to understand that there is no one type of histogram that is right for all photographs. Remember, how you use light and shadow in your photography is a creative choice, not a mathematical one. Some photographs simply require heavy shadows (see Figure 5-28) or highlight spikes (see Figure 5-29).

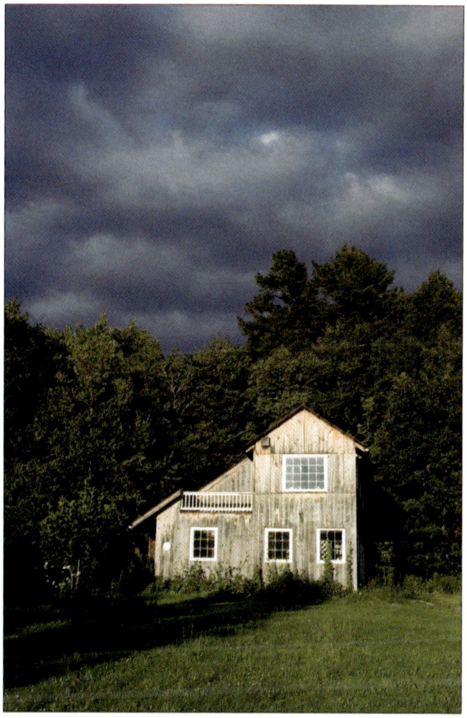

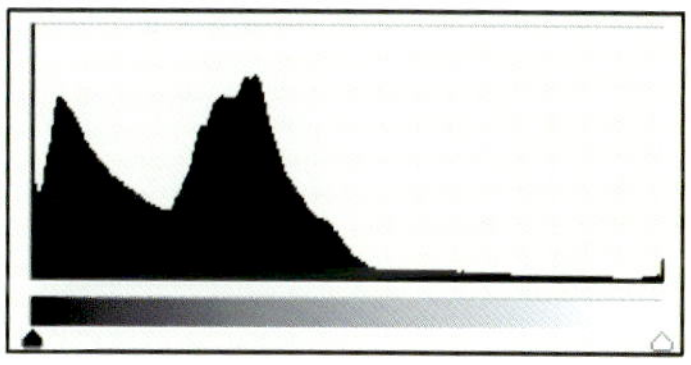

Figure 5-28: With the dark storm clouds, deep greens, and shadows of the forest and the dark shadow in the foreground, this photograph certainly has more darkness in it than midtones or highlights. And that's what makes it a powerful image. If Sally had exposed for a classic "bell-curve" histogram that would have put more of the pixels into the midtones, and a diminishing percentage in the highlights and shadows, the photo would have been washed out and more prosaic. Notice, however, that the histogram does have a small spike in the brightest highlights (to the right), which corresponds to bright white areas on the building. (Photo taken with a Nikon D70, 24–120mm lens set at 40mm, 1/100 at *f*13.)

The histogram on your LCD may be displayed in one of two ways, depending on your digital camera. Some consumer and prosumer models allow you to turn on the histogram while you are setting up your photo. In that case, it is called a "live" histogram because it changes in real time, as you adjust your exposure settings. However, most DSLRs will display a histogram only on playback. That's because most DSLR image sensors are exposed to light only at the instant the shot is being taken. But most DSLRs allow you to immediately check your shot — as well as see an accompanying histogram — within a second of capturing the photo. If the playback histogram looks as though the photo may be too dark or too light, or spread out in ways that don't represent what you were trying to capture, you can quickly adjust your exposure settings and shoot again.

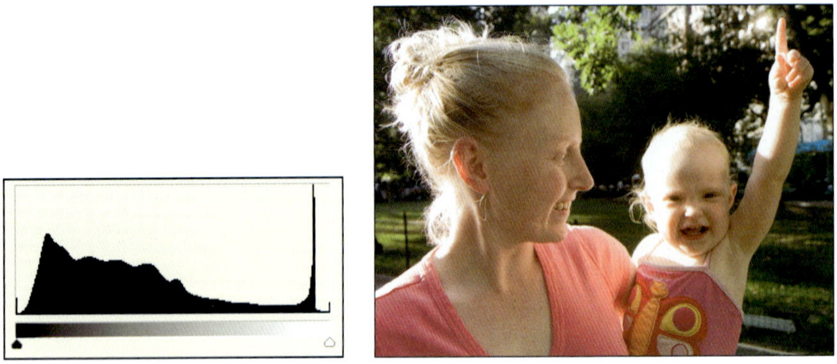

(A) (B)

Figure 5-29: (A) If you were to look at this histogram without seeing the photo it represents, you might question the large spike in the highlights (near the right of the graph). Does it represent a blowout of details, or an unwanted hot spot? (B) Only when you see the photo that corresponds to Figure 5-29 (A), does that histogram make sense. The spike in the highlights is an appropriate representation of the halo effect of the sunlight streaming through the subjects' blonde hair. (Photo taken with a Canon EOS 1Ds Mark II, 16–35mm lens set at 24mm, 1/400 at *f*6.3.)

In viewing a histogram, the trick is to recognize the comparative percentages of pixels in the various areas of the dynamic range scale. How much of your photo should be dark versus light? Should most of your picture be in the midtones? Does your vision for it require that it be skewed to one end or the other of the histogram? When you understand what you want the effect of your exposure to be on your photograph, you will be able to envision the appropriate histogram for it. That, in turn, will allow you to choose the best exposure settings, and then confirm that you have captured the shot you want by viewing the histogram on your camera's LCD screen.

TAKING CHARGE OF YOUR HIGHLIGHTS AND SHADOWS

Histograms have one other very important use in digital photography: to help you make certain that you don't lose details in the deepest shadows or brightest highlights, especially when you output your photos.

When inspecting the histogram of a photograph, look for any spikes at the far end of the highlights or shadows that indicate areas that are pure black or pure white. While some photographs may have such extremes within the composition, we have found that some cameras will often automatically overexpose the brightest areas or underexpose the darkest, whether or not there are true whites and blacks in the scene. That, in turn, causes details to be lost. (See Figures 5-30 A, 5-30 B, 5-31 A, and 5-31 B.)

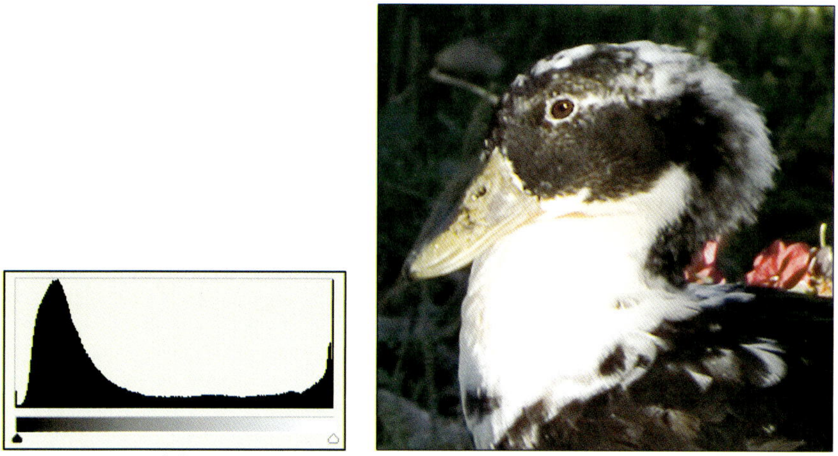

(A) (B)

Figure 5-30: Notice the large spike in the highlights (right side) of the histogram. This indicates that a significant number of pixels in the photo are pure white. Now, look at the duck's neck. Most of the white feathers are a pure white blob with no details. On the other hand, the small spike in the far left end of the shadows is appropriate for the photo, because there are a few places in the background where the shadows are quite dark, including areas of true black. (Photo taken with a Konica Minolta Maxxum 7D, 24–100mm lens set at 100mm, 1/250 at *f*5.)

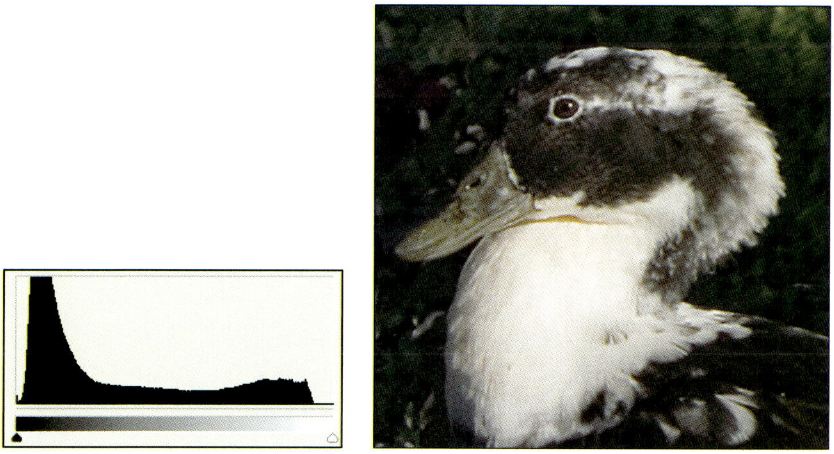

(A) (B)

Figure 5-31: Look at the neck in this picture of the same duck as Figure 5-30 (B). Notice how you can see the variations in white that delineate the individual feathers. Yes, there are some points of pure white, but only where appropriate. Now, compare the histogram to that of Figure 5-30 (A). While there are a few pixels indicated throughout the highlights (the thin line at the bottom of the graph at the far right), the majority of the bright pixels are spread out along a subdued continuum of off-white to midtones. On the other hand, this photo retains the pure blacks (the small spike at the far left), because the background still has deep shadows. (Photo taken with a Konica Minolta Maxxum 7D, 24–100mm lens set at 100mm, 1/1600 at *f*5.)

EXPOSING FOR YOUR INTENDED OUTPUT

In addition to blowing out details, extreme highlights and shadows can be difficult to print. We cover printing in Chapter 12. However, the time to start ensuring that you will get great prints is when you capture your photo. That's why you need to know how your intended output device will handle highlights and shadows.

- Computer monitors and other screens have a wide range of displayable highlights and shadows. If your intended output is the Web, email, or projecting onto a screen, you will want your photo's histogram to show data (pixels) over the entire graph area, from darkest shadows to brightest highlights (that is, if such extremes of light and dark are appropriate for the picture).
- Printers typically "clip" shadows and highlights. That's why many photographers will carefully watch their histograms, to make sure that the pixels don't go all the way to either end. However, the ability of printers to output highlights and shadows varies with each model. The only way to know for sure how certain types of photos will be printed is to output test prints from the specific printer you intend using. Then, with your prints in hand, look at the histograms of the images on your computer monitor. You'll then learn what kinds of histograms work for your specific printer or print service, and which ones don't.

Tip

If you shoot in the RAW file format, you can adjust your histograms according to the intended output in your RAW conversion utility and save out different exposure versions of the same photo. This is useful if you plan to output the same photo as a print as well as post to the Web, or to output the photo with two different kinds of printers, each with varying abilities to reproduce highlights and shadows. (See Chapter 4, regarding RAW.)

Summary

By definition, photography is the control and capture of light and shadow. DSLRs put powerful tools in your hands for taking full control over exactly how light is captured. In the process, you'll be able to make your own creative choices that will affect the composition, style, meaning, and beauty of your pictures.

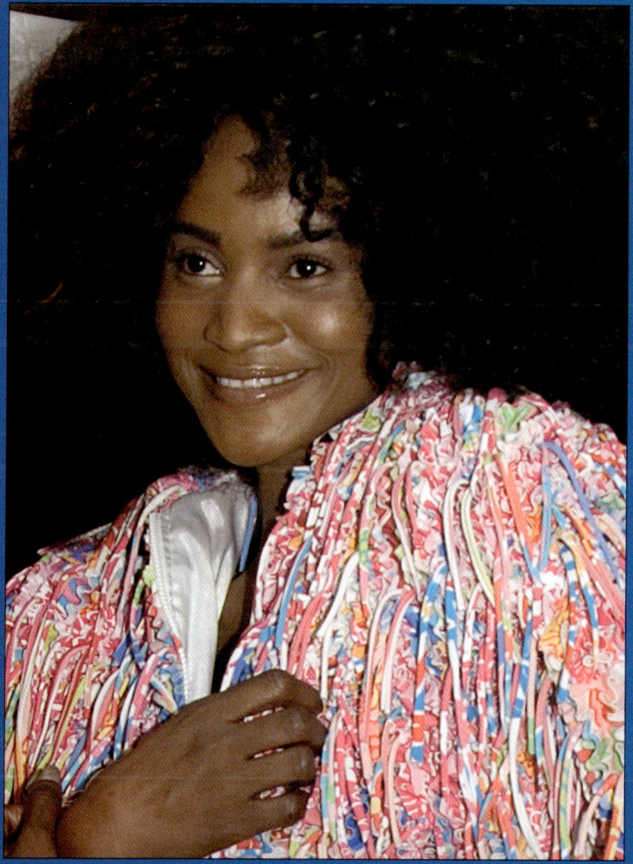

Model Uju Christian relaxes on the set. (Photo taken with a Nikon D2X, 24-120mm lens set at 24mm, 1/60 at f4)

Chapter 6

Camera Controls for Better, More Efficient Photography

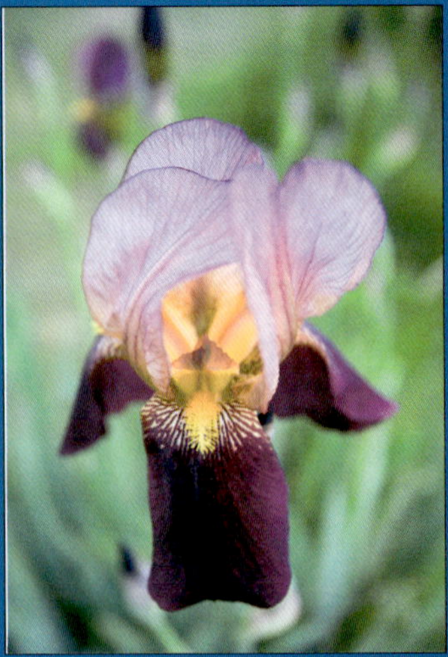

Selective focus, reduced depth-of-field, plus slightly increased saturation and heightened contrast make this iris stand out within a field of irises. (Photo taken with a Canon EOS 1Ds Mark II, 16–35mm lens set at 34mm, 1/200 at f2.8.)

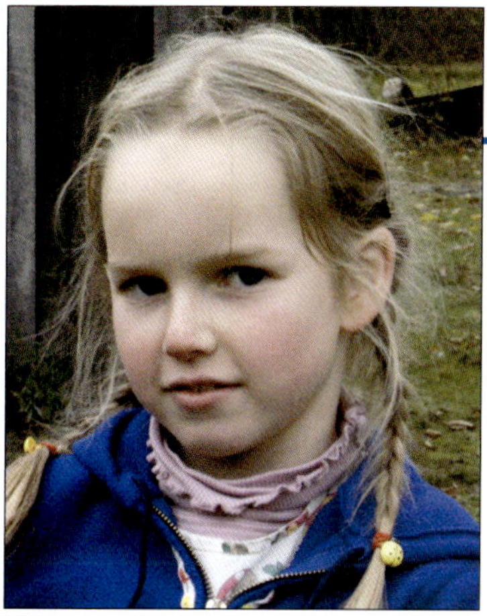

While some photographers tend to use a blur to soften portraits, we tend to prefer more realistic pictures — at least when the model's complexion is as perfect at Rowen's. (Photo taken with an Olympus E-1, 14–54mm lens set at 32mm, 1/50 at f16.)

Digital cameras are hybrid devices — part camera and part computer. The photography portion dictates how the picture is captured, while the computer controls the processing and handling of the captured data. Along the divide of this split personality are the multitude of commands and controls that you, the photographer, use to impose your vision on both technologies.

In this chapter, we delve into important camera settings and options, and help you understand how choosing one over the other will affect your photos. Specifically, we cover:

- Using the different focusing modes
- Choosing the best color model
- Getting the right white balance and colors every time you shoot
- Using other image adjustments your camera may offer

In addition, we'll cover tools that give you control over your files, including:

- In-camera folders to keep projects, types of photos, or different photographers' work separate
- Your file names and method of numbering
- Options available when reviewing your photographs in playback

Understanding DSLR Focus Options

Generally speaking, in a good picture certain areas will be in clear, sharp focus. Other portions of the photo may or may not be softer, perhaps even purposely blurred. How a photographer handles this definitive aspect determines how another person will view the picture.

Where will a viewer's eyes be pulled to look first and most carefully? What will be the path they will follow within the picture? In other words, what will a person tend to look at second, third . . . last? What elements of the composition will have more emotional and intellectual weight than others, keeping the viewer's attention for longer? (See the sidebar "The Weighty Subject of Composition.")

No, focus isn't the only element that dictates the answers to these questions. Color, framing, angles, perspective, lines, and subject also play a role. But focus is one of the most powerful and subliminal of these tools for communicating exactly what you intended your photo to say.

The Weighty Subject of Composition

The *weight* of an item or area within your composition helps determine how a viewer will look at your picture. In other words, the more visual importance an item or area has, the sooner and longer it will hold a person's eye and interest. Factors in giving weight (or priority) photographically include:

- Focus
- Color
- Placement and relationship to other elements

If you keep the impact of these factors in mind when you compose your pictures, you can guide viewers along a path of visual clues that involuntarily make their eyes travel to where you want them first, second, third . . . or last, as they visually absorb what you wish to communicate.

Focus

A high degree of focus — sharpness and clarity — gives an item or area greater weight when compared to softer focus. (For examples of this phenomenon, see the various figures throughout the focus section of this chapter.) Similarly, just as you would use sharp focus to establish visual priority, using blur creatively can isolate, emphasize, and delineate important (in-focus) areas of your picture. There is a middle ground, too, in which an area in soft focus is weightier than one more fully blurred, but still secondary to something that's in crisp focus. Remember, this is controlled not only by how and where you focus, but also by your depth-of-field (see Chapter 5).

Color

Brighter, more vibrant colors have greater weight than cool, subdued colors. For instance, brilliant red will always attract the eye before almost any other color. Soft browns, olive greens, matte blacks, and similar muted colors tend to be less emphatic. It isn't simply the color of the main subject — it's also the contrast and relationship to the other colors in the composition that will make it stand out (see the first sidebar figure).

Placement and Relationship of Other Elements

Ever since the Renaissance, when artists "discovered" visual perspective, the lines, angles, and shapes of a composition have been recognized as literal pathways for directing the viewer's eye. Angles and lines point to the main subject in classic composition. Large shapes demand attention. Foreground tends to be weightier than background.

What's more, certain positions within a picture are considered to have greater strength than others. If you draw an imaginary tic-tac-toe grid on your scene, the "power points" tend to be at the intersections of the lines. But that's only an approximate guide. All such mathematical "rules" exist to be broken. The key is to be aware of how the placement of your main subject and other elements in your picture affect its emotional impact and its weight within the composition.

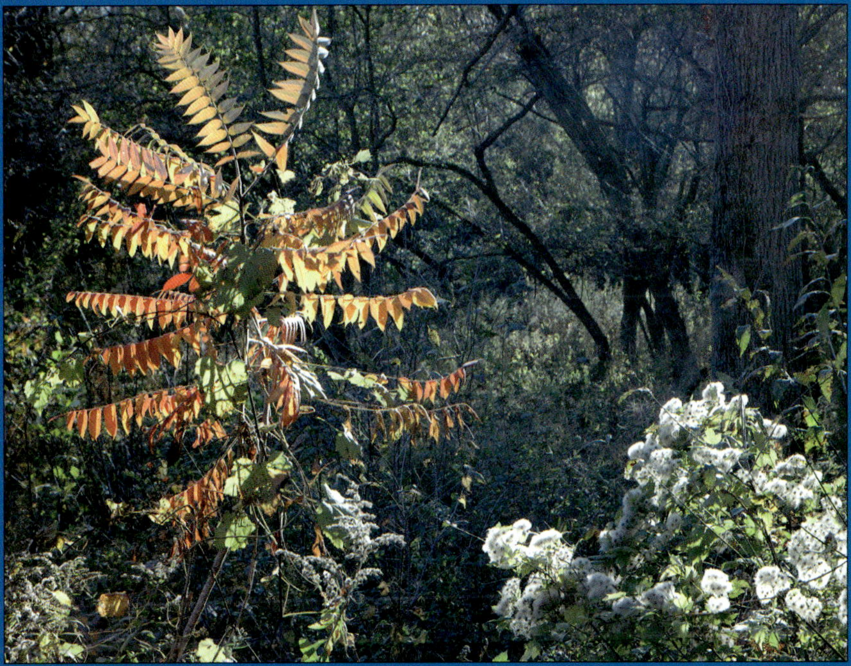

In this photograph of the chaos of the wild deep woods, the eye is pulled first and foremost to the red foliage. It is brighter, bigger, and red. The second area one tends to look is at the white weeds in the right foreground, which is brighter, bigger, and more forward than the other elements. On the other hand, the rest of the picture is made up of cool, dark greens, browns, and blacks, which cause those portions to recede visually, at least in comparison to the red bush. In addition, other elements, such as the white weeds and various dark or black limbs in the background — even the red bush's own trunk — point toward its red and gold leaves. (Photo taken with a Nikon D70, 24–120mm lens set at 52mm, 1/80 at *f*7.1.)

Tension

One other element that dramatically affects the impact of a photograph is its tension. All the above — focus, color, position, perspective, relationship — can contribute to tension. But more than that, it's a result of imbalance, the lack of symmetry, a sudden, sometimes unexpected break in homogeneity. Tension creates a visceral reaction to the picture that draws the viewer, impels him to look, to consider, to be attracted or repelled (see the second sidebar figure).

Continued

The Weighty Subject of Composition *(continued)*

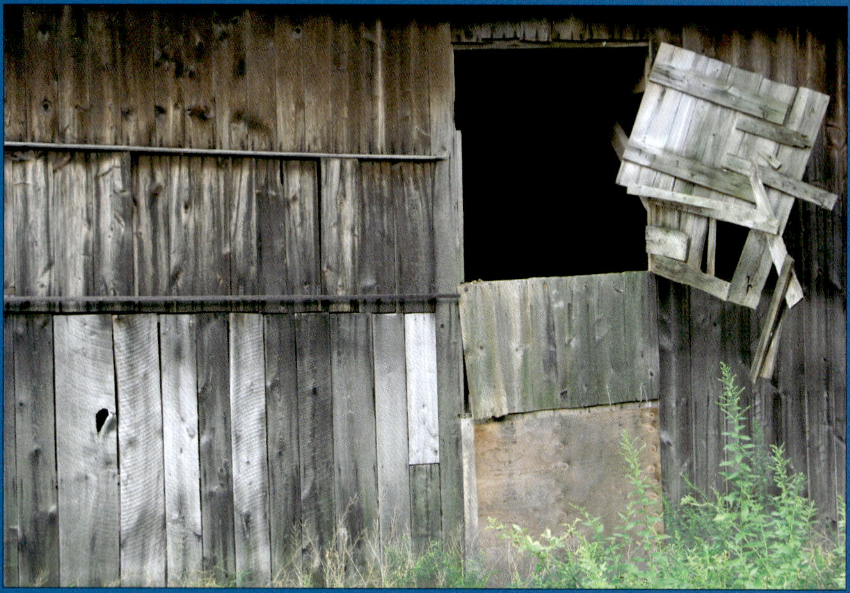

If the broken door of this old barn were in the middle of this composition, the photo would be much less interesting. Putting it in the upper-right corner creates an essential imbalance and tension, giving more visual weight where there is nothing — just the rectangle of black interior. In addition, the other most important areas of the picture (the broken door, the grass, the vertical bars that split the worn wood to the left) all point to that black rectangle. (Photo taken with a Nikon D2X, 24–120mm lens set at 40mm, 1/6 at f8.)

When using a DSLR, you must make three choices regarding focus:

- Whether or not to take full control over focus
- The type of focus tracking
- The point of focus

Unfortunately, many manufacturers confuse the issue by using the word *mode* for the controls of all three focus issues. You'll want to keep the concepts separate to make sure that you are covering all bases.

Tip

While focus defines the center of what will be sharp within your photograph, depth-of-field (which is controlled by the aperture, or *f*-stop) determines how much of the foreground and background will be in focus. Please see Chapter 5, for a discussion of depth-of-field.

Autofocus versus Manual

To shoot using your DSLR's autofocus mode, simply point your autofocus-enabled lens (most are) at a subject or area, press the shutter button down halfway, and the camera will snap into focus on that specific subject or area. This easy procedure works remarkably well in most situations. In fact, even top pros tend to rely on their DSLR's autofocus capability, because the electronics and mechanisms controlling autofocus are usually faster and much more precise than the human eye. (Please see the section "Choosing Your Focus Point or Area" later in this chapter for ways DSLRs help you handle focusing on off-center subjects.) However, autofocus isn't infallible. To understand why, you have to consider how it works.

Autofocus seeks out the darkest point within an area of contrast and then moves the servomotors within the lens to bring that point into greatest clarity. When it can't lock onto such a point, the servomotors will whine in and out, without finding a good focus. Or, it might lock onto the wrong point.

Autofocus can be confused by the following types of scenes:

- A low contrast or nighttime scene that doesn't give the camera anything on which to lock focus. (In the case of a dark scene, the camera may emit a focus assist light to give the lens something to lock on.)
- Other subjects that don't have enough variation in detail or light differentiation.
- Objects between you and your main subject that will draw the autofocus away from your main subject. These can include the bars of the zoo cage behind which a panther paces, a picket fence, or even forest foliage in front of romantic waterfall.
- A main subject that is too small and doesn't fill the focus area.

In addition, you might not agree with the focus the camera chooses because it doesn't give you quite the composition you had in mind.

That's why DSLRs also feature manual focus.

Just as in traditional film photography, DSLR lenses have a focusing ring or collar that you turn when you want or need to take control over focus away from the onboard computer. In some cameras, even if you have autofocus enabled, you can use the lens ring to fine-tune the focus. In other cameras, you have to flick a switch (usually on the front of the camera or on the lens) to use manual focus. Incidentally, many lenses come equipped with a friction-based focus collar that the photographer twists, while other lenses have an electronic "focus-by-wire" mechanism that activates a small motor when you turn the focus ring. Either way, they both accomplish the same thing by allowing the photographer to manually set the distance.

Locking Down Your Focus

If the main subject or area of your composition is off-center, traditionally, you would use the following classic method for choosing and locking in an off-center focus point:

1. Point the camera lens at the key subject or area of the scene.
2. Press the shutter button down halfway, which freezes or locks the focus (and exposure).
3. While still holding the shutter button down halfway, frame the scene (which may displace that key subject out of the center of the scene).
4. Press the shutter button all the way to capture the scene.

DSLRs also have AF-L (autofocus lock) and AE-L (auto exposure lock) buttons. Instead of holding the shutter button down halfway to lock in the focus and/or exposure, simply press the AF-L or AE-L button. Please see the "Choosing Your Focus Point or Area" section later in the chapter for discussions of other DSLR methods of doing so.

You're not entirely dependent upon your eye's visual acumen when focusing manually. As you turn the ring, a small dot (●) will appear in the optical viewfinder when you are in sharp focus and disappear when you aren't. In some cameras, if you are close to focus, the dot in the viewfinder will blink, and it may display arrows showing you which way to turn the lens to get a good focus.

Tip

Focus and depth-of-field are defined optically rather than digitally. Therefore, if you don't get them right when you take your picture, no amount of editing in the computer will fix blatant sharpness or out-of-focus problems — not even in your RAW utility.

Single versus Continuous Focus

With single shot focus, once you set your focus point and either hold your shutter button down halfway or use the focus lock button, the camera will maintain that exact focus point.

With continuous shooting, you set your focus point on a moving object, and the camera will continue to focus on that subject. This is great for shooting wildlife, sports, and running children. Depending on how advanced the camera's programming is, it may even analyze the movement and try to predict where the subject will be going next. In some cameras, you can set the focus point you want, so when the subject moves into the frame to that preselected point, the shutter automatically takes the picture.

In all the DSLRs we have tested, the single or continuous control is a lever or dial on the front of the camera, near the lens, or on the lens itself.

Unless you shoot mostly action subjects, we highly recommend that, after using continuous focus, you reset your camera to single shot before putting your camera away. Otherwise, on your next shoot, when you try to lock down your focus, you'll find your lens servomotor endlessly moving in and out, and not staying focused on the area or subject you have selected.

Choosing Your Focus Point or Area

As we mentioned, the traditional method for focusing on an off-center subject has been to lock down the focus using the AF-L button or to press the shutter button halfway and then to frame the shot. The biggest problem with either method becomes most apparent when you are using a tripod or camera stand. Though fixing a camera to a stand or tripod ensures a steadier, crisper picture, it also introduces a level of rigidity to the process of taking a picture. It isn't easy to physically move around, locking in focus onto an off-center item then reframing with each shot. That's one reason why DSLRs have variable focus points.

Variable (or flexible) focus points are displayed in the viewfinder, usually as small rectangles or circles distributed throughout the frame. How many you have and how they work will depend on your specific camera model. But generally, if you have flexible autofocus enabled, the currently selected area of focus will be illuminated red, while the inactive ones will be small black outlines. Usually, you turn a selector dial or use the jog buttons on the back of your camera to activate other focus points. (By the way, manufacturers tend to call flexible autofocus by a variety of names.) This gives you remarkable control over exactly what is in sharp focus and what isn't. (See Figures 6-1 through 6-4.)

With some cameras, you can allow the camera to use these points to analyze a scene, seeking out the closest subject, or you can manually select them. Another option offered by some cameras allows the photographer to select an area of focus, using these viewfinder indicators, and then the camera automatically focuses on the nearest subject within that specified area.

It takes much longer to explain in words than to perform. As you get used to the controls, you'll find that your fingers will move about them with the same instinctive ease they do when changing the zoom of your lens.

Tip

For those times that you want to be absolutely sure of your focus distance, professional DSLRs, such as the Canon EOS 1Ds Mark II and the Nikon D2X, have a focal plane symbol (ϕ) on the side of the camera cowl. (The cowl is the hump on the top that houses the optical viewfinder in pentaprism cameras.) Measure from that symbol to your subject for precise focus distance.

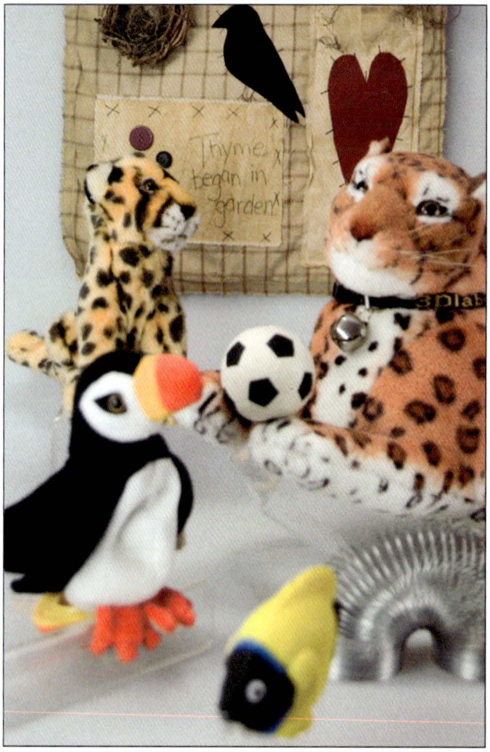

Figure 6-1: To illustrate the concept of flexible focus, all the items in this composition are situated to fit exactly at some of the focus points within the Nikon D2X viewfinder. For all these photos, our focal length was 45mm, and our exposure was 1/60 at *f*5.3, which limited the depth-of-field. Here, we selected the upper point, to focus on the crow in the hanging.

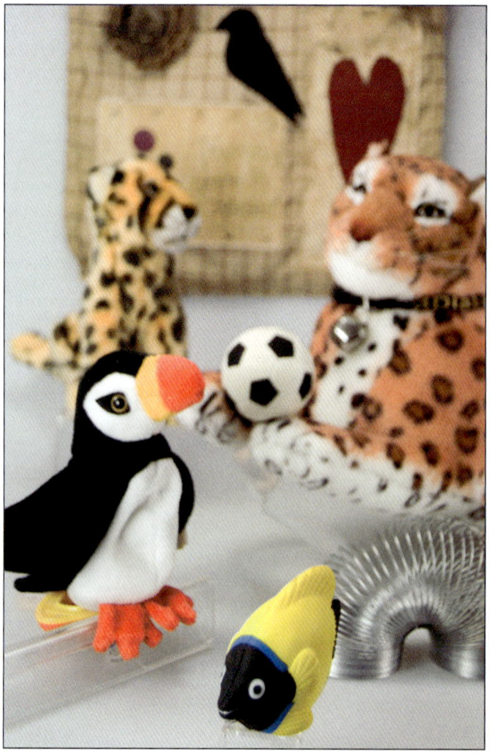

Figure 6-2: In this shot, we focused on the fish in the foreground. Notice that the puffin is soft but certainly closer to being in focus than the elements further toward the background. Given that the puffin is larger than the fish, the puffin tends to have almost the same "weight" as the fish in this version of the composition. That's why the slight softness of the puffin feels somehow wrong when you look at it too long.

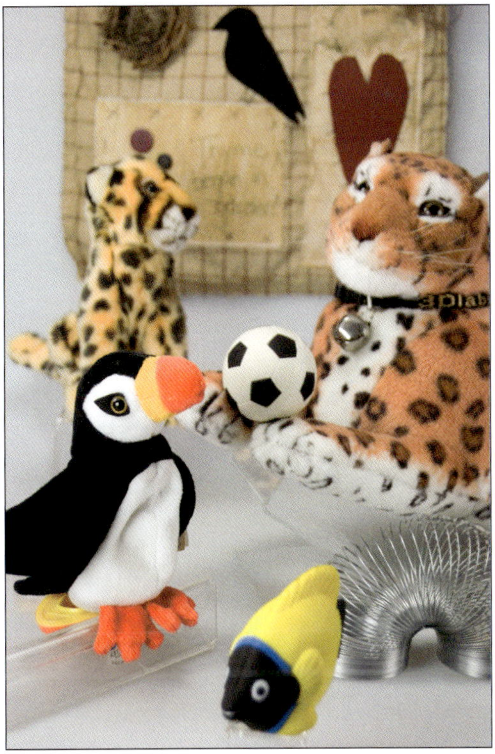

Figure 6-3: When we focus on the puffin and allow the fish to be in soft focus, the puffin becomes unquestionably the most important element in this version.

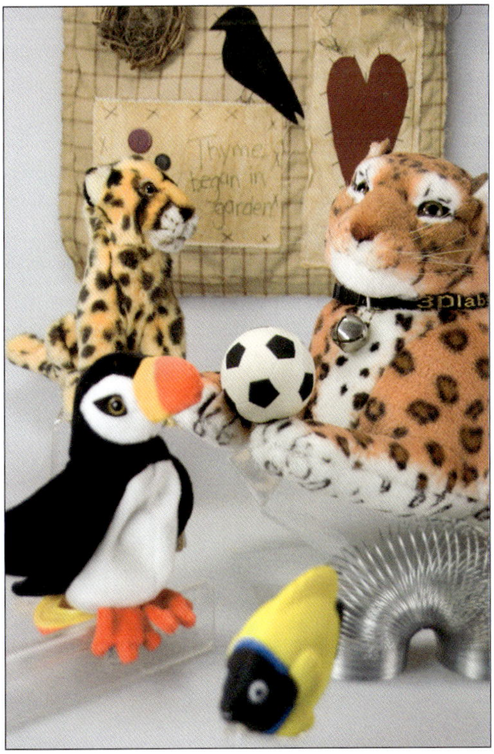

Figure 6-4: Focusing on the big cat's eyes brings its face into sharp clarity, softens his front legs, the small cat, and the background hanging, while blurring the puffin, slinky, and fish.

In-Camera Color Controls

How we perceive color and process it in our brains is one of the more human things we do. The blue of a summer sky, the green of a grassy meadow, the warm skintones of a healthy, happy baby — color is much more than varying wavelengths of light. In addition to being densely packed with information about the world around us, color is visceral and emotional.

Cameras, scanners, computers, monitors, and printers can't possibly see and use color the way we do. In fact, the science of color is, at best, a series of educated guesses that attempt to emulate the human perception and response to color.

And yet, DSLR technology has advanced sufficiently that it can provide various color controls that help you get the image you envision. The two most important in-camera color tools are the ability to select your color model and white balance.

Choosing the Right Color Model

In their attempt to understand and reproduce color, scientists have come up with a variety of ways, or models, to describe how color is created. We go more deeply into color models in Chapter 11. What is important here is to understand the differences between the two color models that all DSLRs offer — sRGB and Adobe RGB — and how to choose the right one for your needs.

Both sRGB and Adobe RGB create photos using the primary colors of red (R), green (G), and blue (B). But they do it in different ways so that the results are different. These differences will affect the way the colors of your photos will be reproduced. So, it's important to select the correct model (or color matrix) for the type of output you plan.

sRGB is best suited for the Web and screen-based presentations. In addition, it's the most appropriate model to use when you plan to output to desktop printers or kiosks without doing any color adjustments in your computer. This is especially true of memory card–enabled or any other direct to print desktop printers that don't require a computer. (See Chapter 12, regarding printing.)

Adobe RGB creates a wider range (or gamut) of usable colors than sRGB. What's more, Adobe RGB imbeds an ICC profile into the photo file that automatically informs some output devices how the colors were defined and created. If you plan to do any color editing on your photo (which, by its very nature, destroys some image data), it's best to start out with as much data as possible by shooting in Adobe RGB. In addition, we recommend using Adobe RGB if you plan to output to professional-quality printers, to printing presses, or through a service bureau.

If you aren't sure which color model you will need, Adobe RGB is the safer bet. That's because you can always decrease the number of your colors to sRGB's more limited gamut. But if you shoot in sRGB and find you need more colors, you'll have to allow the computer to invent (interpolate) the colors. That generally doesn't produce as good quality as capturing all the colors from the start. In addition, the ICC profile is invaluable should you decide that one particular photo would be great for an exhibition print or a book you are preparing.

Tip

If you post an Adobe RGB photo on the Web or use it in a PowerPoint-type or screen-based presentation, the colors will look dull. So, be sure to convert to sRGB first.

Some cameras have more than one version of these sRGB and Adobe RGB color models, designed specifically for portraits, landscapes, and so on. The preceding guidelines still apply, but you'll need to refer to the camera manual to choose among the variations of each color model.

Getting Whites Truly White

One of the things that the human eye does better than any device or machine is see the colors that are meant to be, rather than the colors that are really there. If you work in an office with inexpensive fluorescent lights, you still see your coworker's white shirt as white. The red roses the receptionist received for Valentine's Day will appear brilliantly red to your eyes. But if you take a photo under the same fluorescents, without making the appropriate adjustments to the camera's settings, everything in your picture will have a sickly yellow-green cast. In fact, every type of light has its own inherent color cast. Your eye, in combination with your brain, automatically filters out these color imperfections. A camera cannot, unless you help it along, by using its white balance controls.

White balance is one of the controls that give digital photography an unassailable edge over film photography. It works on the principle that the light in a scene will add the same amount of the same color cast over the entire scene. (This is assuming that the lighting is comparatively uniform. We'll deal with mixed lighting later.) Therefore, to adjust the camera's perceptions of color so that it captures white as truly white (or neutral grey as pure, neutral grey), the camera needs to analyze how much of what color contaminant needs to be removed from the whites and greys. That removal of color is applied to the entire scene, giving you more realistic colors in your photograph.

WHITE BALANCE PRESETS

DSLRs (and most consumer and prosumer digital cameras) have preset white balance settings (see Figure 6-5), which may include:

- Auto
- Daylight
- Incandescent (household-type light bulbs)
- Fluorescent
- Shade
- Cloudy
- Flash

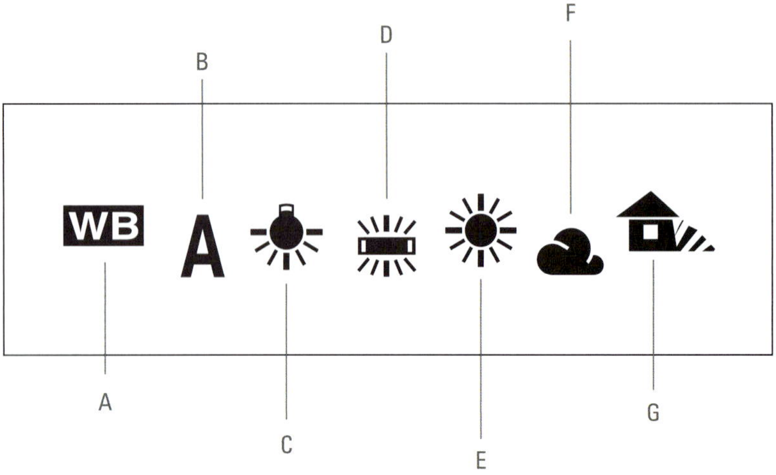

Figure 6-5: White balance preset icons vary on every camera that has them. However, they do tend to be pictographs similar in theme to these from the Nikon D70. (A) WB is usually the designation identifying the button to press to access the white balance controls. (B) Auto white balance is often indicated by a capital A or AWB. (C) A round light bulb is usually used for tungsten, incandescent, household lights. (D) Some kind of tube, often with light rays, is for fluorescent light. Your camera may have more than one fluorescent setting to try to accommodate the variations among standard fluorescent lights. (E) Daylight white balance is typically an obvious sun icon. (F) We've found the cloudy icons used by different camera manufacturers may sometimes be difficult to discern. This one is rather clear. (G) The shade icon can be a house projecting a shadow. (Graphic courtesy of Nikon Corporation)

Auto white balance actually works well in many situations; it's more effective if there is an element of pure white or grey in the scene (though not always necessary) to give the camera something to help it with its color analysis.

With the exception of Auto, you choose among white balance presets based on the primary source of light in the scene. Using the correct white balance for the light is very important, if you want to capture the best color. (See Figure 6-6.)

The problem is that all presets are based on a specific color temperature that the camera's designers determined to be typical. But color temperatures (see the sidebar "Taking the Temperature of Your Lights") vary considerably. For instance, typical light bulbs are not standardized. Their temperature can be dependent on the manufacturer, the day they rolled off the assembly line, their age, the amount and steadiness of the electricity flowing to them, and other factors. Even daylight is a moving target, with different color temperatures depending on the time of day, the season, the weather, even the longitude of the location.

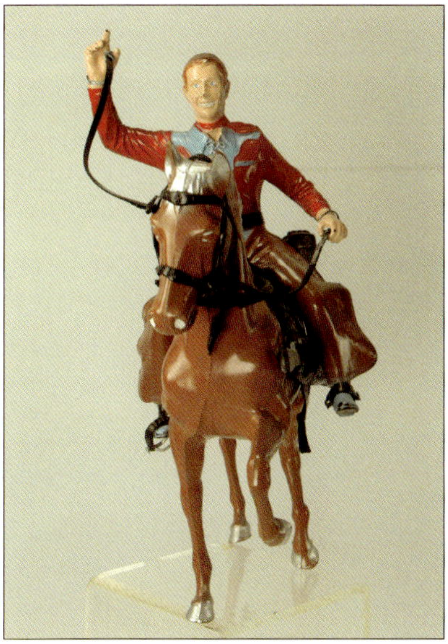

(A)

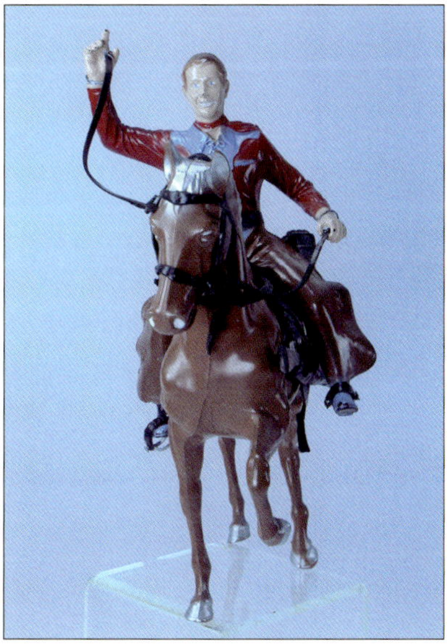

(B)

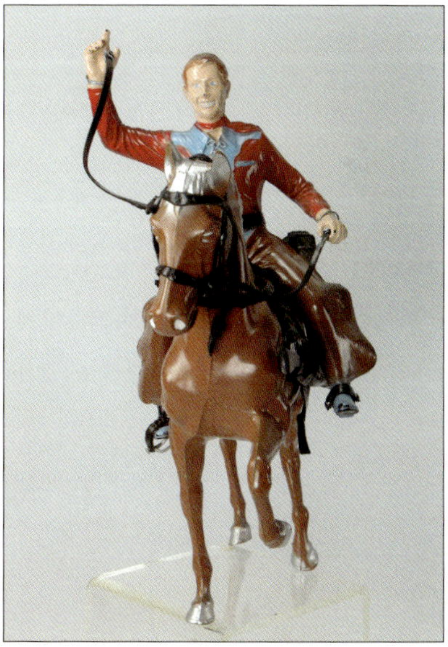

(C)

Figure 6-6: This Roy Rogers doll was photographed on our white shooting table under color-corrected, stabilized daylight (5000° Kelvin) lights. When we used the wrong white balance setting, our colors came out all wrong. (A) This version was shot using a fluorescent preset. (B) Then, we shot it using an incandescent present. (C) For this setup and scene, the Auto white balance setting gave us the cleanest colors. What is interesting is that though the color casts of version (A) and (B) distorted the skin tones of the doll, many people will automatically compensate for it and think they see a healthy face. This is even more true if the person in the photograph happens to be someone they love, such as a child. But serious photographers must see as their cameras see, not as a grandparent might. (Photos taken with a Pentax *ist D, 18–55mm lens set at 33mm, 1/20 at *f*8.)

Tip

On those DSLRs that don't have mode dials with various presets for portrait, landscape, and such, you might find something similar in their menus. Some of the more expensive cameras, such as the Canon EOS-1D Mark II and the Nikon D2X, have combination presets of white balance, color model, saturation, and other image settings that they may identify only by number in the menu and an explanatory chart in the camera manual.

Taking the Temperature of Your Lights

The color of light is measured as color temperature, in degrees Kelvin. The table following this sidebar gives general guidelines on color temperature. However, it is important to remember that no natural light source or general purpose, nonstabilized bulbs give infallible, unchangeable light. The numbers are approximations only. Like most other professional photographers, we use a color temperature meter to precisely measure the color temperature of a scene.

Light source	*Approximate Color Temperature in Degrees Kelvin*
Candlelight	1800
Household tungsten incandescent light bulb	2800–3200
Sunrise or sunset daylight	2000
Midday sunny daylight near New York City in the summer	5300–5900
Average cloudy day	6000

The idealized daylight is often said to be 5000–5500 degrees Kelvin. But a wide range of factors affect the color temperature of light. When shooting outside, it can be impacted by the weather, time of day, season, geographical location, reflectivity of the subject, and so on. When shooting indoors, the age of light bulbs, any dust or dirt on the bulbs, the strength and stability of the electricity, the nature of ambient light coming in from the outside, and other variables directly affect the color temperature.

In Chapter 8, we go into greater depth about controlling, measuring, and using light.

MORE PRECISE WHITE BALANCE CONTROLS

White balance presets are based on idealized scenarios rather than real-world lighting. In the real world, or even in the studio, where you might have a great deal of control over your lighting, the situation is seldom ideal. The color temperature of similar light sources can vary widely. Even the same lights, using the same electricity, can be a specific temperature one day and another the next. You might have mixed lighting from a variety of sources, one of your bulbs may be significantly older than the others, or any of a number of other factors might skew the color temperature.

That's why DSLRs offer additional white balance controls. Depending on your camera model, you may have one, two, or all three of the following tools:

- Custom white balance
- Manual white balance
- Reference image

Custom White Balance

Custom white balance is probably one of the easiest custom tools you'll ever use. Simply do the following:

1. Activate custom white balance in your camera. (Check your camera manual to determine what buttons and/or dials select the command.)
2. Put a piece of white paper in your scene, under the lights you plan to use. We frequently use a sheet of standard photocopy paper for this purpose.
3. Zoom in so that the white paper fills your viewfinder.
4. Press the shutter button.

That's all there is to it. Your camera's white balance is now set to fully understand how to handle the colors of the scene under those specific lights.

Tip

The biggest problem with white balance is to remember to turn any presets, custom, manual, or other white balance settings off when you are no longer shooting under the current light conditions. After every shoot, we try to remember to put our white balance back to Auto. When we forget, we can end up with some rather strange colors in the next shoot.

Manual White Balance

Using a color temperature meter, measure the lighting in your scene. Then, set your camera's manual white balance to the number of degrees Kelvin that the meter indicates would be appropriate to the shoot. If you get several different color temperature readings across your subject (which sometimes occurs when you are using more than one light source), average the readings and use that number to set your camera. (Or, choose the reading that covers the greatest portion of your main subject and use white balance bracketing, as we discuss in the next section.)

Reference Image

Your camera's software may allow you to upload a specific photo to your camera's memory. Or, you may be able to indicate that the camera should refer to a particular photo saved on the current memory card. It would then attempt to emulate the white balance of that reference image.

WHITE BALANCE BRACKETING

Bracketing is a long-established procedure that photographers have used for decades to zero in on the perfect exposure. (See Chapter 5.) Some digital cameras also offer white balance bracketing (and, as we discuss in Chapter 8, flash bracketing).

As its name implies, when you set your camera for white balance bracketing, it will take several photos of the same scene, adjusting the white balance slightly with each shot. The theory is that one of those pictures within the series will be bang-on with accurate colors. (See Figure 6-7.)

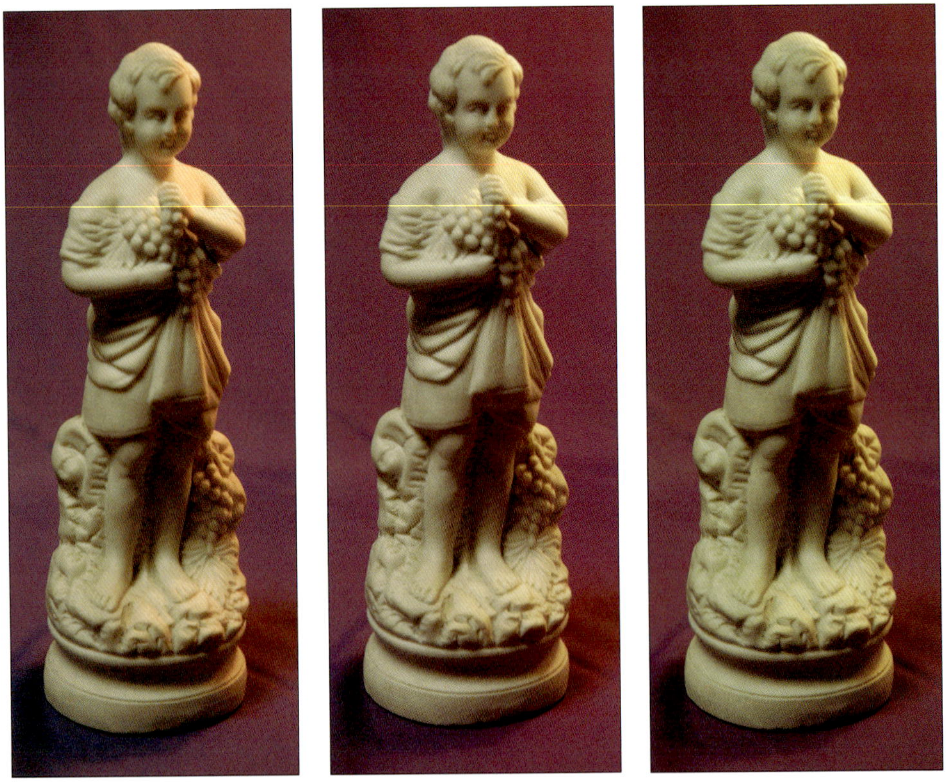

(A) (B) (C)

Figure 6-7: This Parian statue was photographed under a single tungsten light, the white balance was set to tungsten, and then white balance bracketing was used, which automatically created these three versions: (A) with no adjustment, (B) with a magenta bias, and (C) with a green bias. (Photos taken with a Canon 20D, 17–85mm lens set at 68mm, 1/6 at *f*5.6.)

Incidentally, some cameras that don't have white balance auto-bracketing may feature white balance compensation. Like exposure compensation, white balance compensation allows you to manually dial in minus and plus values to the current white balance setting. For manual white balance bracketing, shoot one setting, change the white balance compensation, shoot the same scene again, and change the white balance compensation in the other direction before shooting a third time.

Playing with Colors

One other type of color control some cameras have allows you to directly alter the colors that will be captured. These settings may involve choosing among standard, vivid, or subdued colors, which are exactly as they sound. (See Figures 6-8 and 6-9.)

If you remember the film days, then you might recall FujiFilm Velvia, a film emulsion that heightened colors unnaturally, but beautifully. On the other hand, Kodachrome tended to be more natural and true to life. And some emulsions, such as AgfaChrome, were comparatively subdued. We would choose our film emulsion based on which type of color would be appropriate for the subject and the assignment.

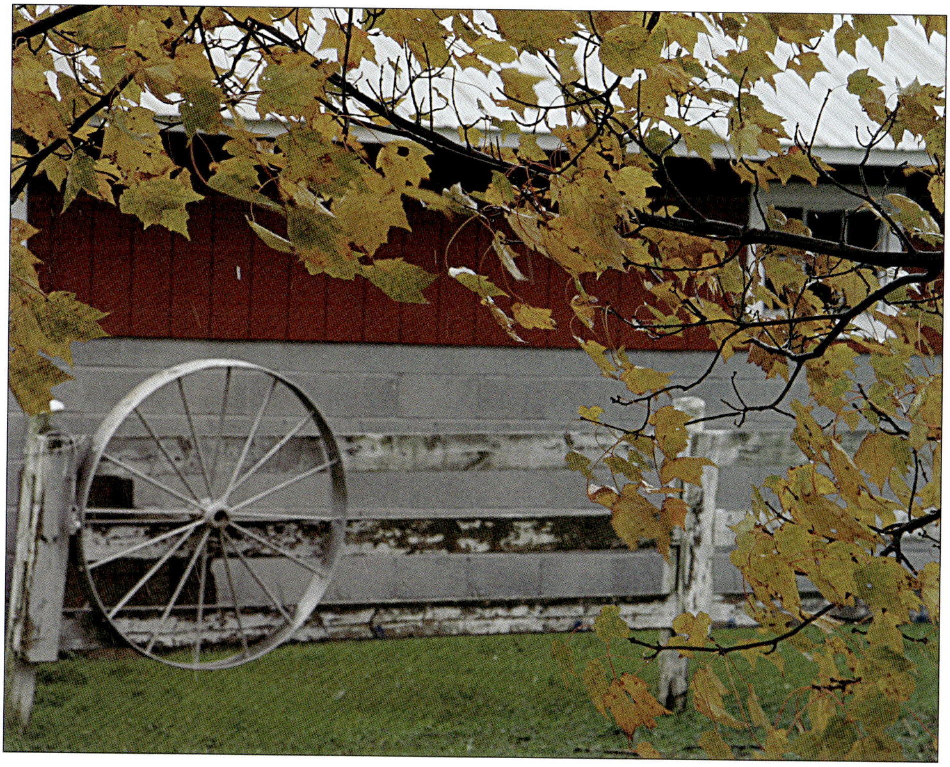

Figure 6-8: Shooting using a standard or normal color setting tends to produce accurate colors. In this situation, in which we were photographing in the rain, that meant that the colors we captured were a bit dull. (Both photos taken with a Canon 20D, 17–85mm lens set at 80mm, 1/125 at *f*8.)

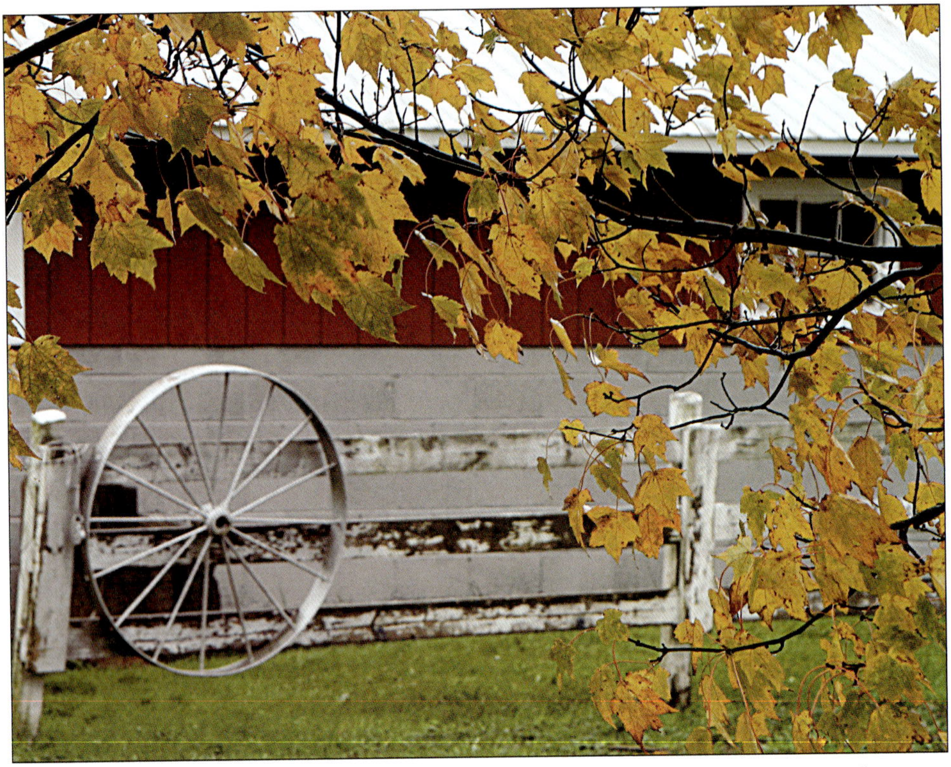

Figure 6-9: Selecting a more vivid color setting, we were able to capture the full vibrancy of autumn.

Choosing the type of color among vivid, standard, and subdued colors on a digital camera works the same way, with one major difference. Every frame you shoot can have a different type color, rather than shooting a whole roll of 12, 24, or 36 exposures of one kind. When we want to play with color, we will often bracket a scene, shooting several frames at different color settings.

Another color control your camera may have is hue adjustment. For instance, in the Nikon D2X, you can adjust the hue of your picture up to +/- 9 degrees in 3 degree increments. To understand what this means, look at Figure 6-10.

Given that there are 360 degrees to the circle of the hue wheel, adjustments of 3 degrees, or even 9 degrees are rather subtle. And in most cases, we have found them unnecessary. However, if you know that such a subtle change is just what you need under certain lights, using it may save you time in postprocessing.

Tip

When you use Auto settings for color controls or image processing, don't expect the same results every time. Your camera will automatically analyze the current scene and then choose the best setting it feels is appropriate for that particular situation. Similarly, More and Less settings can vary with each shoot.

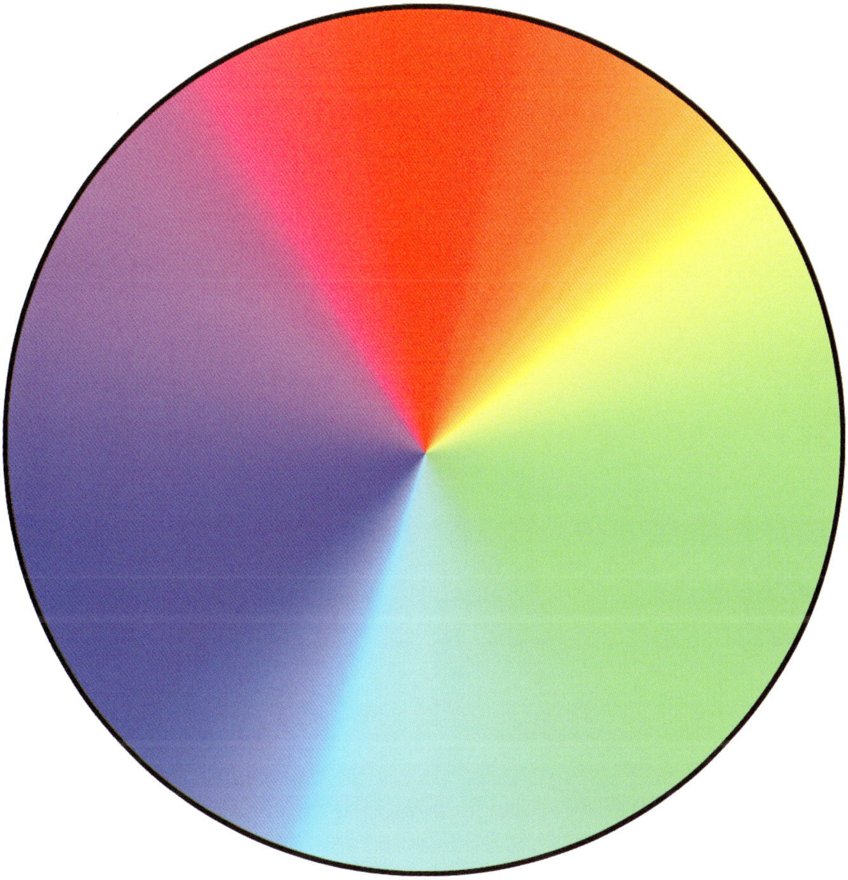

Figure 6-10: This is a hue wheel. When the hue of a photo is adjusted, the colors are displaced in one direction or the other around this wheel. (Actually, most hue wheels you see will also have a continuum of saturation density or lightness from the center to the edge, but that doesn't apply to these camera hue controls.)

Digital Black-and-White Photography

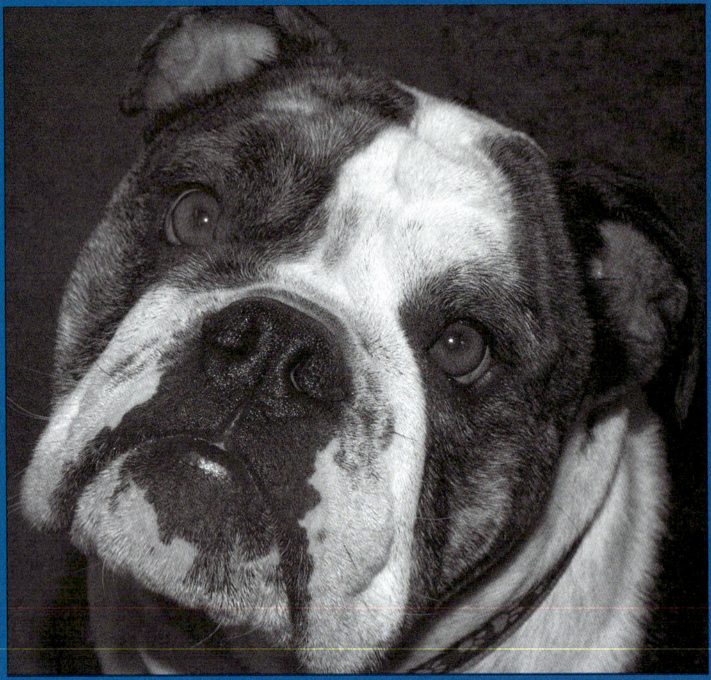

One color setting that has a strong following among fine art photographers is no color — that is, black-and-white photography. In some cameras, b&w is a setting you can choose. Even those cameras that don't offer a specific black-and-white setting can be forced to shoot monochrome by simply toning down the saturation all the way. In both cases, you'll end up with a 24-bit RGB image.

However, it is important to remember that black-and-white photography has very different requirements than color in terms of contrast and tone. You'll probably want to increase contrast and perhaps even use a custom tone curve. If the camera doesn't have color filter options, you might want to use optical filters to bring out specific tones in the greyscale. (Please see Chapter 3 regarding optical filters.)

For our personal fine art work, we prefer to shoot in full color, so we have all the data captured. Then, we use our RAW utility and/or Photoshop's Channel Mixer to convert our photos to monochrome or duotone, with greater precision. That also gives us the option of bringing back small portions of the original color into our black-and-white pictures. (Please see Chapter 10, regarding converting to monochrome in a photo-editing program.)

Other Image Processing

If you don't shoot RAW (or if you shoot JPEG concurrently with RAW), your camera's computer will process the captured image data, converting it into a digital photograph. (See Chapter 4, regarding RAW.) This involves analyzing the data and colors, particularly the relationship of light and dark areas, according to factory (default) settings established by the camera manufacturer. You can override these factory settings by choosing from a handful of other options in your camera's menu, including:

- Sharpening
- Tone compensation (contrast)
- Saturation
- Noise reduction

With all of the preceding image controls, the menu options are typically multiple choice, offering either On/Off, or Low, High, and Auto settings. Some cameras may add Medium Low and Medium High. Others will represent your choices in a sliding scale on which you dial your choice. In the higher-end cameras, you may have the ability to create custom settings.

The problem is the difficulty in determining how much is low or medium low, and so on. And the results of using these relative settings can vary, depending upon the scene you are shooting as well as your other settings. So, for the sake of being able to predict exactly what any of these settings will do to your photographs, we strongly suggest taking some test shots in various situations. Keep those photos on your computer's hard drive, and reference them periodically to help you decide when and if you want to use any of these in-camera image options.

On the other hand, if you are setting up for a shoot using controlled lighting, you can do your test shots, study them in the computer, and then make your adjustments to each of these options. That way, you'll know exactly what you will be getting. It's not that different from setting up your lights, checking exposure, and making sure the model's makeup and clothes are right.

Tip

When you are applying or judging sharpening or focus edits on your computer, be sure to view your photo at 100 percent magnification to have an accurate view of how the photo is changed by these tools.

Sharpening

Every digital camera adds some sharpening to non-RAW images. (Some DSLRs allow you to turn it off, if you wish.) Though the algorithms (internal programming) may vary from model to model, the typical process analyzes the transition areas between dark and light and attempts to enhance the contrast at those points, to give the appearance of greater image sharpness. That's because the human eye sees well-delineated lines of contrast as sharpness. In fact, inexpensive consumer cameras used to put a one-pixel black line where they detected lines. (Some of the really cheap ones may still do that, but we haven't seen this annoying practice in any brand-name cameras we've tested in recent years.)

Oversharpening a picture can severely damage image quality, actually destroying pixels and significantly degrading otherwise smooth photorealistic gradients. Fortunately, the small amount of factory set auto-sharpening that DSLRs do is quite subtle and certainly acceptable under most shooting circumstances when we're shooting JPEG. When we are shooting RAW, we prefer handling sharpening in the RAW conversion utility on our computer. (See Chapter 4.)

On the other hand, we don't adjust the sharpening settings in the camera very often. We prefer to take full control over sharpening in our computer, when we have the color-calibrated, full-sized preview of the photo on our computer monitor where we can judge precisely what level we want to use. Then again, we occasionally break our own rules and do some in-camera sharpening adjustments. (See Figure 6-11.)

As you become more familiar and comfortable with your camera, you may wish to invoke varying degrees of sharpening to handle specific shooting situations. For instance, you might want low sharpening (that is, a slight softness) for portraits or similar situations when you want to diminish the impact of unattractive details (such as wrinkles). Or, you might know (as we did when taking Figure 6-8) that the circumstances of the shoot will be cutting down on your picture's sharpness.

Tip

Sharpening a picture, either using the camera's controls or your photo-editing software, does not remedy poor focus. Achieving proper focus at the instant of photo capture is absolutely essential and cannot be handed off to technology. That's because no amount of correction can properly compensate for an out-of-focus picture. It's always better to reshoot to capture a sharp image. Of course, DSLRs' autofocus options make it much easier to achieve a solid focus lock on the area you want. (See the focus section earlier in this chapter.)

Tone Compensation, or Contrast

Contrast, like sharpening, is an important aspect of every photograph. (See Figure 6-12.) When done right, you don't even notice it, but when overdone, it destroys data. Conversely, low contrast produces flat, uninteresting photographs. We use our in-camera contrast controls very sparingly, but we have found them to be useful in certain situations.

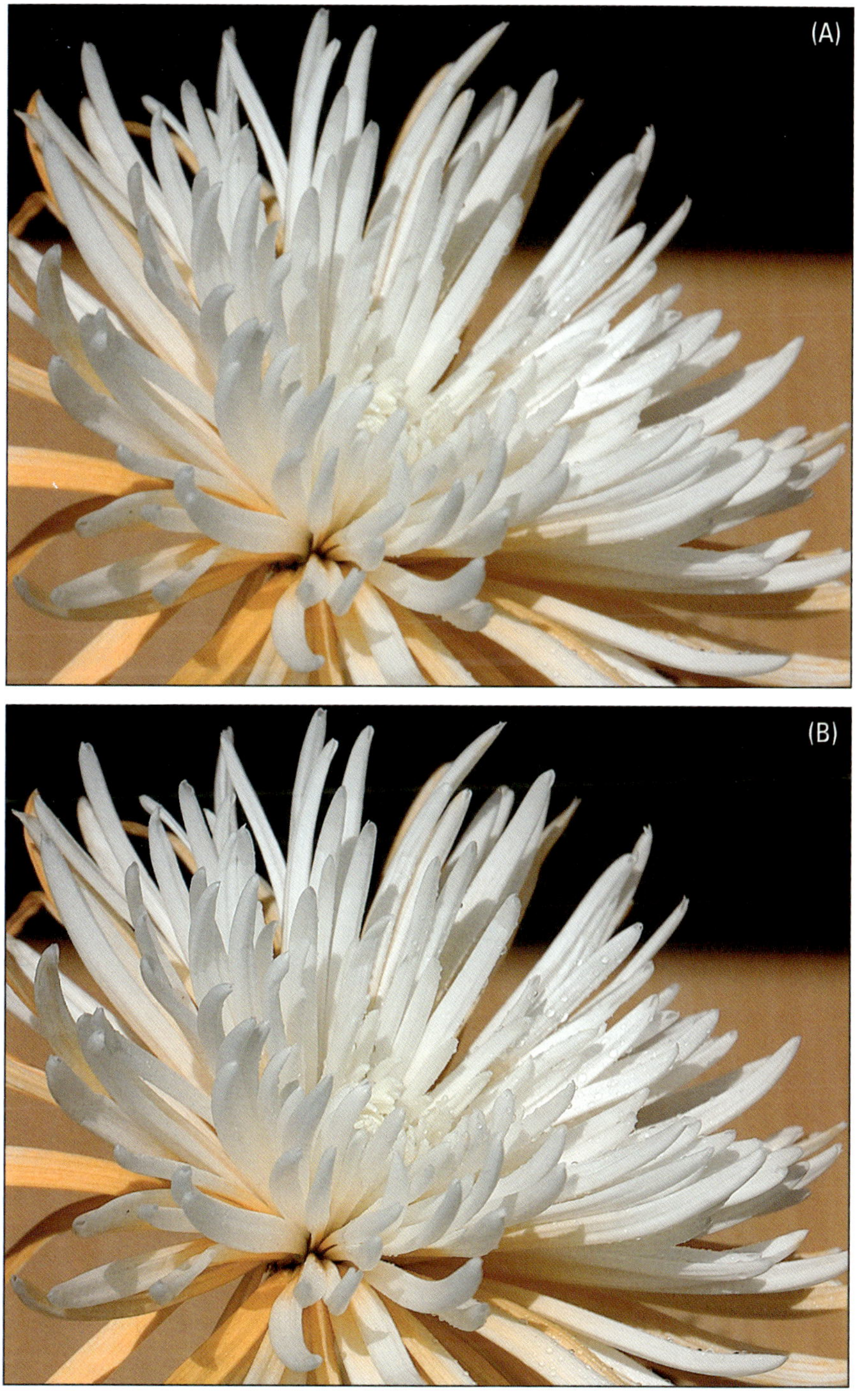

Figure 6-11: (A) We shot this flower through window glass, which cut down on the sharpness of the picture. (B) Setting sharpening at High made the water drops much more distinct and interesting, but the change is subtle and doesn't degrade image quality. (Photos taken with a Nikon D70, 24–120mm lens set at 40mm, 1/2000 at *f*5.6.)

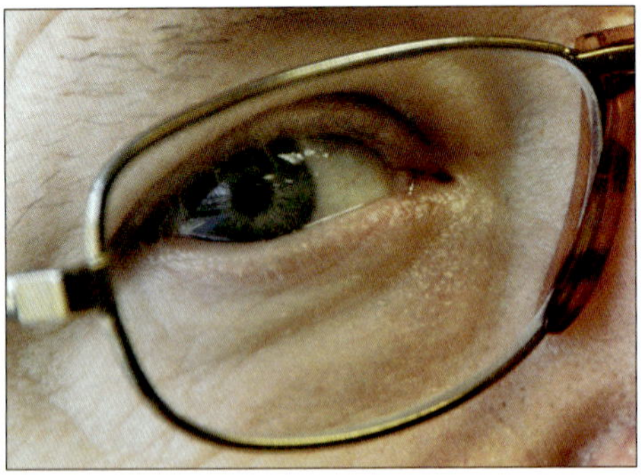

(A) High contrast

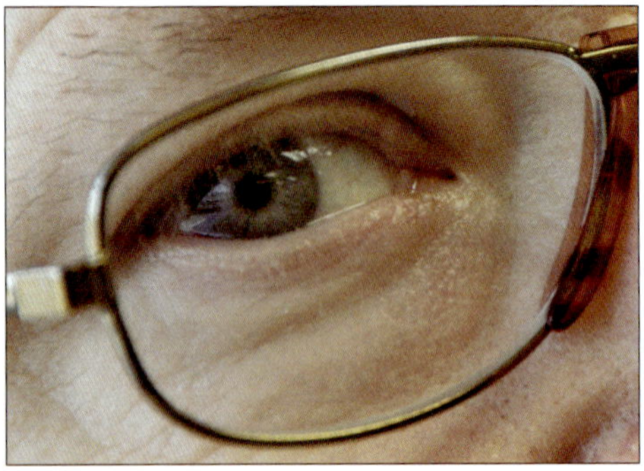

(B) Medium high contrast

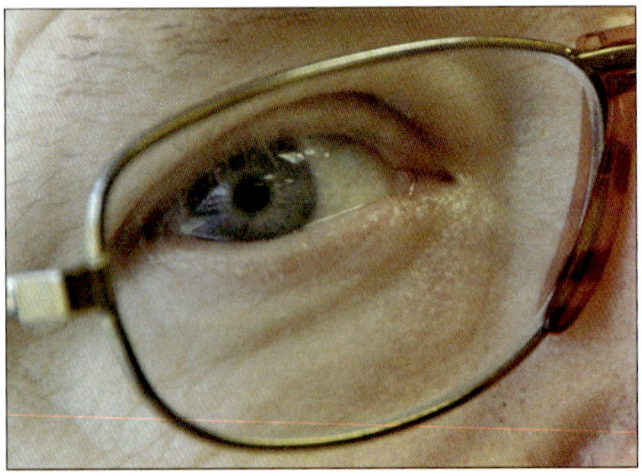

(C) No contrast adjustment

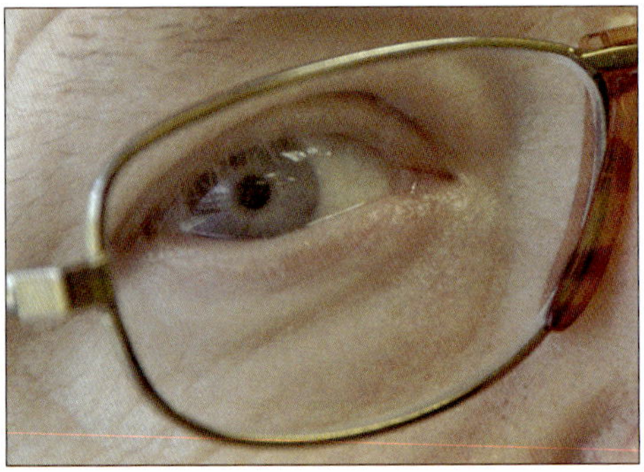

(D) Medium low contrast

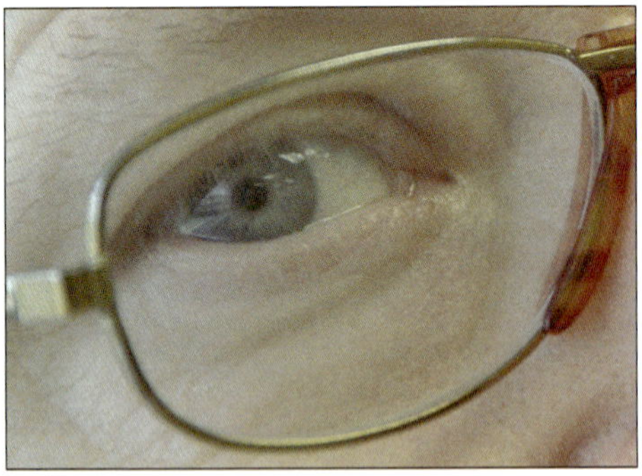

(E) Low contrast

Figure 6-12: Looking at the varying contrast levels of these five pictures, we prefer the one to which we applied a medium high contrast setting. The problem we have using in-camera contrast settings is that we can't really judge which is best unless and until we view the photo on a full-sized calibrated computer monitor. The camera's small LCD screen just doesn't give us enough visual data to make a judgment call. (Photos taken with a Nikon D2X, 24–120mm lens set at 120mm, 1/8 at *f*5.6.)

Having in-camera contrast options can be very useful in certain circumstances. For instance, if we are shooting in a very high-contrast environment, where important scene details are in the extreme highlights or shadows, setting contrast to medium low may bring out more of those details. This is especially useful when we know that our final output device has a limited gamut — that is, it can't reproduce those extreme highlights and shadows.

If the lighting is flat, such as outside at midday or when the sky is very overcast, then we sometimes will increase our contrast. Similarly, a fog scene also may require a contrast boost, though that could counter the effect you are trying to achieve by shooting in fog.

Increasing or decreasing contrast is only one type of tone compensation. In some DSLRs, you can create a custom tone curve in your computer and upload it to your camera. What that means is that you can manipulate the relative values of the entire exposure range from highlights through the midtones to shadows.

To understand this concept, take a look at a few tone curves in Figures 6-13, 6-14, and 6-15.

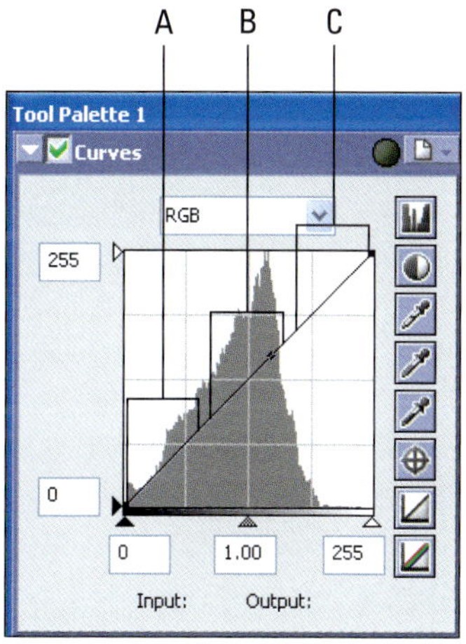

Figure 6-13: This is the tone curve for Figure 6-12 (C). Notice that the diagonal line is a straight 45 degrees, which is the normal state, indicating that no changes have been made to it yet. That line bisects tonal regions of the photo: (A) the shadows, (B) the midtones, and (C) the highlights. (Tone curve screen captures taken from Nikon Capture software)

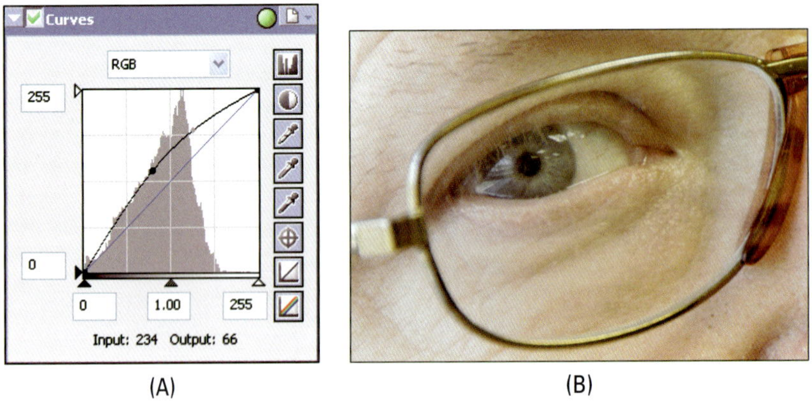

Figure 6-14: (A) We can change the shape of that bisecting line in the tone curve to affect the exposure of pixels in the related exposure range. In this curve, we've pulled down on the midtone section, moving those pixels further toward the shadows. In other words, we've darkened the midtones, while not altering the highlights or shadows. (B) You can see the effect of using this tone curve by comparing this photo to Figure 6-12 (C).

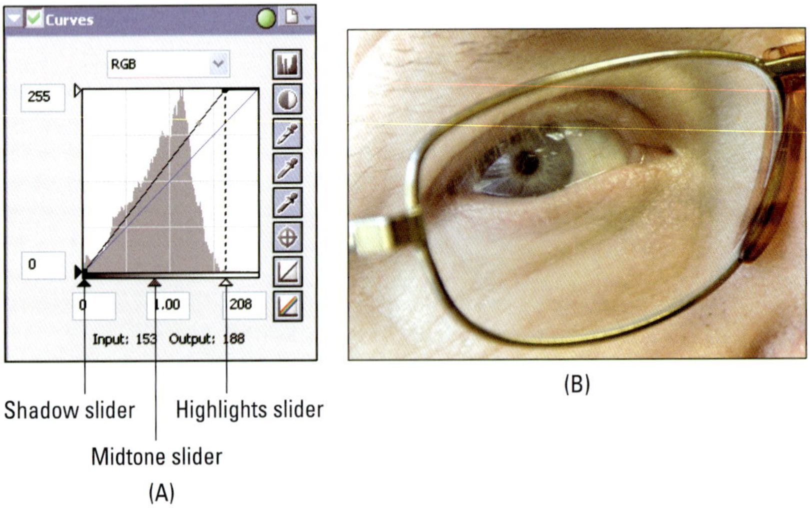

Figure 6-15: You can also adjust a tone curve by pushing on the shadow, midtone, and highlights markers, which force the pixels to remap to new exposure levels. (A) In this curve, we pushed the highlights slider downward, which creates an overall brighter picture, as you can see in (B).

Figures 6-14A and 6-15A are examples of two types of tone curves you might upload into your camera's tone compensation function. It's useful only if you know beforehand the precise lighting conditions and want or need to adjust it in your camera without changing or moving your lights.

Tip

If you get to a point that you've changed so many settings on your DSLR and aren't sure what they are or if they are correct or even relevant, most digital cameras have a reset option that puts everything back to their factory default settings. In many cases (but not all), simply removing the camera battery, waiting a few seconds for the charge to drain, and then reinserting the battery, will also reset the camera.

Noise Reduction

Noise, those ugly misplaced color pixels that mar the smoothness and appeal of your photos, increases with high ISO settings and very slow shutter speeds, such as those below 1/2 second. (See Figure 6-16.)

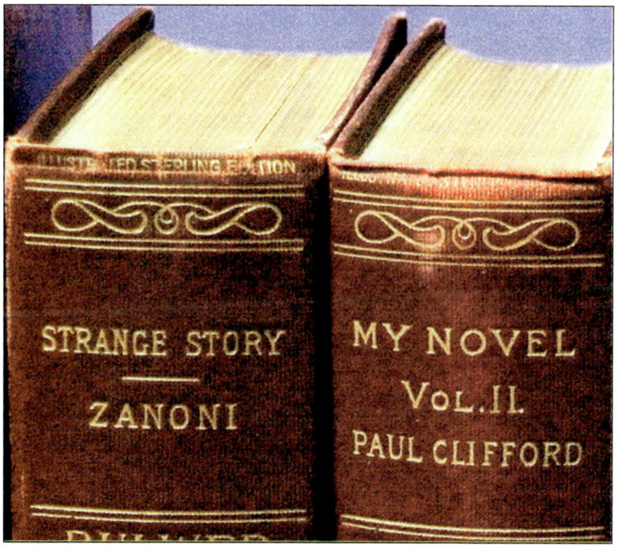

Figure 6-16: Shot in a poorly lit room, with a shutter speed of 30 seconds (and an aperture of *f*5), this photo exhibits considerable noise.

Some cameras have a noise suppression option. Unfortunately, turning it on means that your camera will have to do considerable extra image processing, during which time you cannot continue to shoot. (If your camera is busy reducing noise, it is using memory and other resources that would otherwise be devoted to shooting.) An even greater deterrent is the fact that the noise reduction doesn't always make much of a difference in the quality of the photo.

Whenever possible, we prefer adding light to a scene to counter the potential for long exposure noise. Or, if possible, we open up the lens and shoot at the largest *f*-stop. Of course, if there is no other way to get a photo than using a long exposure, and if it really is a picture that you want, then, by all means, shoot. In those situations, we would take two pictures, one with and one without the noise suppression—just in case we don't like what the noise reduction algorithm does to the sharpness of our photograph.

Custom Defaults

Every camera ships with default settings that were determined by the factory to be what they consider optimum for typical situations. But you can set your own defaults.

Sally often uses spot focus, aperture priority, Adobe RGB, RAW+JPEG (at lowest JPEG compression), and auto-white-balance. So, she has set that as the first user default on all our cameras. That way, whenever we change our settings to something else, to accommodate other shooting conditions, she presses a single button to reset to her personal defaults.

Every DSLR allows its users to set up one or more custom default settings. This allows you to set a separate series of user defaults for specific color settings, such as saturation, color type, white balance, hue, and so on. For instance, if you tend to use the same lighting setups in your studio, define a default profile that stores the specific white balance setting you use with those lights. However, we do recommend checking the color temperature of your studio lights from time to time, since that can become a moving target as bulbs and equipment age, dust settles, or electricity fluctuates. (See Chapter 8.)

Can't I Just Photoshop It?

Photo-editing software makes it quite easy to change all the definitive aspects of a picture — color, smoothness, sharpness, contrast, and so on. But think before you plan to fix a photo in the computer.

As we have said in previous chapters, when you set the parameters of a picture before you shoot, you are creating pixels. If you shoot in RAW, and work on your photo in a RAW conversion utility, you are also defining the pixels of your image. However, when you edit it in the computer in any other program, including Photoshop, you are destroying pixels. Therefore, your image quality will likely be better if you create the best photo you can in the first place.

Then there is the issue of time and skill. It is much easier and faster to get it right in the first place (when you shoot) than to try to fix it later (in the computer). In fact, there's an old-time computer acronym that still holds true: GIGO (garbage in/garbage out.)

But all that is a generalization. The next sections take a look at how this rule of thumb works for various controls we have discussed in this chapter.

Focus

Focus is part of the optical characteristics of the photo. While a tiny bit of softness may be correctable in software, you won't be able to do anything more than apply digital band-aids to photos that exhibit noticeable blur. And we all know that band-aids never really hide anything.

Color Models

As we mentioned in the color model section, it is very feasible and sensible to convert the Adobe RGB photos to sRGB in software. But going the other direction doesn't usually work as well. That's because the Adobe RGB color model encompasses more potential colors than sRGB. (In other words, Adobe RGB has a wider gamut of possible colors.)

Tip

Remember: image settings that you make in your camera affect JPEGs only. If you shoot in RAW, your file will save all information that the camera's sensor captures. You can then apply similar image settings to those in your camera while converting the RAW file in the conversion software. (See Chapter 4.)

White Balance

Getting white balance right when you shoot is a major time saver. Yes, there are some wonderful software grey point and white point tools that do auto color corrections. But when white balance is off, a correction of one set of colors in a picture might not always fix all the colors. (See Figures 6-17, 6-18, and 6-19.)

We have seen photographers spend a half-hour or more in Photoshop trying to correct a white balance problem that might have taken no more than a minute or two to correct when shooting. And the result would have likely been better quality, too.

Sharpening

When it comes to sharpening — which can be such a destructive process — we usually accept the camera's auto setting. We usually resist heightening or reducing the amount of sharpening in the camera, simply because we can't know for certain what such adjustments are really doing to our pictures until we view them at 100 percent on our calibrated computer monitor. On the other hand, if we know a certain lens tends to shoot soft, we may compensate for it with a camera sharpening setting. Note, however, we take this step only after making a series of tests on the lens. The one thing we don't like to do is apply sharpness blind — that is, without knowing exactly what it is doing to our photos. That's why we seldom fiddle with the camera's sharpen options.

Other Image Adjustments

When it comes to the camera's various controls over color type (vivid, subdued, or black and white), saturation, contrast, and tone, we are of two minds. On the one hand, we've been doing these kinds of edits in Photoshop and similar programs for many years. The software tools are very precise and mature. However, the less photo editing a picture needs, the better — not only because editing can destroy pixels, but because it takes time and skill.

Whether you use your camera's built-in image adjustment tools may depend on what your purpose is, as well as how much control you have over the scene and lighting. If you are shooting in a studio, choosing your camera settings and checking them out on a computer monitor is SOP — standard operating procedure. Then, it makes good sense to get as many of the image settings right before you shoot as possible. If you are on location, however, and it's not possible or practical to check your camera settings by previewing a few photos on your laptop, then you might not want to take a chance on guessing which set of parameters is right. That's when you will probably want to bracket your shots with a variety of settings.

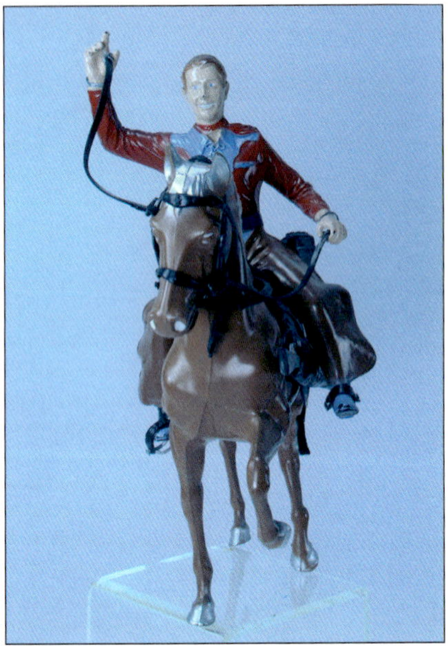

Figure 6-17: This is the same photo as Figure 6-6 (B), which was shot at the wrong white balance setting (incandescent). (Photos taken with a Pentax *ist D, 18–55mm lens set at 33mm, 1/20 at *f*8.)

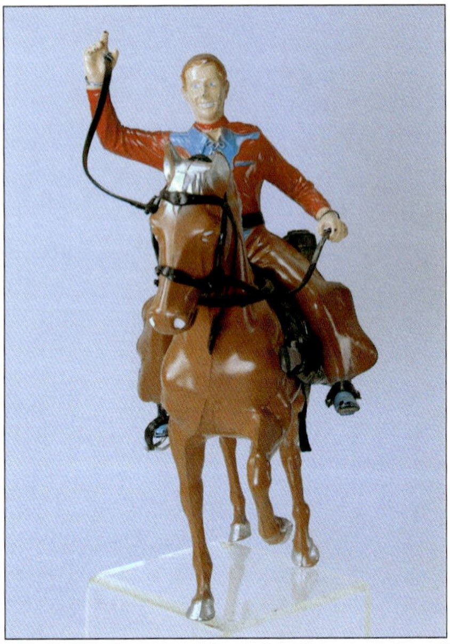

Figure 6-18: Using Photoshop's grey point color correcting tool in Figure 6-17, we got the skin tones to look pretty good. The red shirt, brown chaps, and horse are fairly close to natural (though too saturated). But the background is blue when it is supposed to be neutral. We could use the Replace Color tool in Photoshop to get rid of the blue, but it will take some finessing. It's almost always better to shoot using the right color balance rather than try to correct it later in the computer.

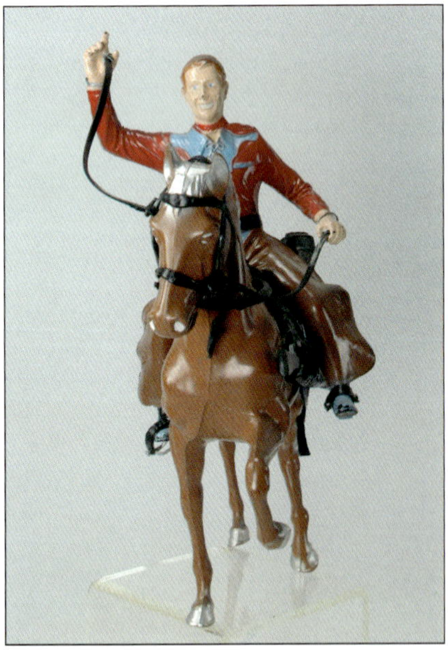

Figure 6-19: This photo, which was shot at the correct white balance for the scene, took only a couple of minutes to set up. Its colors are accurate (far better than in Figure 6-18) and didn't require any editing time or skills.

When Sally is working in photo-editing software, she is also creating, because she's a digital artist as well as a photographer and will often combine numerous images or use them for the basis of something entirely different. Therefore, she prefers to have all the original image data, including full, unmanipulated color and tone. That gives her options in taking the image in any direction she wants. The most important thing for Sally is to have accurate, high-quality, clean, and clear pictures to work on. (In addition, her photos must have the right combination of focus and depth-of-field for the composition.) Actually, that's one of the reasons why she almost always shoots in RAW, so she can save an archive copy of the original image and subsequently adjust the tone, color, saturation, contrast, and so forth on a copy of the picture, in the RAW software, without destroying pixels.

Organizing Your Files

It's so easy to press a shutter button, especially now that there's no need to buy, load, unload, replace, and process film. A good size memory card (2 gigabytes or larger) can hold hundreds of photos and be reused many thousands of times. No cost, great convenience, and high capacity all add up to lots and lots of photos. In Chapter 9, we discuss some of the ways you can get control over this mushrooming volume of picture files once they are in your computer. But you can start taming them while they are still in your camera. DSLRs (as well as some advanced consumer and prosumer cameras) have two very useful tools:

- **Folders** — Folders on your camera's memory card are just like the folders on your computer hard drive. In other words, they allow you to file related photos separately from other pictures. Conventional wisdom typically touts folders as being particularly useful when more than one person uses the same camera and memory card. Each one can then save his pictures to his own personal folder. However, we have found them to be valuable also in helping organize photos, even before you get them on the computer. You can set up a series of folders and decide to save specific subjects, assignments, or clients to particular folders. Then, when you transfer them, they are already sorted.
- **File numbering options** — Cameras automatically assign file names to every photo taken, such as 101000.jpg, 101001.orf, 101002.orf, and so forth. (ORF is Olympus's RAW file format.) The actual format of the name may vary, depending upon your camera model, but the system of using sequential numbers is universal. In DSLRs, you have a choice of how those sequential numbers will be handled. You can have your camera remember the numbers previously assigned to photo files and never repeat a number. Or, you can have your camera reset assigned numbers whenever a fresh memory card is inserted. We prefer the continuous, unreset numbering, because that assures that no two files on our computer will have the same name (although the numbers automatically revert back to zero once you've gone through all the digits, such as 100,000 images on a camera). Yes, we do try to rename our photos to something easily recognizable once we have transferred them to our computer (such as Autumn_Barn_12.jpg), but we don't always get around to it right away. Besides, the transfer process can be slowed down, or files overwritten, if you have redundant file names.

  In some cameras, you may also have some control over the format of the file names. For instance, you can insert the initials of a specific project or location before or after the sequential numbers.

Tip

When checking your photos on the LCD viewfinder, use the zoom and pan tools to magnify the view of the picture and move around it. This will give you a better (though still not honest) perspective on the details that were captured.

Confirming Your Shot (Playback)

The immediacy of digital photography, of knowing that you got a photo, is what really set it on the map. That LCD screen on the back is irresistible. So much so, that wherever we travel, when we take a photo, people — children and adults alike — will crane their necks to see the tiny playback picture. That alone has been one of our advantages in asking for and getting model releases. (We talk more about model releases in Chapter 7.)

However, there's one major problem with the LCD screen — it out and out lies. What you see is definitely not what you got. The problem is threefold:

- The LCD screen is low resolution, which means that it doesn't give you enough data to fully judge the image quality or details.
- Typically, it will brighten automatically to make it easier to see the picture, which means you won't see the true exposure of the photo.
- It is definitely not color calibrated or corrected. So, you can't judge the colors accurately, either.

After awhile, as you become familiar with your camera, you might learn to better interpret the pictures you see on the LCD. However, we suggest that you don't rely on how your photos display on your camera's LCD screen. What it's best for is a quick-and-dirty look at the shot and not a detailed display upon which you might make precise decisions and confirmations. For instance, your LCD screen is useful for confirming that you did get the picture, that the composition is what you wanted, and that the exposure and color aren't so far off as to be next to useless (such as a dramatically underexposed picture).

On the other hand, the LCD screen provides access to various playback tools that make it easier to judge your shoot — at long as you temper what you see by what you know.

Tip

One of the most important playback tools is the histogram. The histogram of a photo is a statistical graph of its exposure. Please see Chapter 5, regarding reading, interpreting, and using histograms.

Metadata

Metadata is literally data about data. It's information about how and when you shot your photograph that is embedded into the photo's file. This includes the aperture and shutter speed, zoom lens setting, focus mode, color model, adjustments to the various image settings, flash mode, time and date taken, camera make and model, and so on.

On playback, you can check the metadata to be sure that the settings you intended were the ones that you used. However, we find metadata even more valuable when organizing, editing, and reviewing our photo files, which is why we cover it in more detail in Chapter 9.

Tip

For flipping quickly through your photos, use your camera's slideshow playback. Typically, you can set the interval time between slides. You can interrupt it at any time to look more closely at a specific photo and check its metadata. Or, on most DSLRs, you can instantly return to the shooting mode simply by pressing the shutter down halfway.

Erase and Protect

When reviewing and checking out your photos on the camera's LCD screen, it's an easy matter to simply erase the ones you don't want to keep — almost too easy. You can choose to erase a single picture, all photos in your camera, or if you have defined folders, entire folders of pictures. If you have taken a definitive photo that you would be loathe to lose, and you can't transfer it immediately to your computer, mark it for protection in the playback options. That will make it undeletable for as long as the memory card remains in your camera.

If you accidentally erase a photo that you really wanted, or if your memory card suddenly becomes unreadable, telling you that it contains no pictures, don't panic. Take your memory card out of your camera, and flick the tiny notched lever on the corner, which locks it. Then try a recovery program, such as ImageRecall (`www.flashfixers.com`) or the utility that comes with SanDisk Extreme III or similar premium-priced memory cards.

Summary

Photography isn't simply about capturing the frozen moment. It's your interpretation of that moment and how you communicate it to others. Learning and mastering the shooting controls of your DSLR expands your visual vocabulary, giving you the tools to define and predict how others will view and respond to your photographs. The various menu options also give you control over your photography, by providing information, allowing you to organize your files, and helping you to confirm that you really did get the picture you intended.

Part III

Digital Photography Techniques and Tips from the Pros

Chapter 7

Getting the Shot

Chapter 8

Lighting

Chapter 7

Getting the Shot

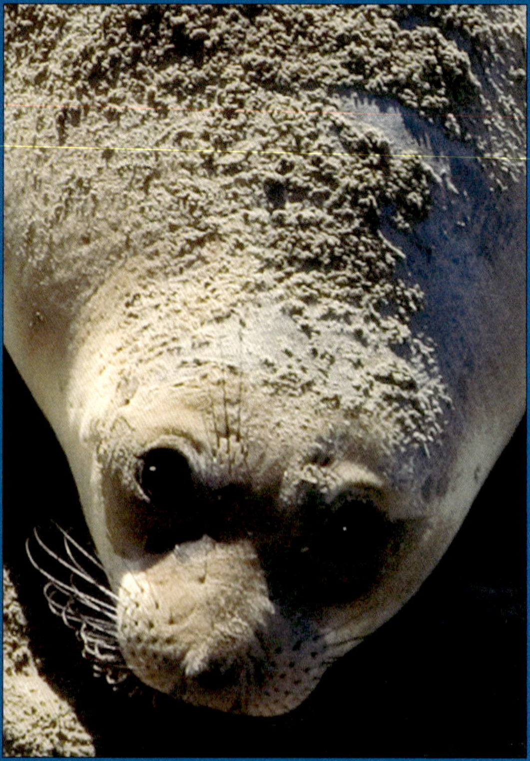

This baby elephant seal happened to look up into our lens at just the right moment. (Photo taken with a Nikon D70, 24–120mm lens set at 70mm, 1/640 at f5.6.)

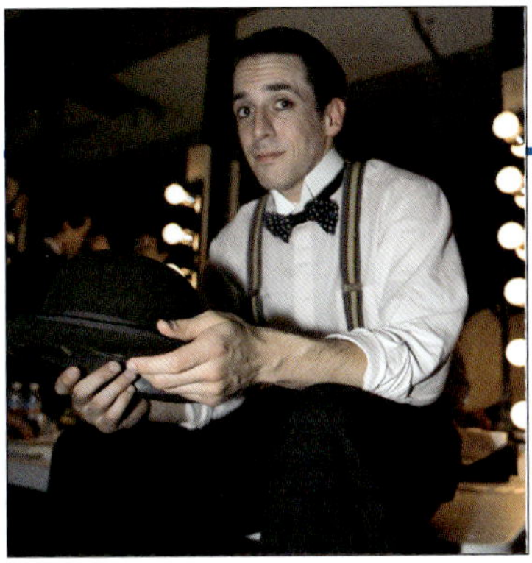

Actor Jeff Wills relaxes backstage at The Northeast Theatre. (Photo taken with a Canon EOS 1Ds Mark II, 16–35mm lens set at 26mm, 1/160 at f2.8.)

We are often asked what camera will take the best pictures. Our answer is . . . no camera. It's the photographer behind the lens who conceives of and then captures truly great images. In fact, we have found our fellow photographers to be remarkably inventive and skillful when it comes to doing whatever it takes to get the shot. When the light is just right, and the moment perfect, they will find a way around almost any obstacle. For instance, Sally is a terrible climber. But put a camera in her hands and a scene that she feels compelled to capture, and she can climb any rock formation or ladder. (Getting back down after she's taken the picture is another matter entirely.)

Getting the shot involves an artistic sense, an understanding of the essence of the subject, a hyperawareness of the ambiance and environment, technical know-how, and determined ingenuity in handling whatever circumstances arise.

In this chapter, we share insights and tips for getting the shot, in all kinds of situations, including:

- Photographing action
- Photographing events
- Photographing close up
- Dealing with the challenges of shooting away from home or the studio
- Photographing strangers
- Securing model and property releases
- Handling hostile environments

Passion, Perseverance, Patterns, and Patience

Richard Ettlinger, the bird photographer (`www.richardettlinger.com`), says that getting the perfect wildlife photo "has to do with passion, perseverance, patterns, and patience . . . . It doesn't happen overnight. You have to go out there day after day, watch the birds, get to know them, learn their patterns, how they fly, how they land. Once you learn their habitats, you can figure out how to shoot them, to anticipate certain action. Eventually, you'll get the shot, but it might take years." He added, that, of course, "you can never know when an amazing shot will happen." (See Figure 7-1.)

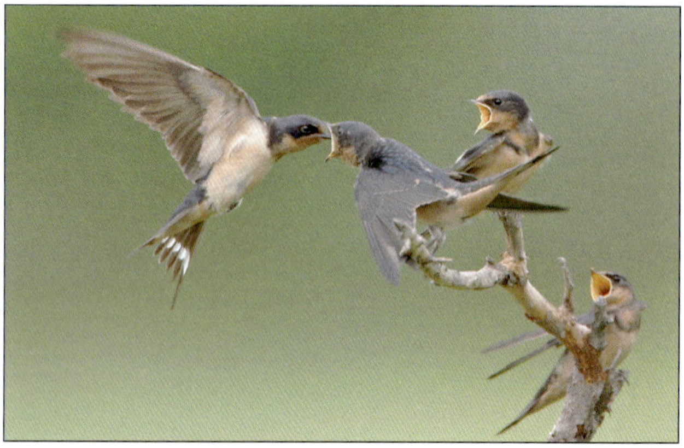

Figure 7-1: Discussing this photo of barn swallows, Richard Ettlinger told us, "It's difficult to catch a bird feeding young. You need to frame exactly right, and try to guess where the bird will go, which young it will feed first. Snap your fingers, and the shot is gone." (Photo taken with a Canon 10D, 500mm lens with 1.4x converter, 1/750 at *f*5.6. Copyright Richard Ettlinger)

As we listened to Richard, we realized that most great photographers say the same thing about their subject — whether it is sports, travel, wildlife, children, flowers, or whatever. "I know my subject, I know what it/he/she is going to do, where the ball will be next, the brief expression that will tell an entire story." Armed with such intimate knowledge, they can not only anticipate the subject but also understand what the definitive moment is, as well as the best framing and angle, how the light affects it, and what position(s) will give them the quintessential shot.

Sally has long had a passion for the circus. Some years ago, when we were out grocery shopping, we saw a circus tent going up in a farmer's field. We attended a performance that night and found out that for the next several weeks, the one-ring circus would be traveling through the nearby Pennsylvania Dutch countryside. The following morning, Sally ran away with the circus, so to speak. She got to know the performers, their animals, and their acts, and she didn't start taking pictures until she could anticipate the essential moment(s) that would best capture each personality and experience. So it was that she was able to capture the instant when the trapeze artist caught his wife with one hand as she flew through the air, or a child's wide-eyed wonder as the elephant rose on its hind legs. What's more, because Sally spent so much time with the performers, they learned to trust her and gave her exceptional access to their private world, too — such as when their august clown allowed her to photograph him as he applied his makeup, transforming himself from a very plain man to a magical creature.

Similarly, every sports photographer can tell you the best position in which to stand to get that impossible rim shot or catch that amazing touchdown pass. Photographers who specialize in architecture know what details and angles best convey the scope and style of buildings. And a great portrait photographer spends as much time as possible talking with the man, woman, or child, trying to understand the personality she wants to capture.

The Art of Stillness

Two physical acts separate professional photographers from amateurs. The first, as we mentioned earlier in this book, is to not be rooted in place but move into whatever position that's needed— higher, lower, closer, further away, to the side, from the back—until what you see through your viewfinder is exactly the picture you envision. The second is the ability to be absolutely still and allow the picture to form around you.

The art of stillness involves patiently blending into the natural habitat of your subject, the ability to get the picture without interfering with or influencing the activities you are trying to photograph.

For the photo in Figure 7-6, Sally knew that dragonflies swarm in the late afternoon at a certain pond near us. She sat in the tall grasses, near a section of the pond where she had seen them previously. When she first settled into position, all the dragonflies (and other critters) scampered away. But then, she became quite still, and eventually, the dragonflies returned, alighting on plants within inches of her lens.

In many ways, photographing people requires a similar ability to blend into a scene, avoiding disrupting their natural habitat and the way they are used to feeling about things around them.

Naturally, no amount of study will make things happen the way you hope they will. Helene Delillo, the New York beauty photographer (`www.helenedelillo.com`), has spent years perfecting her understanding of angles, light, and personalities. As a result, her portraits are quite lovely. But, as she told us, all the planning and study in the world is just preparation. "A lot of great photography is magical accidents. If you are there and you pay attention, follow your passion, and do what you love, things come to you. You just have to be open to listening and seeing things."

Shooting from the hip (taking pictures quickly, because the moment is right there in front of you) is also part of nearly every photographer's experience. It can be quite a successful method, when the photographer has developed her skills of observation and familiarity with her equipment.

Action Photography

Action photography covers a wide range of moving subjects, from high-speed racing to the antics of a restless child, and everything in between.

The first step in setting up your action shot is analyzing what it is about the subject that will make a great picture.

- If it is the subject or person and not the speed that is important, you may want to freeze the action, so everything is crisply in focus.
- If the motion is an important ingredient, then you may want to capture some motion blur, to help convey the sense of speed.
- Do you need a clearly defined background, to give a sense of context and ambiance to the picture? Or would a dark and/or out of focus background be more appropriate?

Tip

Trying to follow any high-speed or erratic action through the lens is difficult. Richard Ettlinger suggests keeping your noncamera eye open, because "you need one eye out of the camera to see where [your subject] is going." It's how he photographs small birds, like warblers, that are constantly jumping all over the place.

Freezing the Action

Naturally, when you want to freeze the action, you need to use a high shutter speed. (See Figure 7-2.) How fast should your shutter speed be? At least, a split second faster than the action you are trying to capture. With an infant who is just learning to crawl, that may mean about 1/125 or 1/250 (depending on how adept the child is at scampering). But if it's a skateboarder, then you would probably push the shutter speed as fast as possible for the light available.

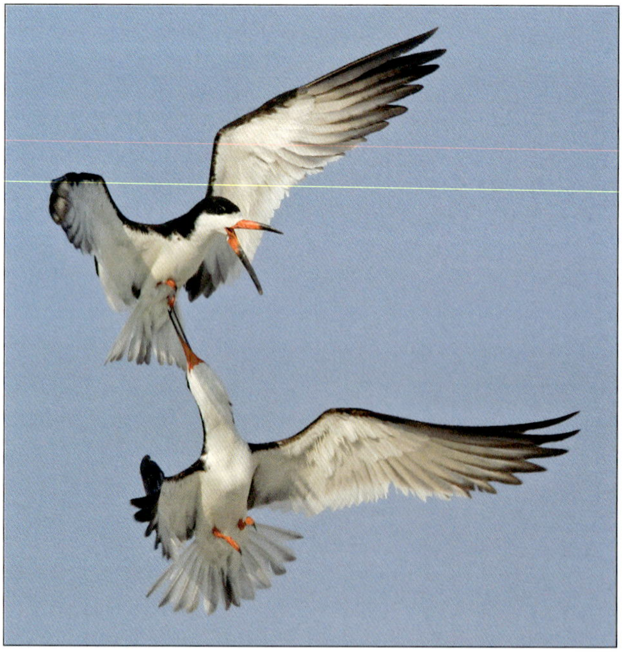

Figure 7-2: When Richard Ettlinger photographs birds, he keeps his shutter speed between 1/800 and 1/1000. For those birds that move really quickly, he may need to use 1/1500 to 1/2000 to freeze their wings. That's why he usually has his ISO set at 400, though if there's lots of light, he might lower it to 320. (Photo taken with a Canon 10D, with a 300mm lens and a 2x converter, at 1/1600 and *f*9.0. Copyright by Richard Ettlinger)

Single Shot or Continuous Autofocus

In default mode, your camera's default setting allows you to activate autofocus by pressing the shutter down halfway. But for really fast action, you might want to set your camera to continuous - autofocus. By switching to continuous focus (usually via a lever or switch on or near the lens), your camera's lens will continuously focus on the subject, and you'll be less likely to miss an important split-second shot. Continuous autofocus works much faster than single shot autofocus, but does require some getting used to for proper control.

In many cases, action isn't a constant. Rather, it reaches an apex that is not only the perfect shot but also a split-second natural freeze. Horse jumping is a classic example of this. The apex is the point in the jump when the horse has reached the top of its arc, with the legs in perfect position, just as it begins its descent. Catching that fleeting moment is difficult, which is why so many sports and wildlife photographers use continuous autofocus (see the sidebar "Single Shot or Continuous Autofocus") and fast burst mode. But it's just as important to recognize and anticipate where and when the apex will be.

Action moving towards you doesn't require as high a shutter speed as something that is speeding across your frame. However, try not to choose your position in relationship to your subject based on your shutter speed. A picture of something rushing toward you can be less dynamic than one in which it is moving across or, often better, at an oblique angle to you.

By the way, another way to freeze action is to use your flash. (See Chapter 8.)

Tip

Remember to use your camera's various focus options to zero in on the most important subject in your composition. This is especially important when using a fast shutter speed means that your depth-of-field will be narrow, blurring the background. If you focus on the background instead of the subject, you can end up with a blurred subject and sharp background. (See Chapter 6.)

Faster Than a Speeding Bullet

When you freeze the action in a picture, it can look quite static, as though nothing is really happening in the scene. It becomes, quite literally, a still life. Think of the old movies in which Superman or other flying heroes were obviously suspended on wires, with their arms and legs stretched out, but laying there, in mid-air. Nothing about those scenes imparted a sense of motion. However, add a bit of blur to the picture, and suddenly, everything becomes alive with action. (See Figure 7-3.)

Burst Speed

Good action photography requires that your camera be ultra-responsive, with no discernable delay between the instant you press the shutter button and when the picture is actually captured. DSLRs are much better suited for action photography than consumer or prosumer cameras, because most DSLRs have virtually eliminated shutter lag. However, their burst mode capabilities can vary widely.

Burst mode is the ability of a camera to quickly shoot a series of pictures, one right after the other, simply by holding down the shutter button. Some DSLRs can shoot continuously at five, six, eight frames or more each and every second (depending on the specific model and the file format you're saving to) for as long as you have space left on your memory card. Because of various hardware considerations, others can shoot only two or three frames per second for a few seconds — then you must wait until the camera saves the captured images and is ready to shoot again. Catching the moment for a great photograph often requires a great burst speed, plus the ability to time your shots carefully. If you don't have a really fast burst speed, you'll need to be even more precise with your timing.

All other things being equal, three issues can limit your camera's burst:

- **Internal memory** — As you shoot, a whole bunch of other processes are simultaneously going on inside your camera. The camera's buffer memory holds photos in a queue, while waiting for their turn to be processed and saved. If your camera has lots of memory, then you can keep shooting. But if your buffer becomes full with photos that have not yet been handed off for processing, your camera will stop shooting and can't resume until space is freed up in the buffer.
- **Processing speed** — Obviously, if photos are waiting in a queue until other pictures are being processed, the faster the camera does all the tasks necessary, the sooner the buffer can release more photos, making room for the next shots.
- **Read/write speed** — Happily, all current DSLRs can take advantage of high-speed memory cards (see Chapter 3). Using high-performance cards enables your DSLR to write the processed images that much faster. And that helps to relieve the traffic congestion that backs up through the entire pipeline, starting with the buffer.

If you plan to do a lot of action photography, we recommend getting a camera with a great sustained burst mode and using only high-performance memory cards. Don't just trust the printed specs of the camera. Go into a store and shoot the camera, holding your finger on the shutter button while tracking some movement. Try shooting off a couple dozen shots to see if there is any lag or interruption.

The key to effective motion blur is balancing enough sharp, clear detail to identify the subject, with enough blur to make it exciting. Often, you have to keep shooting at different settings, because it can be difficult to predict exactly how much detail you'll be able to preserve within the blurred image.

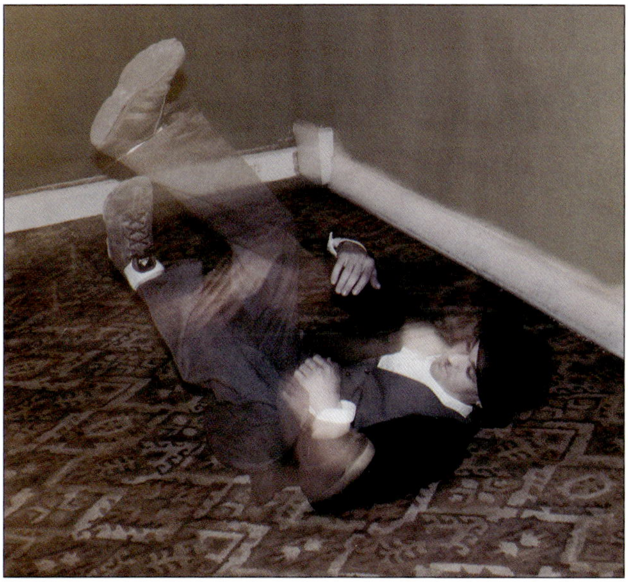

Figure 7-3: When Sally photographed actor Todd d'Amour, in TNT theatre's production of *Silent Lives*, she used a slow shutter speed of 1/25 of a second. That way, she was able to blur the full action of his Chaplinese pratfall. If she had used a faster shutter speed to freeze the action, it would have appeared that Todd was just laying there on the ground. (Photo taken with a Canon EOS Digital Rebel, using an 18-55mm lens at 22mm, 1/25 at *f*5.)

You can set up motion blur shots in one of five ways (or use a combination of some of them):

- **Traditional** — Set your shutter to a comparatively low speed, frame your shot in anticipation of the action, and click the shutter button when it comes into view.
- **Tracking** — Put your camera on a tripod with a rotating head. (Tracking can be done without a tripod, but it is more difficult.) Select a slow shutter speed. Frame the subject before you start, press the shutter button, and track the action by rotating the camera on the tripod head. Tracking takes some practice (as well as trial and error). The key is to keep the subject in the same place within your lens while tracking. (See Figure 7-4.)
- **In-camera composition of two images** — If your DSLR has multiple exposure or image overlay, you can take two photos: one fully blurred and one static but clearly focused. Then, superimpose the static photo over the blurred one in the camera. This method works best when the subject is very predictable. We find athletes and actors are often best at performing the same action over and over again.

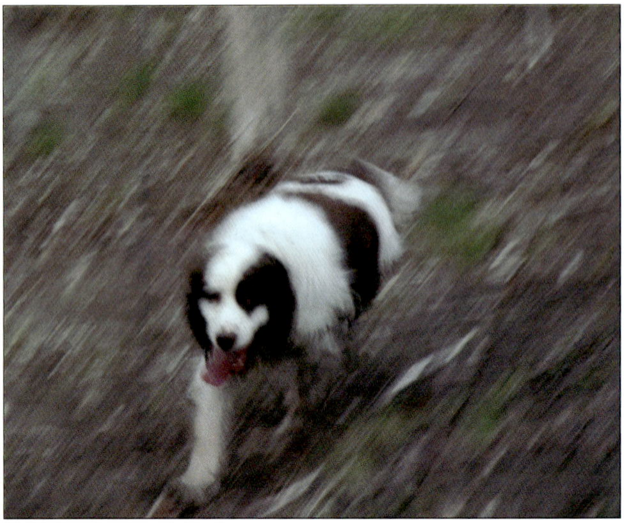

Figure 7-4: In this photo of Cuddles, our English springer spaniel, running through our field, we had to hand-hold the tracking, rather than use a tripod, because we weren't sure in which direction he was going to run. (Taken with a Nikon D70, focal length 70mm, at 1/60 at *f*18.)

- **Digital imaging in your computer** — If your DSLR doesn't have multiple exposure or image overlay capability, or if you prefer working in the computer where you can achieve greater precision and subtlety, shoot two pictures, but combine them in your photo-editing software. Use layers and set the top layer's transparency, so parts of the underlying image show through. (See Chapter 10.)
- **Rear curtain sync** — Your flash fires at the end of an exposure, freezing the final portion of the action, but blurring the rest. (See Chapter 8.)

Event Photography: Getting to Know You

Bruce Dorn (`www.idcphotography.com`) says that good wedding photography is "the art of getting to know people." You can say the same thing about any event photography in which you are called on to shoot people you hardly know or never met. To get great pictures, it's important to develop a rapport with your subjects, as much as possible, and to try to understand them.

We would add to Bruce's comment that good event photography requires recognizing what is appropriate. This usually involves understanding why people are attending an event and making sure that your photography doesn't interfere with their purpose — whether it is to have fun, see something or someone, or achieve a professional or personal goal.

When Sally recently photographed a masters class in film acting, conducted by playwright/director Mark Medoff, she needed to tiptoe around sensitivities. The actors' concentration was so intense, and the opportunity for them so important, that Sally understood flash would be both distracting and would disturb the lighting ambiance of the theater. That meant shooting available-light candids, which required setting the ISO higher than she typically uses. In addition, DSLRs tend to be noisy devices. Sally carefully avoided shooting whenever a student was actually performing. (Mark was quite comfortable being photographed, so Sally could shoot anytime he was speaking.) Simply being respectful and unobtrusive disarmed all reservations or possible objections by the students, allowing Sally to do her thing while they did theirs.

Here are a few suggestions for good event photography:

- **Gauge the temper of the event** — Some people would rather you fade into the background. Others react well to having a personable individual interact with them and photograph them.
- **Get help** — Ask your client to provide an assistant to point out who is who and to help you get the correct spelling of names and titles for later picture identification. Try to find out what the interests are of the important folks and what their names are. In a family-type event, young teenagers and maiden aunts can be a big help in filling you in about the people around you.
- **Match the mood of the event** — If it is a happy occasion, such as a wedding, get on the dance floor, capture the way people are swaying to the music and holding each other. If it is a formal conference, be reserved and respectful, but not intimidated.
- **Don't let your lens or your body become fixed** — Paint the scene with both broad strokes, capturing the full sweep of the event, and then zoom into the tiny details. Check out all the angles and perspectives.
- **Vary your photographic style** — Try using a higher ISO so that you can shoot romantic moments by available light. Blur the action to show the energy of the scene. Freeze the action, to capture the impact of a gesture. Ask people to pose, but also take candid pictures.
- **Time your intrusions and interruptions carefully** — If you need specific group shots, try to arrange when and who will be in them beforehand. Make a list of the people who should be in each shot, and get some assistance in assembling them.
- **Be sure of your equipment** — Important events are not when you should be testing new equipment or trying unused settings and techniques for the first time. Do a test run of all your stuff. Make sure that the cameras and lights are on your preferred default settings (no EV or other adjustments from the last shoot). Clean and format your memory cards. Use fresh batteries and have chargers plugged in somewhere convenient. (As we mentioned in Chapter 3, when it's convenient to the shoot, we use an AC converter in our car's lighter, so we can lock our battery chargers in there.)
- **Keep your cool and sense of humor** — Things go wrong, usually at the worst times. But that's when a good photographer smiles and then figures out a solution.
- **Take lots and lots of pictures** — After all, it's digital, not film. So, the only added cost is the extra time you will need to spend in sorting and editing the photos.

Background Decisions

Whether you want to freeze or blur your action, once you have chosen your shutter speed, your choice of the corresponding *f*-stop becomes limited. (See Chapter 5 for discussion of the relationship of shutter speeds, *f*-stops and ISO.) Yet, some photos require a blurred background, while others demand a background that is sharp and clear.

You can widen your choices of *f*-stop, for a given shutter speed, in the following ways:

- If you need a fast shutter speed and a greater depth-of-field than is possible with the current light, add light or increase the ISO.
- If you need to reduce the shutter speed and/or the depth-of-field, but there's too much light to attain the effect you want, reduce the ISO or add a neutral density filter to your lens. (See Chapter 3 regarding filters.)
- With DSLRs and RAW file format, it is possible to shoot a usable underexposed picture (with a faster shutter speed and/or greater depth-of-field than appropriate for the light), then brighten it a bit in the RAW conversion utility. Of course, you don't want to lose details or increase the noise in the shadows. (See Chapter 4 regarding RAW.) On the other hand, overexposing a picture (with a slower shutter speed and/or narrower depth-of-field than appropriate for the light) will almost always result in lost details in highlights that are blown out (too bright).

Tip

Be aware of how perspective is affecting your composition. As we discussed in Chapter 2, the entire composition and comparative impact of the visual elements of your photo will change depending on the focal length of the lens you use. For instance, you'll get one picture if you shoot a photo close up with a wide angle lens, and a very different one if you take the same subject from further away using a telephoto lens.

Close-Up Photography

Moving in close to capture the fine details of life can be a very satisfying artistic experience. It can pare things down to the bare essentials, or turn the familiar into something almost alien. (See Figure 7-5.) Tuning down, to look closer, we aren't just changing our lens focal length and focus distance, but our viewpoint and the way we see things.

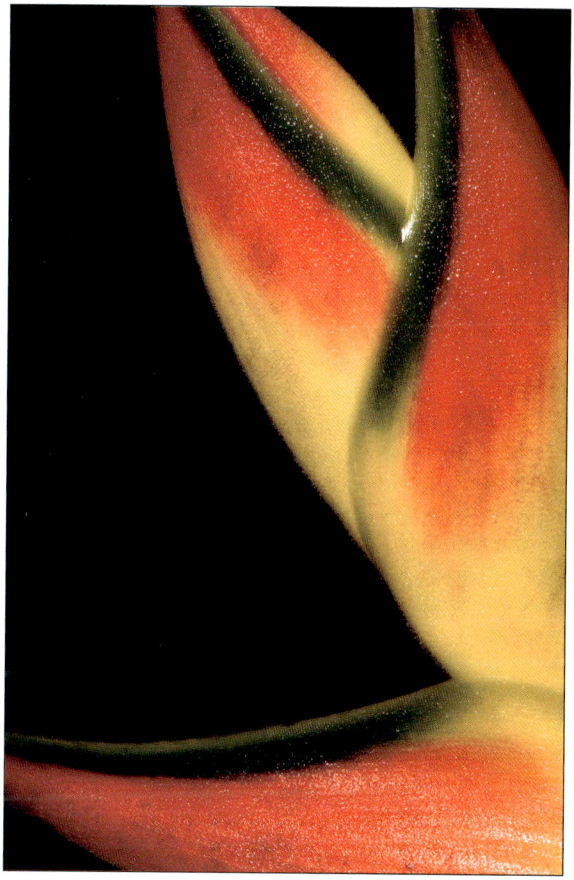

Figure 7-5: For her 2005 New York exhibit "Aumakua, Passion and Portraiture," beauty photographer Helene Delillo created very large prints of her close-up flower photos. Some looked quite alien or abstract, while others looked like animals. For the waxy (versus the "furry") flowers, she took makeup artist Mark DeHaven's advice and sprayed them with oil, to bring out the color and details. (Copyright by Helene Delillo. Photo taken with a Canon EOS 20D, 50mm lens, 1/250 at *f*18.)

Close-up photography also has its own unique challenges:

- The closer you focus, the more your depth-of-field will be reduced. This means that the background will almost inevitably be out of focus, blurred. What's more, much of your main subject may not be sharp, unless you're careful and use a very small aperture (high *f*-stop number). (See Figure 7-6.)
- Using a small aperture usually means that you will need to either use a comparatively slow shutter speed or up your ISO, or both. You may also need to throw more light on the subject or shoot using a tripod, or both.

- When the entire frame is only inches wide, the image's tolerance to camera shake decreases significantly. If you aren't willing to increase your ISO (because you don't want image noise), then it is likely that your shutter speed won't be very fast. That, in turn, means that even the act of breathing can introduce some motion blur. Therefore, using a tripod is virtually mandatory. If you can't use a tripod, because you're trying to remain flexible and follow a moving target (or you forgot the tripod), then try to use an anti-shake lens, and be sure that the anti-shake is turned on. (With Konica Minolta DSLRs, the image stabilization is in the camera body, not the lens.)
- Distortion is magnified, too, when you're in close-up. Try to keep your camera parallel to the plane of your subject, to reduce perspective distortion and maintain optimum sharpness.
- Any imperfection, even the smallest speck of dust, is a larger percentage of the image, and can look like an ugly boulder. So, examine your subject and the area surrounding it to see if anything needs to be cleaned, dusted, or otherwise made neater.

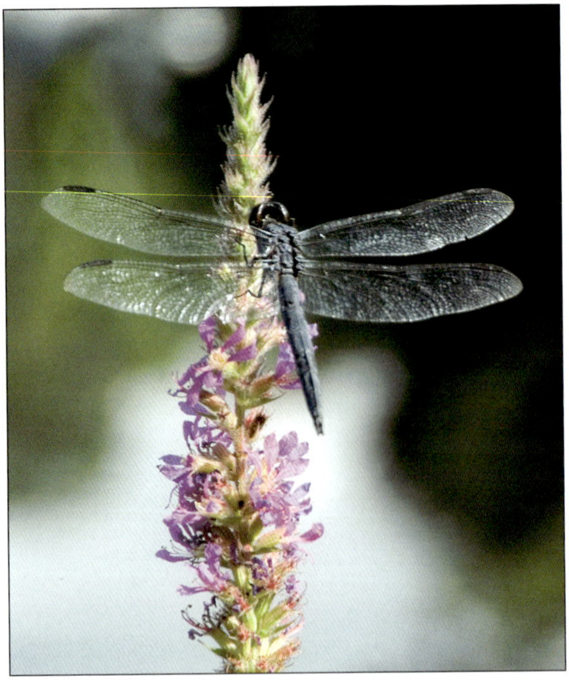

Figure 7-6: This dragonfly alighted on the purple loosestrife branch long enough for Sally to hand-hold her camera, and, using a Nikkor VR antishake lens, capture it at 1/180 of a second. Since the focus point was so close to the lens, the depth-of-field was extremely limited. However, by not using a very fast shutter speed, she was able to set the aperture at *f*9.5, which made the entire dragonfly and most of the plant sharp. (Photo taken with a Fujifilm S3 Pro, 24–200mm lens at 120mm, 1/180, *f*9.5.)

Tip

Go ahead and break any and all "rules" when composing your pictures. For instance, while good architectural photography requires that you maintain accurate perspectives, good visual energy can be achieved by pushing distortions and making them even more pronounced.

Around the Block, Around the World

We used to travel frequently all over the world on assignments, everywhere from Antarctica to the Amazon, Africa to China, the South Sea islands to the Caribbean islands, and of course Europe and the Americas. We'd fly, sail, or drive into strange environments, and within a comparatively limited time, we would have to end up with great photos of people we'd never before met, wonderful landscapes, and intriguing city scenes, regardless of the weather and conditions.

Whether you are going for a walk around the block, flying off to foreign lands, or sailing the high seas, whenever you leave home or the studio, you will encounter new photographic opportunities and challenges.

Photographing Strangers

We have been in areas of the world where people think that anyone who takes their picture is stealing their soul. In some ways, we agree. Not about the theft of souls, but when we look at strangers through our lenses, we see much more deeply than they may want anyone to look. Their uncertainties and fears, joy and pleasure, confusion and assurance . . . photographers can see what strangers may not even want to acknowledge to themselves. That's why, when people indicate that they don't want their picture taken, we put down our cameras.

However, we try to avoid reaching that point.

It probably helps that we actually tend to like people, even strangers. Smiles go a long way, especially if you are smiling at something that the stranger takes pride in, such as a pet, a garden, or a child. Being pleasant and asking questions without being intrusive. Often, when we are photographing *things*, people will come up to us and ask us what we are doing, and that leads to a convivial conversation that naturally evolves into our taking their pictures. (See Figure 7-7.)

We have found that kids are usually easier to meet than adults in strange areas outside the United States. Street urchins can be sticky fingered, but if you hire or temporarily "adopt" one, he/she may protect you from the rest, while helping you meet and get to know the community. As Philippe Tarbouriech, the French photographer (`www.phitar.com`), said to us, "A kid is like a *laissez-passer,* a master key, for meeting people." When he travels with his own children, he finds that strangers are drawn to them and, no doubt, feel less threatened by him and his camera.

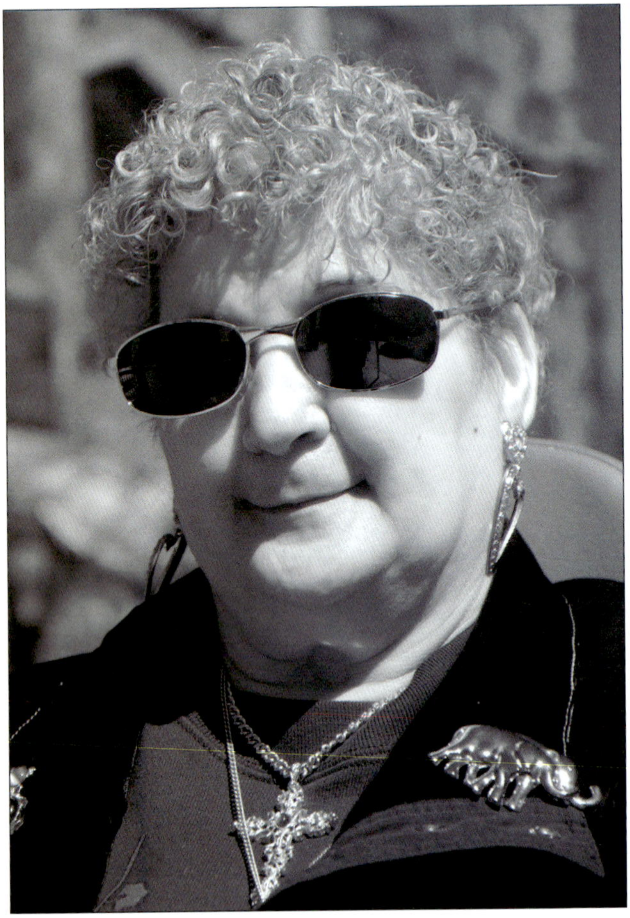

Figure 7-7: Sally was shooting architectural details in Scranton, Pennsylvania, when this lovely lady rolled up in her wheelchair and started chatting. Soon, she was asking why Sally wasn't taking photographs of her. And, yes, she was quite happy to sign a model release. (Taken with a Nikon D70, 60mm, 1/1260 at *f*4.5, converted to greyscale in Photoshop.)

In the United States, the climate has changed considerably regarding talking with and photographing kids. We won't even try, as a rule, until after we've first made a connection with the parent. We've been pleasantly surprised at how many strangers are more than happy to have us photograph their children once we have spoken to them for a few minutes, and they understand why we want to take their pictures.

Being sincerely interested in what strangers are doing and asking intelligent questions is another way of gaining entré. (See Figure 7-8.)

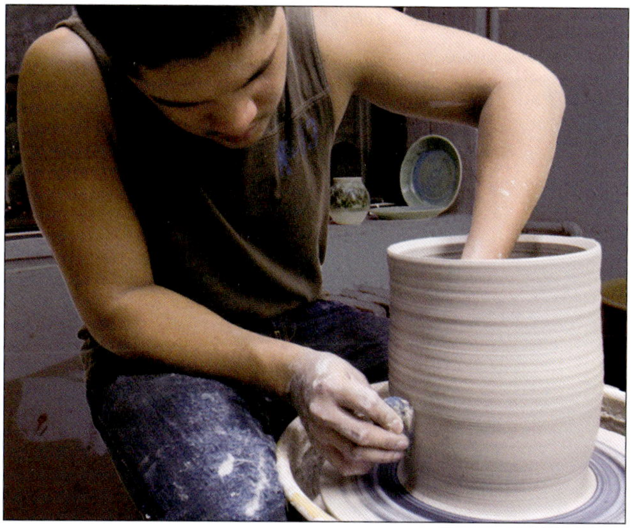

Figure 7-8: Late one night, as we walked through Manhattan, we saw a small shop with two men working at potters' wheels. Curious, we walked in, started talking with them, asking questions about their work. Soon, Sally had permission to take their photographs. Because it was done in a friendly manner, we had no problem obtaining signed model releases. The picture was taken in a dark room by available light, so we upped the ISO to 1250 and, to show the motion blur of the wheel, we used a slow shutter speed. (Photo taken with a Canon EOS-1Ds Mark II, 35mm, 1/20 at *f*10.)

Similarly, if you are or look interesting, you'll find that people naturally gravitate around you. Philippe Tarbouriech always travels with a 3-foot wide reflector, which folds into a small circle in his bag. "I sometimes use it for photography," Philippe told us. "And, sometimes for entertainment." When it pops open, it "makes people laugh and establishes a relationship with them."

Tip

Philippe Tarbouriech told us that one of the most difficult things for him while traveling around the world is recharging his batteries. Sometimes, there are no plugs or the wrong kind of plugs. So, he put together a cable that fits into any standard light bulb socket, into which he can then plug in his battery rechargers. If you decide to do anything like that, please be sure to confirm that it is safe and won't electrocute you or start a fire. By the way, the standard for light bulbs does vary around the world, so you'll probably want to have more than one kind.

Hostile Environments

Extreme temperatures, excess moisture, wind, and dust — these are hostile environments to your camera equipment. We frequently shoot outdoors, and preparing our equipment carefully for whatever the weather might bring is as instinctive as dressing properly for the cold or heat. (See Figure 7-9.)

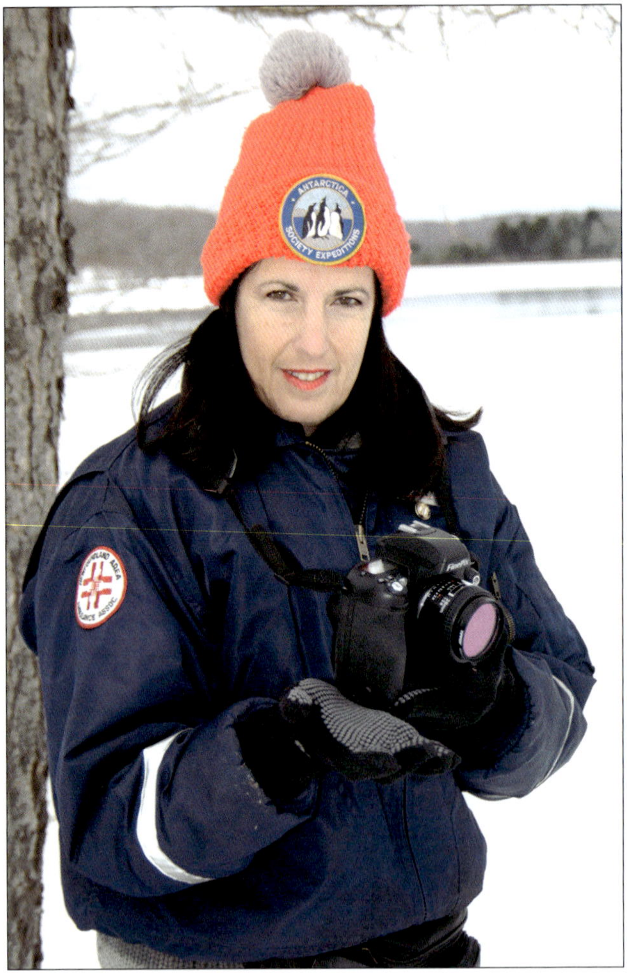

Figure 7-9: Though it has been years since we were last in Antarctica, we still do a considerable amount of cold weather photography, and therefore prepare and dress accordingly. Notice the Lowepro gloves Sally is wearing. They have rubberized dots on the palm and fingers, to make it easy for her to handle the camera controls without having to expose her hands to the cold. In really extreme cold, she will wear thin silk or nylon liner gloves under the Lowepros. (Photo taken with a Nikon D2x, 24–120mm lens zoomed to 42mm, 1/60 at *f*4.5.)

Model and Property Releases

We are fortunate to live in a society whose legal system upholds the individual's right of privacy, including protection from embarrassment and defamation. What's more, business entities (and celebrities) have the exclusive right to benefit financially from those icons and images that are uniquely theirs, such as a trademarked logo, a recognizable building, or, in the case of a celebrity, a face.

If you are using your photographs only for private enjoyment or exhibitions, it is unlikely that you will need any model or property release. But not having a release can severely limit how you might use, display, or sell your photos should you decide later that you want to publish it in a book, sell it through a stock photo agency, paste it on mugs or T-shirts, and so forth.

Whenever possible, we try to get releases for all our photos. In fact, we tend to not take pictures in situations in which a release would be appropriate, but we are unable to obtain one. We keep blank model releases in all our camera bags and car glove compartments. Our forms are short and simple. The key phrases state the following:

- We are professional photographers
- We have taken photographs of the person, property, or child (specifically named)
- We have taken these photos with permission from the person, owner, or guardian
- We may use these photos in articles, lectures, books, exhibitions, or for commercial purposes (we scratch out the commercial phrase when dealing with a famous individual and in other sensitive situations)

The form has a place for a date, signature, printed name, email address, and phone number, as well as our contact information. (We offer the person a copy of the release for their files, after they have signed our copy.) We are not attorneys, so, please, check with experts in this field for what the specific wording of your releases should be. This is especially important if you plan to use your photographs in any way that the people or business entities represented might consider impinging upon their rights. A good place to start for advice is the American Society of Media Photographer's Web site — `www.ASMP.org`.

We are often asked how we persuade people to sign model releases. Quite simply, we ask. But then, we usually have already asked for their permission to take their photo (or that of their child or property). At the very least, we probably held up our camera, pointed it at them, and waited to see if they minded. We explain that we are professional photographers, and if the picture turns out well, we might want to use it in our books, lectures, exhibitions, or other purposes. But we should have it in writing that we had their permission to take the picture.

Rarely have people refused. Of course, it is helpful that we live in this digital age, so we can show them the photo on the LCD. What's more, we often offer to email them a link to the photo on our Web page if it's good enough to post. Everybody loves looking at photos of themselves. (What we DON'T do is promise them a print of any photo we take. Because of the time and expensive involved, that's a promise that we can rarely keep, so we rarely make it.)

When you go from cold air to warm, damaging condensation can form on your equipment. This is true whether you are in the cold outside, going inside to get warm, or if you are in air-conditioned comfort, headed out into the heat. Putting your stuff inside airtight plastic bags can help, but make certain that your camera body and lenses have acclimated to the new temperature before removing them from the bags.

In freezing weather, LCDs become increasingly less visible and unreliable, and batteries don't last as long in the cold. We usually keep our extra batteries in an inside pocket, where our body warmth can help protect them against premature depletion from the cold. But be careful of that condensation, again. You don't want to get moisture inside your camera's battery compartment.

If you tend to shoot in very warm or cold climates, always use environmentally optimized memory cards, like SanDisk's Extreme III series. They will function properly when other cards become erratic or unreliable. However, they aren't protected against moisture, so always store them in their hard plastic cases when not in use, and avoid getting them (or your camera) wet when swapping them in rainy or snowy weather.

Dust is a major concern, since every time we change lenses, we open up our DSLRs to the elements, exposing their inner workings — including the image sensor. When changing lenses, we always seek a protected area away from the wind, or, at the very least, use our own bodies to block the wind. Ideally, we use a lint-free changing bag in dirty, dusty, sandy, windy areas. Philippe Tarbouriech told us that he tries to avoid changing lenses as much as possible in dusty areas. "When in Bangladesh," he said. "I didn't change at all."

Recently, Josh Marten gave us a great tip for shooting in the rain and snow: he uses a gator to protect his cameras in inclement weather. For the uninitiated, gators are elasticized waterproof leggings that outdoorspeople wear over their boots. He puts his camera inside the gator; the lens can see through one end, and you can see into the viewfinder through the other. "I've carried a gator in my camera bag for the last 7 years," Josh said, "And I've never had to go in from the weather." We plan on buying a gator next time we go down to the hardware store.

Security Issues

Daniel started his career as a war correspondent and photojournalist, dodging bullets, crazy mercenaries, and children with automatic weapons. Since we've been together, the dangers we've faced have been much less incendiary. Still, security and safety remain an important consideration, for two reasons:

- Photographers carry equipment — equipment that is perceived by others to be expensive and therefore valuable.
- As photographers, we tend to follow our lens without thinking where we are going. If the opportunity for a great image presents itself, we tend to walk into alleyways, through jungles, even across a busy street without regard for traffic.

Protecting Our Images

Few things are more valuable to photographers than their picture files.

When taking photos on location or otherwise away from our studio, we have adopted a simple technique Jay Maisel, the famous New York photographer (www.jaymaisel.com), once showed us. We put colored stickers on the small plastic memory card holders. When the card is empty, we put the card in the holder in such a way that we can see the size of the card. When the card is full of photos, we flick the write-protection switch, and put the card into the holder so that the colored sticker obscures the card size.

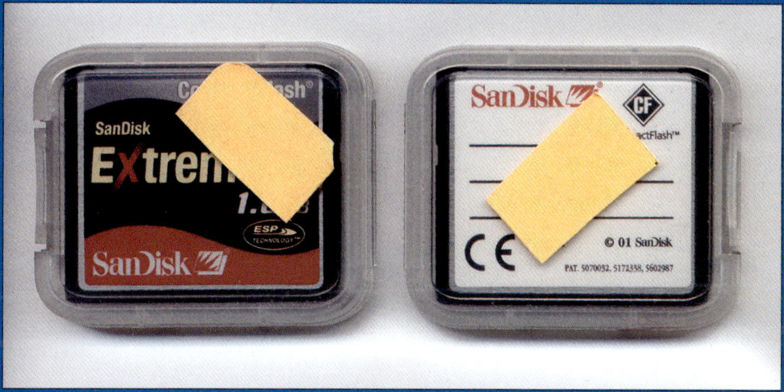

We put a colored label on only one side of the plastic memory card holders. Just by looking at the card on the left, we know it is filled with pictures. That's because we can't see the card's size through the holder cover; the label is covering it. The card on the right is facing away from the colored label, which means, on the other size of the holder, we would be able to see the size of the card. Therefore, at a glance we know that the card on the right is empty and can be used.

While shooting, we always keep our used memory cards on our person, rather than in the camera bag. If we are away from home, once we get to the hotel (or wherever we are staying), we stash the filled cards into a room safe or the hotel's safe deposit box. If possible, we copy them into our laptop, but don't erase the cards while still on the road — in case something happens to the laptop. Once we get home, the photos are emptied right away into our computer and queued for archiving. (See Chapter 9, regarding transferring and archiving photos.)

Here are some of the ways we try to protect ourselves:

- Stay alert to everything around you. Don't fixate on a single image and angle. Awareness doesn't only make for good photography; it's good security.
- Remember that even isolated roads can have traffic. Please look and listen both ways before crossing a street or path.
- Be aware that your perception of distance can be distorted when looking through a wide angle or telephoto lens. Frequently glance away from the viewfinder.
- When Sally has a camera in her hands and/or a camera bag on her back, she never carries a purse. Instead, she uses a belly bag around her waist. Although ugly and unfashionable, it leaves her hands free to protect the equipment and take her shots. (By the way, her wallet and passport are seldom in the belly bag, but secured elsewhere on her person.)
- When shooting by herself in urban areas or anywhere she is worried about someone sneaking up behind her, Sally will open up her tripod or monopod, and carry it on her shoulder, with the leg(s) sticking out behind her (usually protruding over her backpack).
- If we put our camera bag on the ground, where other people might run up and grab something, we don't turn our back on the bag or walk more than a couple of steps from it. More often, when shooting with a tripod, we will wrap the camera bag's strap around one of our own legs.
- We carry lockable steel cables with us. That way, we can lock our bags closed and attach them to a nearby immovable fixture (such as a telephone pole), when we do need to turn our backs to our equipment. You can find lockable cables at `www.kensington.com`.
- We use a tiny, two-part electronic gizmo called the Security Force Wireless Separation Sensor (`www.digitalinnovations.com`) that beeps loudly whenever our camera and camera bag are moved more than 10 feet away. That way, we can't forget about the bag while shooting, nor can anyone walk away with it without alerting us.

Finally, we have both agreed that in a truly dangerous situation, we will throw our equipment or wallets in one direction and run the other way. Most thieves will go for the valuables rather than the victim, given that clear a choice.

Summary

By definition, photographers are people who get the shot by whatever means it takes. The best, most successful photographers are those who plan carefully but are ready to take advantage of any shooting situation or opportunity. This they do by keeping their equipment ready at all times, making optimum use of the environment, using their senses and common sense, and interacting successfully with those whom they are trying to photograph.

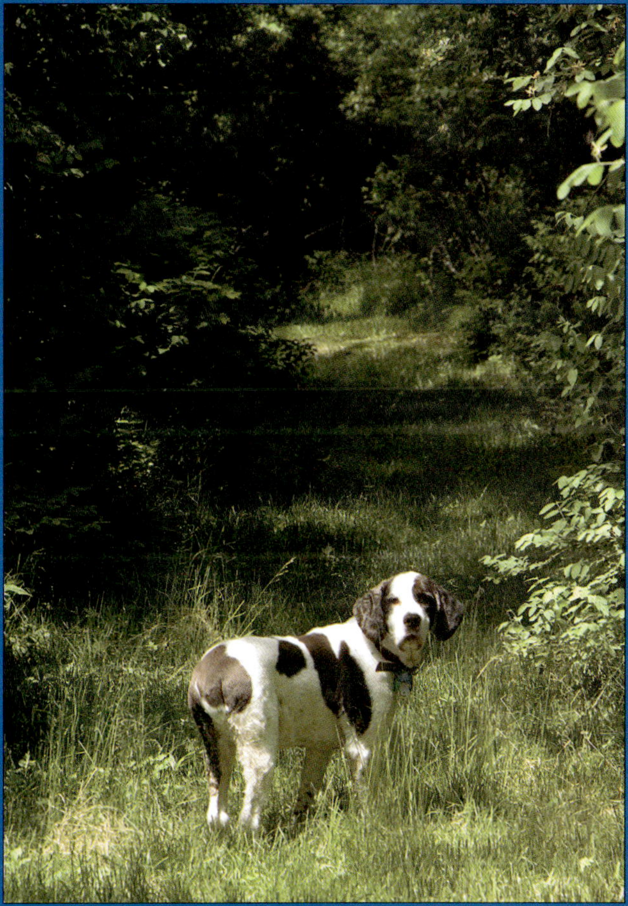

Sometimes, the light is simply perfect, and your subject glances back toward you; that's when you have to grab your camera and shoot, before the moment passes. (Photo taken with a Nikon D70, 24–120mm lens set at 70mm, 1/125 at f5.6.)

Chapter 8

Lighting

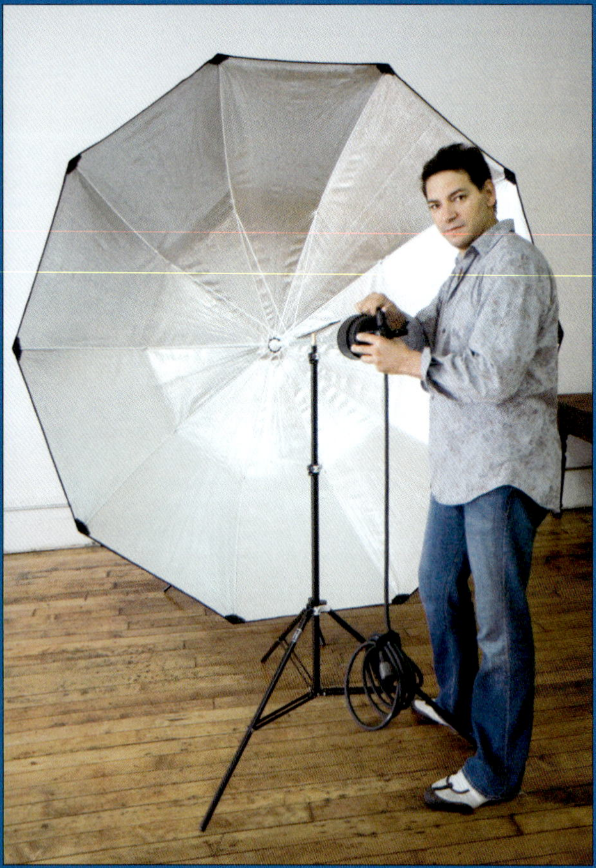

New York photographer Joseph Cartright setting up a large umbrella to reflect light from his studio strobe. (Photo taken with a Canon 1Ds Mark II, 16–35mm lens set at 27mm, 1/250 at f2.8.)

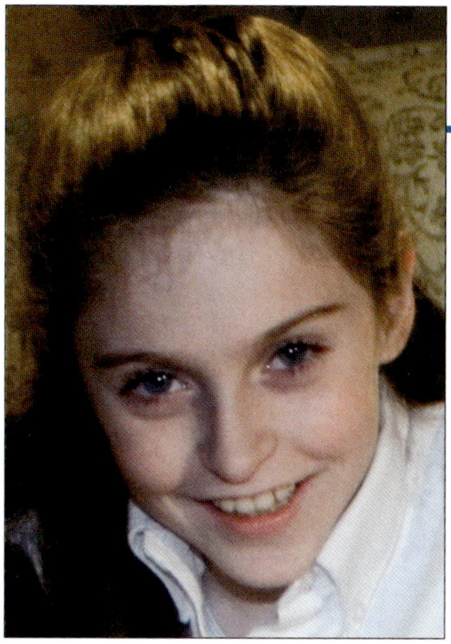

Often, the best lighting is lighting that you don't notice. (Photo taken with a Nikon D2X, 24–120mm lens set at 38mm, 130 at f2.4, with an SB-800 Speedlight on the camera, and another SB-800 slaved on an umbrella reflector.)

Hanging in our hallway is a beautiful picture, a wedding gift to us by Daniel's childhood friend, renowned photographer Siegfried Halus. It is one of his signature Flashlight series, most of which were shot at night in the New Mexican desert. Leaving his camera on a tripod with its lens wide open, he painted the scene, literally, with a flashlight, illuminating those areas he wanted captured on film. It is a masterfully executed painterly photograph.

While most of us set up lights and keep them in place for each frame, Siegfried's method demonstrates a universal truth about photography: images are created by striking the image sensor or film with light. Without light, there is no picture.

In this chapter, we discuss:

- Using light and shadows to sculpt and contour
- Reshaping faces and moods with carefully placed lights
- Using studio lights with DSLRs
- Taking advantage of DSLRs intelligent two-way communication with matched TTL strobes
- Tips and tricks for great lighting

Shadow and Light

Just as light is the essence of photography, shadows are equally important. Together, the two give us the ability to create contours and textures, make our physically flat pictures appear three-dimensional and alive. (See Figure 8-1.)

It doesn't matter if the light illuminating your subject is sunlight streaming in through a nearby window, a desk lamp brought closer to your subject, an intelligent TTL flash communicating with your DSLR, or a full set of studio strobes. The key to great lighting is controlling the light, as well as how it defines and delineates the shadows. (Later in this chapter we discuss TTL and studio lighting.)

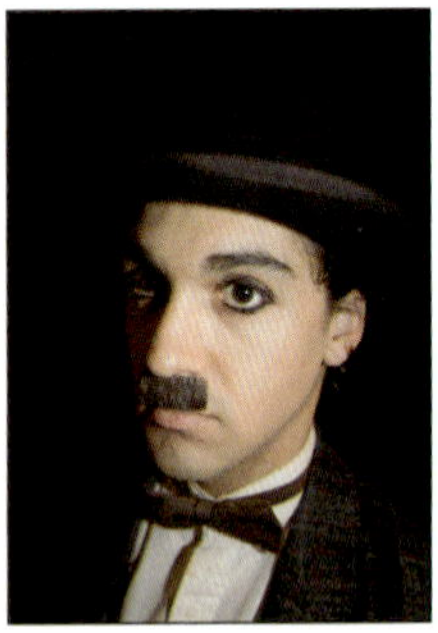

Figure 8-1: In this portrait of Todd d'Amour in the role of Chaplin in TNT Theatre's production of *Silent Lives*, it's the shadows that define the photo, capturing the dark side of The Little Tramp's dreaminess. The careful lighting, combined with the deep shadows, gives contour and shape to the image. (Photo taken with a Canon EOS-1Ds Mark II, 16-35mm lens set at 30mm, 1/160 at *f*2.8.)

You can control five aspects of your light:

- The power
- The distance to your subject
- The quality
- The color
- The angle

Power and Distance

The first two aspects — your light's power and distance to your subject — are linked variables. The intensity of the light depends on its own power rating (measured in lumens or watts). However, the closer your light source is to your subject, the brighter it will be. Pull it away, and the amount of light falling on the subject diminishes.

In addition, the distance of the light also affects how much of the subject it will illuminate. Think of light as a cone, whose starting apex is the source. The closer the light is to the subject, the smaller the area covered on your subject. The further away, the larger the coverage. (See Figure 8-2.)

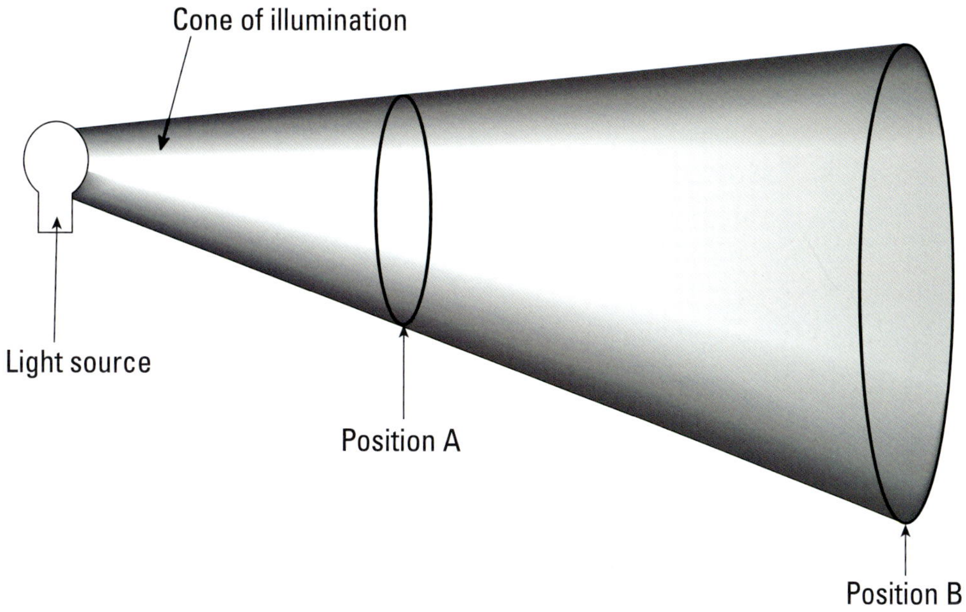

Figure 8-2: Picture your light as a cone of illumination projected by the light source onto your subject. The power and area of coverage of the light is relative to the physical position of the light to the subject. If the subject is close to the source (Position A), the illumination will be stronger and brighter, but the area of coverage will be smaller. On the other hand, if the subject is further away (Position B), the illumination will be not as bright but will cover a larger area.

Many photography textbooks abound with mathematical formulae for setting up studio lights. We don't subscribe to formulaic photography, however. What's more, in an informal survey among our photographer friends, none use equations to set up their lights. Lighting for a great photo goes well beyond mathematics. Every scene and person is different, requiring an aware eye, a discerning sense of artistic value, and an intuitive understanding of photographic dynamics.

However, we realize that some photographers like numbers, so here they are, courtesy of photographer Dan Clark (`www.weinberg-clark.com`). "The relationship between light and distance follows the inverse square law. Halve the distance between the light and the subject, and the light is 4 times brighter (2 *f*-stops). Since each *f*-stop is 1.4 (the square root of 2) times the preceding *f*-stop, they follow the same pattern. So, if you have a light that's 4 feet (think *f*4) from the subject, you can drop it down one stop by moving it to 5.6 feet (think *f*5.6) from the subject, or two stops when it's moved to 8 feet."

In other words, if you need to increase the amount of light, either up the power (wattage) or bring it closer to the subject (or, of course, add lights). Or vice versa. If you want to increase or decrease the area of coverage, move the light from or closer to the subject (or add/remove lights).

The Quality of Light

Lighting is said to be flat or contoured, hard or soft. These are qualities that are neither desirable nor undesirable. Instead, they are choices you make, which can change the impact and message of your photographs.

FLAT OR CONTOURED

Flat light is created by direct illumination, face on — either by a flash attached to the camera or some other light source angled along the same path as the lens. Contoured light creates shadows, giving more definition to details and textures, and making the subject appear more dimensional. (See Figure 8-3.)

Contoured lighting directs one's eye towards the details, forcing the viewer to pay close attention to certain areas. It not only adds dimension but can create a mood and ambience. (See Figure 8-1.)

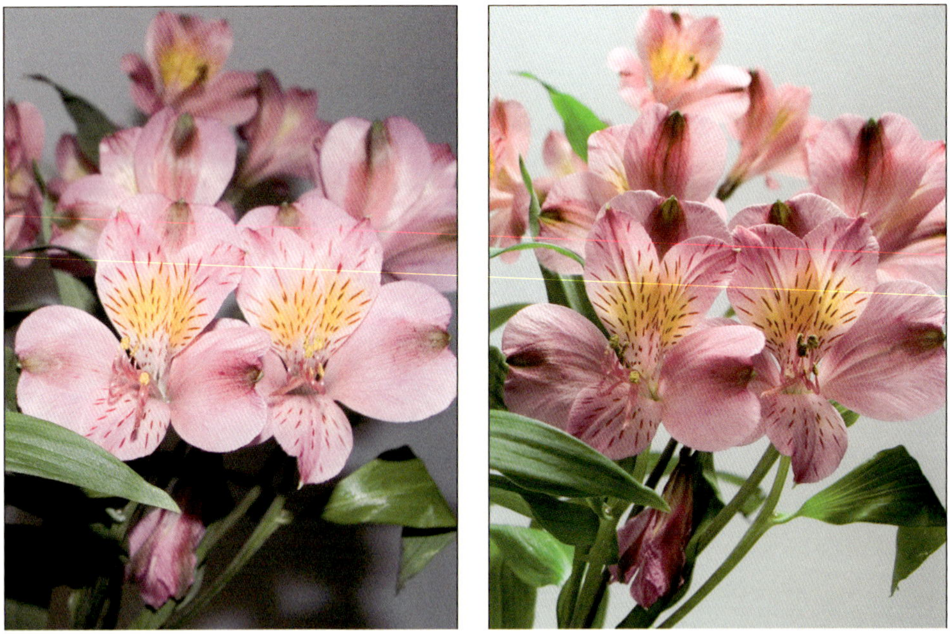

Figure 8-3: (Left) Using the camera's built-in flash creates a very direct and flat light. That simplifies this image, so it emphasizes shape, color, and light, rather than details or textures. (Photo taken with a Pentax *istD, with an 18–55mm lens set at 24mm, 1/45 at *f*8.) (Right) We closed the built-in flash for this picture, lit these flowers from the side, and added a backlight. The resulting shadows made the petals and leaves appear much more textured and contoured, almost three-dimensional, pulling the eye to pay attention to the small details. (Photo taken with a Pentax *istD, with an 18–55mm lens set at 24mm, 1/15 at *f*8.)

Flat lighting can direct one to take in a fuller, wider view, rather than one where the viewer is distracted by the details. We sometimes use flat lighting to diminish blemishes, for example in a portrait where scarring or pockmarks are not a statement of character and life. In that case, we might make the light on the face flat, but add highlights (and shadows) to the hair.

HARD OR SOFT

In hard lighting, the transitions between shadows and light are sharp and abrupt. Soft lighting diffuses the transition, making it more gradual and less obvious.

We often use hard lighting when we want to make a statement or create a mood with the shadows. (See Figure 8-4 left.) But when the subject and not the shadows are the point of the picture, we generally prefer soft lighting. (See Figure 8-4 right.)

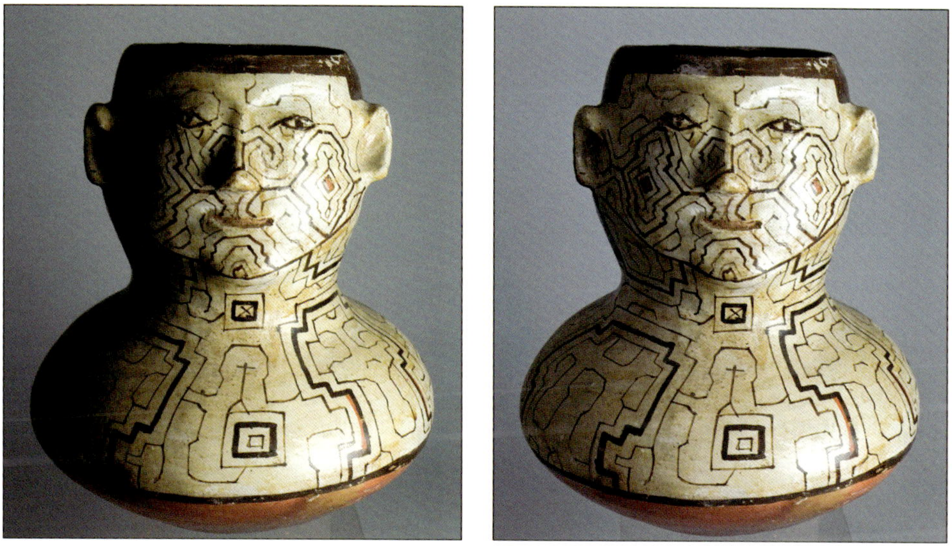

Figure 8-4: (Left) The lighting in this photo is "hard." The shadows are much darker than the bright areas, and the transitions between the two are abrupt. The severity of the shadows draws the eye to the lighting and creates a mood. (Photos taken with a Pentax *istD, with an 18–55mm lens set at 33mm. This photo was shot at 1/30 and *f*8.) (Right) For this photo, we softened the light by putting a diffuser on the lamp. (See Figure 8-6.) The shadows and highlights aren't as severe, plus the transitions are softer. The eye is drawn to the urn itself, rather than the lighting. The diffuser cut down on the amount of light, too, so we had to slow down the shutter speed. (Shot at 1/10 and *f*8.)

In our work, we use four methods to soften light, sometimes combining more than one:

- Rearrange the lights, moving them around to redirect the illumination, and pulling the ones that are too strong further away from the subject.
- Use a diffuser over the light. (See Figures 8-5 and 8-6.)
- Reflect the light, using an umbrella or other reflecting surface. (See Figure 8-7.)
- Fill in the shadows with more light, which might be reflected or another light source added to the scene. (See the next section about reflecting light and Figure 8-8.)

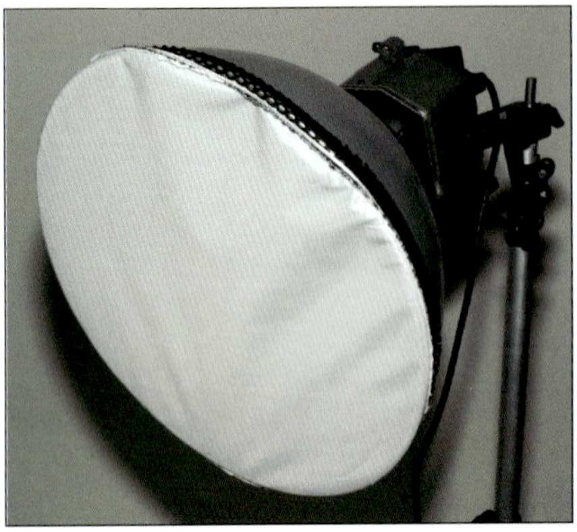

Figure 8-5: We slipped a diffuser bonnet over our light to create the softer illumination of Figure 8-4b. It fits like a shower cap and is quite inexpensive. (Photo taken with a Nikon D70, 24–120mm lens set at 42mm, 1/20 at *f*20.)

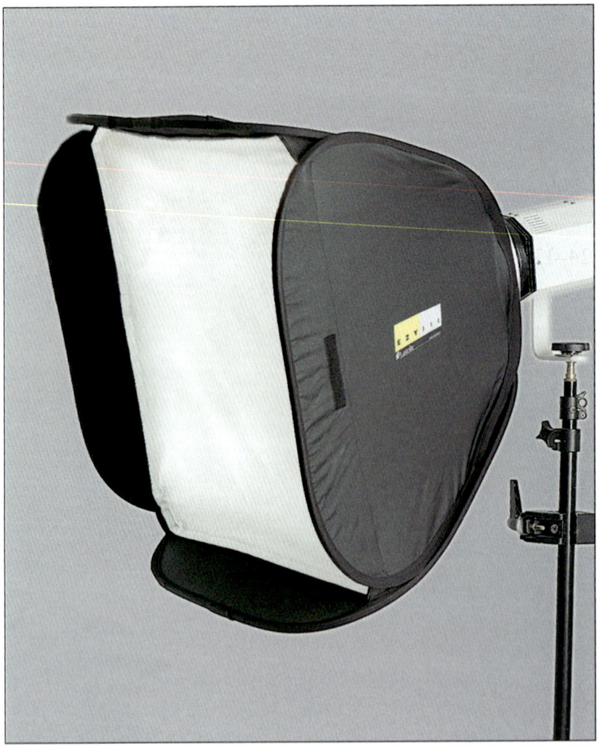

Figure 8-6: Soft boxes, which fit over your entire light, come in all sizes, up to those large enough to light an airplane. (Photo courtesy of Bogen Imaging)

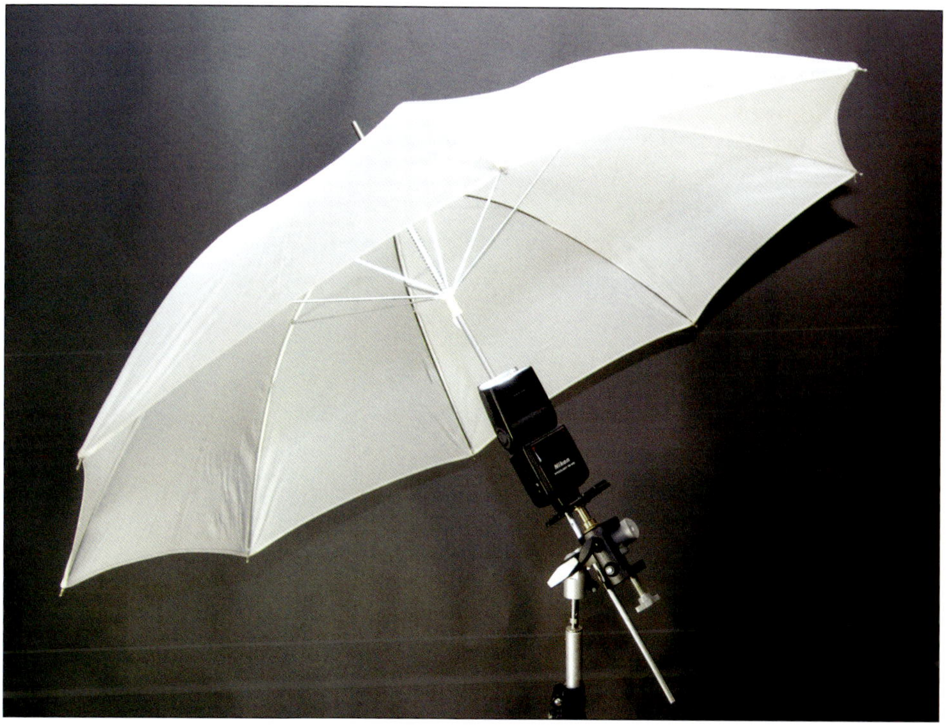

Figure 8-7: To use an umbrella for diffusing your illumination, aim the light up into the cloth, which you then angle to shine on your subject. Like soft boxes, umbrellas come in all sizes and various colors. (Photo taken with a Nikon D2X, 24–120 mm lens set at 1/60 at *f*4. SB-600 Speedlight on umbrella fired wirelessly by an SB-800 on the camera.)

DON'T ADD LIGHT — REFLECT IT

To create pleasingly soft illumination, consider reflecting rather than adding more physical lights. (See Figures 8-8 and 8-9.)

The quality and color of the reflected light is dependent on what you use as your reflector. Photographers often carry pieces of aluminum foil in their camera bags, or get plain metallic wrapping paper on sale after Christmas. However, we tend to use traditional reflectors like the one in Figure 8-8. They fold up compactly and last much longer than foil or paper without creasing or tearing.

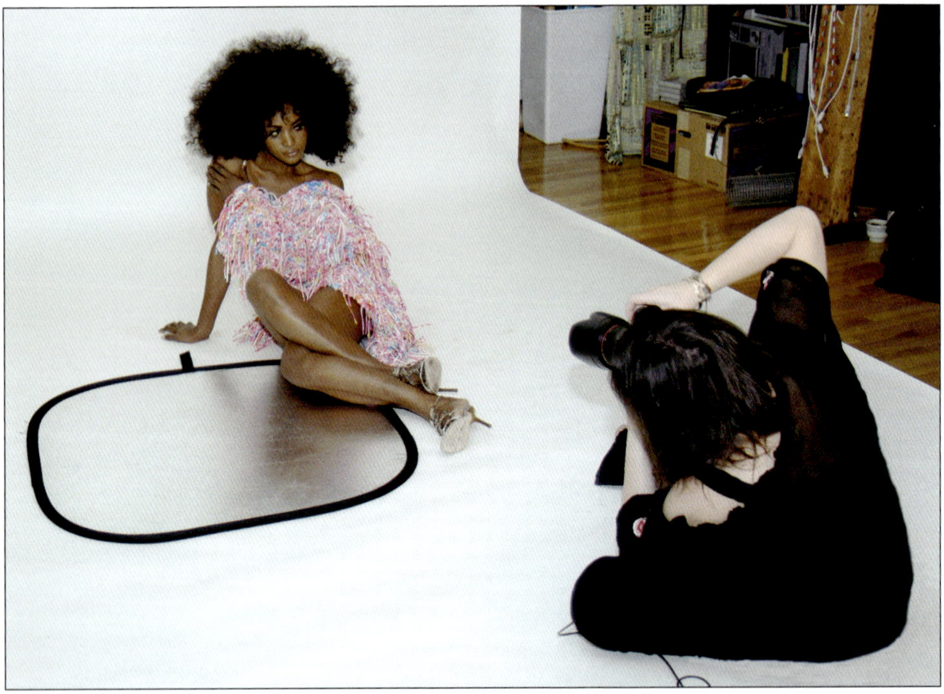

Figure 8-8: For a series of photos that Helene Delillo shot of the model Uju Christian, she used one large rectangular softbox over a studio strobe (positioned just behind Helene in this photo) as her only source of light. Then, she placed a silver reflector on the floor to reflect additional light up onto Uju, to produce cool, sparkling highlights. (Photo taken with a Nikon D2X, 24–120mm lens set at 29mm, 1/30 at *f*4, with SB-800 TTL flash.)

Typically, reflectors are white, gold, or silver. White tends to be neutral, brightening without adding any color. Gold reflectors add a warm color, and silver is cooler. (See the discussion in "The Color of Light," the next section.) Many reflectors have one surface on the front (such as gold or white), and another on the obverse side (such as silver)—two reflectors in one. However, we also like using plain white reflectors with no metallic liner. The white reflector not only is useful as a neutral reflector, it also can double as a diffuser or softener when placed it in front of a light.

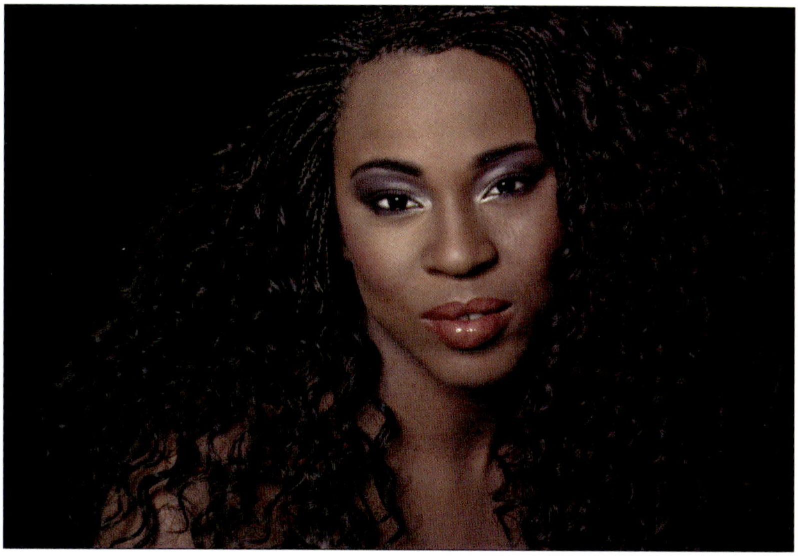

Figure 8-9: For this portrait of the singer Tiyee Champagne, Helene Delillo pulled out the ironing board she keeps in her studio specifically for this type of lighting. As she often does, Helene put a reflector on the board and had Tiyee lean forward over it, with her hands braced on the board. (The ironing board allows Helene to put the reflector at any height for a sitting or standing subject.) It reflected luminous light upward into the face and hair. (Copyright by Helene Delillo. Photo taken with a Canon EOS 10D, 70–200mm lens set at 120mm, 1/125 at *f*11, using a single Briese studio strobe with a large 5-foot umbrella and a silver reflector.)

The Color of Light

As we discussed in Chapter 6, all light has color, and your DSLR has excellent white balance controls to help you remove any color shift introduced by different kinds of light. However, sometimes you want to take advantage of the color of light. Most photographers consciously decide to make a picture warmer (shifted toward the reds) or cooler (toward the blues). Similarly, you might want some other slight or significant hue shift. You can choose your light source based on the color influence it will add to your photos. (See Figure 8-10.)

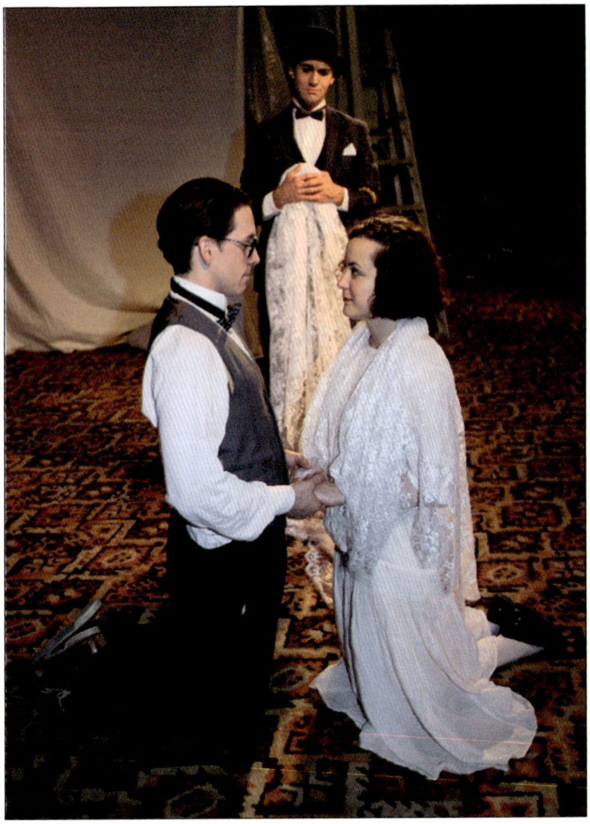

Figure 8-10: To photograph Heather Stewart, Jeff Wills, and Todd d'Amour in this scene of TNT Theatre's production of *Silent Lives*, we took advantage of the stage lighting. For romantic scenes such as this one, the red hue shift adds the right touch of emotional, as well as visual warmth. (Photo taken with a Canon EOS-1Ds Mark II, 16–35mm lens set at 33mm, 1/125 at *f*2.8.)

Chapter 6's guidelines of what type of lights add which colors (such as yellow-green for fluorescents) are not hard-and-fast rules. Unless you are dealing with color-corrected bulbs whose manufacture is well-controlled and stabilized, each factory run of lights can produce different hue shifts. That's not unlike the emulsion problems we used to have with film. What's more, the color of the lights will shift as they age.

To solve the problems of color film variances, we used to buy large quantities of film from the same emulsion lot and do test shoots of one roll to establish a baseline of color for the rest of the lot. Similarly, we recommend that you do test shots with your lights to determine what their color characteristics are. Yes, your camera's white balance will zero out any color contaminants, but you might also want to use those same "contaminants" in some of your pictures, to add atmosphere, mood, humor, or other artistic or subliminal messages.

As with traditional film lighting, you can also add colored gels to your lights. The difference is that we don't recommend gels for correcting white balance (which is done much better by your camera). Instead, use them for drama, to draw attention to a specific area of your image or for other artistic reasons. (See Figure 8-11.)

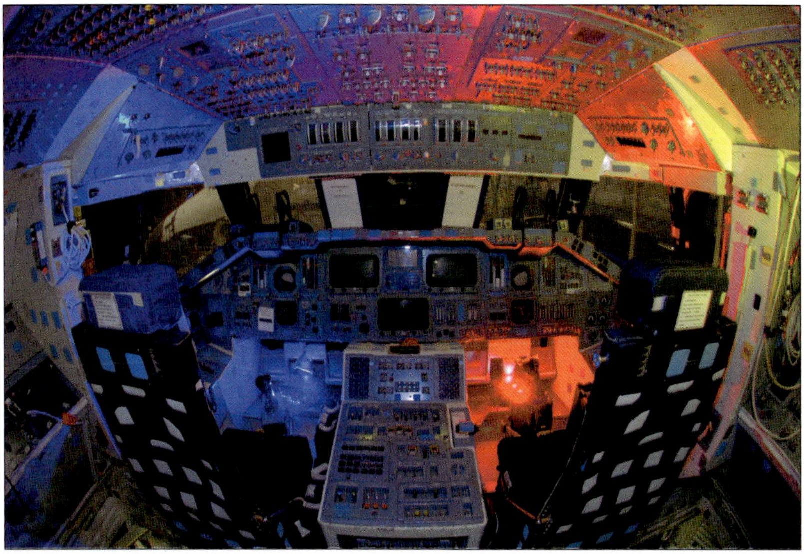

Figure 8-11: Lindsay Silverman took this photo at NASA in Houston, Texas, inside the command module of the space shuttle. The color gels on his lights add interest and intrigue to the picture, pulling the eye to look more closely at various areas in the picture. (Copyright by Lindsay Silverman of Nikon. Photo taken with a Nikon D2H, with a fisheye lens, 1/20sec at *f*5.6, plus four Nikon SB-800 speedlights, one on the camera for bounced fill light, two within the cockpit with red and blue gels, and one behind Lindsay with a blue gel.)

When using color gels on studio lights, we recommend setting up the scene in the following order:

1. Set up your basic lights, with no gels.
2. Use your camera's white balance controls to zero out any color influence those lights might introduce. We recommend using your camera's manual white balance tool, which is much easier than it sounds. (See Chapter 6.)
3. Place your color gels on various light heads after you have set your white balance. That way, the only color that will be introduced into your photo will be that which you purposely added. By the way, make certain that the gels are placed far enough away from hot lights that they won't melt.
4. Take some test shots to make sure that the color you are getting is the color you want. View the test shots on a color calibrated computer monitor to be certain. (See Chapter 11.)

If you are shooting with portable flash strobes, set the white balance to the temperature of any uncolored strobes, and then add the color. But we start with auto white balance, because that will often work just fine.

Color Temperature

As we discussed in Chapter 6, the color of light is physically measurable (in degrees Kelvin, or K) using a color temperature meter. The Kelvin scale is based on the fact that when a flame burns at certain temperatures, it emits specific colors.

We already talked (in Chapter 6) about how different light sources (sunlight, fluorescent tubes, incandescent bulbs, and so forth) can be identified by how cool or hot they are on the Kelvin scale. We can also use the scale to determine what kind of color is emitted by light. For instance, 900K is a dull red, 1500 to 2000K is a yellow-red, 3000K is a yellow-white, and 5000K is a bluish white.

Many DSLRs allow you to use the Kelvin scale to set your white balance. We take a reading with our Minolta color temperature meter of the light falling on our scene. If it is a small scene or one in which a portion is significantly more important than others (such as a face), then we measure only one area, and select that K number in our camera's white balance controls. That way, the camera knows how to interpret the scene, to eliminate any color contaminants introduced by the lighting. If we want several areas in our scene to have the same color values, we use the meter to read the color values of those areas and adjust our lights until they are similar (usually within 50K–100K of each other).

Conversely, if we want the colors in the scene to vary, we first take a reading of the most important area that we want to have no hue shift and input that K number into our camera's white balance control. Then we take readings of other areas to confirm that they, indeed, have a different color temperature than the primary one.

Tip

Classical portrait lighting involves a main light, a side light, a background light and a hair light. We often feel that can add up to too much light and not enough interesting or defining shadows. Experiment with lighting angles to see how they affect you final picture.

The Angle of Light

Change the positioning of the light source and the angle of the path of illumination in relationship to the subject, and you can alter the entire feeling and impact of the picture. You can even reshape the subject with the judicious use of shadows and light, which is very useful when doing portraits. (See Figure 8-12.)

You can also change the entire mood of the photograph, depending on the angle of your lights. (See Figure 8-13.) Notice also, how the different angles of the light actually change the color of the hair, the fairness of the complexion, and the contrast between the hair and face.

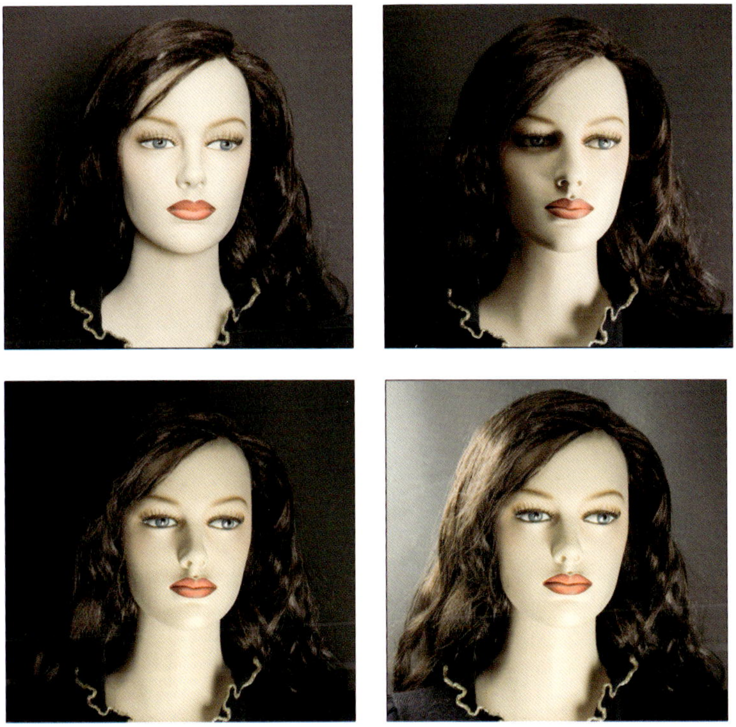

Figure 8-12: Meet Vanessa Quinn, the mannequin we use to test digital cameras. She's never late for work, always has the same predictable (though wooden) personality, and her dress size, complexion, and hair never change. Yet, by using different angled lights, we can literally sculpt her face to reshape it, diminish blemishes (she does have a ding on her forehead), and even make her molded face appear as though her expression has actually changed. It's all done with light and shadows. (Photos of Vanessa taken with a Canon EOS 20D, 17–85 mm lens set at 64mm, 1/10 at *f*5.6.)

(Top left) For this photo, we used a single light, positioned right next to the camera, so it came straight onto Vanessa's face, at her eye level. This creates classic flat lighting, which can broaden the face and make the complexion appear smooth and flawless.

(Top right) Moving the eye-level light to the side created some dramatic shadows and made her face appear narrower. Be careful with this kind of lighting, and be sure the shadows that are produced are attractive rather than distracting.

(Bottom left) Lowering the single light and angling it upward made the light appear luminous, almost as though it is internal to Vanessa. Unlike the direct, flat lighting in the top-left picture, this angle creates interesting contours but still can diminish blemishes.

(Bottom right) This portrait was done with a three-light setup. One light was angled to illuminate the background and add highlights to Vanessa's hair. Another was in front and below her, angled upward (as in the bottom-left picture). The third was on the opposite side to the background/hair light, at about a 45-degree angle to Vanessa's face and almost at eye level.

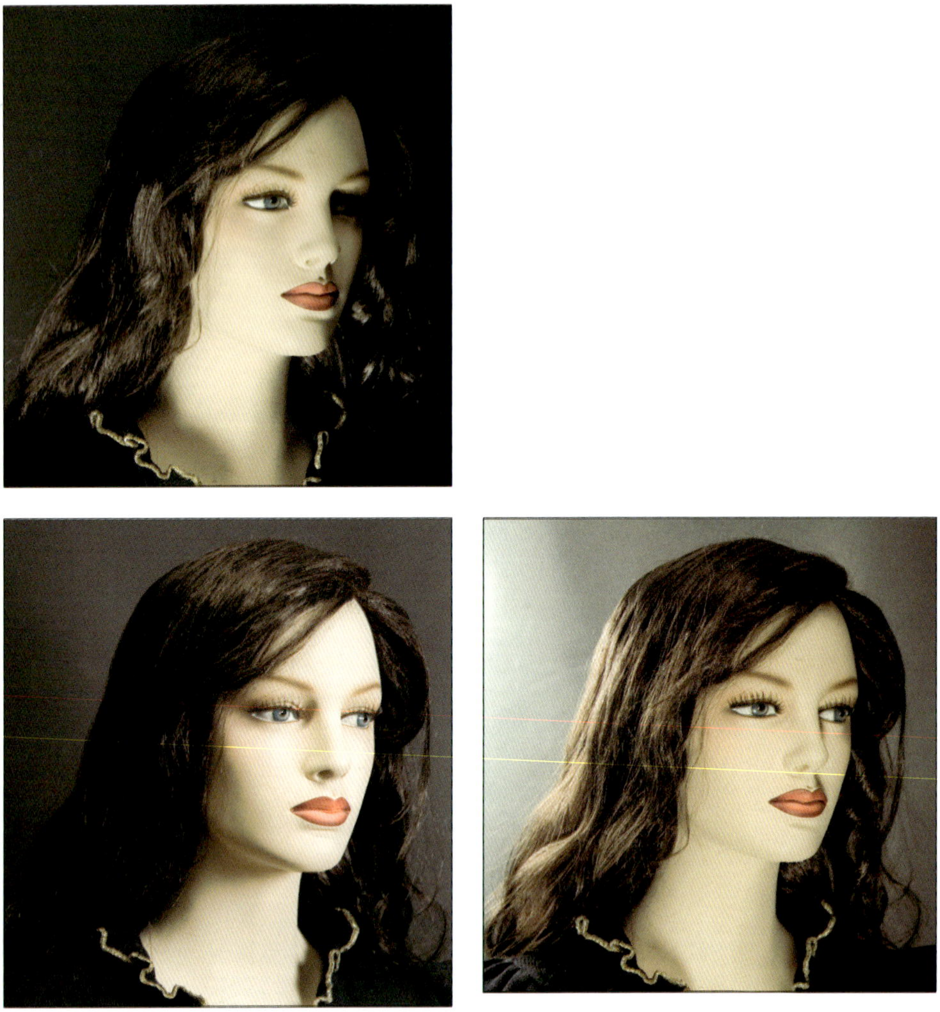

Figure 8-13: (Top) Using a single light from the side and angled upward from below gave Vanessa an aura of mystery.

(Bottom left) Moving that lower light toward the front of Vanessa spread the highlights to nearly cover her face. While it is the same relationship of light angle to Vanessa's face as the top-left picture in Figure 8-12, because of the different camera angle, it makes her seem more aloof, almost a cool personality.

(Bottom right) Adding a background/hair light to the lower-front light of the bottom-left picture makes Vanessa seem more natural, accessible, and warm.

Tip

Anytime you have an unwanted reflection, such as in eyeglasses, reangle the light and/or the camera. For other shiny objects, reangling may work, but you can also try using reflectors, diffusers, or baffles to block whatever is being reflected on the surface. For instance, when photographing silver serving pieces, such as a teapot, we will place cardboard covered with aluminum foil between the serving piece and whatever is showing up as an unwanted reflection in the silver.

Lighting Practicalities

DSLRs work well with three kinds of lighting:

- Whatever lights happen to be available
- Traditional studio lights
- Matched TTL strobes

Available Lights

Let's be honest: our choice of lights often has as much to do with what happens to be at hand and/or is easy to set up as it does with some more esoteric technical or artistic issues. We turn ceiling lights on or off. We move household or desk lamps closer to our subject. We direct our subject to move closer to the lights and/or window.

The great thing about DSLRs is that they don't really care what the light source is — once you set your white balance correctly to give you the colors you seek. (See Chapter 6.) All that matters is getting enough illumination where you want it — and, of course, creating the shadows that are most appropriate for the picture you have in mind.

Tip

When using studio lights, cords can end up snaking all over the place. You'll save a lot of confusion, time, and effort by simply putting matching labels on the plug end of the cords and on the light heads. That way, we know at a glance that a specific cord (marked A) matches a specific strobe head (also marked A).

Traditional Studio Lights

You can use almost any kind of traditional studio lights with DSLRs, including:

- Color-corrected fluorescents
- Studio strobes
- Tungsten halogen lights

COLOR-CORRECTED FLUORESCENTS

For most of our still life work, we use flicker-free, color-corrected fluorescents that are rated to deliver consistent 5000K or 5500K light. (See "The Color of Light" section earlier in this chapter.) We plug them into line stabilizers so that any fluctuations in the electricity are smoothed out, to avoid any change of color that dips or spikes might cause.

This is our preferred still life set up for several reasons:

- It delivers reliable, consistent, daylight-simulated light.
- Fluorescent lights are cool, which is more comfortable for working. It also means that we can use nearly any kind of material over them as diffusers or color filters.
- It involves no guesswork. We turn on the lights and can see exactly how the illumination and shadows will affect our scene before we press the shutter button.

One limitation of fluorescents is that they tend to be dimmer than strobes or tungsten halogens. But that's easily taken care of — just add more lamps.

Warning

Some older studio strobe systems are too powerful for use with digital cameras and can even burn your camera's flash contacts. Be sure to check your camera's documentation and your lights' voltage rating before plugging them together. You may need to use a device such as Wein's Safe Sync (`www.weinproducts.com`) to protect your camera.

STUDIO STROBES

On the side of many (but not all) DSLR bodies is a pc plug port. (See Figure 8-14.) As you probably know, pc, in this case, has nothing to do with personal computers or political correctness. It's the name of the port into which you can plug the cord for syncing the firing of studio strobes with your camera shutter button.

With the pc cord plugged into the side of your camera, and your studio strobes set up as they usually are, pressing on your shutter button will automatically fire the lights.

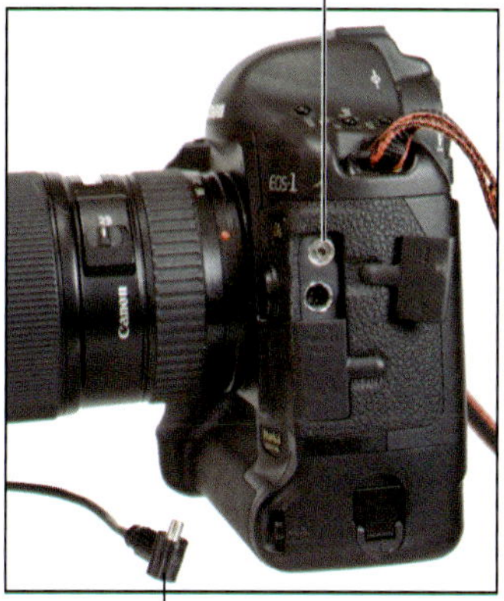

Figure 8-14: If your camera has a pc port, it is likely under a small flap on the side of the camera body, as it is on this Canon EOS-1Ds Mark II. (Photo taken with a Pentax *istD, 18–55mm lens set at 55mm, 1/2 at *f*5.6.)

Studio strobes are great for portraits and any other live subjects. That's because the firing freezes any movement. They can also be used for still life setups, but they are not significantly preferable to other types of lights. In addition to being expensive (a pro light setup can run into the thousands), strobelights are more difficult to deploy and balance. They are hotter and brighter than fluorescents. The heat doesn't come from the flash tube — it fires for only a split second — but from the halogen modeling lights (they remain on continuously, for focusing and framing), which warms up the strobe head considerably — so much so that many heads have built-in fans.

Setting Your DSLR Exposure for Strobes

Using studio strobes requires setting your DSLR to manual mode. It also requires reading the documentation to determine the fastest shutter speed that you can select while syncing with strobelight — the so-called "x-synchronization" speed.

Here's why you'll need that information. All DSLRs have what is called a focal plane shutter (as opposed to most consumer digital cameras, which have leaf shutters). At slower speeds, a lightproof curtain opens fully, exposing the image sensor; once the exposure time is reached, a second curtain moves in the same direction to close off the image sensor. But at higher speeds (usually somewhere above 1/150 and 1/250, depending upon the specific make and model), there's not enough time for the two-curtain shutter to remain completely open through the full exposure. What happens is that the first curtain is still opening while the second one begins its movement to close. The net effect is that instead of having an instant at which the entire shutter is open to the image sensor (that's the point when the strobelight is triggered to fire), the two curtains move in tandem as a slit, exposing the image sensor in segments. Why? Because at higher speeds, the mechanical shutter can't move fast enough to fully open and close.

However, studio strobelights flash at anywhere between 1/750 and 1/10,000 of a second. When the strobes fire, you want your entire image sensor exposed. So, you need to know the x-sync speed of the camera — the fastest shutter speed at which the full sensor is exposed long enough to capture all the light of the strobe.

Shoot any faster, and you'll light only part of the picture. The faster you shoot, the narrower the picture frame will be.

On the other hand, you don't want to set the shutter any slower. That's because you could pick up "ghost" images that occur when your shutter remains open after the flash has fired, if there's enough ambient light to illuminate the subject. (Unless you want to use blur as part of your composition.)

You also will have to set your camera's *f*-stop manually. We use a 40-year-old Wein flash meter (`www.weinproducts.com`) to determine the correct *f*-stop by putting it in front of the subject and manually triggering the studio strobelights. The meter reads the amount of light and instantly shows us what *f*-stop to use. You can buy more sophisticated (and expensive) flash meters from Konica Minolta (`www.konicaminolta.com`), Sekonic (`www.sekonic.com`), and other manufacturers, but the Wein flash meter works so well that is has changed very little over the decades.

Or, if you don't want to use a flash meter, you can use trial and error, looking at your just-shot image in the LCD screen and examining the histogram to determine what *f*-stop gives you the best exposure. If the image is too bright, use a smaller *f*-stop; if it's dark, open the lens up one or more stops.

If you can't get the right exposure by varying your *f*-stops (remember, you don't want to change your shutter speed from its optimum setting for strobelight synchronization), then you will have to change your lights. This you do either by moving them closer to or further from the subject, or as is possible with many different units, upping or lowering the flash power.

Once setup and the correct exposure are established, studio strobelights work fast and efficiently. Many units recycle in only a second or two. It used to be that your camera had to be tethered to the pc connector via a long cord, but it's possible to buy adapters that allow you to shoot wirelessly. We don't use them, because a 25' cord costs about $20, while a radio or photoelectric wireless trigger will cost many times that amount.

TUNGSTEN AND HALOGEN LIGHTS

We usually don't use tungsten or halogen lights because they are so darn hot. What's more, they suck up lots of electricity, plus the bulbs are expensive to replace. But many of our fellow photographers prefer them because of their excellent quality, consistent color (about 2800K to 3400K), and versatility. They pump out a lot of power, which means that you can attain greater shutter speeds and higher *f*-stops than with other lighting options. Tungsten halogen lights are best used for still life setups rather than live models, since they won't give you the freeze action capability that studio strobelights can.

Tip

All the methods that you would use to diffuse or reflect traditional studio lights usually work well, if not identically, with TTL strobes. This includes umbrellas, soft boxes, reflectors, and so forth.

Matched TTL Strobes

One of DSLR's major advantages is their matched intelligent TTL flash systems. (TTL stands for "through-the-lens.") Essentially, as the flash is firing, sensors inside the camera read the light reflected from the film's surface, and when the camera's intelligence has determined that enough light has reached the subject, it will turn off the flash. This was a vast improvement over earlier automatic strobelight schemes, such as embedding a sensor in the flash and measuring the reflected light. (Alas, external sensors could be easily fooled.)

TTL works somewhat differently with most digital cameras because there's no film to bounce the light off for the sensors to read (most image sensors don't reflect light). However, the same TTL principle applies; only, instead of reading the light from film, it triggers a series of rapid preflashes that feeds back information from sensors positioned near the CCD or CMOS sensor itself, or, in some models, positioned inside the optical viewfinder. TTL is also much smarter than before, since it can profile different shooting situations, compare them to built-in algorithms, and miraculously come up with what it thinks is the best lighting solution. Another major advantage is that multiple TTL lights can be used to illuminate a subject, without blowing out the image. Modern TTL also allows special effects, like front or rear curtain sync (or both), flash compensation, fast curtain sync, and so on.

Tip

TTL has been around for a long time, even before strobes acquired intelligence. If you are looking for the most advanced flash strobes for your DSLR, be sure the name or specifications has something about intelligence or 3-D in it. (For instance, Nikon calls it iTTL, while Canon's is eTTL.) We highly recommend buying the matched flash units for your camera from your camera manufacturer. That way, you can be sure that you'll be able to use your system to its full potential. In fact, since TTL capabilities vary considerably, if you absolutely must have a particular feature in your flash (the so-called "killer app"), it may actually determine what camera you will buy.

FILL FLASH

Where TTL excels isn't as a primary source of illumination (any flash or lighting system can do that) but for fill flash — pumping out just the right amount of lumens to brighten a scene without significantly increasing contrast or saturation. Like many photographers, we have long been a bit snobbish about flash photography, preferring the look of natural light when we couldn't carry our studio lights around with us. We especially don't like it when a flash adds too much illumination, drowning out the appeal of streaming sunlight and contrasting shadows. However, we have found that the control that a really good TTL flash gives allows us to put just the right amount of light where we want it. This it does by reading the ambient light and adjusting the flash intensity accordingly. When done properly, the effect is subtle, yet spectacular — you're not even aware that flash was used, but the subject looks much better when it's not lost in distracting shadows. Fill flash works best brightening backlit subjects. More often than not, we shoot with a TTL flash on our camera — even in bright sunlight. (See Figures 8-15.)

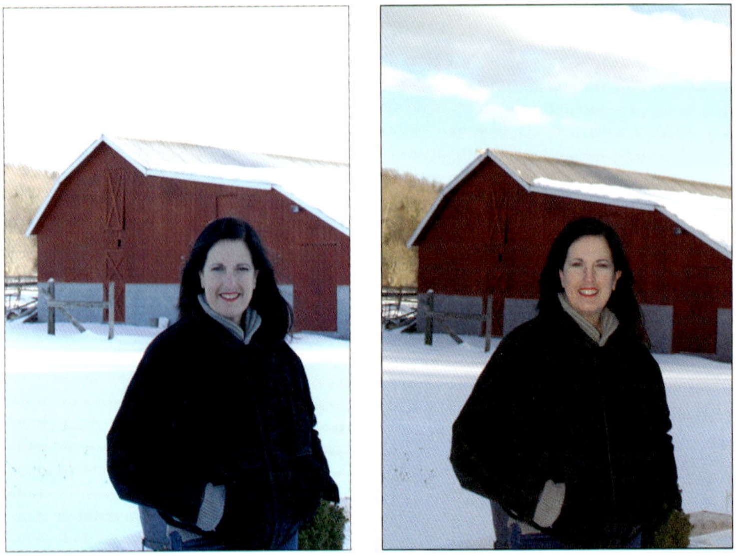

Figure 8-15: (Left) Even though Daniel used spot metering to expose for Sally's face, this portrait is dull, with no visual life or excitement to it. The clear blue sky and the reflections on the white snow are so much brighter than her face that the background lost almost all detail in the highlights and brighter midtones. (Right) When Daniel used an intelligent TTL flash to increase the illumination on Sally's face, it automatically pumped out the right amount of lumens needed to offset the ambient light in the scene, thereby greatly reducing the difference between the light on her and on the background. Exposing for her face, which is now much brighter and colorful, still gave us a great deal of lively detail in the background. (Photos taken with a Nikon D50, 18–55mm lens set at 55mm, 1/60 at *f*11.)

The reason using fill flash works so well in bright sunlight is that it compresses the ratio of the background brightness to the foreground midtones and shadows. That more limited dynamic range allows the cameras to capture the details in both. In mathematical jargon, it reduces the *f*-stop range between the two, so that a good exposure of foreground doesn't blow out the exposure of background (as in the picture on the left in Figure 8-15).

Tip

Helene Delillo suggests that if you are using a flash mounted on your camera for shooting a portrait, consider holding the camera upside down. "Most people have circles under their eyes," she told us. "If you flip the camera upside down, it makes the circles disappear, and they appear very much younger." She acknowledged that this technique works great with little point and shoot cameras. "It's a bit more challenging to hold larger cameras upside down."

WIRELESS CONTROL OVER REMOTE STROBES

The two-way communications between intelligent TTL strobes and your DSLR can control up to three banks of remote strobes, with several units in each bank — wirelessly. These remote flash units can, for example, be deployed around a large room, and with each one controlled from the strobe (flash control unit) attached to the camera. For instance, if you decide that bank A needs to be dimmed, you can dial in a negative exposure compensation without walking over to wherever you have placed bank A. Of course, capabilities and features vary depending on your camera manufacturer and model. The point is that the best of these systems are so sophisticated, capable of very creative and controlled lighting, with greater ease than ever before, that we tend to use them everywhere — including in our studio. Our traditional studio strobelights are beginning to gather dust.

BOUNCE FLASH

As we discussed earlier in this chapter, a light source illuminating the subject from an angle approximately parallel to the lens creates flat lighting. (See Figure 8-16.) That applies to any flash mounted onto a camera — unless you bounce the light. (See Figures 8-16 and 8-17.)

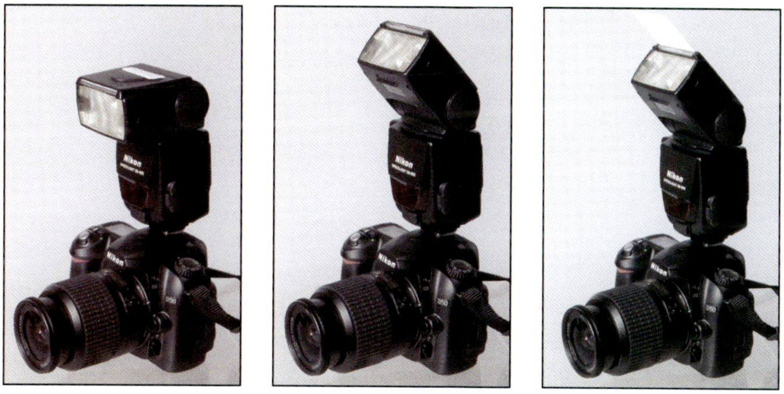

Figure 8-16: (Left) When a strobe is mounted onto a DSLR in its normal position, the flash's illumination follows a straight path to the subject parallel to the lens. Often, the result is flat lighting, as in the left-hand picture in Figure 8-17. (Middle) The heads of many DSLR strobes can be swiveled or tilted upward or sideways to bounce the light so that it reflects on the ceiling or wall. This indirect lighting can create a more dimensional photo, as in the right-hand picture in Figure 8-17. Of course, it requires that there be a surface within range of the flash that can be used to bounce the light onto the subject. (Right) Some DSLR strobes have small white cards built into their heads that can be pulled out to create a de facto reflecting surface to bounce the light when no other suitable surface is available. If your strobe doesn't have one, simply tape a small piece of paper above your flash head, and it will serve the same purpose. (Photos of a Nikon D50 with an SB-800 Speedlight taken with an Olympus E-1, 14–54mm lens set at 38mm, 1/2 at *f*20.)

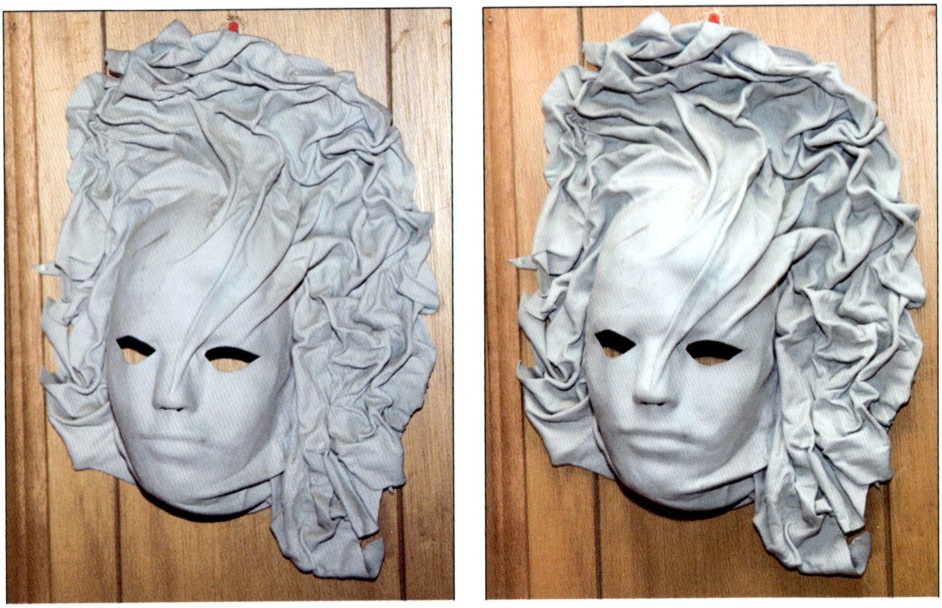

Figure 8-17: (Left) This flat photo was taken with the flash squarely in its default position, as shown in Figure 8-16 on the left. (Right) Tilting the 580EX Speedlite's head upward, to reflect the light on the low ceiling (as in the middle picture in Figure 8-16), created a more contoured photo, with more distinct shadows that are clearly differentiated from the highlights. (Photos taken with a Canon EOS 20D, 17–85mm lens set at 68mm, 1/60 at *f*5.6, 580EX Speedlite.)

Tip

If you do a lot of close-up photography, you might want to invest in a set of ring lights that mount around the camera lens. A ring light gives even 360-degree illumination from as close to the lens as possible, eliminating parallax shadows that a flash positioned away from the lens will produce. In other words, using a ring light creates virtually shadowless close-up pictures.

Tip

The names for flash modes may vary from manufacturer to manufacturer, but the functions are very similar in how they work and what they do. However, not all flash models have all the modes we list in the "Flash Modes" section.

What Exposure Mode Should I Use?

The best exposure for taking flash pictures depends upon your particular model, what you are trying to capture, and your comfort level (or sense of adventure) with your equipment.

In program mode, the camera automatically detects the flash and sets the shutter speed and *f*-stop it thinks appropriate. If you wish, you can change shutter speed and aperture parameters by moving your camera's subdial. Letting the camera and an intelligent TTL flash do their own thing in program mode can produce excellent illuminated pictures. If you don't like the results or want to experiment on your own, that's when you'll want to switch to aperture, shutter, or manual mode.

If you wish to use shutter priority, never set your speed faster than your camera's top speed for x-synchronization. (See the discussion of x-sync in the "Studio Strobes" section earlier in this chapter.) Otherwise, part of the image won't be illuminated, and, at top speed, only a tiny slit will be lit. Conversely, don't set your shutter at a slow speed, unless your subject is motionless and you are on a tripod — or you want to create a blur or ghost images. (See the "Front and Rear Curtain Sync" section later in this chapter.) You may use aperture priority to control your depth of field, but keep in mind the same strictures against using too fast or too slow a shutter speed. If your flash doesn't produce enough light to use the *f*-stop you wish, try boosting the power by upping flash compensation. (See the section on flash exposure compensation later in this chapter.)

On manual, you can get great shots if you know what you're doing. But even if you don't have a clue, the only way to learn is to try. Experiment with pushing the exposure and letting the intelligence of the flash compensate. The worst that can happen is that you'll delete the picture and have to reshoot.

FLASH MODES

In addition to the various functions we've already discussed, most TTL strobes offer other features for more precise control. These include, but are not limited to:

- Flash exposure compensation and bracketing
- High-speed sync
- Front and/or rear curtain sync
- Multiple flash
- Red-eye reduction
- Autofocus assist
- Modeling light

Flash Exposure Compensation and Bracketing

Just as with exposure compensation (EV) in your camera (see Chapter 5), you can manually adjust the power of your flash by the buttons on the back of the head to set plus or minus EV on your flash. Flash bracketing, if your model has it, adjusts the amount of light fired with each of a series of three to five shots. The amount of light illuminating each frame will vary from 1/3 to 3 stops, depending upon the model and the increment selected by the photographer. Bracketing assures that at least one of your frames will have just the amount of light you want.

High-Speed Sync

Remember when we said that you shouldn't use a shutter speed faster than the one your camera is rated for x-synchronization? That doesn't apply when you shoot in the high-speed sync mode, which is sometimes also called focal plane (fp) sync. Instead of a single, bright flash, in high-speed mode, the flash strobes rapidly many times (so fast that it appears to be a single flash), each small spike of light illuminating the open slit area of the focal plane shutter as it moves across the image sensor. This ensures that light falls on the image sensor at every point that the shutter moves, regardless of speed (which can be as high as 1/8000 of a second). When viewed, the light looks seamless. However, there is a tradeoff for this technological magic: each rapid spike of light is only a fraction of the total power of the flash, so its range is much more limited.

When a camera has the feature, we tend to keep it set at high-speed sync continuously. When we use normal to moderately fast shutter speeds (1/250 to 1/1000), it will give us just the right amount of fill light to balance the foreground subject to a well-lit background. When we use it at high shutter speeds (up to 1/8000), the foreground will be perfectly illuminated, and the background will tend to go dark. (See Figure 8-18.)

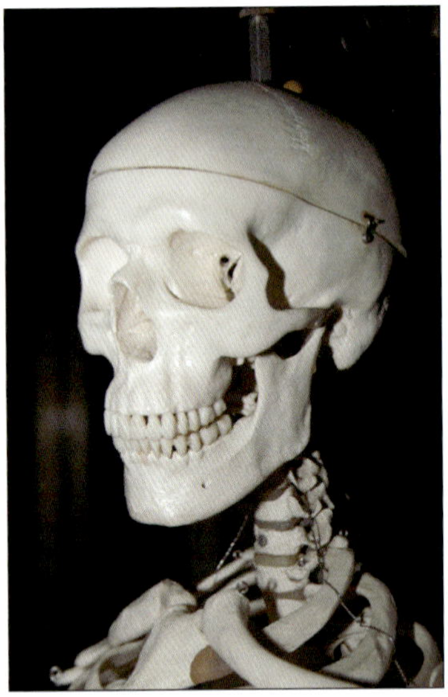

Figure 8-18: The background behind this skeleton was very busy and would have ruined our picture. Shooting at high speed illuminated the skeleton, but made everything else black, which in this case, was a very desirable effect. (Photos taken with a Nikon D2X, 24-120mm lens set at 45mm, 1/8000 at *f*4.5, SB-800 Speedlight.)

Front and Rear Curtain Sync

Still cameras are designed to capture static images—that is, unless you want to show motion in some way that is dynamic and dramatic, artistic and effective. For that, we have front and rear curtain sync. Rear or front curtain sync works by setting the camera at a slow shutter speed (from 1/10 second down to 30 seconds, so it's best done using a tripod), so the camera can capture a continuous motion or action. In rear curtain sync, the flash fires weakly at the instant you press the shutter, to freeze the beginning action, the shutter remains open, recording the image in motion, and the flash fires more strongly at the end, freezing the motion. (See Figure 8-19.) The result is a streaky picture that captures the motion blur but with a perfectly illuminated subject at the end of the frame. Front curtain is the opposite: a strong beginning flash, shutter open to record motion, and a weak end flash. It's a technique that takes some practice to perfect, and it's often a situation in which you just have to keep shooting until you get the timing exactly the way you want it. But when done well, the results can be spectacular.

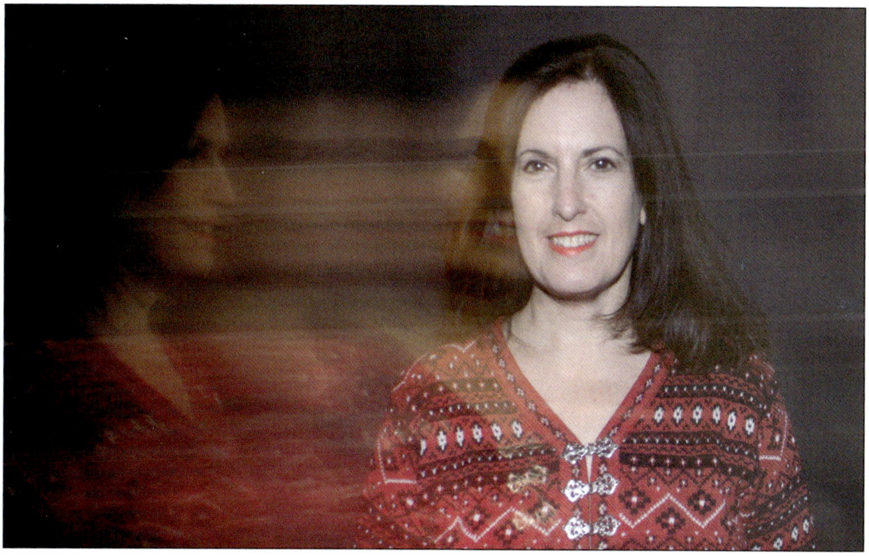

Figure 8-19: An example of rear curtain sync. During the 3-second exposure, Sally walked forward, pausing a couple of times to burn her profile into the blur, then spun around, facing forward where the flash fired. There was enough ambient light in the studio to allow the camera to record her forward motion as well as her face at the beginning and end of the frame. (Photo taken with a Nikon D2X, 24-120mm lens set at 24mm, 3 seconds at *f*2.8, SB-800 Speedlight.)

Multiple Flash

Multiple flash, sometimes called stroboscopic flash, fires a number of very short duration spikes (usually 16) in rapid succession. Unlike high-speed sync, the shutter is limited to no faster than its fastest x-synchronization speed. This means that any motion within the frame is frozen in position 16 times. Why would you want to do that? To create an effect or a record of something in motion, such as a tennis swing, a ball being thrown, and similar actions. It can make a rare, but effective shot, as long as you don't overuse this technique.

Red-Eye Reduction

We all know what red eye looks like—a demon-looking red eye on people and animals, caused when the light from the flash reflects straight back into the lens. Most strobes, TTL or otherwise, come equipped with some sort of red-eye reduction scheme, such as firing off a rapid series of preflashes, to force the iris to dilate and therefore reduce or eliminate the amount of light reflected back into the lens. Unfortunately, most preflash red-eye reduction modes don't work well, but they certainly annoy your subjects facing the lens. To eliminate red eye, either use a bracket to elevate or otherwise reposition the flash, bounce the flash head, or take the red-eye shot and get rid of it with image-editing software.

Autofocus Assist

Most DSLR lenses come equipped with an autofocus mechanism that works by moving the front element of the lens until a light sensor inside the camera says that the subject is at its darkest, or most contrasty, point. But to focus, the lens needs light. This isn't an issue when you're shooting outdoors or have bright available light, but if you're in a dark room, you're out of luck. Many strobes have a built-in illuminator—often called an AF assist—that can be set up to project a red, white, or green light when you press the shutter halfway; the light is just bright enough to allow your camera's autofocus to work properly. Once the lens focuses, you then take the picture by fully depressing the shutter.

Modeling Light

The modeling light is different from the AF assist, because it's designed to aid you, the photographer, rather than help the autofocus. The modeling light is a bright light that you can turn on briefly, usually for about one second at a time (it uses a lot of battery power) to show you where and how the flash will illuminate the subject. If you are shooting with TTL slaves, they will automatically turn on as well, and at whatever intensity you have preselected so that you can see the total effect of your lighting scheme. If you're satisfied where the light falls, then you take the shot. Otherwise, you can adjust the strobes' positions or power until you're satisfied. While modeling lights sound good in theory, unless you are working in a semidarkened room, it may be difficult to discern what the lighting effect will be. The best way is to take a shot and look at it and its related histogram on playback.

Summary

Creating or capturing the perfect illumination for your pictures shouldn't be overly complicated, but it does require some knowledge and experimentation on your part. Your choice of lighting equipment, as well as where you place the lights, will determine what kind of illumination you can throw on your subject and what effect you will create.

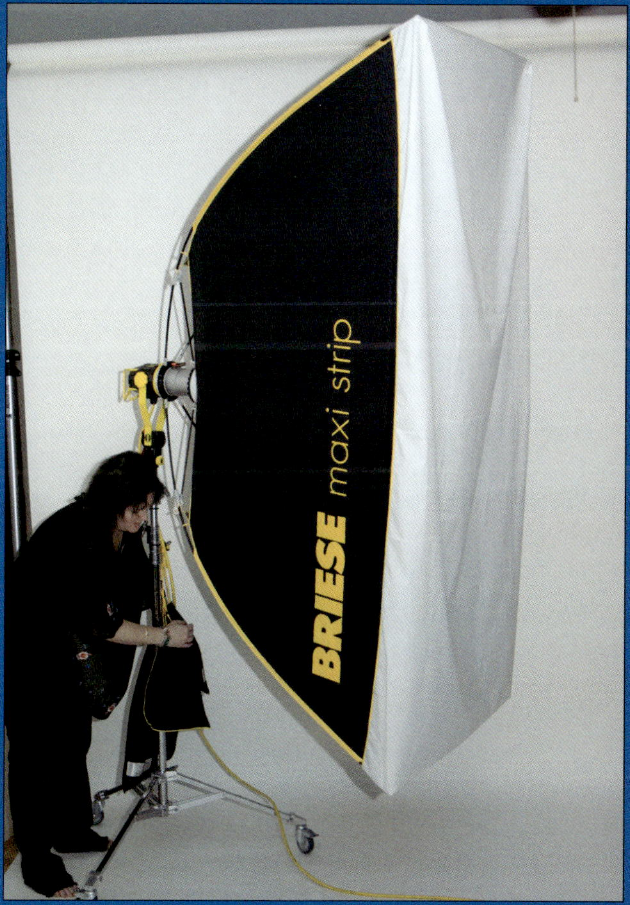

New York photographer Helene DeLillo sets up the large soft box strip light that she often uses as her single light source for her beauty and fashion shoots. (Photo taken with a Nikon D2X, 24–120mm lens set at 24mm, 1/60 at f4, one SB-800 Speedlight on the camera.)

Part IV

Digital Photography Beyond the Camera

Chapter 9

Taming Your Digital Photo Files

Chapter 10

Perfecting and Extending Your Photos

Chapter 11

Understanding Color Management

Chapter 12

Preparing Your Photos for Output and Sharing

Chapter 9

Taming Your Digital Photo Files

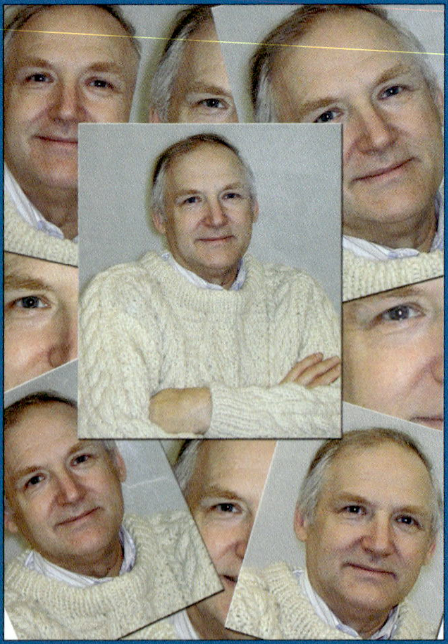

Considering how many pictures most of us take, it's important to develop a system for sorting, organizing, and filing them in a way that we can find any specific photo quickly and easily.

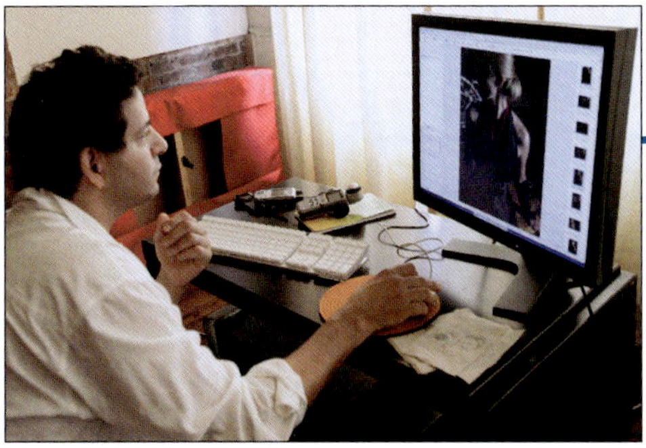

Photographer Joseph Cartright sorts the pictures he just shot. (Photo taken with a Canon EOS 1Ds Mark II, 16–35mm lens set at 33mm, 1/60 at f3.5, ISO 400.)

Back in the 1980s and early 1990s, when we were traveling around the world on assignments, we took advantage of hotel safe deposit boxes whenever they were available. No, we didn't keep our passports and money in the safes. Instead, we put what is most valuable to any photographer under lock and key — our exposed film. Everything else was replaceable. But if we lost our photographs, they would be gone forever.

If only it were that easy to secure digital photos.

Unfortunately for us, we started with digital photography long before there were any really good solutions to help us secure our picture files. What's more, organizing and managing our photos was something of a nightmare. When we uploaded our pictures from our camera to our computer, we would sort them into various folders on our network. We tried giving the folders descriptive names, which often helped us with general searches, such as when we were looking for photos from a trip to California or an assignment on robots. But what if we were looking for a specific picture that was taken of a child picking flowers, but we couldn't remember when or where we shot it? That was difficult. We'd sometimes spend long minutes or even hours, browsing through all our pictures until we found it.

Thank goodness, we now have a choice of mature, intelligent software solutions that make managing, organizing, using, searching, and securing our photo files far more efficient and effective. Some of the tasks that are now easier, deeper, and, in some cases, automated, include:

- Uploading to the computer
- Sorting, rating, and selecting photos
- Keywording, cataloging, and searching
- Leveraging and extending metadata
- Batch processing
- Archiving
- Sharing

Moving Your Photos from Your Camera to Your Computer

In the dark ages of the late twentieth century, when digital cameras were in their infancy, getting photos from a camera to a computer used to be one of the major stumbling blocks for folks just learning digital photography. Transferring data now is such an easy task that it quickly becomes second nature to every photographer, even those who have been at it for only a short while. For that reason, moving photos from your cameras to computer is a step that is sometimes overlooked in many explanations of working with digital photography.

There are two ways to move your photos from your camera to your computer:

- The tried-and-true drag-and-drop method
- Using an automated software wizard

The Tried-and-True Method

The tried-and-true method is quite simple and has worked well for years.

1. Attach your camera to the computer (via USB or FireWire, depending upon your hardware configuration) or take your memory card out of your camera and insert it into a memory card reader that is attached to your computer (also, via USB or FireWire cable). Incidentally, some computers and laptops come equipped with built-in memory card readers.
2. Whether you are on a Mac or a PC, as soon as your computer detects that a camera has been attached or that a memory card has been inserted, it will recognize it as a storage device. In other words, your camera or memory card will be indistinguishable from any hard drive or other external storage device (such as your CD/DVD drive, floppy drive, etc.). If you have created folders in your camera or memory card (see Chapter 6), these subfolders will also be recognized. (See Figure 9-1.)
3. Select all the photos in your camera or memory card, by clicking on the first one and, while holding the Shift key on your keyboard, clicking on the last file.
4. Drag the selected photos into the folder on your computer's hard drive or network drive where you want your photo files to be stored.

You can, of course, choose to move various photos to different folders. Once the camera or memory card is attached to your computer as a storage device, all operations you usually perform on your folders and files can be used on your photo files.

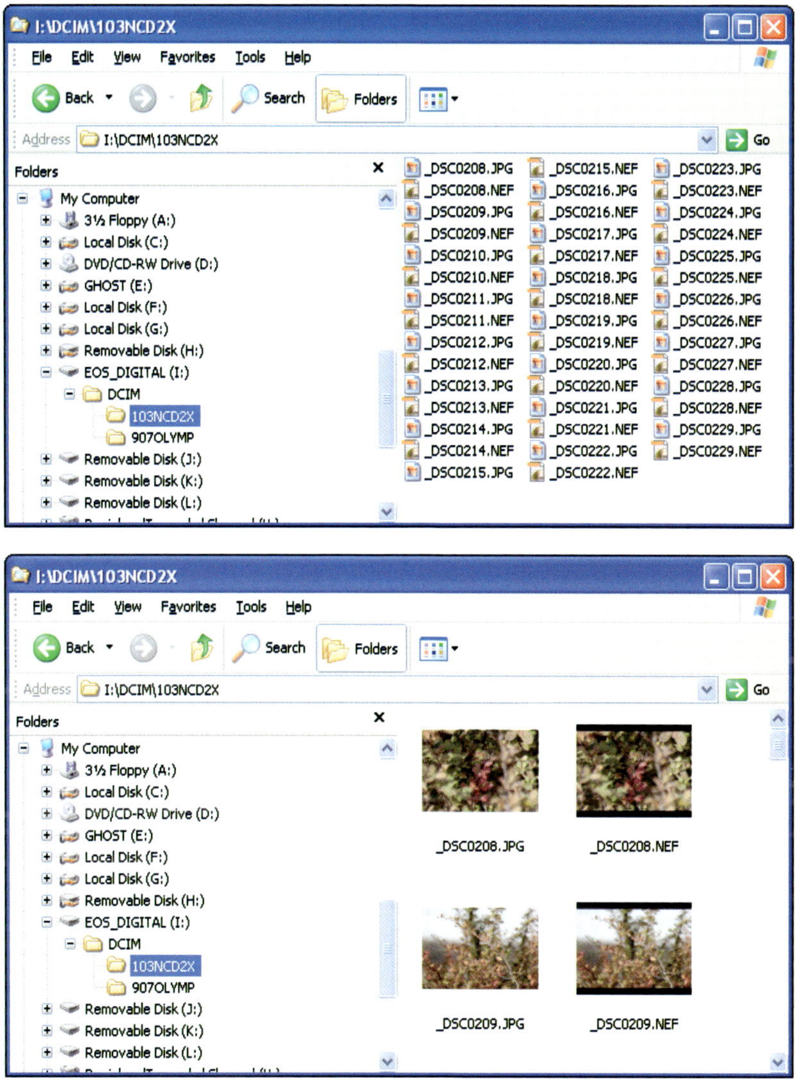

Figure 9-1: (Top) When you attach a camera to your computer, or insert a memory card into a card reader attached to your computer, it shows up as a normal external drive. This screen capture is of Windows Explorer on a PC. In the left pane is a list of all the drives and storage devices attached to the computer. Notice that the A: drive is the floppy disk drive, D: is the CD-R drive, and C:, F:, and G: drives are the system's hard drives. We have several "removable drives" (that is, various storage devices) attached to this system, including a camera memory card as our I: drive. Most memory cards have a folder called DCIM, which will contain the folder or folders of your pictures. Here, the folder 103NCD2X (from a Nikon D2X) is highlighted. In the right pane is a list of all the picture files in that memory card folder. All we have to do is select them, and we can drag and drop them into any other drive attached to the computer or network. Macs recognize memory cards and attached cameras as folders in the same manner. (Bottom) On both Macs and PCs, you can choose to list the files on the attached card or camera as names or as thumbnails. Here, you can see the thumbnails of the photos taken with the Nikon D2X and saved to the attached memory card.

Automated Transfer of Photo Files to Your Computer

Professional software has taken a cue from entry-level programs by automating the downloading process as much as possible. Some programs have wizards that pop up the minute a memory card is inserted or a camera is attached. Others' downloading interfaces are accessed through an icon or a command — typically an import command in the File pull-down menu.

As part of the process, you can usually set where the files will be saved and batch rename all of them to the same root name (plus an incremental number). In addition, you might be able to add annotations, a copyright notice, and other metadata type of information. (See Figure 9-2.) We discuss metadata and batch renaming later in this chapter.

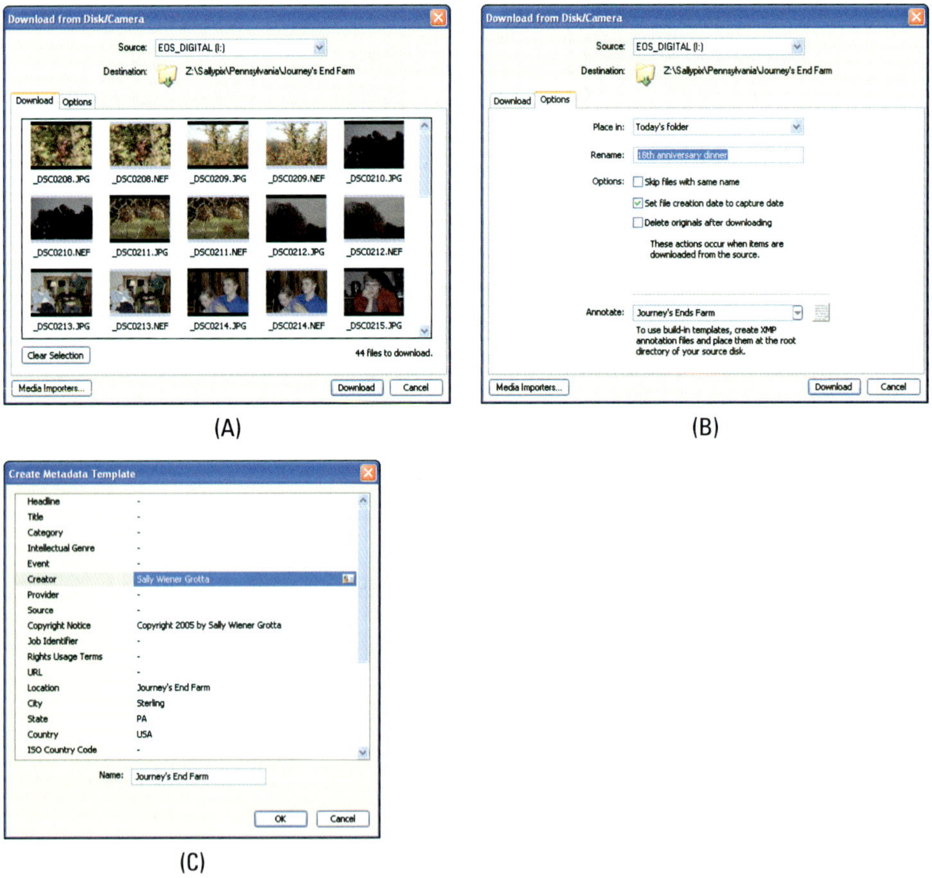

Figure 9-2: iView MediaPro's download interface. (A) You can choose the source of your files and the folder where they will be saved. (B) Other options include batch renaming, selecting what date to associate with the file, and applying a user-defined annotation file. (C) The annotation file is essentially an automated filling in of essential metadata information. (Courtesy of iView Multimedia)

Photo Management Programs

Numerous programs exist to help you tame and organize your photo files. Called by various names — photo management, digital media asset management, photo organizers, etc. — the most popular programs among serious photographers include:

- ACDSee Pro
- iView MediaPro
- Extensis Portfolio
- Adobe Bridge
- Apple Aperture

Deciding which one program is right for you is a personal choice that takes into account how you like to work, whether you are in a collaborative environment, the kind of computer you use, your budget, and which interface best fits your personality and the way you think.

Among these programs, ACDSee Pro (PC only) and iView MediaPro (Mac and PC) are very good for independent photographers and small studios. While the two are different in the details of how they work, they offer comparable power and versatility. Serious and professional photographers who use either program tend to be very happy with them.

Extensis Portfolio is more appropriate for the collaborative network environment (such as a professional studio or magazine office) in which one person is responsible for administrative issues (such as creating new keywords).

Apple Aperture, which is available only for the Mac, is for serious photographers who demand speed and lots of power, and are willing to pay for it. Yes, iPhoto (which comes installed on Mac systems) may be adequate for the occasional photographer, but Aperture offers much more.

Adobe Bridge is included with Photoshop, so you may already own it. Like iPhoto, Bridge is not as full featured as the others, but it is tightly integrated with Photoshop, making it easy to move between your organizer and your photo editor quickly and easily.

Incidentally, as we go to press, Adobe announced Lightroom, which should be released in late 2006. Reportedly, it will function similarly to Apple's Aperture, with the one advantage of being cross-platform (working on both PCs and Macs).

As with all software, we highly recommend that you download free trial versions of photo management programs to try them out. However, be aware that once you start cataloging and keywording your photo library with a specific program, you are making a commitment to that software, and it will be that much more difficult to switch to another at a later date. So, test the program out thoroughly, and try the others, before deciding which one fits your needs, budget, and personality. But don't spend too much time and energy using one unless you intend to buy and use it permanently.

Tip

Digital camera manufacturers come out with new RAW file formats faster than software engineers can develop support for them. What's more, camera manufacturers will often create new variants of RAW for new camera models. So, even if a program supports some formats from a specific manufacturer, that doesn't mean that it necessarily covers others from the same company. Before you buy a photo management program, be sure to confirm that it supports your camera's RAW file format.

Sorting, Selecting, and Rating

If you shoot like us, then you have lots of versions of the same scene, object, or person, each image with a slightly different pose, exposure, lighting, framing, or other variable settings. (See Figure 9-3.) So, the first task (after getting your pictures into the computer) is to sort and select the photos you like the best and which ones you may want to discard.

We used to sort our film slides on a large light table, using a magnifying loop to study each one carefully. Usually, we would put all similar pictures together, then compare them two at a time, replacing the one we liked the least of the two with another, and so on. The duds were quickly thrown into the trashcan, while the good-but-not-best were put aside for reconsideration, labeling, and filing. This "bubble-up" method was the quickest way to sort and prioritize our slides.

The digital process of sorting is quite similar. (See Figure 9-4.) However, on the computer screen, you can usually compare more than two photos at a time, each at a zoomed in view, if you wish. In addition, while you sort, you can rate your pictures, do some basic editing, assign keywords and/or categories, and in some programs, do basic editing. (See Figure 9-5.) See the sidebar on batch processing for a discussion of applying these functions and others to groups of photos.

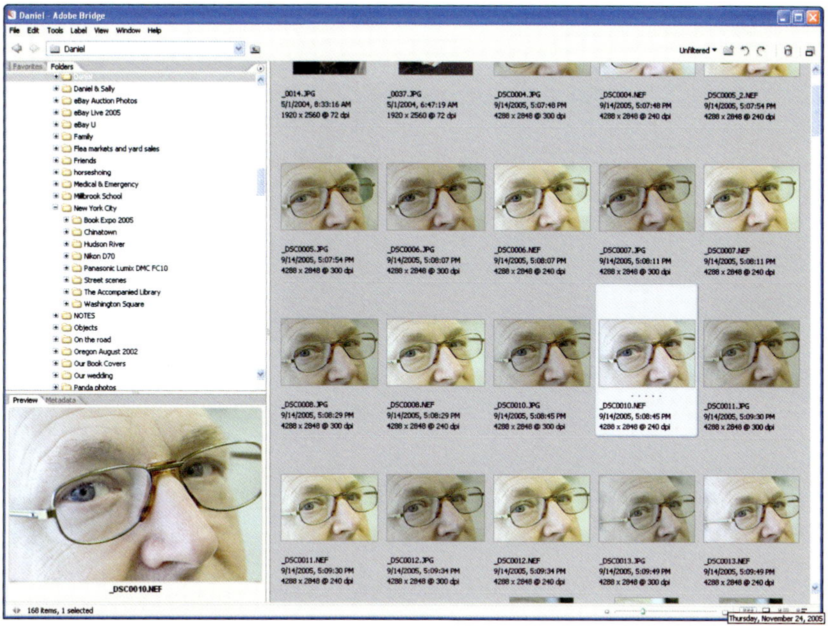

(A)

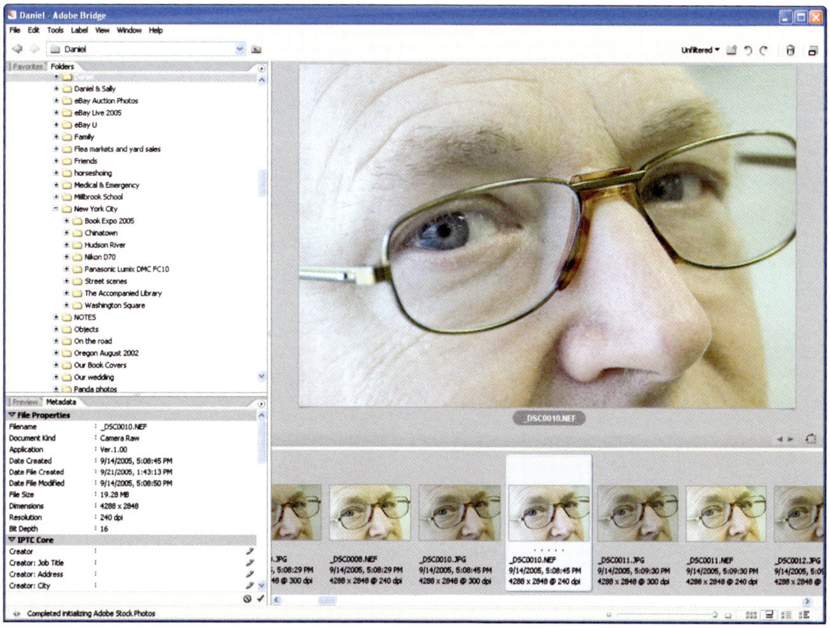

(B)

Figure 9-3: (A) In a photo management program, paging through the many thumbnails of your photos provides a quick overview of what you have in your photo library. You can make the thumbnails smaller for even faster paging, or larger, so you can see more details. (B) The filmstrip view, in which the selected picture is displayed in a large preview, provides more visual information for individual photos. (Screens of Adobe Bridge, courtesy of Adobe Systems)

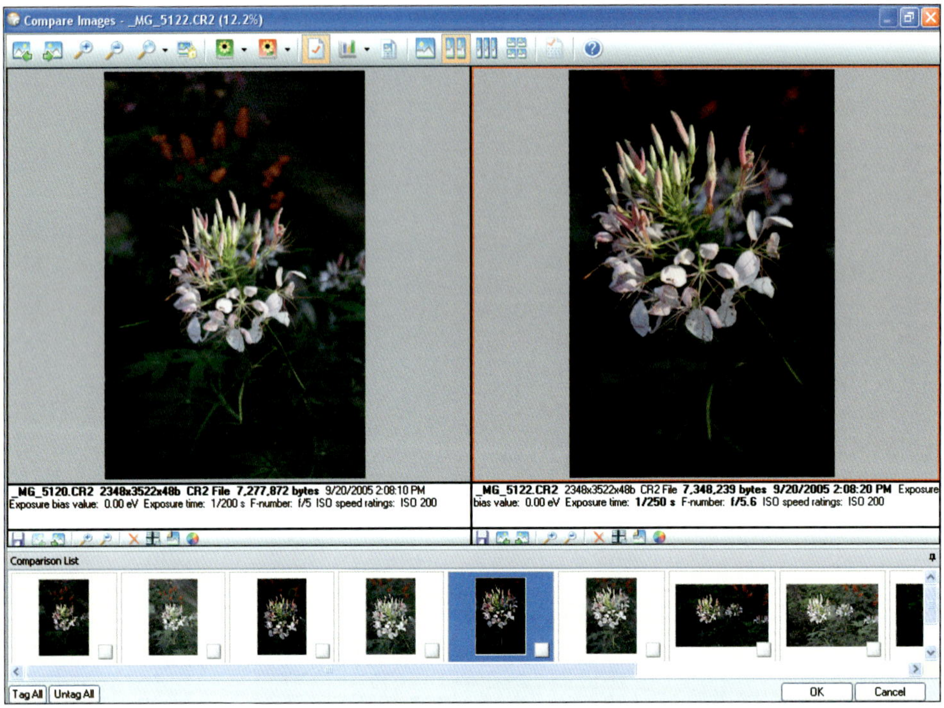

Figure 9-4: Sorting images usually involves comparing them two or more at a time, replacing the one(s) you like least with another from the film strip (bottom of this screen), until you decide which one(s) from the shoot you like the best. Notice the file information (properties) displayed under each photo; we can customize it to include any information from the picture's metadata. (Screen capture from ACDSee Pro, courtesy of ACD Systems)

Tip

While software demonstrators like showing photos against a black background because it is more dramatic, we recommend setting your program preferences to a medium grey background. That way, the background will have no influence over the visual impact of your image or your evaluation of its exposure and color.

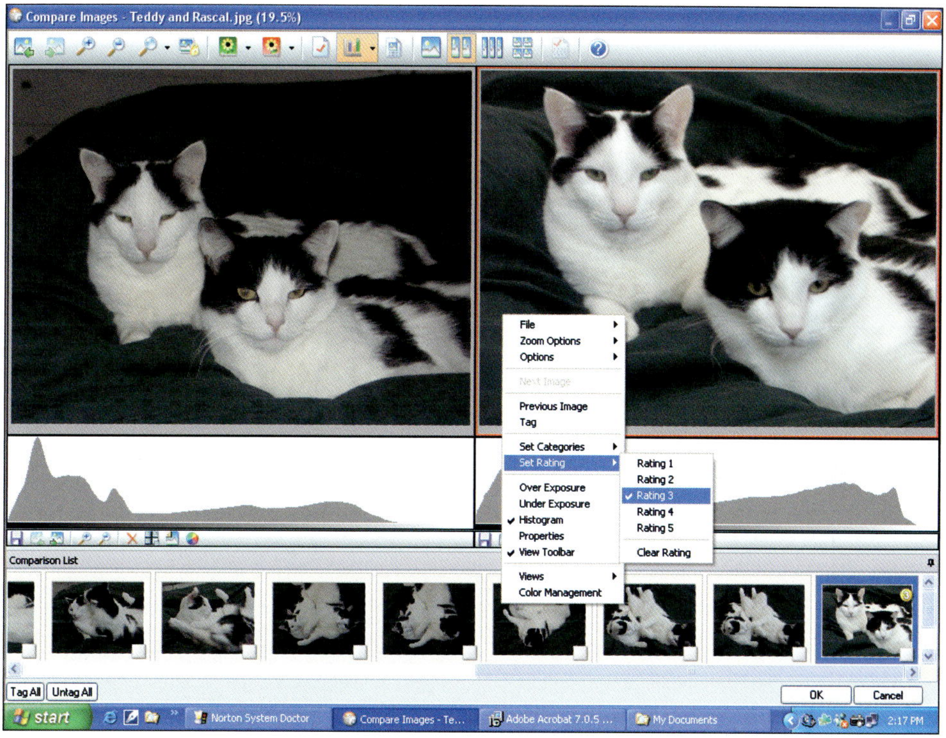

Figure 9-5: You can set the rating of each of your pictures while you sort them. This is far superior to our old slide light table because we can always search for any pictures from the shoot that we gave, for instance, 4 or 5 stars. Notice that we have turned off the properties and turned on the histogram for the previewed image. (Screen capture from ACDSee Pro, courtesy of ACD Systems)

Tip

All these programs have a 5-star rating system. We suggest that you establish criteria for what each level of the 5 stars represents to you. For instance, we seldom give any photo 5 stars. That's for those pictures that are as good as they get and are potential exhibition prints. We consider 3 stars a decent picture that could be tweaked for further improvement — such as adjusting the exposure, color, sharpness, and so forth — in a photo-editing program. But we seldom use any 3-star photos, unless we absolutely need them and have nothing better. We don't bother with 2 stars, even though we may keep some of the photos as points of reference. Most of the photos that we would rate 2 stars and any that deserve 1 star are usually thrown away, unless they would be useful in our books and seminars, as examples of what not to do.

Batch Processing

One of the great time-savers that we have learned to depend upon is batch processing — the ability to apply an edit simultaneously to several pictures. For instance, we use batch processing for the following common edits:

- Rotate photos that were taken with the camera held sideways, producing a tall (portrait mode) picture rather than a wide (landscape mode) one. (See the first two sidebar figures.)
- Rename all the photos, converting the nonsensical alphanumeric names given by digital cameras (such as 1003521.cr2 or DSC52981.jpg) to something that makes sense to us. When you batch rename, you create a root name (such as TrainYard) and the software will use that name, plus add an incremental number. Therefore, your photos may end up being called TrainYard01.nef, TrainYard02.nef, and so on.
- Apply the same keywords to a series of photos.
- Insert information into the metadata of a series of photos. This can include your copyright notice, the client's name, the name of the assignment, and so forth. (See the section on metadata later in this chapter.)
- Apply basic image edits to a series of photos, such as color, exposure, or a sharpening algorithm.

Batch processing works in one of two ways, depending on the complexity of the edit and on the software.

- Select all the photos you want to apply the edit to, and then either click and drag a command to one of the selected photos, or invoke the command or dialog.
- Apply a series of edits to a single photo, save the settings, and then select a group of photos and apply those settings to the group (see final sidebar figure).

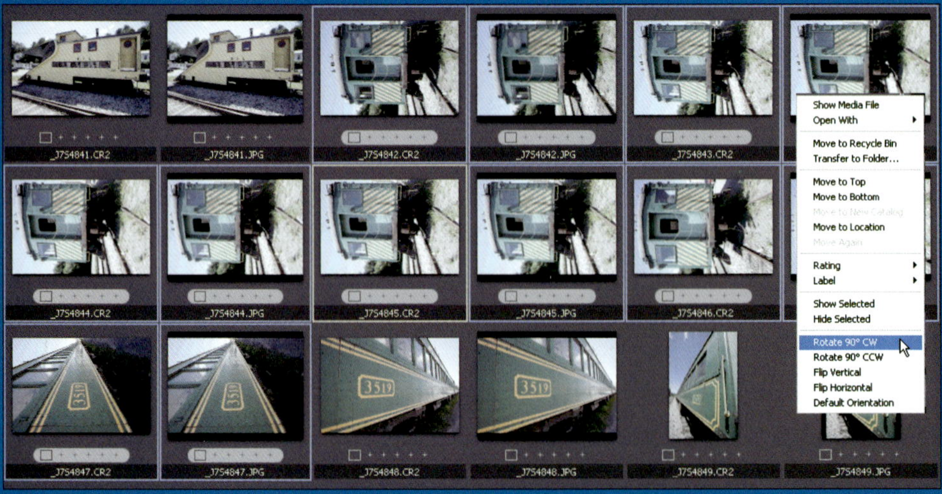

We selected all the photos in this shoot for which we held our camera on the side, and then invoked a rotation command. (Screens courtesy of iView Multimedia)

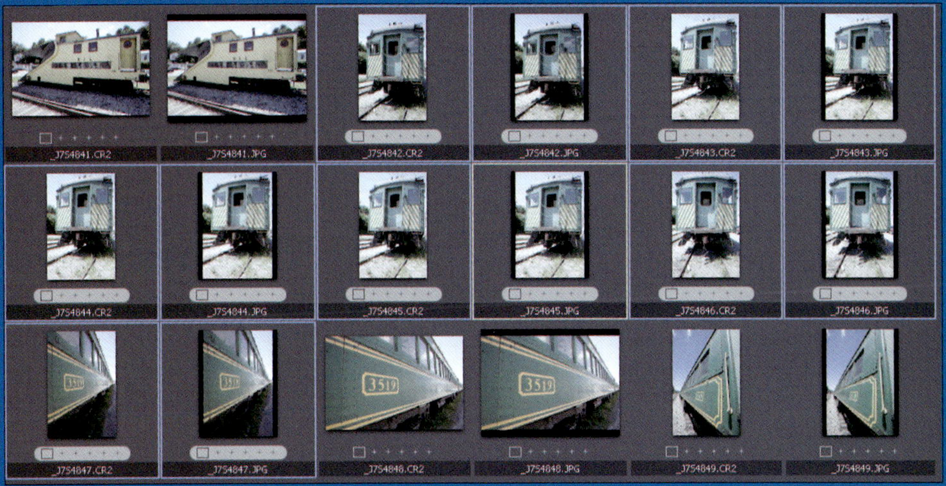

With only two mouse clicks, a batch rotation turned all the selected photos upright.

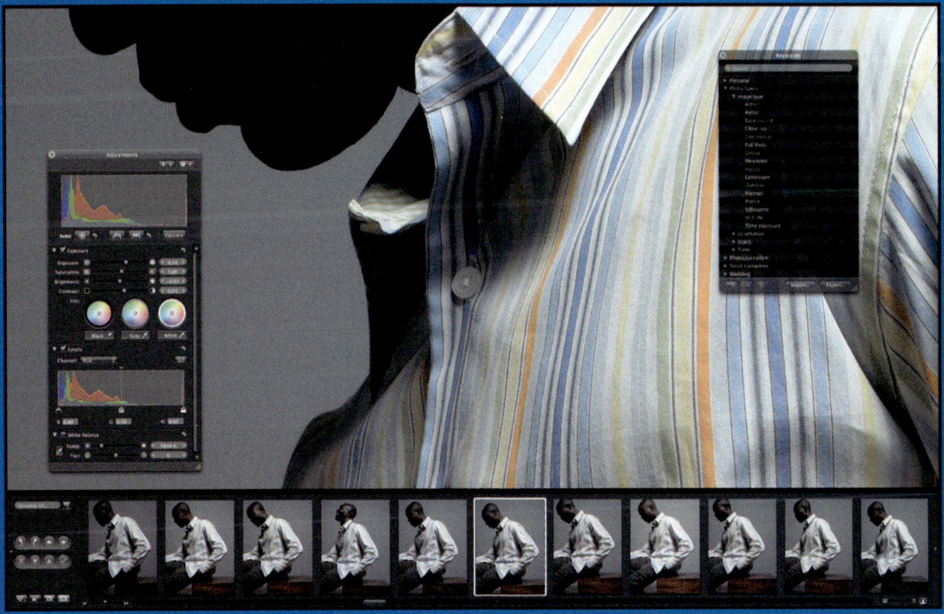

In this view of Aperture, you can edit the color and exposure of one photo in the series and then apply that edit to all the other pictures. (Courtesy of Apple)

Keywording, Cataloging, and Searching

Sorting and filing photos is all well and good, but the central purpose of these programs is to make it easy to find specific photos when you need or want them. In addition to the rating system we discussed previously, you should assign keywords to your photos. You also may want to develop categories, which are like folders for your keywords (see Figure 9-6).

As you add photos to your library, consider what concepts they represent in your mind and why you might search for those specific pictures. If those keywords don't yet exist in your database, create them. We find that it helps to think in terms of the journalistic mantra: who, what, where, when, why, and how. For instance, the following are the typical types of information you might want to include:

- Geographical location (neighborhood, city, town, state, country)
- Type of place (beach, park, city, farm, etc.)
- Time of year or day (spring, Easter, dawn, night, etc.)
- Person (child, father, mother, proper name, etc.)
- Animal (elephant seal, horse, dog, pet's name, etc.)
- Activity (skiing, driving, eating, etc.)

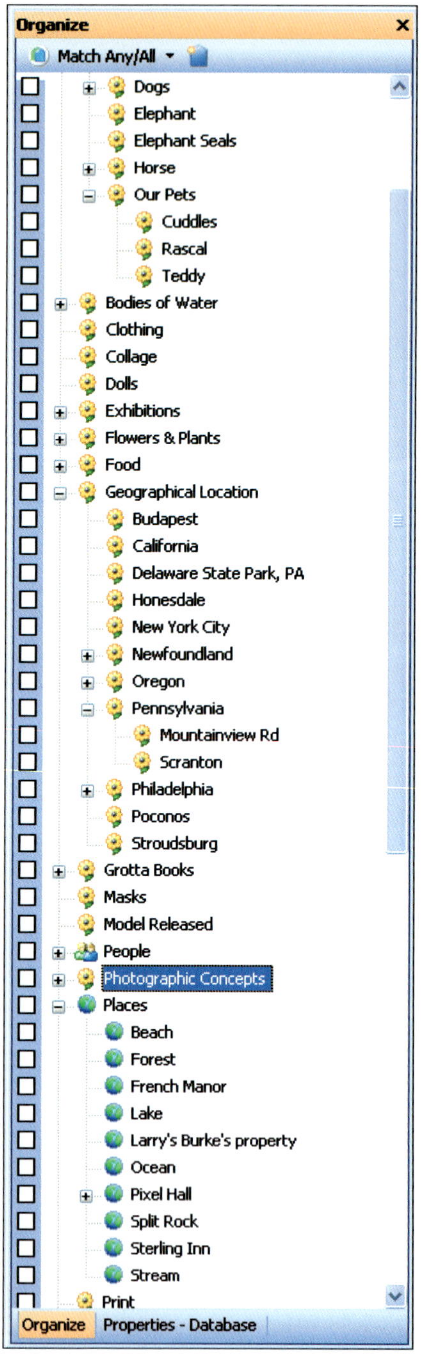

Figure 9-6: Define your keywords according to the concepts that you would be mostly likely to search. You can add keywords to your master list as you add photos from different shoots. (Courtesy of ACD Systems)

- Photographic concepts (blurred action, rear curtain sync, greyscale, imaged composite, etc.)
- Status of the picture (model or property released, published, etc.)
- Any other subject, name, concept, or visual information you might wish to search

We prefer a hierarchical organization of our keywords, to make it easy to zero in on the exact one(s) we need. For instance, in Figure 9-6, notice the cascading organization of our geographical locations category.

Assigning keywords generally works one of two ways, depending on the program. After you have selected the photo or photos, you either click and drag the keyword onto one of the selected photos, or click inside the checkbox next to the word within a list of keywords.

Where Should I Edit My RAW Files?

You may have as many as four choices of where to edit your RAW files before they are converted to standard TIFF or, eventually, JPEG. (See Chapter 4.)

- The conversion utility from your camera manufacturer
- A third-party conversion utility, such as SilverFast
- Your photo-editing program, most notably Photoshop's Camera RAW utility
- Advanced photo management programs, such as Aperture and ACDSee Pro

The fact is that the utility developed by your camera manufacturer is based on intimate knowledge of exactly how the RAW file was created. Every other utility has to reverse engineer that information. But camera manufacturers are usually much better at creating hardware than software. So, we have found their utilities to be uneven in speed, power, convenience, quality, and ease of use.

When on a Mac, we will work with Aperture because it is convenient, fast, and powerful. When on a PC, we will use Camera RAW because it is so tightly integrated with Photoshop. However, when we shoot with Nikons, we will almost always use Nikon Capture Editor because we haven't found any other utility that does as good a job interpreting their NEF RAW file formats. When we need distortion correction, we use DO Optics.

Of course, as Joe Schorr, Apple's product manager for Aperture, said, "What constitutes a good RAW decoder is so subjective. Every RAW decoder is a starting point." The whole point about RAW is that it delivers all the captured data. The first view of that data, in whatever software you are using, is simply that — a view. The reason we shoot RAW is so that we can interpret the image data according to our own standards. Therefore, when editing your unconverted RAW, use the software that fits your personality, gives you the tools you want, and is organized in a manner that makes sense to you. Then, go to work making it the best darn photo possible.

When you want to search for a photo, you can be very specific, combining several keywords and a rating level (that is, 3 stars or better), as well as metadata information, such as the date a picture was taken. (See the next section, regarding metadata.) For instance, we could search on the keywords *Pennsylvania*, *resort*, *Sterling Inn*, *stream*, *Sally*, *dog*, *Cuddles*; furthermore, we could limit the search to photos that we rated 4 stars or above, and to pictures taken in December 2004.

Tip

We use a flatbed scanner to scan our model and property releases. Then, we save them in the same folders and under the same keywords as the related photographs. That way when we search for the photo in our photo management program, we can also access a copy of the release.

Leveraging and Extending Metadata

Metadata is information about your pictures that is saved with the picture file. For instance, when a digital camera captures and then stores a photograph, it also saves information about which camera took the picture, the time and date shot, using what *f*-stop and shutter speed, whether or not a flash fired, the color model used, and other parameters you set when taking the photo. (See Figure 9-7.)

Studying the metadata from the camera is useful when comparing different photos and analyzing what settings produced what results. Even expert photographers with many years of experience can learn a lot from the feedback metadata can provide.

Metadata Jargon

Various acronyms are associated with metadata. EXIF, IPTC, and XMP are three of the more important ones.

- **EXIF**, which stands for Exchangeable Image File Format, contains information about how your camera created the picture. This includes settings you applied and others that are defined by the camera's manufacturer. In fact, EXIF holds the information that helps desktop printers interpret how a photo should best be reproduced to recreate color and exposure as the camera had first defined it. (See Chapter 12.)
- **IPTC** refers to fields that conform to standards set by the International Press Telecommunications Council. These can include headlines, captions, copyright notice, location, specific codes for subject and scene, and so forth. If you work with a newspaper, they may require that the IPTC fields be filled out in certain ways to make it easier to slot your pictures into their databases. But you don't have to work for a newspaper to take advantage IPTC metadata files.
- **XMP** is Adobe's Extensible Metadata Platform, which is used to organize and store data in Adobe Bridge, Photoshop, and the rest of Creative Suite.

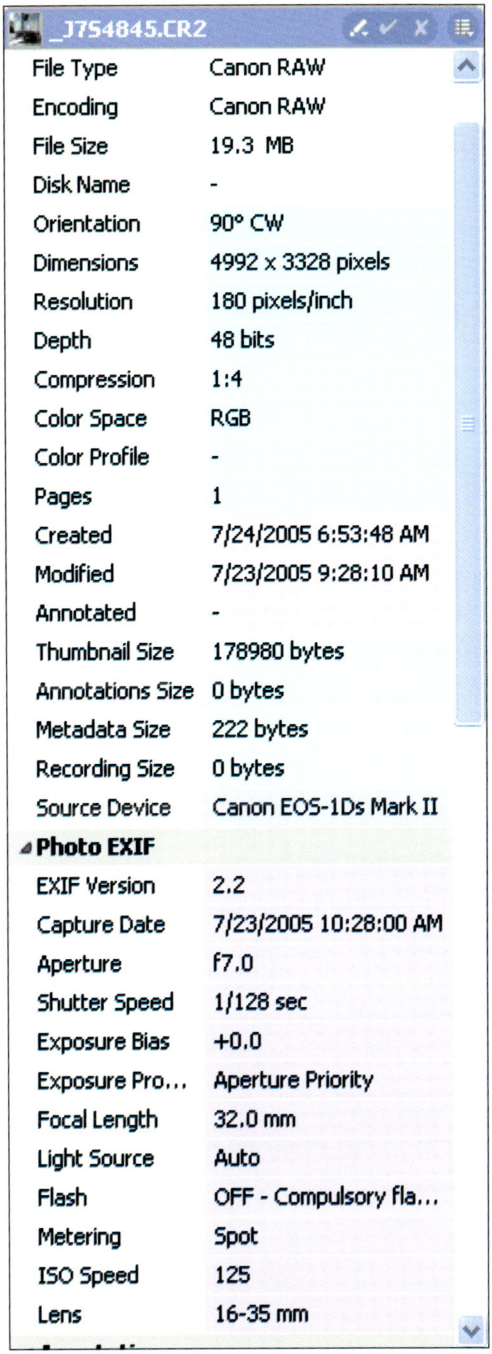

Figure 9-7: Digital cameras save metadata with every photograph, providing information about how a picture was taken. (Courtesy of iView Multimedia)

When you bring your photos into the computer, you can extend the metadata, to include a wide range of standard and custom information. Your ratings and keywords become part of a picture's metadata. We've already shown you how metadata can (and should) hold your copyright notice. (See Figure 9-2(C).) In addition, you may be able to create a standard set of data containing your contact information that will be attached to your photos whenever you apply your copyright notice to a picture.

You can customize some fields, according to your own needs. For instance, if each of your model and property releases has a unique number, you can create a field in which you might input the form number. Then, when you need to produce the release for a specific picture, you can find the number right there, as part of the photo's metadata. With the number in hand, you can easily find it in your files.

Other fields can be freeform, allowing you to insert notes about the shoot, such as where the photo has appeared or the people who were on the set with you.

Generally, you can view a photo's metadata in your photo management program (or in your photo-editing program) by selecting Properties or File Info. Metadata is searchable; how comprehensive and quick such searches are depends upon what software you use.

Archiving

The more you know about computers, the more you realize how unreliable they are. As Ray McGoldrick, NTI product manager, says, "It's not a question of *if* your hard drive will fail, but *when* your hard drive will fail." If you care about protecting your pictures, you will want to archive them. Professional photographers usually archive their photographs onto CDs or DVDs at two points in their production process:

- When they first transfer the photos from a shoot, before editing them. That way, whatever happens in the editing process, they have protected backups of the original pictures.
- When all the editing is finished, and the job is delivered.

In both cases, we recommend archiving from within your photo management software. Most such programs will keep track of all the photos on external drives, including CDs or DVDs burned within their interface. In other words, the software will maintain the thumbnails, names, keywords, and other metadata information about the archived pictures. If, when you do a search, the software determines that the picture you seek is on a CD or DVD, it will prompt you to insert that specific disc into your drive to access the archived file.

We find this functionality so valuable that we even use our photo management program to archive nonphoto files, such as stories we've written, research notes, letters, and other important documents.

Backing Up Your Data and System

Archiving your pictures (and other files) is only one portion of a good backup system. The others are:

- File-level protection
- A mirror image of your hard drive
- Backing up the database data

For file-level backups, we recommend using an external hard drive (typically one attached to your network hub via USB 2.0 or FireWire) that will monitor important folders on your computer. The external drive's software detects when a new file has been saved to a monitored folder and will automatically back it up.

The mirror image of your hard drive is needed in case your system fails and you have to restore your operating system and applications.

Finally, the information maintained by your photo management program — the keywords, metadata, location of files, and so forth — should be backed up periodically.

Sharing

Photo management programs aren't only for organizing your photos any more. Increasingly, they also provide tools for sharing your pictures. Depending on the program you use, it may provide some or all of the following features:

- Photo Web pages
- DVDs or CDs
- Assembly of photo book pages

Simple photo Web pages are generated from selected pictures. (See Figure 9-8.) Usually, you have a choice of templates to use, and whether or not to include metadata and other information about the pictures. Clicking on a thumbnail picture typically opens up a larger view.

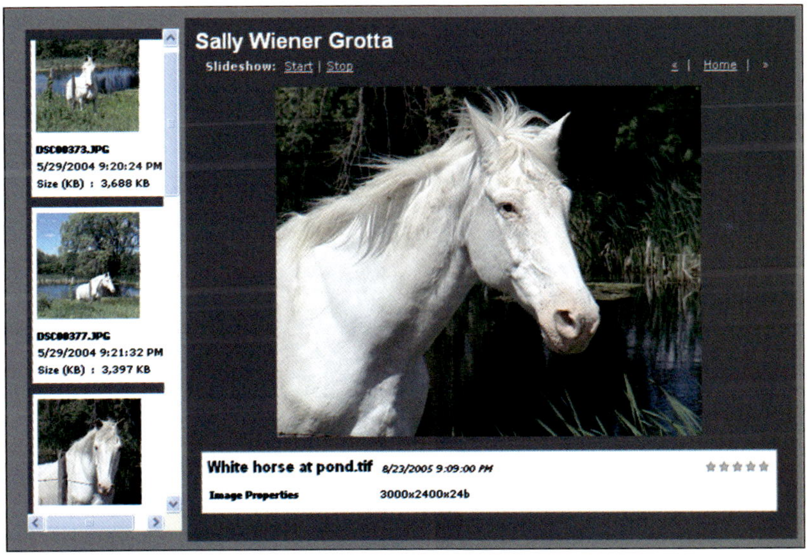

Figure 9-8: Web gallery pages can showcase your work on the Internet or provide an attractive format for delivering low-resolution photos to clients and associates. (Courtesy of ACD Systems)

When you create a sharing CD or DVD (as opposed to an archive disc), it can include interactive menus that the viewer can use to play specific galleries or slideshows

As we discuss in Chapter 12, one of the big sellers for professional photographers are personalized, hardbound photo books. At the time of this writing, output to these photo books is unevenly supported by these programs. However, Aperture has a nice light table for photo book layout. (See Figure 9-9.)

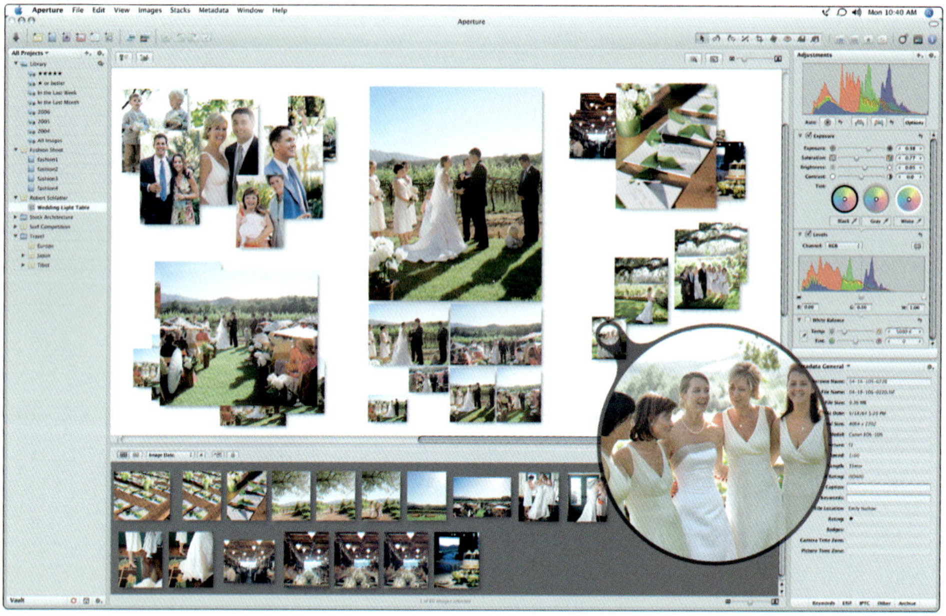

Figure 9-9: Aperture's light table is an intuitive interface for pasting up pages and photo books. (Courtesy of Apple)

Two other output tasks that these programs do well are creating contact sheets and emailing photos. The emailed pictures can be automatically resized and attached to a memo in your default emailing program.

Cross-Ref

For a more in-depth discussion of output and sharing, please read Chapter 12.

Summary

One of the most important pieces of software a photographer can have and use is a photo management, or digital asset management, program. It will help you maintain control over any size library of digital images, while also providing the tools to easily organize, sort, manage, and archive your pictures. Equally important, the software's keywording, rating, and cataloging, plus the way it uses metadata, make it easy to find a specific photo among the hundreds or even thousands you might have on your hard drive, network, external drives, and archived on CDs and DVDs.

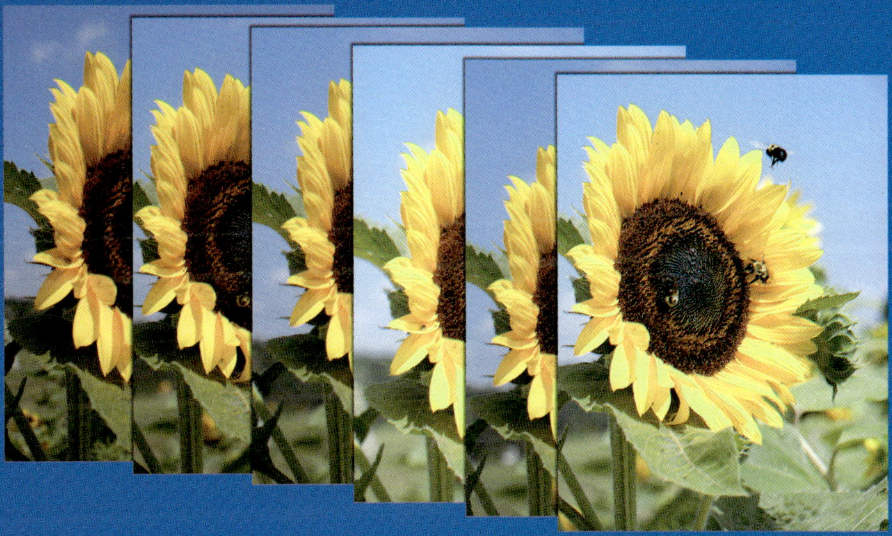

A good photo management program helps you select the one best photo out of several with an intelligent viewing, sorting, and rating system. (Photos taken with an Olympus E-1, 14–54mm lens, at various zoom and exposure settings)

Chapter 10

Perfecting and Extending Your Photos

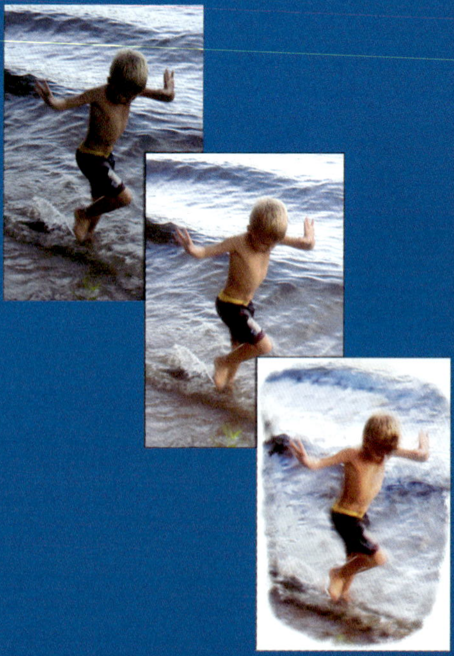

With photo-editing programs, you can perfect your photos and/or use them to create something completely different.

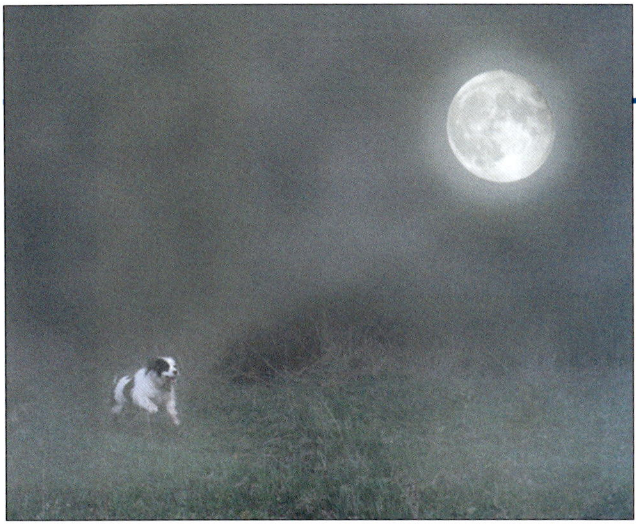

Sally created "Moondoggie" from several photos, using Photoshop's layers. Before combining them, she edited their exposure, tone, and color to make them similar enough to fit in a single image.

We have stressed throughout this book that it takes less time to shoot a good photo than to correct a bad one in photo-editing software. Moreover, the image quality will usually be far better when you create and work with the best possible photo from the very beginning. However, even great pictures can be improved, enhanced, and extended by photo editing.

In this chapter, we cover:

- Choosing the right editing software for your needs and budget
- Perfecting exposure and color with simple, powerful software tools
- Tips and techniques for efficient, creative editing
- Using time-saving macros
- Taking advantage of layers and adjustment layers for combining and controlling image elements
- Going beyond the basics to create fine art images

Choosing the Right Photo-Editing Software

It's often said that among photo-editing programs there's Photoshop and then there's the rest of the pack. But we're going to challenge that conventional wisdom by saying that not every serious photographer needs to know or use Photoshop. For many, some other less complex, much less expensive software may be preferable.

Choosing your photo-editing software, like selecting your DSLR system, is both a personal and professional choice, relevant to:

- What you need and want to do with your pictures
- Whether you are in a collaborative environment, working with clients, art directors, and other associates in developing the image
- Your familiarity and comfort with computers and software photo tools
- How much time you want to spend learning and using the software
- Your budget

Do I Need to Learn a Photo-Editing Program?

Jay Maisel, the famous New York photographer, claims that he barely understands computers. Or, at least, he prefers to not use them for his photography. Sure, he finds them useful for reviewing his shoots, sorting out the best pictures, and deleting the rest. But as far as Jay is concerned being a photographer means shooting great photos, not manipulating them in the computer. (Fortunately for Jay, he does have assistants capable of using computers and image-editing software.)

Before the digital age, we maintained what was then a state-of-the-art, chemical-based darkroom in the basement of our old home. (We eventually donated all our film-processing and -printing equipment to an arts center.) Sally used to spend untold hours tweaking and pushing her photographs to the limit in an attempt to make them even better. Not surprisingly, she threw herself into Photoshop (and Painter) as soon as they became available in the early 1990s. For her, manipulating pictures in the computer is an extension of the darkroom creative experience, without the chemical smells or darkness.

Yes, it is possible to be a serious photographer without ever learning Photoshop or any other photo-editing program. But if you are comfortable with computers and wish to extend your photography with all the nifty software tools of the digital age, then you'll want to master a photo-editing program.

Here are some of the image-editing programs that you might want to consider:

- Adobe Photoshop
- Other high-powered programs, such as Corel PhotoPaint, Corel Paint Shop Pro, ACD Systems Canvas, Ulead PhotoImpact
- Adobe Photoshop Elements
- Entry-level programs, such as Roxio PhotoSuite, Microsoft Digital Image

One other program, which we discuss later in this chapter, is Corel Painter, with which you can create natural media fine art from your photographs.

Tip

Most software, including the programs we mention in this book, is available as free limited trial downloads from the manufacturer's Web site. Usually, trial versions are disabled in some way or will work for only a set length of time. After you use it for a while, you have the option to buy it or have it turn into a useless pumpkin.

Since picking out the right photo-editing program for your needs, style, and budget is a very personal choice, we highly recommend downloading the free versions and trying them out on your own photos, before spending your hard-earned money.

Adobe Photoshop

It's a fact of life: if you're a serious professional photographer who routinely performs heavy-duty, production-level photo editing, or your job requires you to communicate and collaborate with other graphics professionals, you are expected to know and use Photoshop. It also happens to be an incredibly powerful, deep, and rich program with so many features and functions that few people ever master it all.

At first glance, Photoshop gives you little guidance. However, if you are new to the program, the best way to beat Photoshop's steep learning curve is to work through the tutorials and check out the How-Tos. The Help menu can be useful, too.

Photoshop is available as a standalone program or as part of a couple of different Adobe suite packages that include Adobe Illustrator, which is the professional's standard for vector drawing programs. (See the sidebar "Photo versus Illustration Programs.")

Other Powerful Photo-Editing Software

One of Photoshop's greatest drawbacks is its steep price. If you aren't collaborating with other graphics professionals, and don't really need to "speak" Photoshop, consider using one of the other high-powered photo-editing programs.

Corel PhotoPaint provides the high degree of the professional-level photo-editing and image-creation tools that we expect and need, in an interface that offers more guidance than Photoshop—at a fraction of the cost. PhotoPaint is available only as part of the CorelDRAW Graphics Suite and is no longer sold as a standalone program. However, the price of the suite is still far cheaper than Photoshop CS, and it includes CorelDRAW, one of the best illustration programs on the market.

Paint Shop Pro (originally from JASC, but now owned by Corel) is another good program. It's particularly well suited for executives and others who want to do things with their pictures, and quickly, using versatile presets and customizable tools.

ACD Systems Canvas (originally from Deneba) has a loyal following among some technically oriented photographers, typically pros who love mechanics and engineering. It's a deep program that provides tools for drawing very precise illustrations within the same interface (and, if you wish, in the same image) as you would use for editing your photos.

You might also want to check out Ulead PhotoImpact, which is something of a sleeper of a program, which often falls under the radar of most serious photographers.

Adobe Photoshop Elements

Photoshop Elements is similar to its big sister Photoshop (it's based upon the same code), but is more directed towards nonprofessionals who want and need lots of guidance. Like Photoshop, it provides lots of tools for editing individual photos (though not as many or as deep as Photoshop). On the other hand, Elements has some functions you won't find in Photoshop, such as the ability to create projects (like making greeting cards and calendars from your photos). And—bottom line—Elements costs far, far less than Photoshop.

If you are a Photoshop user, you will be frustrated by Elements' lack of key tools that you may be accustomed to using. But if you want to learn Photoshop, Elements is a great (and very inexpensive) introduction to the way Photoshop works. What's more, though you may buy Elements with the intention of eventually upgrading to the full Photoshop, you may find you never need anything more than Elements for perfecting and using your photos.

Photo versus Illustration Programs

Adobe Photoshop and Corel PhotoPaint both are packaged with award-winning illustration programs — Adobe Illustrator and CorelDRAW. The difference between photo-editing and illustration programs relates to the elemental building blocks of an image.

In photo editing (which is also called bitmapped editing), the software manipulates the individual pixels (or bits) that make up the image. Each point of data among the millions in any typical photo is a separate entity that must be analyzed, compared, and adjusted. While some functions may consider neighboring pixels when doing their calculations, as a rule, photo-editing software isn't aware of the composition of the photo. When you zoom into a photo or other bitmapped image, or when you enlarge the picture too much, you will see the individual pixels. In extreme magnification, the picture appears to break up into the pixels, like an impressionistic painting (see the first two sidebar figures for an example).

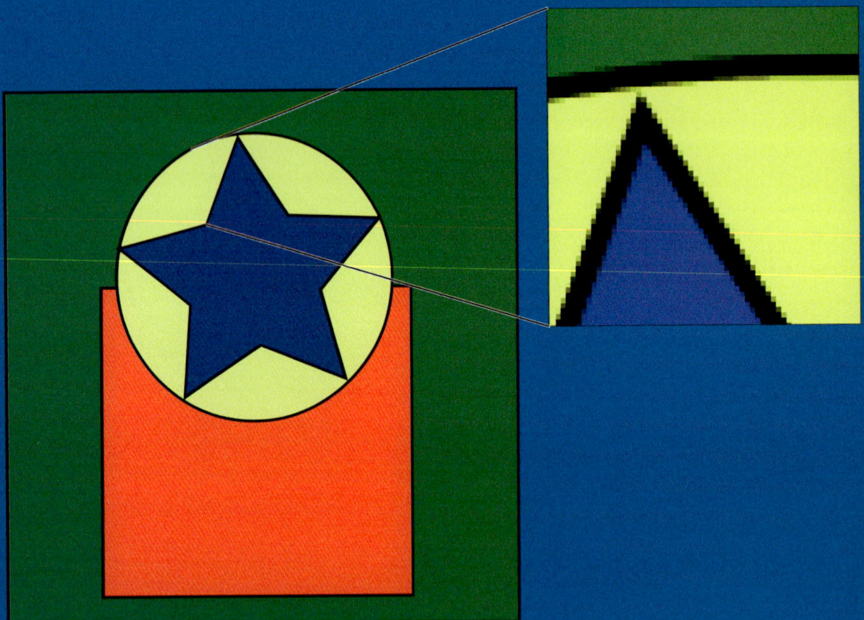

This figure was created in Photoshop and is made up of pixels. When we zoom into the edges of the shapes in the bitmapped image that was created in Photoshop, we can see the step-like pixels.

Illustration software is vector-based, rather than bitmapped. What that means is every shape is defined mathematically. For instance, a circle is a shape defined by πr^2 with specific colors as its fill and outline. Since the shape is the elemental component, zooming in or enlarging the picture results in the same smooth, unbroken edges as the original size (see the final two sidebar figures for an example).

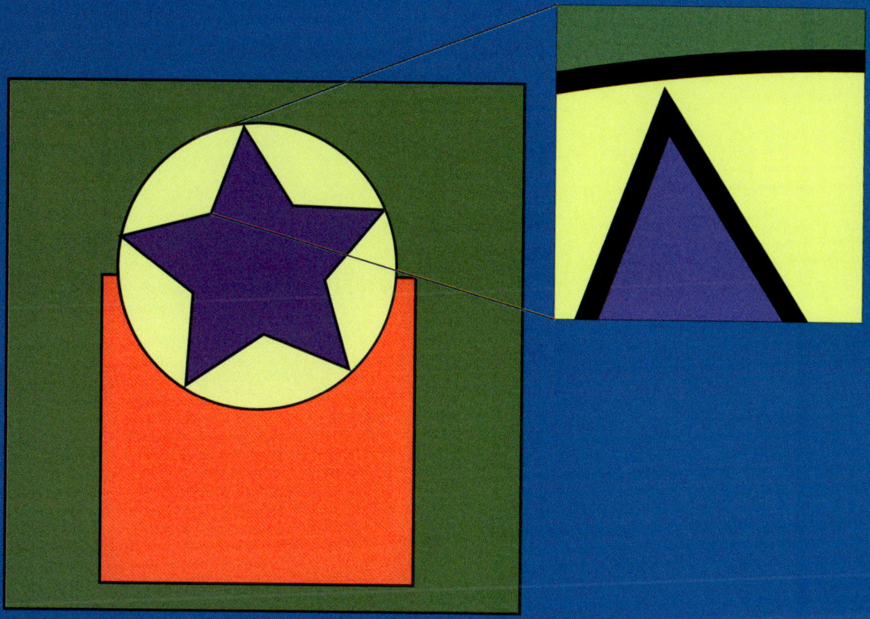

This identical image is composed of vector shapes created in Adobe Illustrator. When we zoom into the edges of the vector shapes, the edges are smooth and unbroken.

Think of bitmapped pictures as being made up of atomic particles, while vector illustrations are composed of infinitely expandable containers of color. The hundreds of thousands or millions of tiny pixels that make up bitmapped images produce the smooth transitions and realism of photos, while the edges and transitions in vector images tend to be abrupt and sharply delineated.

There is some crossover between the two kinds of programs. For instance, because it is cleaner and crisper, type in photo-editing programs is usually vector. Professional-level image-editing programs allow users to create some basic vector shapes (squares, circles, stars, etc.) and drop them into a bitmapped image. Similarly, you usually can insert bitmapped photos into vector graphics produced by illustration software, just as you can insert a vector shape from an illustration program into a bitmapped image. However, the placed graphic is re-editable only in the original type of software. In other words, if you place a photo into an illustration and decide you want to edit that photo, you will have to do so in a photo-editing program. There are exceptions to this. Some programs, most notably Canvas, combine vector and bitmapped capabilities in a single interface.

By the way, Elements often is a proving ground for some of Adobe's newer features and technologies. Photoshop's great healing brush (Sally's favorite tool for removing wrinkles and other imperfections) was first introduced in Elements. We wouldn't be surprised to see some of Elements' current unique tools introduced into future versions of Photoshop CS.

Other Entry-Level Programs

There are a whole slew of consumer level programs on the market offering varying degrees of flexibility, power, and versatility. Entry-level programs are designed to give the typical amateur photographer easy-to-use tools that automatically perform the most needed tasks (such as fixing red-eye, basic exposure adjustments, cropping, creating photo projects, and sharing photos). Therefore, they offer a more limited set of features and commands than the high-powered programs.

In some programs, everything is automatic, with no user control over the effect. Others, such as Microsoft Digital Image or Roxio PhotoSuite, provide greater user control over both the tools and the application of them.

If all you want to do is a bit of quick photo editing before moving on to actually use your pictures, one of these programs might be quite adequate for your needs. However, most DSLR users are relatively sophisticated and discriminating about their photos (which is why they bought a DSLR in the first place) and would probably feel that entry-level photo-editing programs are too limited or juvenile for regular use.

Tip

The best way to learn any program is to use it. As long as you work only on copies and not your original photos, you won't break anything by just clicking on buttons or applying edits. If you don't know what a command or dialog does, try it out. Push the sliders and controls around and see what effect it has on your picture. Explore every option it offers, viewing the results as you go. Zoom in on your photo to check for any destructive consequences (such as with oversharpening). Compare the edited version to the original or to another copy on which you applied a different edit. When you want to understand what the feature really does, look at the Help menu.

Tip

If you want to create things with your photos — business cards, party invitations and favors, calendars, and such — you might want to take a look at the various crafts programs, such as Print Artist or Print Shop. They often include a very simple (and limited) photo editor.

Stay in 16-bit As Long As You Can

As we discussed in Chapter 5, DSLRs are capable of delivering 16-bit images to your computer. That is twice the data that you will actually need for a good photo-realistic 8-bit RGB picture. But given that photo editing destroys original image data, working on a 16-bit image when all you want is 8-bit is simply common sense.

Unfortunately, not all photo-editing programs have the ability to work on 16-bit pictures. That's one of the dividing lines between consumer and professional software. What's more, in those high-powered programs that do support 16-bit editing, typically, only a subset of the tools and features can be used in 16-bit mode. Also, you'll probably need a better computer with a faster processor, more RAM, and a bigger hard drive.

We suggest that you work on your photo in 16-bit as long as possible, using those tools that are available in that mode. Then, save the edited 16-bit version and work on a copy that you convert to 8-bit for the finishing touches and output.

Tip

Many of the exposure- and color-editing tools we discuss in this chapter are also found in RAW conversion utilities (Chapter 4) and in advanced image management programs (Chapter 9). If you are shooting RAW, the rule of thumb is that you may achieve higher image quality if you apply these types of processes before converting the RAW files into TIFF or JPEG.

Correcting and Perfecting Color and Exposure

One of the biggest problems with digital cameras is that it can be difficult to accurately judge the color and exposure of a just taken photo on the camera's LCD screen. So, it isn't uncommon that the photo you shot isn't quite the photo you envisioned. Many digital pictures can be improved by a slight tweak to their color and exposure.

In the following sections, we demonstrate some of the many exposure and color tools available in pro-quality software. (Some of the same tools may also be found in certain entry-level programs.) While the screens in your software may look different from those in our illustrations, the concepts behind them are universal.

Note

The poorly exposed photos in this chapter were purposely shot that way to provide samples for the following exercises, and do not relate to the quality or capabilities of the stated cameras.

Tip

Before you do any color or exposure editing on your computer, be sure to calibrate your monitor. (See Chapter 11.) Otherwise, you will be judging your photos and how much editing they actually need based on an inaccurate view of the pictures. While a bright, contrasty picture might look great on a monitor, you need to take into account the characteristics of your printer, paper, and inks to ensure a good print. Often, a more subdued dynamic range works better in print. (See Chapter 12.)

Correcting Exposure

The most common tool for correcting exposure is a simple double-slider dialog for adjusting brightness and contrast. It's found in almost every photo-editing program, from the very simple to the most powerful. What is important to remember is that brightness and contrast are always fellow travelers. As a rule, when you increase or decrease brightness, you will want to be sure to apply a comparable (though not always identical) change in contrast, and vice versa. (See Figures 10-1, 10-2, 10-3, and 10-4.)

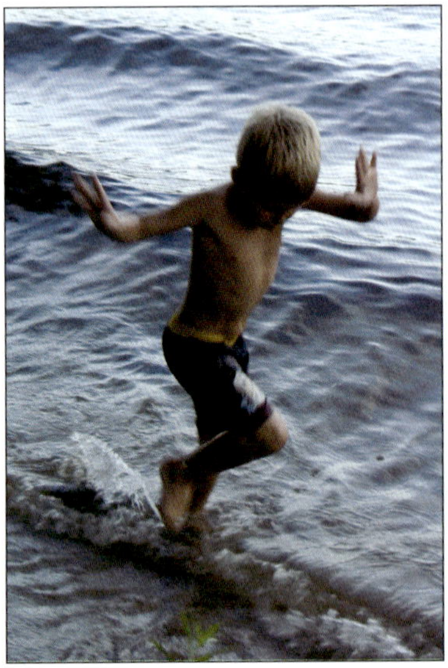

Figure 10-1: This picture of Nick playing at the water's edge is definitely too dark. (Photo taken with a Canon 20D, 17–85mm lens set at 44mm, 1/80 at *f*7.1.)

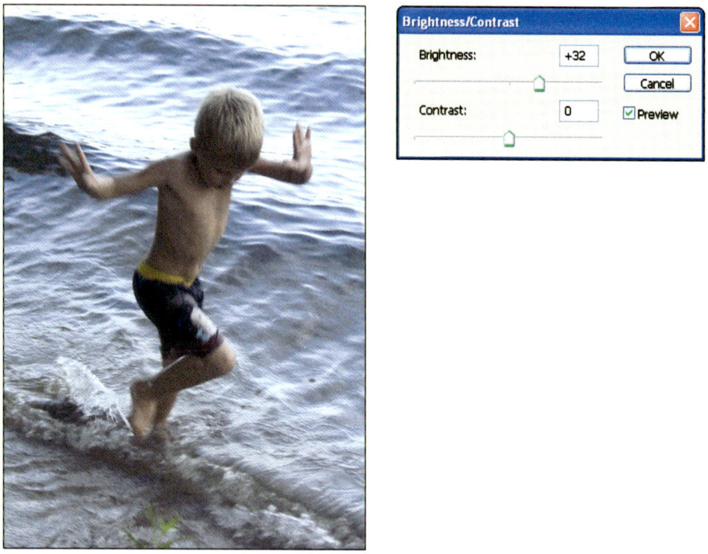

Figure 10-2: Brightening the photo of Nick makes his skin tones more appealing, but without a comparable adjustment to contrast, it destroys the shadows and sense of definition. In many instances, it can make it appear as though you shot the picture through gauze. (Brightness/Contrast dialogs from Photoshop CS, courtesy of Adobe Systems)

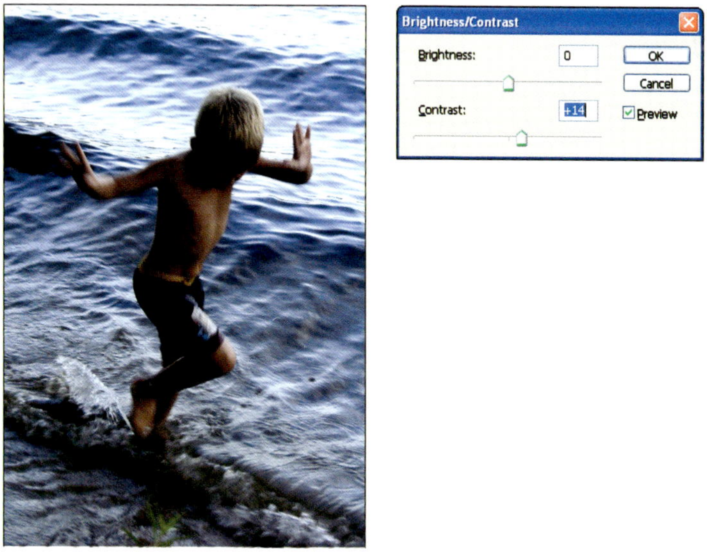

Figure 10-3: Increasing the contrast without also upping the brightness drops out all the details in the midtones and makes the photo look almost posterized rather than photo-realistic.

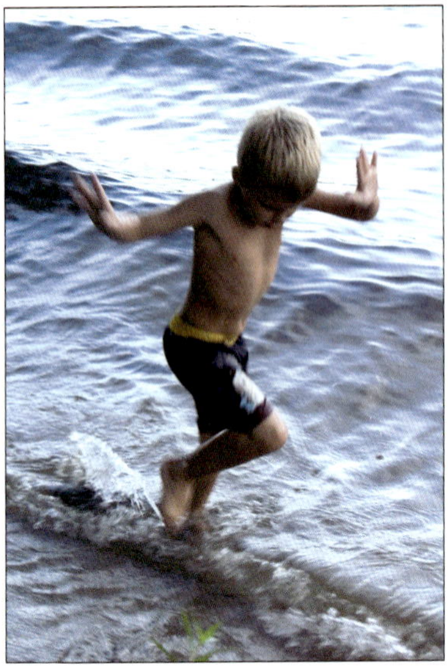

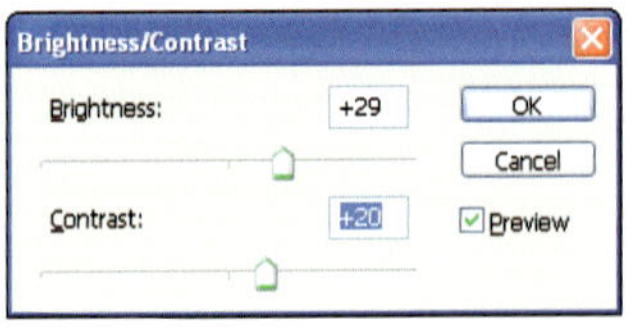

Figure 10-4: Using the Brightness/Contrast sliders is a balancing act. By increasing both the contrast and the brightness on Figure 10-1, we have produced a much better exposure. However, there are limits to this specific exposure tool. Notice that the highlights in the water are now blown out, so you can't see the details of the surface or any color. What's more, the photo still doesn't look lively in terms of exposure (though the photographic moment is certainly a lively subject).

The Brightness/Contrast sliders work best when all you need is a very slight boost or reduction in overall exposure values. We often find that an increase of 10 on both sliders will give just that extra liveliness on generally well-exposed photos. (See Figure 10-5.)

Tip

When adjusting exposure, keep a careful eye on the details in highlights and shadows of your photo. Increasing brightness can blow out highlights, turning nicely detailed bright areas into blobs of white. (See Figure 10-4.) Similarly, increasing darkness can destroy details in shadowy areas, which then become blocks of pure black. Upping the contrast too much can do both — blow out highlights and/or destroy shadow details. (See Figure 10-3.)

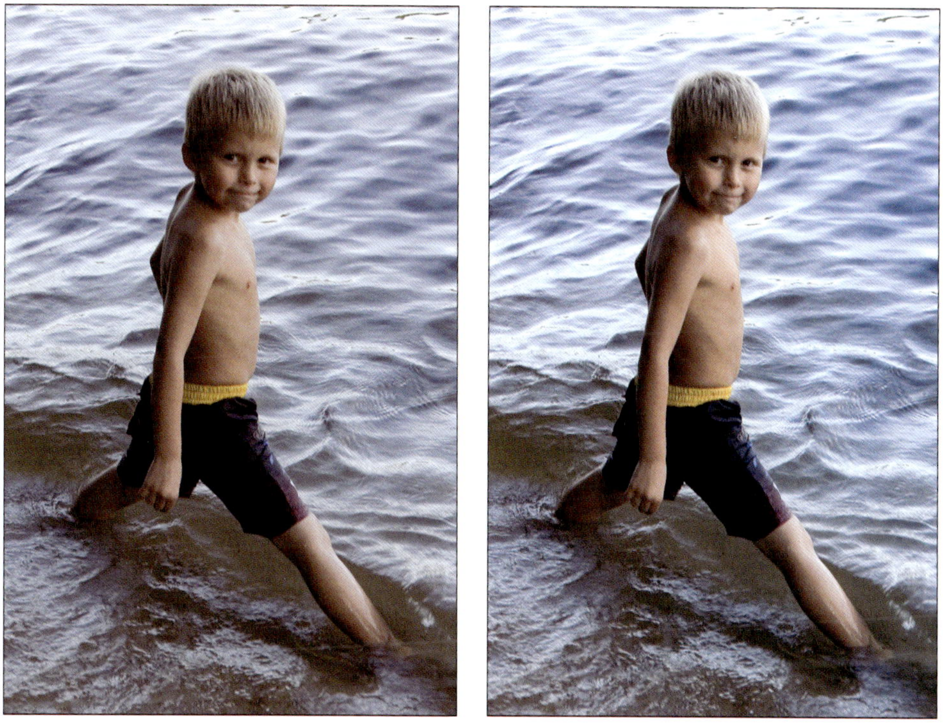

(A) (B)

Figure 10-5: (A) This photo is rather well exposed. (B) However, a slight boost of 10 in both contrast and brightness makes it a cleaner, stronger picture. (Photo taken with a Canon 20D, 17–85mm lens set at 44mm, 1/100 at *f*8.)

Histograms and Gamma Curves

Histograms and gamma curves are more precise exposure-editing tools than the simple brightness/contrast sliders. Both allow you to individually edit specific areas of the greyscale of a photo — in the highlights, midtones, or shadows — without affecting any other portion of the tonal range. (See Figure 10-6.) In addition, you can edit these values in the individual color channels of the picture (that is, the red, green, and blue channels), which also allows for very precise color adjustment.

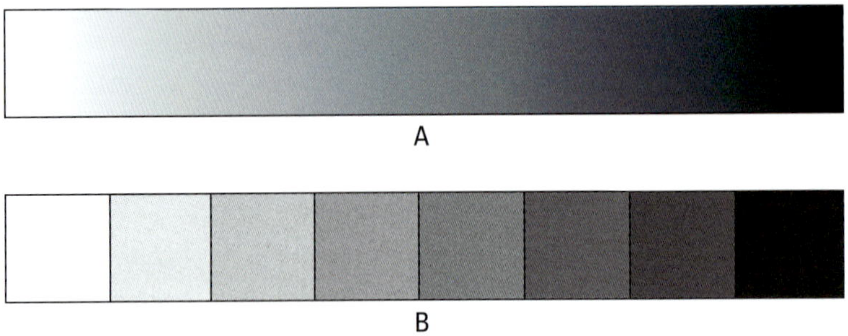

Figure 10-6: The underlying greyscale of even a color photo defines its exposure values throughout the dynamic range, from highlights, through the midtones, into the shadows. Greyscales are often represented as (A) a photo-realistic gradient or (B) a stepped scale.

HISTOGRAMS

Essentially, a histogram is a graph that represents a statistical analysis of how many pixels of your photo are in each value level of the tonal range. In Chapter 5, we discussed the histograms that you can use to judge the exposure of your just-shot photos on your camera's LCD screen. The same tool (which is called Levels in Photoshop) can be used to manipulate your exposure in photo-editing programs (as well as in RAW utilities and better scanner drivers).

Looking at the histogram of Figure 10-1, it becomes possible to analyze why a simple brightness/contrast adjustment wasn't the optimal fix for that photo. (See Figure 10-7.) The highlights and shadows (which are what is affected the most by the brightness/contrast sliders) were well exposed and fully represented in the histogram. It's the midtones that need to be adjusted.

When you click and drag on the controller points for the black point, white point, and midtone (the small arrows under the graph in Figure 10-7), it tells the software to remap the graph to new values. For instance, pulling the black point controller toward the right by, say, 10 redefines all the pixels from 0 to 10 as black. While this may be useful or even necessary, it is important to understand that the original dark grey pixels in that range would now be completely blacked out. (See Figure 10-8.)

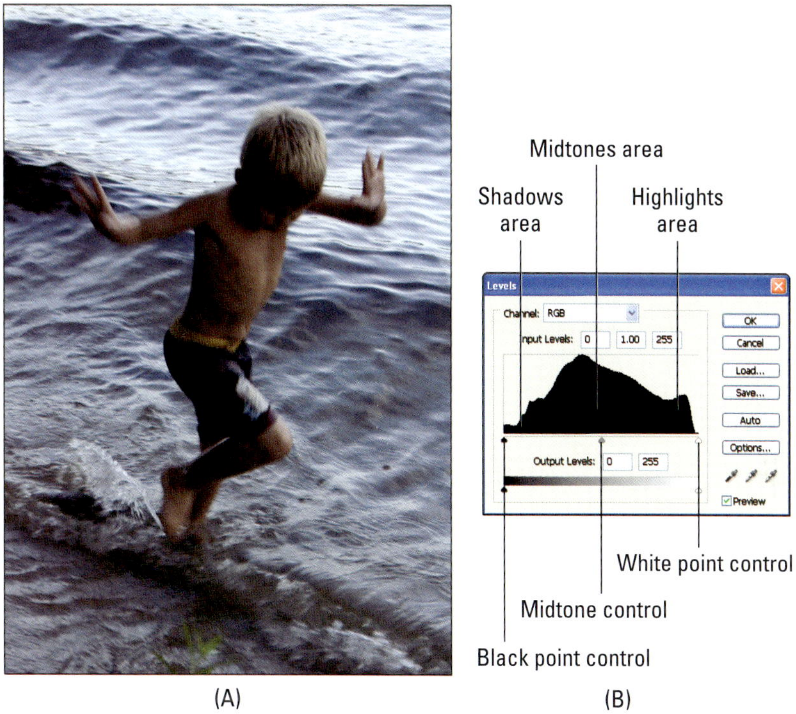

Figure 10-7: This is the same poorly exposed photograph as you saw in Figure 10-1, which we tried to correct with the brightness/contrast sliders. If you look at the histogram, it becomes obvious that the problem wasn't in the shadows or highlights. You have data throughout the tonal range, including at the ends of the dynamic range. (Histogram screen captures from Photoshop CS, courtesy of Adobe Systems)

In the same manner, clicking and dragging the white point controller inward toward the midtones, resets the highlight point in the photo, so more of the bright midtones become pure white.

Similarly, moving the midtone pointer toward the shadow area compresses the dark areas, increasing the bright areas. (See Figure 10-9.) And, moving the midtone pointer toward the highlight area compresses the bright areas and increases the dark.

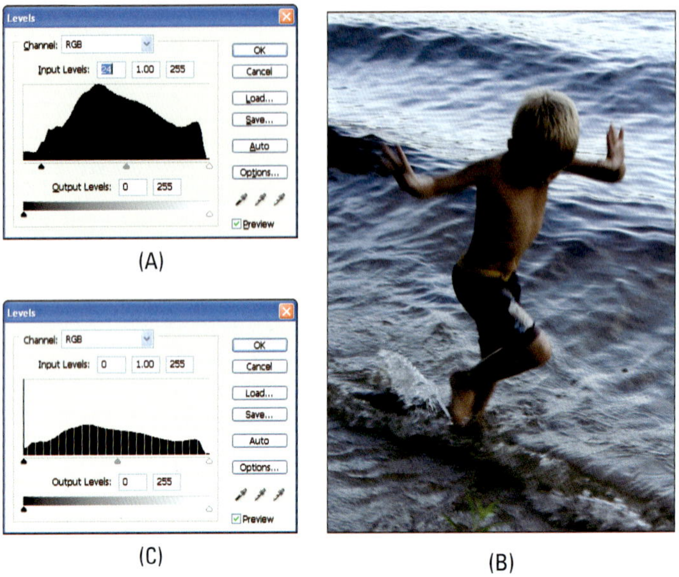

Figure 10-8: (A) We pushed the black point controller inward toward the midtones, remapping all the pixels from 0 to 24 to black. (B) That caused a significant percentage of the dark colors in the original photo to become black. (C) The remapped histogram of (B) is much flatter than that of the original photo (A). In addition, notice the empty areas (the white stripes in the graph) where there is no longer any data. That's indicative of the destructiveness of photo editing that we've been mentioning throughout this book.

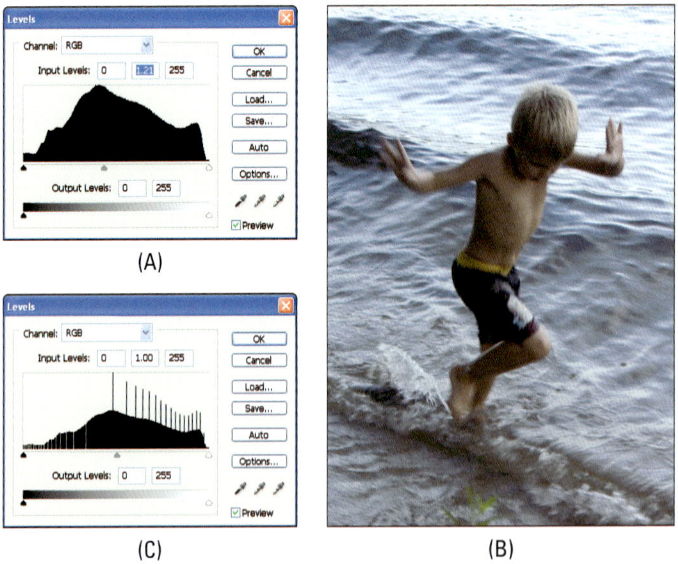

Figure 10-9: (A) We pushed the midtone point from the default 1.00 value down toward the shadows and a 1.21 value. (B) That brightened the midtones, by compressing the shadows. (C) The remapped histogram (B) shows much more data in the brighter side of the graph than in the dark side. Notice also the spikes of data in the bright section, as well as the empty stripes in the dark area.

White Point, Grey Point, Black Point

Throughout this section of this chapter, you will notice these small eyedropper icons in the various screen captures of Photoshop's histograms and gamma curves.

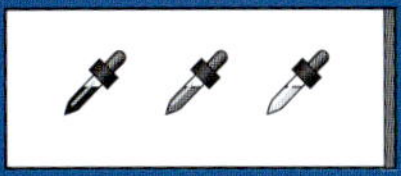

These are the icons for the black point, grey point, and white point tools. We often use the grey point to quickly color correct our photos, by clicking on a pixel that should be neutral grey but that displays a color shift. That click gives the software the information necessary for subtracting the same amount of color shift from the overall picture.

When a photo didn't capture any true whites (and the scene has some white elements), we use the white point tool to identify the brightest pixel. The software then sets that point as white and remaps the tonal range accordingly. Similarly, we use the black point tool to identify the darkest point as black.

Other high-powered programs have the same tools, though they may be represented by different icons. Your software may even have the ability to average the values of several points, as Paint Shop Pro does.

Be very careful how you use these tools. If you click on the wrong point in your picture, the exposure and/or color can be completely skewed. For instance, suppose you click the grey point tool on a pink pixel that really should be pink. All the pink in the picture will be removed. Or, if the pixel you use the white point on isn't the brightest in your picture, you will wipe out all the details in those highlights, turning them to pure white.

Tip

Whenever you are editing a photograph, be sure you have preview enabled. That often involves clicking on a box next to the word "preview", so a checkmark appears in that box. (See Figure 10-9 (A) and (C).) With preview enabled, you can try out various values in any of the editing dialogs (such as histograms, curves, hue/saturation, etc.) and see their effect directly on your photo before applying any change.

We will be covering color corrections and adjustments later in this chapter. But you should be aware that histograms can also be used for that purpose, by giving you the ability to adjust individual color channels of the photo. (See Figure 10-10.)

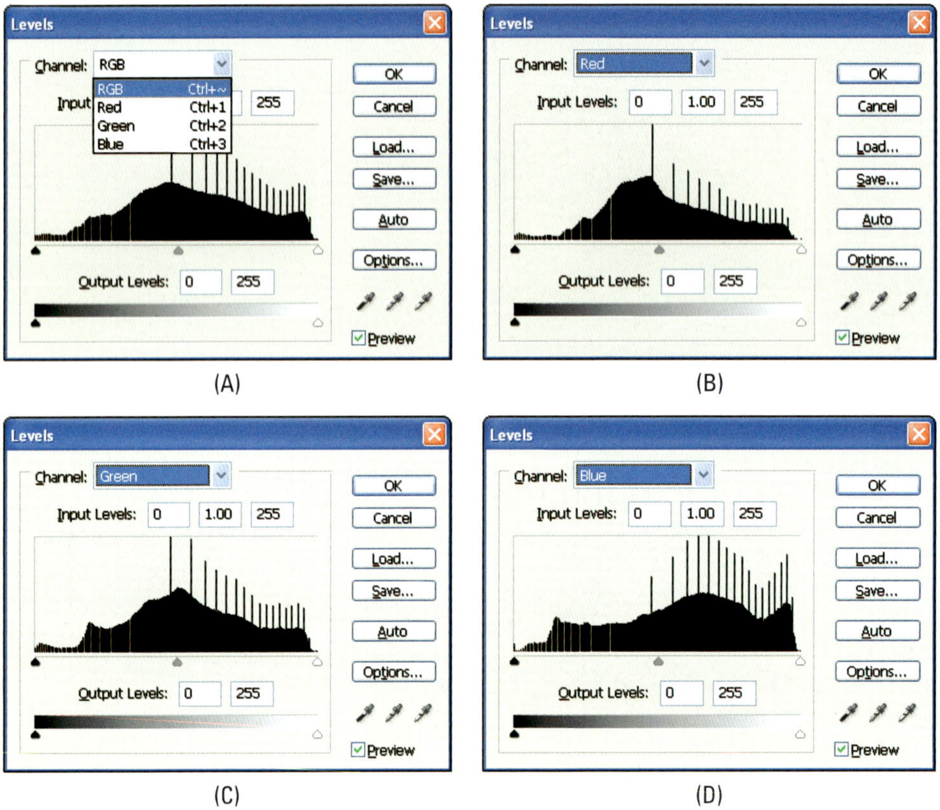

Figure 10-10: (A) While we've been looking at the overall histograms of our RGB photo, you can also examine and manipulate the histograms of the individual color channels of the photo. Comparing the histograms of the red channel (B), the green channel (C), and the blue channel (D) of Figure 10-9(B), you can see much more blue in the photo than red or green.

Manipulating the tonal range of each color channel will alter the color balance of the overall picture. Quite frankly, we very seldom use histograms for color correction, because there are much easier ways to achieve better results.

Tip

We are focusing on RGB images in our discussions. However, all the exposure and color tools we demonstrate on RGB photos, and on the red, green, and blue channels, also can be used on CMYK pictures, and their cyan, magenta, yellow, and black channels. (For information on CMYK, see Chapters 11 and 12.)

Auto Tools Often Work Well

Even if you are very accomplished at editing your photos on the computer, and you enjoy doing it, we suggest that the first step on any exposure and color edit is to see what your program's Auto tools can do. Not only are they quick and easy fixes that often work with a single click, they can sometimes do a better job than intense, multi-step manual editing.

Many programs, including Photoshop Elements, Paint Shop Pro, and PhotoPaint, have a single-click Smart Fix. The software analyzes the picture and automatically makes all the exposure and color adjustments it deems is necessary. In some tools, you can adjust the amount of the edit and other parameters, if you wish. When it works well, the result can be spectacular. When it doesn't, you can undo the edit and proceed with manual editing.

Two other common tools available in just about every program, including Photoshop, are Auto Levels and Auto Color. Called various names, they function much more precisely than any manual edit, analyzing the values of the pixels in your computer and applying edits based on the probability that those values are meant to be something else.

- **Auto Levels** seeks out the darkest and brightest points in the photo and sets them to black and white, respectively. Then, it remaps the rest of the tonal range between those two points. (See the two accompanying sidebar figures.)

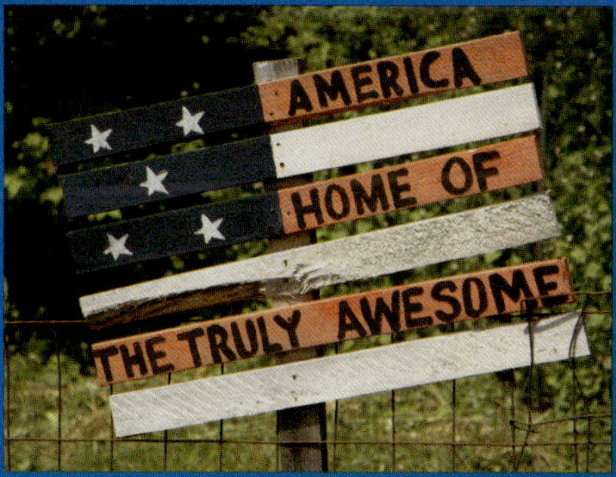

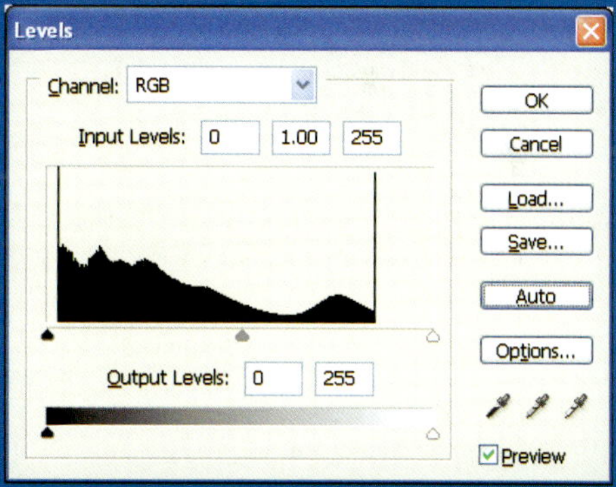

The histogram of this underexposed photo shows that there is no image data in the highlights, and therefore no pure white. (Photo taken with a Nikon D70, 18–70mm lens set at 70mm, 1/320 at *f*9.)

Continued

Auto Tools Often Work Well *(continued)*

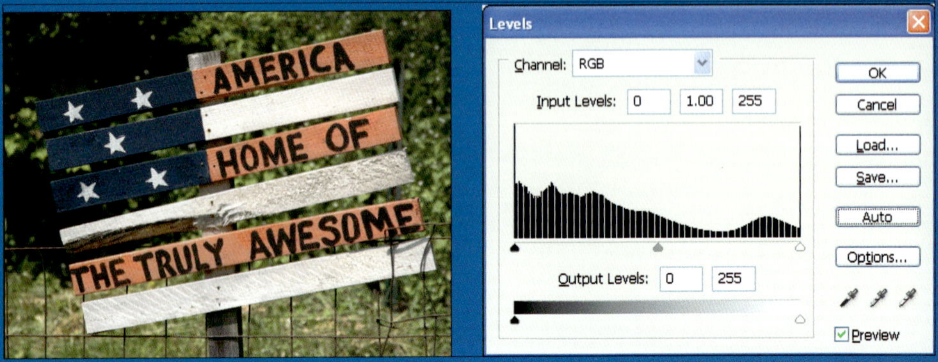

Using Auto Levels on the photo sets the brightest point in the underexposed image to white and remaps all the other pixels, spreading them out through a wider tonal range. The photo looks better, but, as you can see from the histogram, the data isn't as dense.

- **Auto Color** identifies what it believes is a color shift (or tint). Typically, it finds the brightest point in the picture, assumes that it is meant to be white, and then subtracts whatever color is evident at that point throughout the picture. For instance, suppose your photo has a yellow-green shift because it was shot using daylight white balance under fluorescent lighting. Auto Color will calculate how much yellow-green contaminant is in the whites and subtract that amount from all the other colors. (Some Auto Color tools work on greys rather than whites.) In recent years, Auto Color tools have become quite intelligent, seeking out flesh tones, sky, or other definitive colors and balancing the photos to make such important elements realistic and/or more appealing.

GAMMA CURVES

Gamma curves are based on the same concepts as histograms, but they are graphed in another manner. This differentiation affects the way you manipulate your exposure and, sometimes, the results.

Anytime you open the gamma curve of a photo (also called a curves dialog) it looks the same, regardless of how many times you have edited it — a straight diagonal line that goes from the lower-left corner to the upper-right corner of the graph box. (See Figure 10-11.)

If you look at the horizontal and vertical greyscale bars under and to the left of the graph, it becomes obvious what areas of the graph correspond to which portions of the greyscale tonal scale. In the lower left are the shadows, the middle of the graph are the midtones, and the upper right are the highlights.

To manipulate the tones of your photo using the curve dialog, click on the line and drag it. Generally speaking, when you pull the curve downward, you are remapping the pixels in that region so they are darker. Conversely, when you pull it upward, you are pushing the pixels in that region to be brighter. (See Figures 10-12, 10-13, 10-14, and 10-15.)

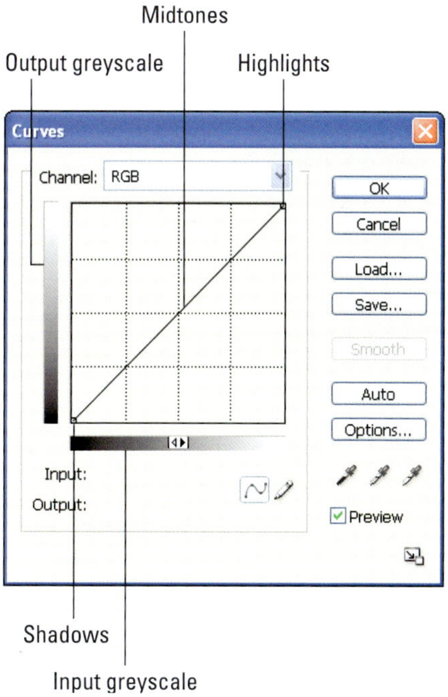

Figure 10-11: When you open a curves dialog, it always displays a straight line graph, indicating that the tonal values of the image (the input greyscale) you have opened is identical to that which the image will output. When you click and drag on the line, to curve it, you are remapping the greyscale pixels, as we explained in the histogram section previously, so that the output values are different from those of the original image. (Curves dialogs from Photoshop CS, courtesy of Adobe Systems)

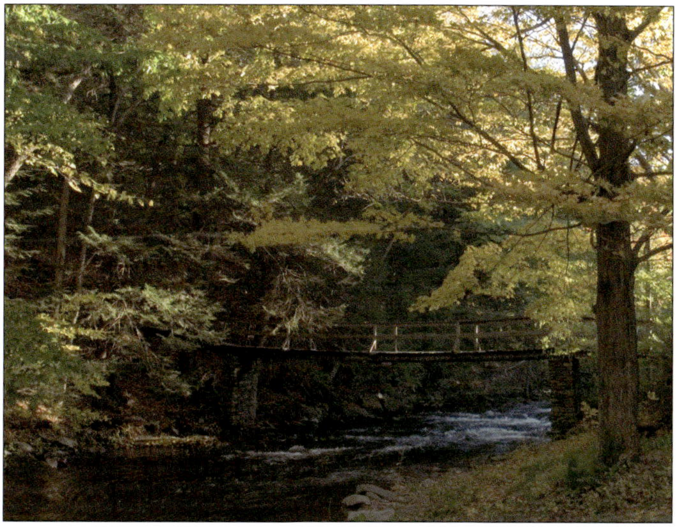

Figure 10-12: This photograph of the Sterling Inn bridge is too dark, and the colors don't have the pizzazz we've learned to expect in Pennsylvanian autumn foliage photos. (Photo taken with an Olympus E-1, 14–54mm lens set at 23mm, 1/180 at *f*10.)

nik Filters

Every so often, an imaging product comes along that quickly becomes an integral part of our workflow, simply because it does what we need it to do.

nik Color Efex Pro is a set of software filters that plug into any photo-editing program. (In other words, it works on your photos, within your photo editor interface.) It applies the same kind of color and light effects we get with glass filters that we screw in front of our lenses. This includes polarizing light, graduated colors (such as adding blue to a sky), dynamic skin softener, various monochrome conversions, and many other effects. We've even seen photos taken in the evening brightened with a nik filter so they look like daylight pictures.

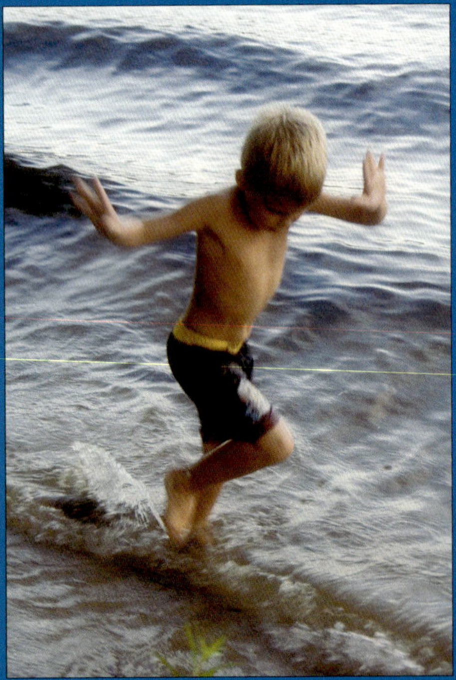

Applying nik's Sunshine filter to our underexposed photo in Figure 10-1 added just the right amount of lively color and adjusted the exposure nearly perfectly.

What makes the nik filters really versatile is that they are added as separate layers that float over the original photo (not changing it). Then, you can use your photo editor's brushes to selectively brush the effect where you want it on your picture, while the rest of the image remains unchanged. (See the section on layers and adjustment layers later in this chapter.) Try a free trial download from `www.nikmultimedia.com`. We think you'll be as impressed as we were.

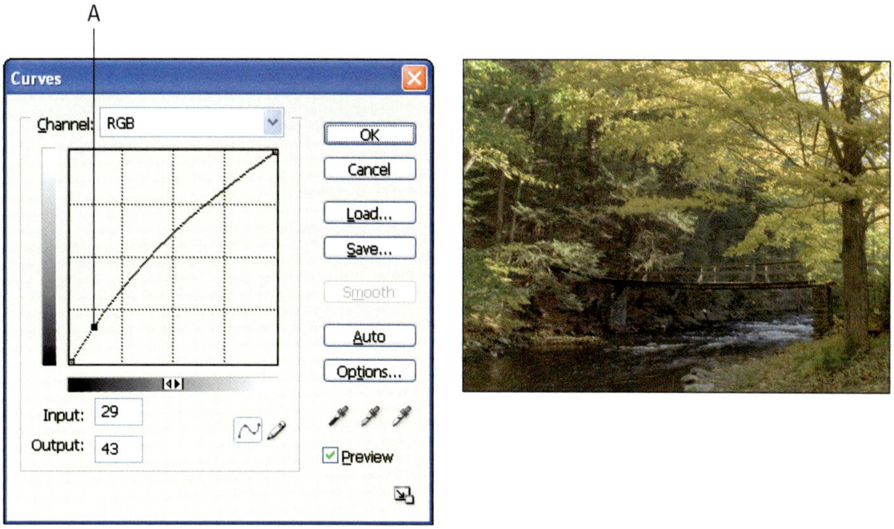

Figure 10-13: (Left) In this curves dialog we clicked on a point (point A) in the darker shadows area of the line and pulled it upward to increase the brightness of the shadows in the photo. Notice how the entire line curved with that one action. (Right) The curve edit made on the left created this brighter picture. (Compare it to Figure 10-12.) However, the picture has lost some snap.

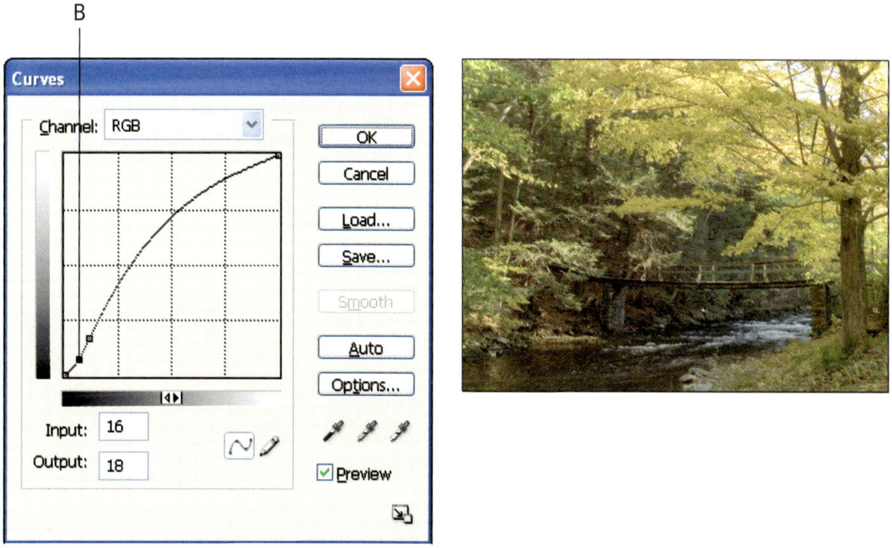

Figure 10-14: (Left) To add more contrast to the figure, we clicked on the gamma curve line in the darkest shadows (point B) and pulled it down to make them even darker. Notice that the first point we edited (point A in the previous figure) acted as a fulcrum. So, when we pulled down on point B, the line on the other side of point A curved upward to further brighten the already bright midtones and highlights. This action and reaction process of the gamma curve is something we'll often use to our advantage, anchoring a point along the line to act as a fulcrum between shadows and highlights. (Right) Now the lower half of the photo is nice and crisp, with good contrast, but the foliage is more washed out.

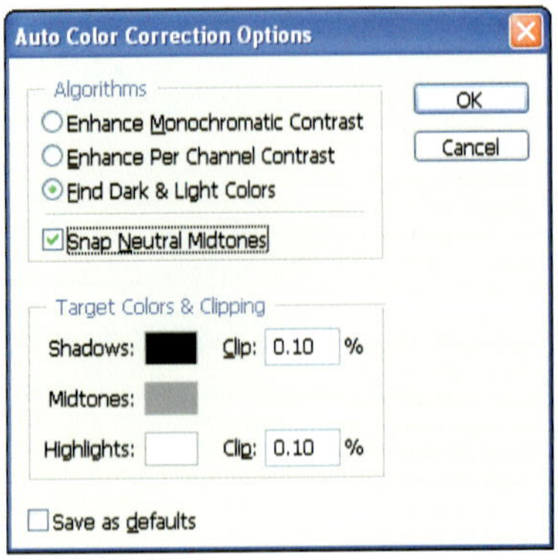
Auto Color Correction Options
Algorithms
Enhance Monochromatic Contrast
Enhance Per Channel Contrast
Find Dark & Light Colors
Snap Neutral Midtones
OK
Cancel
Target Colors & Clipping
Shadows:
Clip: 0.10 %
Midtones:
Highlights:
Clip: 0.10 %
Save as defaults

(A)

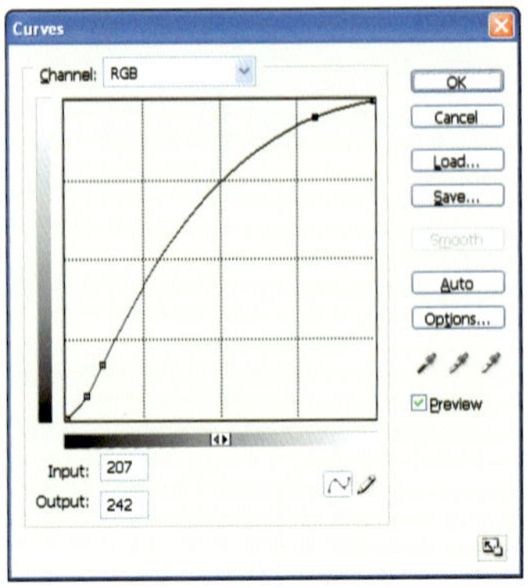
Curves
Channel: RGB
OK
Cancel
Load...
Save...
Smooth
Auto
Options...
Preview
Input: 207
Output: 242

(B)

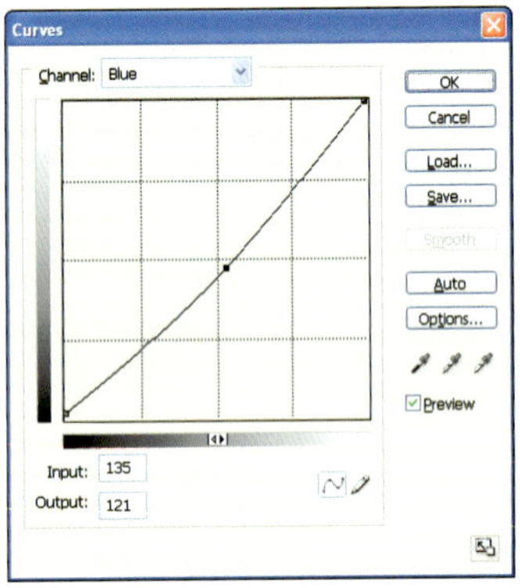
Curves
Channel: Blue
OK
Cancel
Load...
Save...
Smooth
Auto
Options...
Preview
Input: 135
Output: 121

(C)

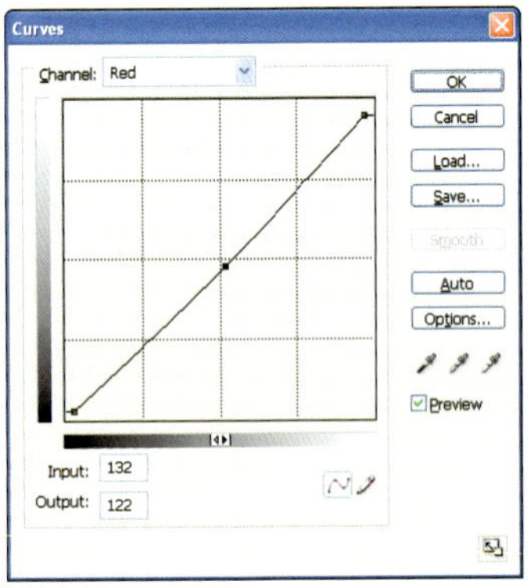
Curves
Channel: Red
OK
Cancel
Load...
Save...
Smooth
Auto
Options...
Preview
Input: 132
Output: 122

(D)

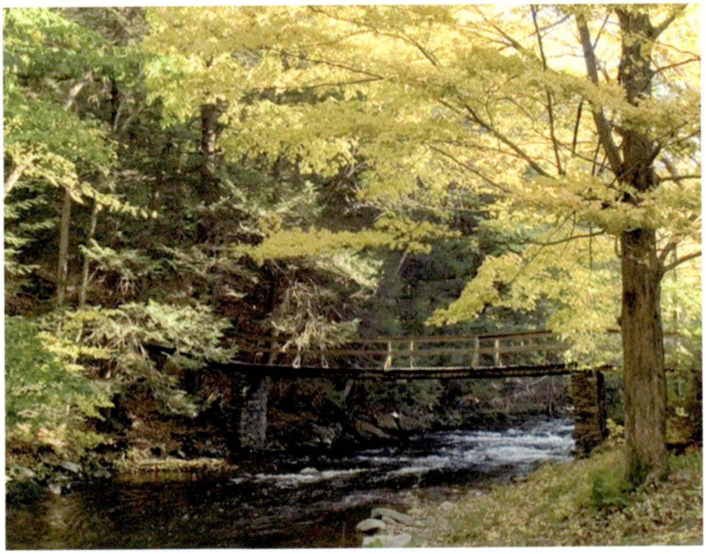

(E)

Considering all that we had to do to get Figure 10-15(E) to look the way we wanted it, we hope you understand and appreciate why we frequently say that it is often much faster and easier to reshoot a photo to get the best exposure and color possible than it is to "Photoshop" it. If we had simply used a fill flash when we had taken the photo, we would have gotten perfect exposure and color right away, with no fuss. (Please see Chapter 8, regarding fill flash.)

OTHER EXPOSURE TOOLS

Most image-editing programs offer additional exposure tools. (See the sidebar on Auto tools earlier in the chapter). One type of interface we have found particularly useful are slider controls for shadows, highlights, and other tonal adjustments. Variations of this are available in Photoshop, Photoshop Elements, Paint Shop Pro, and PhotoPaint.

Essentially, these tools take the capabilities of histograms and gamma curves and convert them to linear controls, which are easier for some people to understand and use. More importantly, the default settings with which the dialogs open up are often so close to what is needed for a photo, that a few minor tweaks of the sliders may be all that are needed to get the best results. (See Figure 10-16.)

Tip

Later in this chapter, we demonstrate how to use selection tools so that your exposure, color, and other edits can be applied to very specific areas of your picture.

Correcting and Editing Color

While histograms and gamma curves can be used for color correction and editing, we have found that the software tools dedicated to color are much more intuitive and precise, giving us results faster with less tweaking.

COLOR BALANCE

Typically, color balance linear sliders adjust the primary colors of red, green, and blue toward or away from their complementary colors. (See Figure 10-17.)

Figure 10-15: (A) Starting with the same dark photo as Figure 10-12, before we used the curves dialog, we first set the options to find and maintain the brightest and darkest points in the picture, and to snap the neutral midtones. That created a more contrasty picture. (B) Then we applied the same edits to the RBG curve as we had for Figures 10-13 and 10-14, but we also boosted the highlights a bit. (C) Switching the curve dialog to represent only the blue pixels of the image, we reduced the blue midtones, which slightly diminished the overall blue component of the photo. (D) When we looked at the red curve, we saw that setting the options in the Auto Color Correction dialog (in 10-15(A)) reduced the amount of red in the photo, as well as clipped the red highlights and shadows. However, an autumn picture requires an extra bit of red, so we pulled the red midtones back up a bit. (E) For the final picture, we also use the brightness/contrast sliders to give it a slight boost of 8 in both brightness and contrast.

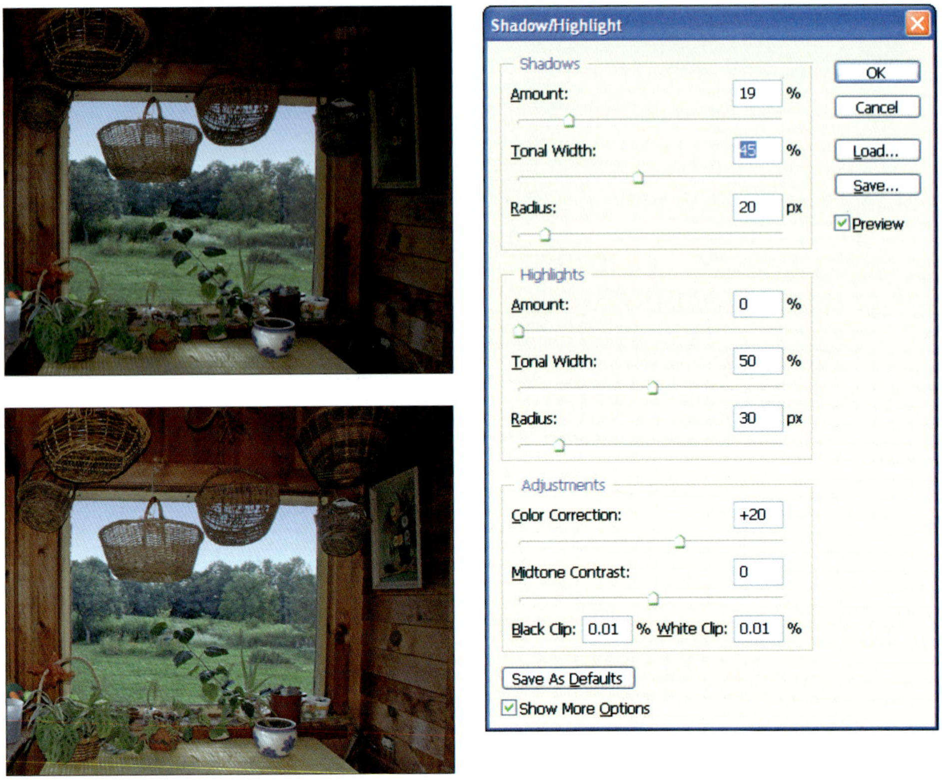

Figure 10-16: (Top left) This scene presents a classic exposure problem in which the landscape outside the window is significantly brighter than the room. If you don't have the ability to light the inside to balance it with the outside, you must make a choice. Either expose for the inside, in which case the outside landscape will be far overexposed and, likely, completely blown out. Or, expose for the outside, as we did here, in which case the room is far too dark. We almost always choose the latter option, so we won't lose the details of the landscape. (Photo taken with a Nikon D70, 18–70mm lens set at 18mm, 1/140 at *f*7.1.)

(Right) Photoshop's Shadows and Highlights dialog. (Courtesy of Adobe Systems)

(Bottom left) If we had used a basic brightness tool on the top-left photo to lighten the interior, the outside landscape would have become washed out. By applying the Shadow/Highlights settings, we ended up with a well-balanced exposure of both the inside room and outside landscape.

Using a color balance dialog is rather intuitive. The arrow on the slider line acts as a balance beam fulcrum, weighing the picture's colors more toward one end or the other of the represented color continuum. (See Figure 10-18.)

When using a color balance dialog, you can usually apply separate color balance adjustments to the midtones, highlights, and shadows independently of each other. Keep preserve luminosity checked if you want the tonal range of your photo to remain unchanged. For instance, with Figure 10-18(C), if we didn't have preserve luminosity checked, the depth of the night shadows could have been lost.

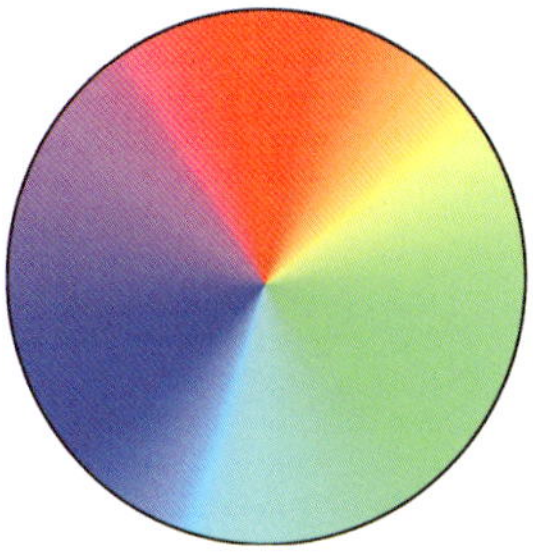

Figure 10-17: On this hue wheel, you can see the relationships of complementary or opposite colors. Blue is directly opposite yellow, red is across the wheel from cyan, and green is on the other side from magenta.

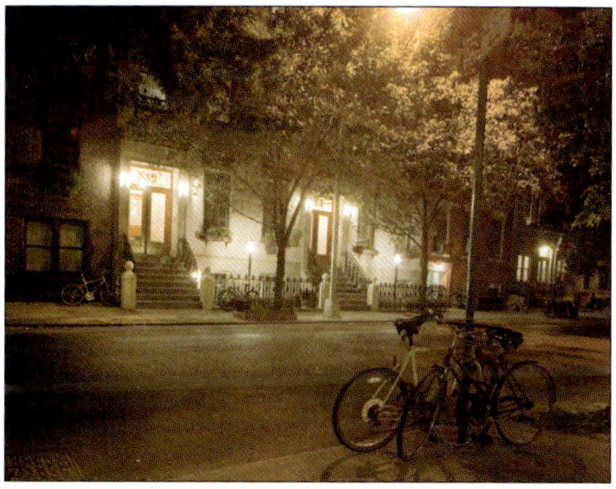

(A)

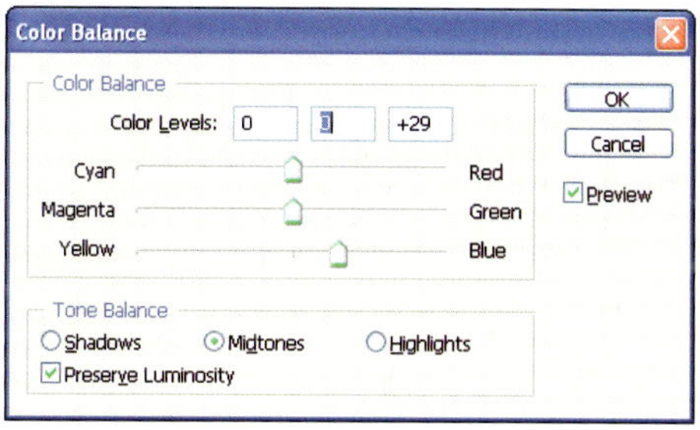

(B)

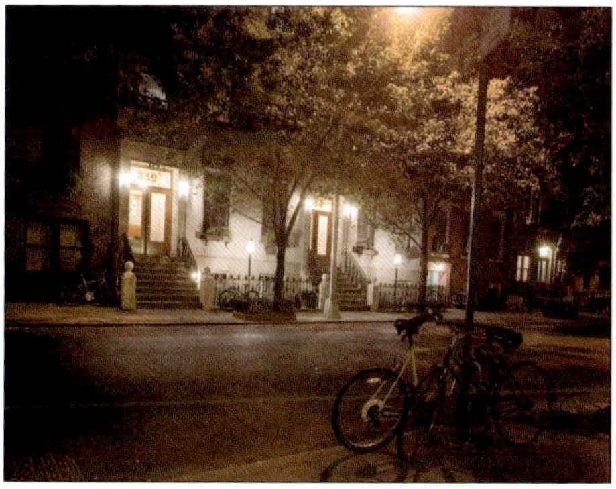

(C)

Figure 10-18: (A) This photo has a significant yellow cast. (B) We pushed the blue/yellow slider in Photoshop's color balance dialog toward blue. (C) That neutralized the yellow color shift, allowing the natural warmth of the scene's colors to come through. (Photo taken with a Canon EOS 1Ds Mar II, 16–35mm lens set at 25mm, 1/2 at *f*10. Color balance dialog screen capture courtesy of Adobe Systems)

HUE/SATURATION

With a hue slider, you can push all the colors in a photo toward another area in the hue wheel (Figure 10-17). Sliders to control the saturation (or intensity of the colors) and their lightness (or darkness) are usually in the same dialog. (See Figure 10-19.)

In Figure 10-19(B), we used the hue and saturation sliders on the full picture (the master), but it can be limited to work on only certain ranges of your picture's colors. (See Figure 10-20.)

Hollywood Squares

For those photographers who prefer visual aids for editing their photos, the Hollywood squares interfaces that several programs offer are highly intuitive and easy to use. Like the Photoshop Variations, these dialogs display different versions of the current picture, often in a tic-tac-toe arrangement, similar to that used on the old Hollywood Squares TV quiz show. (See the sidebar figure of Adobe Photoshop's Variations dialog.)

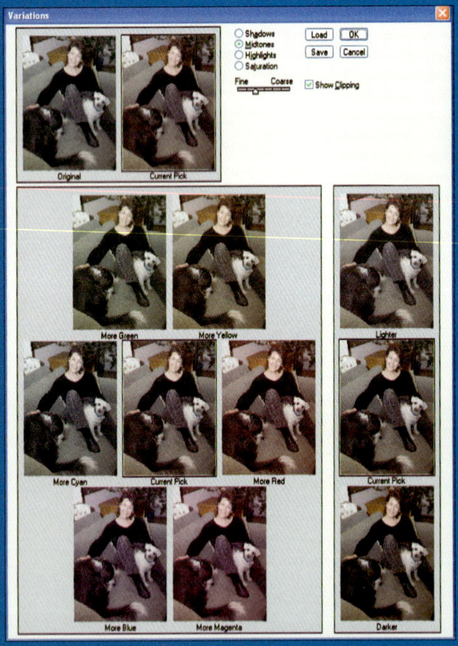

Each version of the picture shows you what it would look like if you pushed it toward a specific color, darkened it or lightened it. Click on the version that is closest to the one you envision to choose it. You can compound the effect by clicking on one version and then another. You can usually set whether it would be a subtle or strong color or brightness shift, and if it would be applied to the midtones, shadows, or highlights.

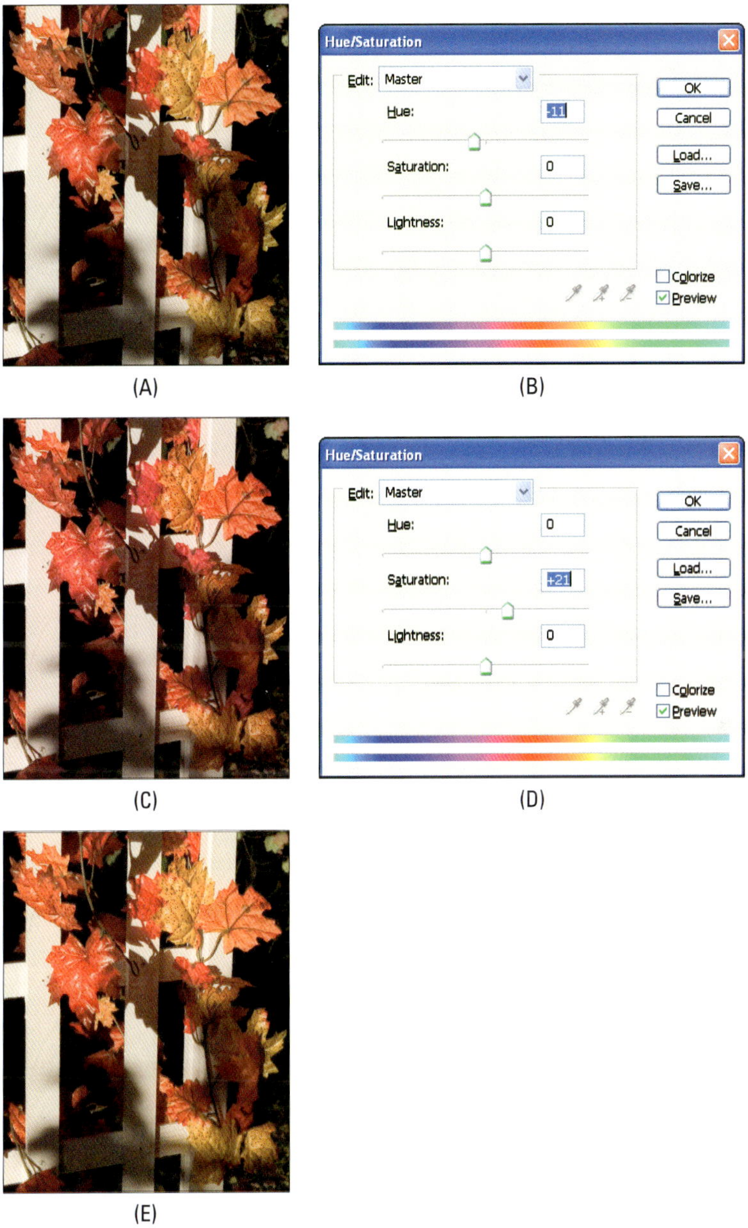

Figure 10-19: (A) This photo of autumn leaves is colorful, but it isn't exciting. (B) We applied a slight hue shift toward the magenta portion of the spectrum. Notice how the spectrums at the bottom of the dialog realign to show you how the original colors (on the top) are remapped (the bottom spectrum bar). (C) That makes the photo's colors more dramatic, but not as realistic. (We could have just as easily gone toward the greens and made it look like a springtime picture.) (D) Undoing the hue edit, we instead gave the photo a saturation boost. (E) That increases the intensity of the colors, without introducing any color shift. (Photo taken with an Olympus E1, 14–54mm lens set at 38mm, 1/4000 at *f*10. Screen captures of the Hue/Saturation dialog from Photoshop, courtesy of Adobe Systems)

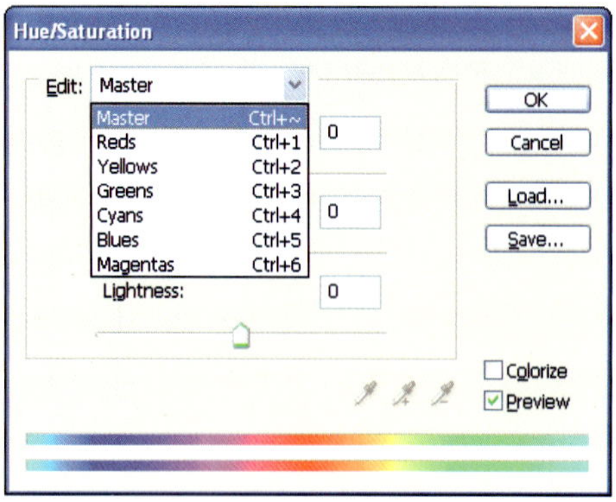

Figure 10-20: The hue, saturation and lightness sliders can be limited so that they work only on specific color ranges within the picture — the reds, yellows, greens, cyans, blues, or magentas.

CONVERTING COLOR PHOTOS TO MONOCHROME

One popular use of the saturation slider is to convert color photos into 24-bit black and white. (See the sidebar on 8-bit versus 24-bit black-and-white photos later in this chapter.) Simply reduce the saturation all the way down. (See Figure 10-21.)

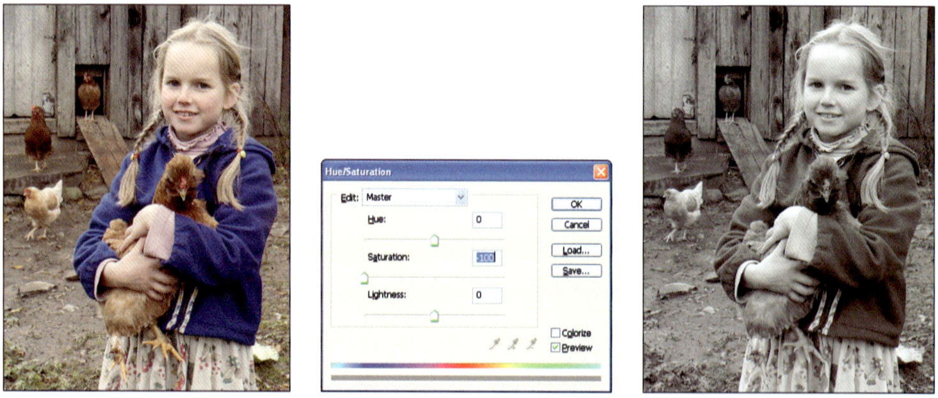

(A) (B) (C)

Figure 10-21: Photographers often reduce a color photograph's saturation all the way down to produce a 24-bit greyscale image, as we did with this picture of Rowan. Notice, in the hue/saturation dialog, that the lower spectrum is now a grey bar. (Photo taken with an Olympus E-1, 14–54mm lens set at 45mm, 1/50 at *f*16. Hue/saturation dialog screen capture from Photoshop courtesy of Adobe Systems)

If you want to leave a slight amount of color in your photo, to give it the sense of an understated color wash, push the slider down, but not all the way.

For more control over how the greyscale image will be created, try using a channel mixer dialog. Remember, color pictures are made up of color channels. In the case of an RGB image, it has three channels — red, green, and blue. When you use the channel mixer to create your greyscale image, you can choose how much of each channel will be applied to the final picture. We have found that those greyscale images we've created via channel mixer tend to be smoother, with greater dynamic range that can make flesh appear luminous. (See Figure 10-22.) On the other hand, the saturation reduction method often produces more texture and is more appropriate for documentary style photography. We have been known to create two versions of the same picture, using both techniques, then selectively combined them using layers, blend modes and/or a clone or history brush. (See the section on "Unleashing Your Creativity" later in the chapter.)

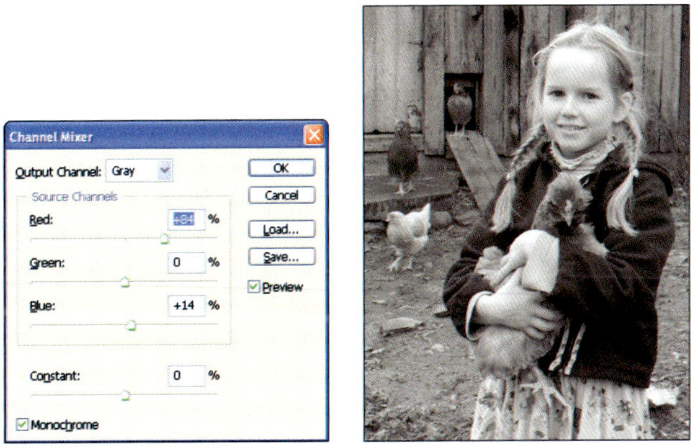

(A) (B)

Figure 10-22: Using the channel mixer on Figure 10-21(A) gave us a livelier photo, shown as Figure 10-22(B), than the one in Figure 10-21(C). For beauty photographers, the smoother complexion produced in this manner can cut down on the amount of digital air brushing that might be necessary. (Screen capture of the Channel Mixer dialog from Photoshop courtesy of Adobe Systems)

Tip

After you have created a monochrome photo, try painting back in a bit of color. In Photoshop, you can do this using a history brush. In other programs, create the black and white as a layer over the original color image, then use an eraser to bring back some of color. Another method would be to use the clone (rubberstamp) tool. (See the section "Unleashing Your Creativity" later in this chapter.)

8-Bit versus 24-Bit Black-and-White Photos

Photo-realistic color photos are, at the very least, 24-bit color — that is, they have 8 bits of information for each of the primary colors of red, green, and blue. (If you are working with CMYK pictures, then it would be 32-bit color.) One of the easiest ways to convert a color photo into a monochrome picture is to turn it into an 8-bit greyscale image. It's a single-click option that throws away 16 bits (or, in the case of a CMYK image, 24 bits) of information.

However, the methods for monochrome conversion that we use and demonstrate in this chapter give you 24-bit (or 32-bit) greyscales. That means they will have that much more data for smoother transitions and richer depth — and be as large a file as any color photo.

Tip

As you edit your pictures, you will end up with various versions of your images. If nothing else, you should preserve the original photo file, which should remain untouched, and a copy that you edit. When we work, we often save our original image, a 16-bit version that we edit, and an 8-bit version for further editing. If we output to various printers at different sizes and/or for the Web, we have those files, too. Plus, as we work on a photo, we may try different editing paths and compare the results. If your program has version control, turn it on, and it will keep the various versions linked, so they are easy to find. If not, then be sure to use related names and save them to the same area in your computer. We cover methods for filing, organizing, and finding your photos in Chapter 9.

Use Macros to Save Time and Effort

Anytime you find that you are doing the same process over and over again, it's time to create a macro (or action). To record a macro, simply start the recording (the controls often look like the record, play, and stop buttons on a DVD player), and then go through the various editing steps on one of your photos. When you are finished, stop the recording and save the macro with a descriptive name. Then, whenever you want to apply the same edit to another picture, simply play back the macro on that image. Macros can reduce a time-consuming, multi-step edit to a single mouse click. We have macros for inserting our copyright into the metadata of our pictures, converting from 16-bit to 8-bit, and so forth. For a discussion of time-saving batch editing, go to Chapter 9.

Other Important Photo-Editing Tools

These programs are so very deep and complex that we cannot possibly cover all the tools you may want to use on your pictures. However, three types are particularly relevant to DSLR photography:

- The new sharpen tools
- Noise reduction
- Lens correction

The New Sharpen Tools

For many years, we have used the Unsharp Mask as our preferred tool for sharpening. Unsharp Mask detects where there are significant differences between neighboring pixels (which should be the definition of a visual edge) and increases the contrast. In other words, the dark pixels get darker and the light pixels get lighter. Since the human eye sees contrast as sharpness, this effectively increases the sharpness of the picture. In addition to the amount of the contrast, you control how far afield the software looks for differing pixels through the radius slider and how wide a differentiation it seeks among pixels through the threshold slider. (See Figure 10-23.)

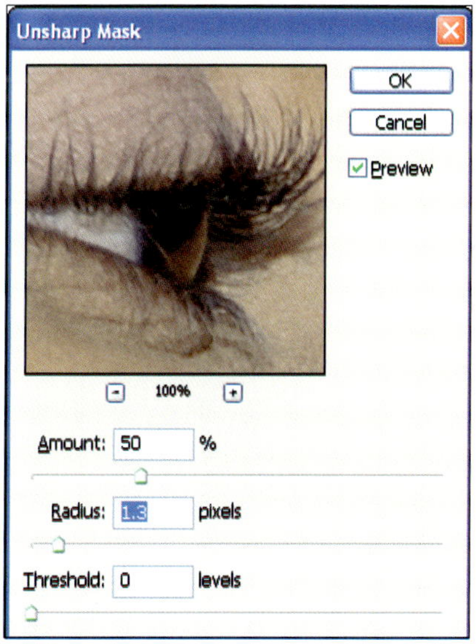

Figure 10-23: This dialog from Photoshop is typical of an Unsharp Mask tool. (Courtesy of Adobe Systems)

The problem with the Unsharp Mask is that it can increase the noise in your picture because it is increasing the contrast among pixels that may not be part of an edge. For that reason, software engineers have developed new sharpening tools that give you more control over what is sharpened, and, just as importantly, what isn't. Two such tools are Photoshop's Smart Sharpen and Paint Shop Pro's High Pass Sharpen.

So, don't automatically go to the Unsharp Mask when you are working on your pictures. Instead, check out the new tools your program may offer. The difference in image quality can be significant.

Noise Removal

Noise comprises those image-degrading stray pixels that come from shooting at high ISO, from oversharpening, or from trying to lighten a dark area that doesn't have sufficient image data. (See Figure 10-24.)

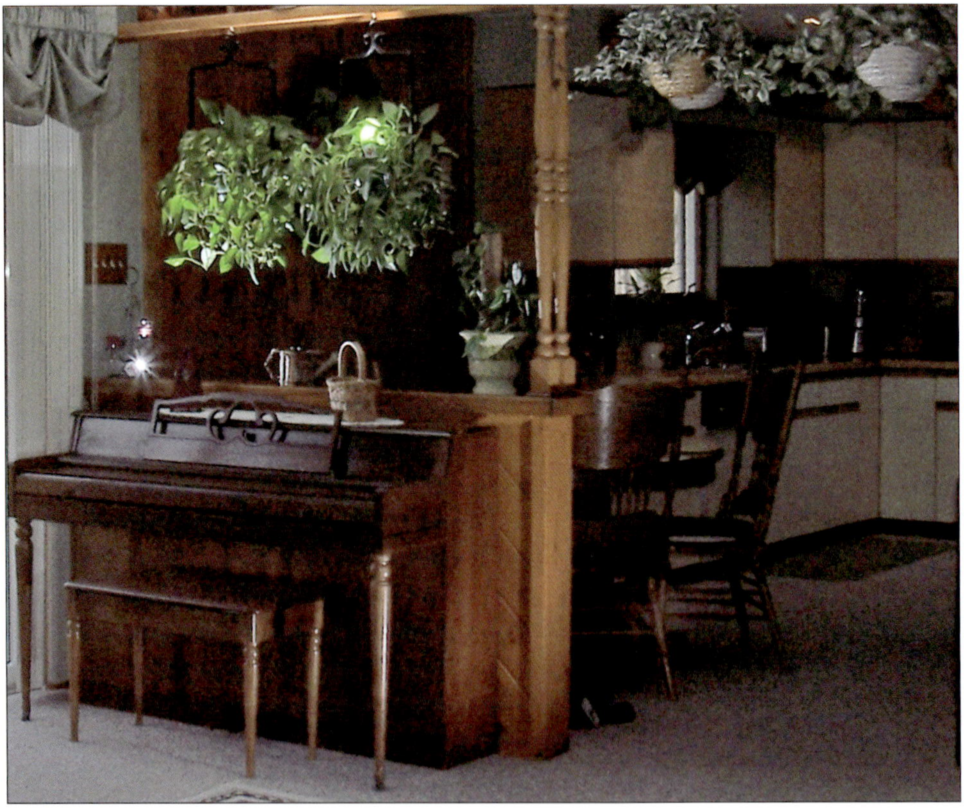

Figure 10-24: This photo was taken inside with not enough light, so most of it was dark. When we lightened it, we ended up with severe noise, most notably in the right side of the picture.

The traditional method for reducing noise in a photo has been to blur it slightly, reducing the contrast between the stray pixels and their surroundings. But that also softens the photo. We often must choose between balancing the amount of noise we want removed against the amount of sharpness we're willing to sacrifice. Like the new sharpening tools, noise removal has come a long way, too. But at the end of the day, it is still a balancing act. The best solution is to avoid shooting in situations or using settings that will produce significant noise, if at all possible.

Lens Correction

As we discussed in Chapter 2, lenses can create optical distortions. This is especially true of extreme telephoto or ultra-wide angle lenses, which can produce pin cushioning or barrel distortion. Another common lens aberration produces *vignetting*, or light or sharpness falloff on the edges of your photo. (For a discussion of the various types of lens distortions, please read Chapter 2.)

Lens correction tools allow you to interactively try to adjust the perspective, light falloff, and other lens-created aberrations in your picture. (See Figure 10-25.)

Tip

If you plan to mat and/or frame your printed photos, you will save money by thinking ahead when you crop your picture, and constrain your crop to standard sizes (such as 4"×6", 8"×10", 12"×18", etc.). Otherwise, you will have to pay dearly for custom frames and mats, or cut your own.

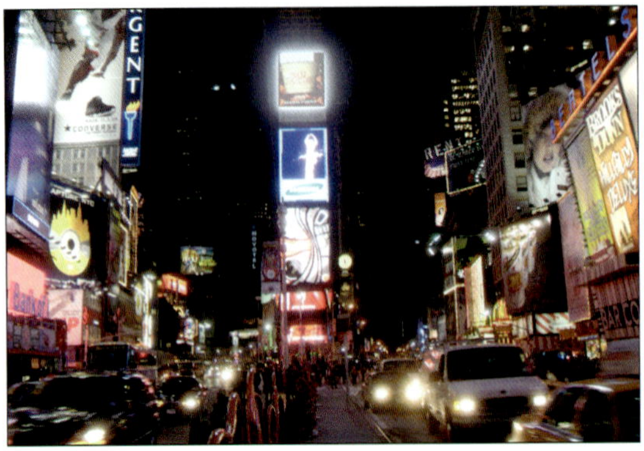

(A)

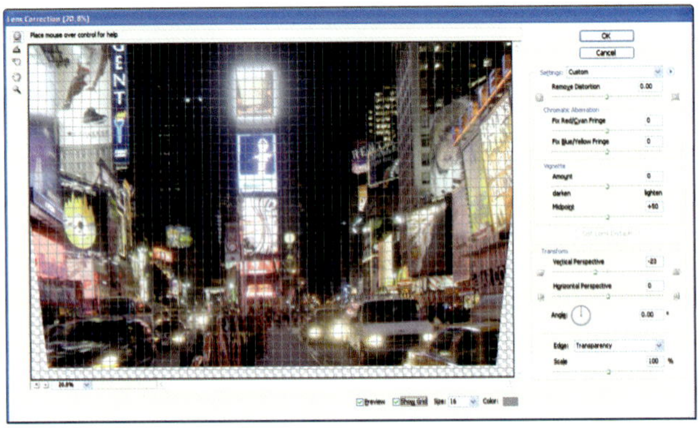

(B)

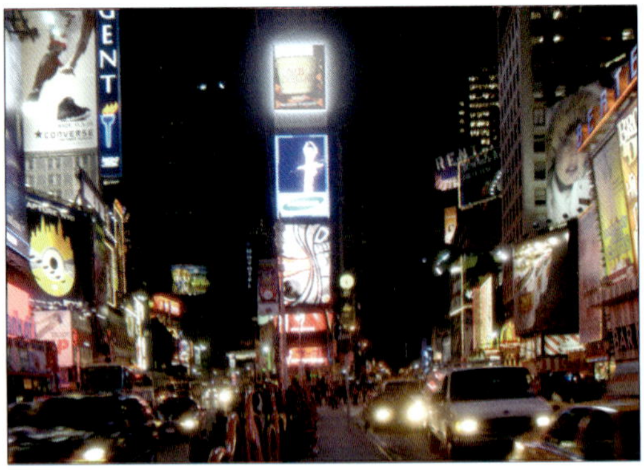

(C)

Figure 10-25: (A) Because we used a wide angle lens for this night photo of Times Square, and we tilted our camera upward to capture the skyscrapers, the buildings look like they are falling inward toward each other. (B) Using Photoshop's Lens Correction tool, we corrected the vertical perspective of the photo, which straightened the buildings and signs. However, that also forced the ground area inward, which means the bottom portion of the picture now has empty areas with no image data. (Courtesy of Adobe Systems) (C). After correcting the perspective of (A) using Photoshop's Lens Correction tool, we had to crop the photo so that we could end up with a rectangular image again. (Nikon D2X, 24–120mm lens set at 24mm, 1/10 at *f*3.5)

Unleashing Your Creativity

Image editing involves much more than simply correcting your photographs. These programs give you the means to take your pictures — and your imagination further, challenging and enabling your creativity to see how far you can go and what sort of images you can create.

What follows is a very basic survey of some of the more important functions for unleashing your artistic self. We suggest that you try them all to see what effect they might have on your pictures.

Selection Tools

Selection tools give you the power and control over your edits that we dreamed of but could never achieve, in our chemical darkrooms. Sure, we knew photographers who would spend the hours to cut masks and silhouettes to limit the developing of their pictures to certain areas. And we had other tricks for burning and dodging, which included interrupting the light with our fingers or using hot chemicals on a dabber. But that was far from the precision and comparative ease that digital selection tools provide.

Essentially, selection tools have two purposes:

- Defining an area in your picture to which an edit will be applied, protecting all the rest of the image (see Figure 10-26)
- Tracing an area of your picture that will then be combined in some creative way with other visual elements (see Figure 10-27)

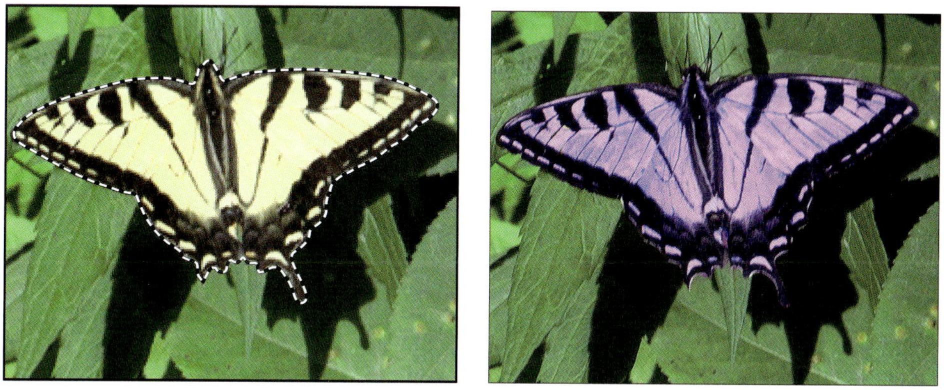

(A) (B)

Figure 10-26: (A) The dotted line around the butterfly indicates that the butterfly is selected. (B) With the butterfly selected in (A), we applied a hue shift; the only colors affected by that edit are those within our selection outline. (Photo taken with a Nikon D70, 18–70mm lens set at 65mm, 1/250 at *f*9.)

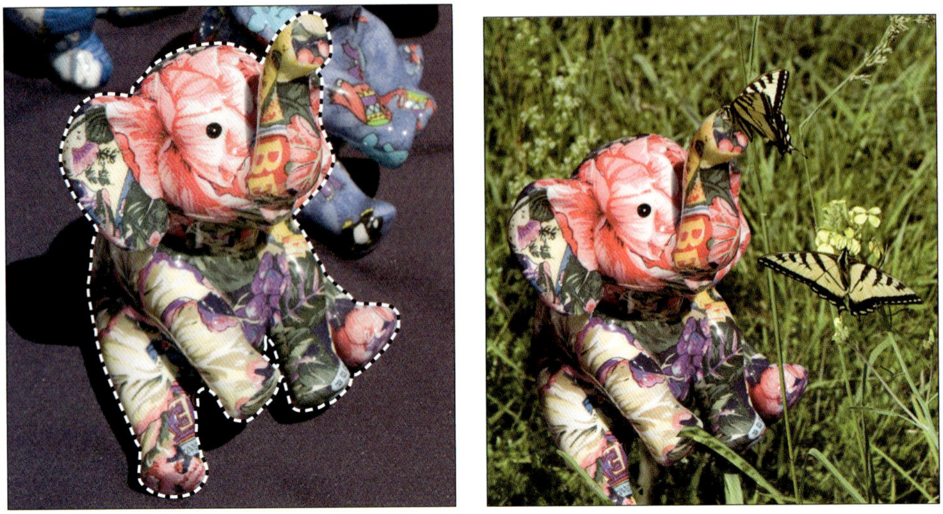

(A) (B)

Figure 10-27: After selecting the elephant in (A), we copied and pasted it into the collage in (B). (Photo of elephant taken with an Olympus E-300, 14–54mm lens set at 54mm, 1/640 at *f*9. Photo of the grassy background with the butterfly taken with a Nikon D70, 18–70mm lens, 1/250 at *f*9.)

Generally, you will find the following selection tools in any advanced photo-editing program:

- **Shapes** — You draw your selection as a specific shape, such as a rectangle or ellipse.
- **Magic wand** — Click on a point in your picture, and the program will select all other pixels that are similar to it, either contiguous to the original pixel or throughout the image. You select the tolerance, or how similar the pixels must be to the original.
- **Outline** — Draw your selection freehand, or use a magnetic tool that attempts to automatically snap your freehand drawing to visual edges.
- **Color range selection** — A selection is created based on a specific color range, such as all the pixels of a certain red hue.

We often use more than one selection tool on an image, adding to and subtracting from a selection until we're satisfied with it. Once we've perfected a selection, we save it with the image so that we can reload it at a future time. A saved selection is also called an *alpha channel* or *mask*.

Mastering selection tools takes time and patience, but it's a skill that becomes invaluable when you want to go beyond the basics of photo editing and image creation. Unfortunately, we don't have the space to cover this subject fully. We highly recommend that you take whatever tutorials your software offers on this subject. For really precise selections, try out the painting on mask tool that high-powered programs have.

EXTRACTION TOOLS

Extraction tools are a special type of selection utility, such as Corel KnockOut, a plug-in that works in any photo-editing program. Within the interface, you draw rough lines, dots, or loops around the areas that you want included in your selection and those you wish left out. Then, the software will analyze the image and create a selection for you.

Extraction tools, while not foolproof, can work well, especially where there are distinct lines and high contract transitions. Of course, if your background is uniform (such as when you shoot on a "blue screen" or other solid color that isn't represented in the subject), then the right utility can even extract the background from smoke, flyaway hair, and glass.

Eventually, you can expect to see extraction tools in most photo-editing programs. As they mature, they should become more efficient and accurate, eventually handling even complex objects on busy backgrounds with greater ease than traditional selection tools.

Layers and Adjustment Layers

Back in the early 1990s, when Sally had her first one-woman digital art exhibition in New York City, photo-editing and imaging programs were in their infancy. One important feature they didn't yet have was layers. So, every edit she did to a picture permanently changed the pixels. There was no such thing as going back and adjusting the parameters of the edit or removing it at some future time. The upshot was that Sally had to save dozens of versions of the same picture under different names, just so she could go back to interim stages, if she wanted. To store all those versions, we used up lots and lots of hard drive space.

Layers keep individual components of an assembled image separate so that they can be further manipulated, adjusted, or removed, without affecting the rest of the collage. Layers may include pasted-in portions of images, text, or other visual material. In addition, adjustment and special effects layers (called Lenses by Corel) can contain edit information, such as an exposure or color correction, which may be applied to only one layer or all layers just below it. Double-clicking on the adjustment layer in the layers palette reopens the dialog, so you can change the settings at any time. (See Figure 10-28.)

Blend Modes

You can use blend (or merge) modes to control how a layer or a painted stroke will interact with the underlying image or color. For instance, while normal will completely cover up pixels from the layers or colors below, darken will cover up only those underlying pixels that are lighter than the ones from the applied layer or brush stroke. Most of the blend mode names are self-explanatory, but as with any software tool, we find that simply trying them out one at a time on our own pictures gives us a greater understanding of what they do than any verbal description of the visual effect.

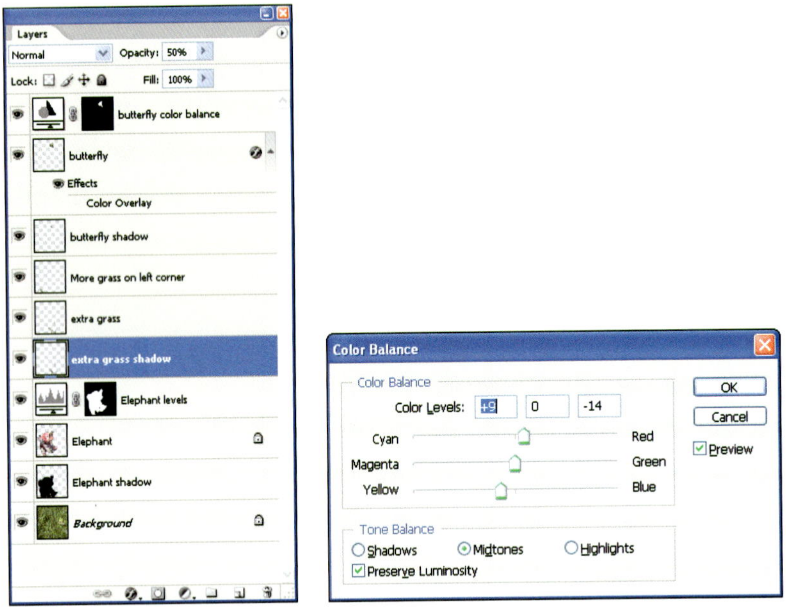

Figure 10-28: (Left) This is the Layers palette for the collage in Figure 10-27(B). You can see from the descriptive names we have given our layers how we assembled this image from various parts of other photos, manipulations (such as the cloning of the grass to extend it), and original imaging. Notice in particular the adjustment layers (the levels edit applied to the elephant and the color balance applied to one of the butterflies) and the effects layer (the color overlay applied to the other butterfly). (Layers palette from Photoshop, courtesy of Adobe Systems)

(Right) Double-clicking on the color balance adjustment layer in the Layers palette opens up the Color Balance dialog. We can see what settings we had used to change the colors of that butterfly, plus we can adjust them now or any time in the future, without damaging or changing the original pixels of the butterfly. (Color Balance dialog from Photoshop, courtesy of Adobe Systems)

Tip

Whenever possible, use adjustment layers to apply an edit to your picture. That way you can always adjust the settings of the edit. Unfortunately, not all edits can be contained in an adjustment layer.

Your Photo As an Artistic Canvas

Software paintbrushes are much more than tools for applying strokes of color to your photos or to a blank digital canvas. With cloners, you can paint with portions of an image. Dodge and burn tools paint with light or darkness. You can even apply special effects, magically remove imperfections and wrinkles, or selectively erase back to a previous image state.

Rather than go through all the many variations of brushes, let's look at a few of the effects you can achieve to get you started thinking of other projects you might want to try on your own.

Tip

To gain control over your software's brushes, create an empty blank image and simply doodle. As you play, change brush types, colors, transparency, blend modes, and other parameters to see what effect they have.

LOADING YOUR PAINTBRUSH WITH IMAGE DATA

Clones are specialty brushes that paint not with color, but with image data. (They are sometimes also called *rubber stamp tools*, because the icon looks like a rubber stamp.) The basic clone tool works in the following manner:

1. Click on a point in the image from which you want the brush to pick up image data. This is called the source point. (Typically, you will need to hold a keyboard key—most often, the Shift key—when you click to define the source point.)
2. Then, click and drag where you want that image data to be applied. This is called the destination.
3. If you set the clone to be aligned, then as you move the destination point, the source point will move, too, keeping the same spatial relationship with the destination.
4. If you set the clone to be unaligned, the source point will move only as you drag the brush, but between strokes, the source will snap back to the original point where you clicked.
5. As with other brushes, you can set your clones to varying levels of transparency and to use different blend modes. (See the earlier sidebar "Blend Modes.") You may also have a choice among various special effects. For instance, an impressionistic clone will recreate the source image data in such a manner as to make it look like an impressionistic painting.

Clones are great for removing distracting background elements and even old boyfriends. Or, you can use them to add elements, such as increasing the number of wildflowers in a field. (See Figure 10-29.)

Very close cousins to clones are those brushes we now use for removing wrinkles and other imperfections. Called by various names (healing brush in Photoshop, touchup brush in PhotoPaint, etc.), all you do is paint over the imperfection, and the software will calculate values appropriate for blending the imperfection into the surrounding areas. (See Figure 10-30.)

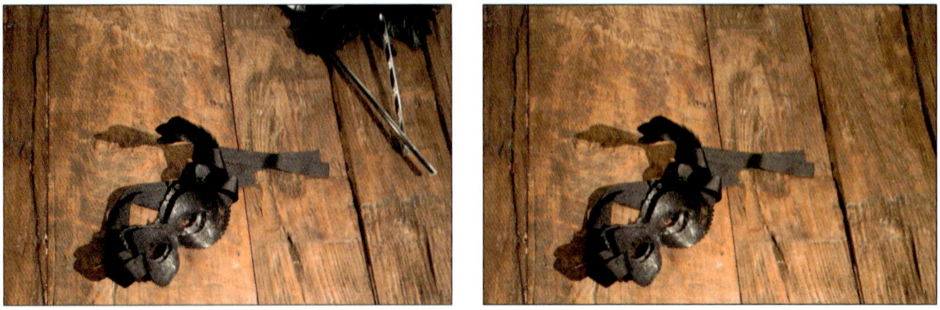

Original After using a clone tool

Figure 10-29: We often use clone tools to remove elements that distract from our composition, such as the sticks and mask in the upper-right corner of the original photo. (Photo taken with a Canon EOS 1Ds Mark II, 16–36mm lens set at 35mm, 1/30 at *f*2)

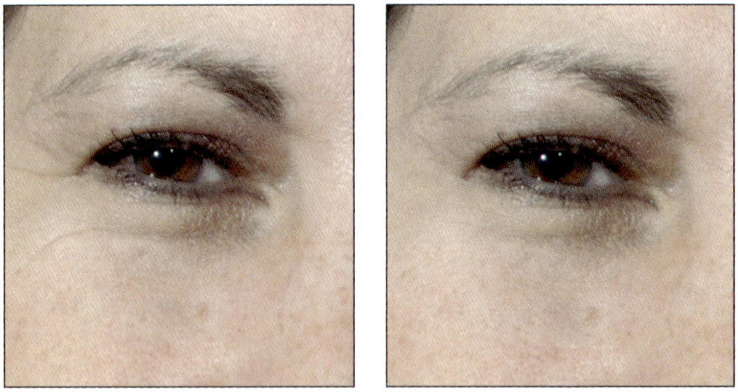

Original After touchup

Figure 10-30: Healing or touchup brushes do a great job of easily painting away wrinkles . . . um, smile lines, that is. (Photo taken with a Nikon D2X, 24–120mm lens set at 40mm, 1/60 at *f*4.2)

Tip

We always go into a program's preferences and change our brush cursor to a circle that represents the actual size of the brush. That way, before we even start painting, we can see exactly where the brush will work and how much area it will cover.

HANDCOLORING USING A PICTURE'S PREVIOUS STATE

One effect we like playing with is converting a photo to monochrome and then painting back some of the original color. (See Figure 10-31.)

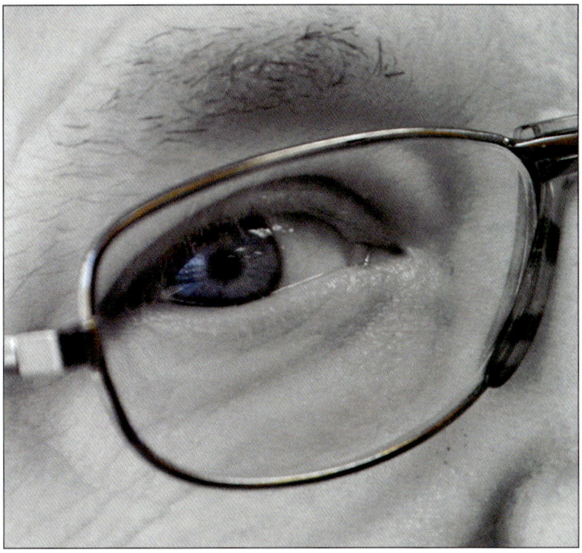

Figure 10-31: Painting back a small amount of color from the original color photo onto a greyscale version can be an effective way to give extra weight and interest to important areas of a picture. (Photo taken with a Nikon D2X, 24–120mm lens set at 120mm, 1/8 at *f*5.6)

Depending on what program we are in, we will use either Photoshop's history brush, PhotoPaint's undo brush, or other programs' eraser to achieve this effect.

Here's how we use the eraser:

1. In the layers palette, create a duplicate of the original picture. (See Figure 10-32.)
2. Convert the upper layer to 24-bit greyscale using either the saturation slider or the channel mixer. (See our discussion on monochrome earlier in this chapter.)
3. With the greyscale layer active, use the eraser to reveal portions of the color photo in the lower layer.

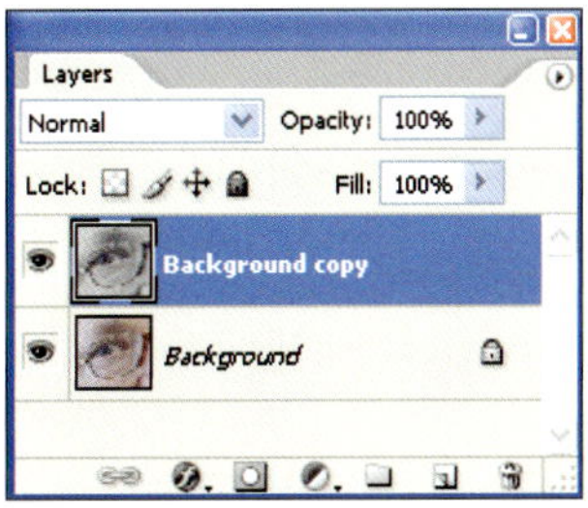

Figure 10-32: In the Layers palette, duplicate the original photo and convert the upper layer to greyscale. Then, when you use the eraser on the upper layer, it will reveal portions of the original color photo. The result can look like Figure 10-31. (Layers palette from Photoshop, courtesy of Adobe Systems)

To use Photoshop's history brush:

1. Convert the photo using either the saturation slider or the channel mixer.
2. Open up the History palette.
3. Click in the box to the left of the original photo (or the state of the photo that you want to paint from). A brush icon will appear in that box. (See Figure 10-33(A).)
4. Select the history brush from the toolbox. (See Figure 10-33(B).)
5. Then, just paint back the color into the monochrome image.

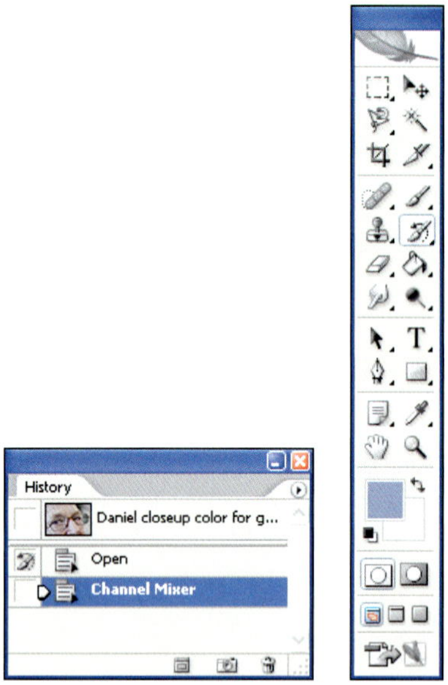

(A) (B)

Figure 10-33: Activating Photoshop's history brush is a two-step process. (A) First, click in the box next to the image state from which you want to paint. (In this case, we wanted to paint from the original photo, which is the state it was in when it was opened.) That puts a history brush icon in that box. (B) Then, choose the history brush icon in the toolbox. The history brush is the icon that is currently depressed (selected) in this toolbox. (Courtesy of Adobe Systems)

When working with either the eraser or a history-type brush, a reduced opacity can create a hand-colored look. With history-type brushes, you might also want to experiment with different blend (or merge) modes. While you paint, adjust the brush size frequently to give you full control over how much color is applied and where. You will probably also want to vary the level of zoom (using the magnifying glass icon) to move in closely to details and then pull out to see the full effect.

Tip

If you intend using brushes frequently, or even if you plan to simply create selections, we recommend working with a stylus and a drawing tablet rather than a mouse. Shaped like a pen, a stylus fits your hand more naturally and allows you to be much more precise with your strokes. The best are those associated with Wacom pressure-sensitive tablets. Please see Chapter 3 for information about drawing tablets.

Corel Painter

Among the numerous photo-editing and image-creation programs on the market, there is only one Corel Painter. Many have tried to imitate its natural media brushes, canvas textures, and colors that act like real paint, but none have the full range and power of Painter.

Bruce Dorn and Maura Dutra (`www.idcphotography.com`) are photographers who now work extensively in Painter, creating a signature style that is uniquely their own. (See Figure 10-34.) "We're at the dawn of a new medium that is yet to be defined," Bruce told us. "We should start to look at Painter as a medium unto itself."

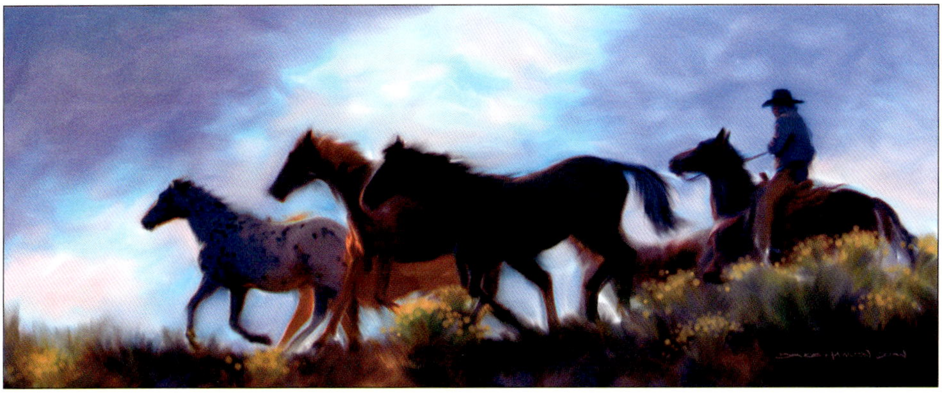

Figure 10-34: "As dusk light painted the approaching storm front, I spotted this sweep-man rounding up a few frisky strays," Bruce Dorn described capturing the moment on Ponderosa Ranch in Seneca, Oregon. "After importing the file into Corel's Painter IX, I hand-rendered the image using a Variable Flat Oil Brush and a bit of Small Palette Knife. The image was printed to twenty by fifty inches on a Canon imagePROGRAF W8400 wide format printer using our own Photo Impressions(r) Select Canvas." (Copyright by Bruce Dorn, courtesy of IDC Photography)

You don't have to have experience as a painter to turn your photographs into natural media works of art. As a photographer, you already have an artist's eye. One key is to let go of your sense of control over your environment that you need for good photography and allow your hand to move freely over the digital canvas. Paint with broad, quick strokes. As Maura explained, “Painting is not a precise thing; it’s a gestural movement.” She likes to express the energy of her picture through her brush strokes and makes sure that she doesn’t overpaint, which would make the picture look too photo-realistic again.

One method is to use Painter’s clone brushes (loaded with digital watercolor, oil, impasto, or other types of natural media), reproducing the approximate colors of your original photo onto a blank canvas.

For Bruce and Maura, creating their own painterly styles has made their work stand apart from the crowd, which has led to more interesting bookings and assignments. “We have determined that there is a tremendous added value of working it by hand,” Bruce said. “Filters and mechanics don’t separate you from the herd. In this era of digital cameras, making the process unique, seeing the thumbprint of the artist, is what turns it from a mechanized medium to an artistic medium.”

Summary

Photo-editing programs provide such a wide range of tools for perfecting and extending your photos that it is impossible to cover them all in one chapter. The most important key to getting control over the considerable power and versatility of these programs is to use them, trying any command you don’t know, doodling with the brushes, testing out the tools and dialogs, and just seeing where they take you. If you’re like us, you’ll soon be pushing your images and your artistic vision further than you expected. Or, you might end up with simply a perfect photo.

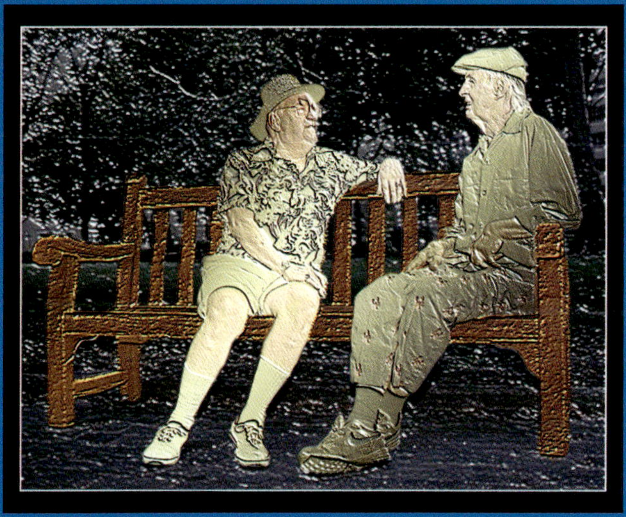

Sally used both Photoshop and Painter to create "Friends."

Chapter 11

Understanding Color Management

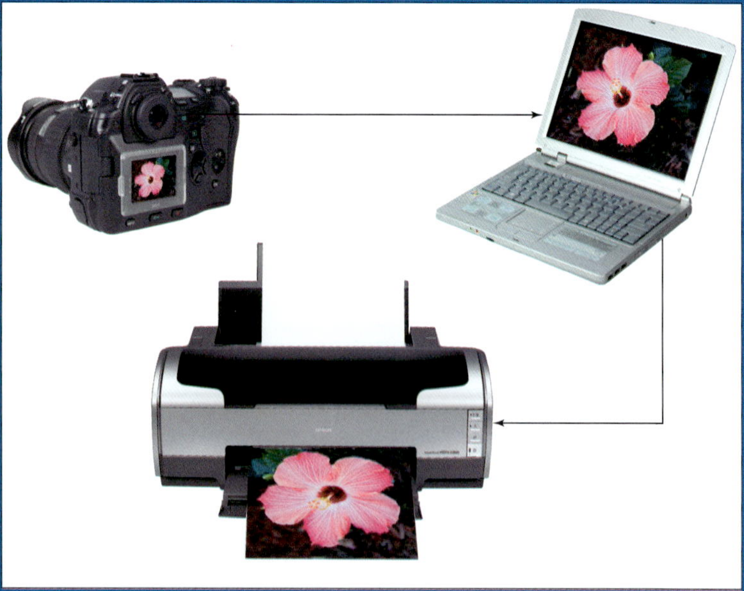

Good color management practices will help you maintain consistent colors and exposure of your images through the entire process, from capture through editing to output

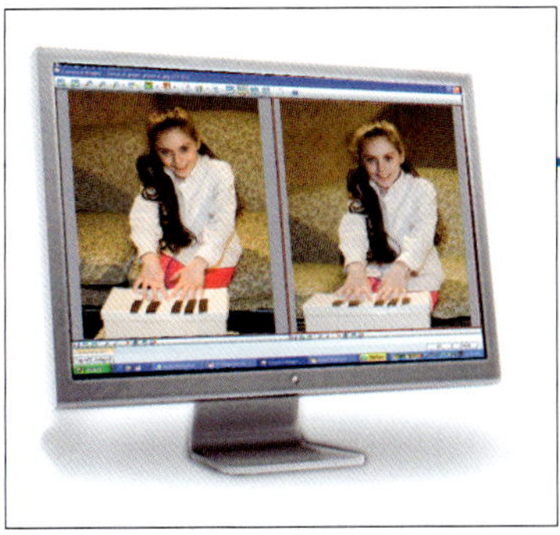

You can be sure what the monitor displays is an honest representation of your pictures' exposure, tone, and color only if your monitor is color calibrated.

Color, like light, is intrinsic to photography. Even if you work only in black and white, being able to rely on accurate reproduction is key to getting the greyscale tones just right. The problem is that the colors your camera sees and captures are not necessarily the same as those displayed on your computer monitor, which in turn can be quite different from those output on a printer.

In this chapter, we discuss:

- Why the color you see isn't always the color you expect
- The differences among the various RGB color models, and CMYK
- Color calibration devices and profiles to insure that your colors are accurate and consistent throughout your photography workflow
- Workarounds to try, if you don't have calibration devices

What Is Red?

Try to describe red to a blind person, and you'll probably resort to the way the color makes you feel. What's more, your description will likely be very different from that of your neighbor's. The human perception of color is a highly personal synthesis of visual input, neural stimulation and processing, intellectual interpretation, and emotional reaction.

Similarly, every device "sees" and describes color in its own unique way. It depends on how its ability to perceive and communicate is engineered, down to the "language" or color model that it uses. In addition, the method by which color is created can differ, throwing yet another monkey wrench into the mix.

- **Transmissive color** is created from light that comes directly to your eyes, such as viewing a computer monitor. This is also called additive color. (If you are a stickler for accurate terminology, monitor color is actual emissive, not transmissive, since light doesn't come through it but from it. But common usage in the industry has blurred the two terms.)
- **Reflective color** (also called subtractive color) is made by light reflecting off a surface, such as paper, and then into your eyes.

The essential differences between these two types of color are among the problems inherent in trying to making color consistent from camera to monitor to printer. Printers use ink and paper, whose colors can vary with each batch and are overlaid onto each other, mixed in different manners. Monitors project bright points of color that are pure light. Cameras take pictures by capturing different wavelengths of light and converting them to electrons and then digital information. The three technologies simply do not normally speak the same language; they need guidance and translation.

For photographers and graphics arts professionals, getting the various devices in the imaging chain to communicate with each other, unambiguously, is a critical step in making certain that color — and everything else in our pictures — is exactly right.

Quantifying Color

The impossible challenge of developing a universal mathematical model for color has fallen to scientists and engineers, who continue to fine-tune their theories, using a wide variety of color models. No one color model tells the whole story. It's simply the attempt to quantify something that is only partially numerical.

Two color models dominate digital photography:

- **RGB**, an additive color model, in which red, green, and blue are the primary colors. When you mix pure red, green, and blue together in this model, you get white. Black is the absence of color. (See Figure 11-1.)
- **CMY**, a subtractive color model, whose primary colors are cyan, magenta, and yellow. In this model, white is the absence of color, and black is the result of mixing all three primaries. (See Figure 11-2.)

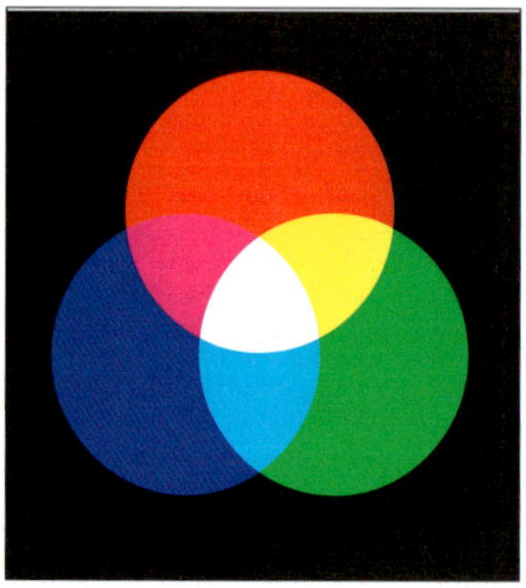

Figure 11-1: In the RGB color model, the primary colors are red, green, and blue, the combination of all colors equals white, and the absence of color is black.

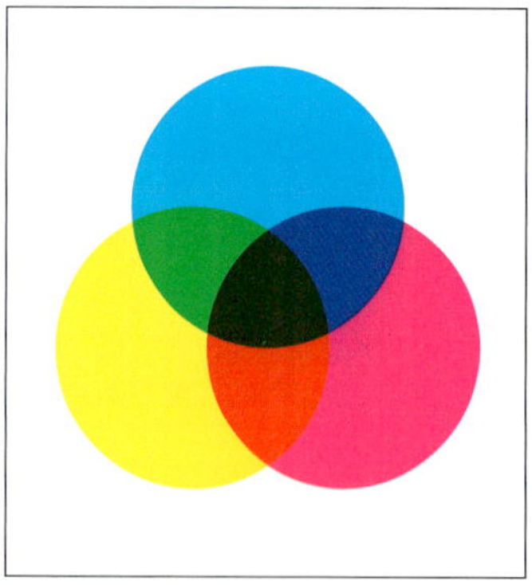

Figure 11-2: In the CMY color model, the primaries are cyan, magenta, and yellow, the combination of all colors equals black, and the absence of color is white.

The Black Realities of CMYK

Looking at Figures 11-1 and 11-2, it becomes quite obvious that the RGB and CMY color models are the exact opposite of each other. Therefore, in an ideal world, it should be a simple matter to translate a color defined by CMY into one defined by RGB, and vice versa.

Alas, ours is not an ideal world.

Traditionally, CMY is the color model used for printing, especially for output on large professional printing presses. The scientifically defined CMY color model says that if you combine equal parts of pure cyan, magenta, and yellow, you'll get black. However, if you mix cyan, magenta, and yellow inks or pigments, you end up with a muddy mess. That's why we have the CMYK color model. The K stands for black ink, which is added to the CMY mix to produce true blacks and to increase the depth of other dark colors. (Incidentally, *K* is used to represent black, so it would not be confused with the *B* for blue, as in RGB.)

That extra K in the CMYK color model skews the relationship to RGB, so that it is now impossible to make a direct translation between the two color models.

When RGB Isn't RGB

RGB is the dominant color model in photography, determining how color is captured by digital cameras and scanners, viewed on monitors, and output on desktop printers. But RGB is what is known as a *device-dependent* color model. That means it's a moving target, defined in different ways by various technologies and companies. Take an RGB image created by a specific camera or scanner, bring it into a particular RGB monitor, or output it to a certain RGB printer, and your colors will very possibly go through disconcerting transformations — unless you have a good color management system in place. (More about that later in this chapter.)

RGB comes in many flavors, including:

- sRGB
- Adobe RGB
- ProPhoto RGB

And there are many others. But that's not all. For instance, Adobe RGB is usually followed by the designation 1998 because that's the version of Adobe RGB that has proven the most popular. Therefore, it is the one you will typically find available in DSLRs and photo-editing software. Similarly, sRGB has several versions, though the one that we've encountered the most is sRGB IEC6 1966-1.

What's important to understand about all the various RGBs is that they have different *gamuts*, or range of colors that they create. The human eye has a remarkably wide gamut, in that we can perceive an incredibly large number of different colors — most of us can distinguish over 12 million different colors and shades. Computer monitors have less of a gamut, and printers even smaller.

So, too, each color model is distinguished by its gamut. Since, in this book, we are dealing with a printed page, in which all the photos have been put through the same color management, it is difficult for us to show you the full differentiation among pictures using different color models. However, in Figures 11-3, 11-4, and 11-5, you can see how different the histograms are. (Please see Chapter 5 on how to read histograms.)

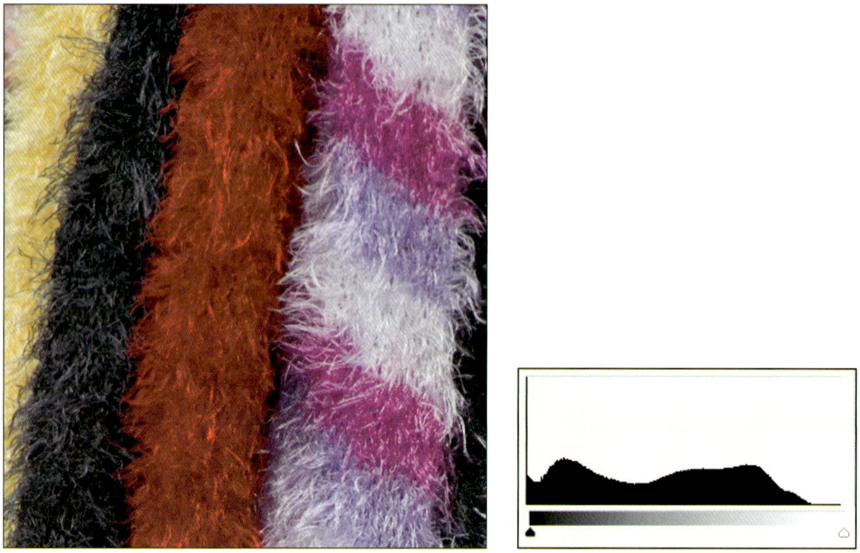

Figure 11-3: In this sRGB picture, the histogram has no image data in the highlight end of the greyscale, and the graph is compressed (displaying a low profile rather than any spikes or high mounds of data). (Histogram screen captures courtesy of Adobe Photoshop)

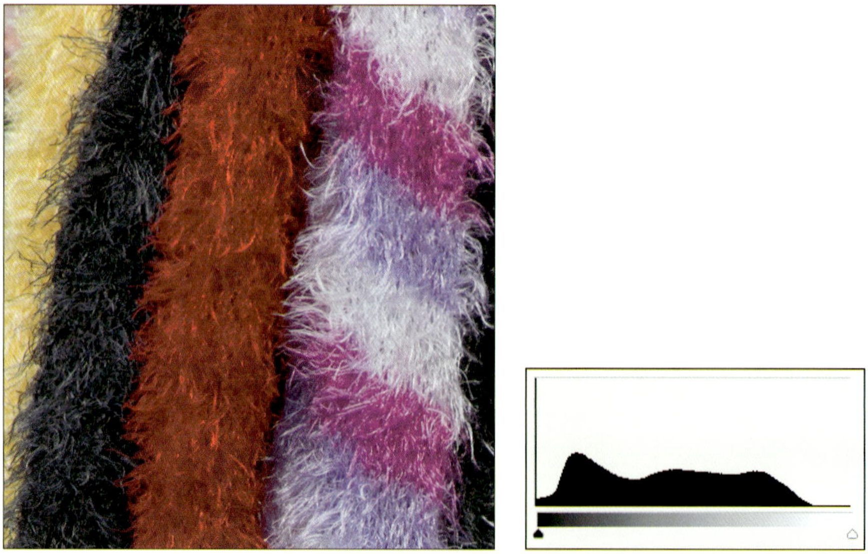

Figure 11-4: This Adobe RGB version of the same picture has a similar general profile to the sRGB, but if you look closely, it becomes obvious that has organized the image data in a very different manner. Certain areas of the greyscale are more dense, while others are less, but the overall graph indicates more data than in the sRGB picture.

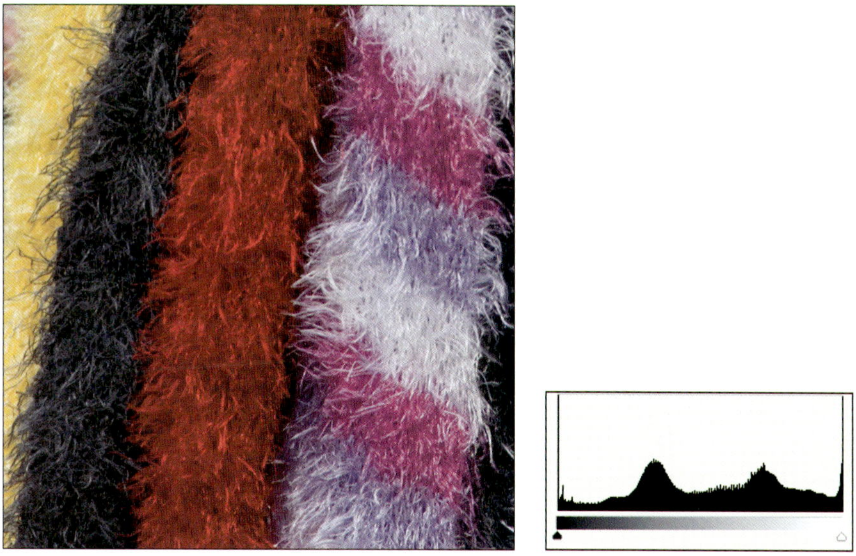

Figure 11-5: In this CMYK version, notice how the histogram shows image data throughout the full greyscale range. In addition, the graph spikes and reaches in some areas to the full height of the data range.

sRGB is the universal color model for the Web; it will usually give you the best color on the unknown, uncalibrated computer monitors of the Internet audience. (See the section later in the chapter about calibrating your monitor.) But sRGB has a much smaller gamut than Adobe RGB. If you output an sRGB photo to a high-quality, high-gamut desktop printer, the printed picture will not reproduce as many colors as it potentially could have, if it had been an Adobe RGB picture. ProPhoto RGB has an even wider gamut than Adobe RGB, which is why many discerning photographers like using it for their output. However, some of the colors it can represent or display on your computer monitor cannot be reproduced by your printer. Whenever this happens, those colors that cannot be reproduced are said to be out of gamut.

Some Other Color Models

Other color models you may encounter include HSB and CIE L*a*b*.

- **HSB** stands for hue, saturation, and brightness. While we never use it as a color model in our pictures, it can be a helpful tool in some photo-editing programs, allowing you to selectively edit those attributes of your picture. (See Chapter 10.)
- **L*a*b* (also written as LAB or Lab)** is an important color model that you may never use (unless you're involved in scientific imaging or other very demanding work with atypical colors). It is device independent, based on what the human eye can see. Therefore, it has a remarkably wide gamut. *L* stands for *luminance*, or the level of brightness. *A* and *b* are ranges of colors, with *a* going from green to red, and *b* going from blue to yellow. It's a three-dimensional color space, with *ab* gradients

Be Protective of Your Color Model

It is remarkably easy to convert your picture's color model in most photo-editing programs. Too easy. With the click of a mouse button, you can convert a beautiful RGB photo into CMYK, and back again.

Think carefully before you attempt it.

If you are going from a larger gamut color model to a smaller one, you are throwing away image data. In the other direction — from a smaller gamut model to a larger one — you are asking your program to invent colors for you, which can result in reduced smoothness and inaccurate tones. One thing you want to avoid at all costs is roundtripping (converting back and forth between color models), which invariably ends up degrading image quality.

We often have to reduce the gamut of a picture, such as when we are uploading a picture to the Web, which requires the sRGB color model. But we never convert upward. If our photos are headed for a printing press, which uses CMYK, we leave that conversion to the people running the press, because they usually have greater knowledge about the inks and paper they will be using. (See Chapter 12 about using service bureaus and print shops.)

In either case, the first step is to *always* save your original picture and work on a copy.

defined at different levels of luminance. LAB is often used internally in programming code to provide an enormous color space through which conversion and other tasks can be facilitated. By the way, it's also called CIELAB, for the Commission Internationale d'Eclairage, which developed it.

Making Color Behave

In the early days of digital photography, getting consistent, reliable color was a hit-or-miss proposition. It required considerable expertise and not a little luck to get it right. More often than not, whatever we did, we tended to waste untold amounts of expensive paper and inks when the pictures coming out of our printer didn't meet our expectations of excellence.

Today, color technology has evolved considerably, and with a little care, there's no reason why a serious photographer can't achieve consistent, high-quality color output. All it takes is some regular color management housekeeping.

Metadata and Color Profiles

The first pieces of the puzzle that help make everything work are metadata and color profiles.

- **Metadata**, as we discussed in earlier chapters, is technical information about a digital picture automatically imbedded into the file by the camera when it saves a photo and includes obvious shooting information such as shutter speed, *f*-stop, ISO, metering mode, and so on. In addition, the metadata handles communications among devices, describing how a photo file was created and how it should be interpreted.

- **Color profiles** are files that contain the color and brightness characteristics of a device — camera, scanner, monitor, desktop printer, and the like. Since device profiles conform to the ICC (International Color Consortium) standard, they can be read and used by both Windows and Apple operating systems, to help correlate colors across the entire digital photography workflow.

Here's how metadata and color profiles work with your computer operating system to color manage your photographs from capture through editing to output:

1. At the time of capture, the digital camera or scanner's ICC profile is embedded into the photo file's metadata.
2. When you open the photo on your computer, the operating system, in conjunction with the other software you may be using (such as your RAW conversion utility or photo-editing program) coordinates the image file's ICC profile with the computer monitor's profile, so that you can see accurate colors of the picture file on the screen.
3. When you output the picture to a desktop printer, again, the computer's operating system correlates the printer's ICC profile with the image file's.
4. If you send your image file to a service bureau or printing service, their computers can read the ICC profile of the picture to make sure their output represents the colors and brightness that is correct for that image. (See Chapter 12.)

Installing ICC Profiles

Armed with accurate color profiles for your digital camera, scanner, monitor, and printer, a modern Windows or Apple computer can eliminate any color contaminants introduced into your photo by each of those devices' specific characteristics. In other words, ICC profiles create a level playing field for you, in which the only colors in your pictures are those that are part of the original picture and not introduced by inaccurate display or output.

- Printer and scanner manufacturers provide factory default profiles as part of the bundled software that comes with the product; they install automatically with the driver. These manufacturer-provided profiles usually work quite well; however, for truly precise color work, you'll want to do your own calibration.
- Camera profiles are embedded in the camera's firmware, but you might want to create your own custom profile. (We discuss custom calibration in the following section.)
- Monitors should be custom calibrated every few weeks because they are a moving target, with light and color values shifting over time.

What about EXIF?

All modern digital cameras and recent photo-quality desktop printers support EXIF, which stands for Exchangeable Image File Format. Buried in the EXIF portion of your pictures' metadata is the ability to communicate with the printers about the color the camera used to capture the picture.

EXIF is limited in that it deals with standard RGB rather than customized color profiles. Still, it generally works very well if you simply shoot your photos and then output them to a good desktop photo printer without making any changes to the files in your computer. However, whenever photos are edited on a computer, it introduces the human element to the color equation. We make inherent changes to the image file, choosing how it will be defined in terms of color, tone, and dynamic range. And all our decisions are based on what we see on a computer monitor. If that monitor isn't standardized to represent colors, brightness, and shadows accurately, all our edits will be seriously flawed. (See "Calibrating Your System" later in this chapter.)

Tip

Profiles are often updated. Periodically check the manufacturer's Web site, and download new profiles as they become available.

For those profiles that don't install automatically, or those that you download from the Web, make certain that you install them into the correct folder on your system.

- On a Windows system, simply use your right mouse button on the profile file (which will have an `.icm` extension on its name), and choose install. That should slot it correctly into the operating system. Or, click and drag the file to the folder `Windows\system32\spool\drivers\color`.
- On a Mac, click and drag it into *library/colorsync/profiles*.
- In your photo-editing program, you may also be able to specifically designate the profiles you want used for input, monitor, and output. The settings for this would be found under the program's color management options.

Calibrating Your System

Manufacturers sometimes create custom color profiles for each individual device that rolls off the assembly line. More often, they provide factory default profiles that are based on the nature of the average device they sell. To be fully assured that you'll get consistent, reliable color, it's best to calibrate your system.

Tip

The first step in calibrating your monitor is to set the color temperature down from the stratospheric 9000 to 9500 degrees Kelvin that most use as their default to a more reasonable 6500 K. That will give you more realistic colors and tones relevant to print output. The other parameter you may need to adjust is the Gamma, which should be set at 2.2. For those laissez-faire photographers who don't do any other monitor calibration, those two adjustments should help a great deal in getting your on-screen photos a bit closer to your printed output.

NUMBER 1 PRIORITY: CALIBRATE YOUR MONITOR

At the very least, anyone who does any image editing must work on a calibrated monitor. Otherwise, you would be working blind, not knowing what your edits are really doing to the colors, contrast, brightness, and shadows of your pictures.

The concept of how it works is quite simple:

1. A sensing device (a colorimeter or spectrophotometer) is placed against the computer screen. (See Figure 11-6.)
2. The sensing device's cord is plugged into a USB port on the computer.
3. Software (which comes with the sensor) displays a series of specific colors at different levels of brightness, plus a full range of greyscales from pure white through the midtones to black.
4. The sensor reads how those colors and tones are displayed on the monitor and feeds that information back to the computer via the USB port.
5. The calibration software compares the ideal colors that were output to the monitor with the sensor's reading of what was actually displayed. Then it automatically calculates a precise, custom ICC profile for that specific monitor.
6. You are asked to give the profile a name (use one that you'll readily recognize), then the software saves it to your computer's hard drive.
7. In all the calibration programs we have used recently, the newly calculated ICC profile is automatically applied to the operating system, adjusting the monitor's display to remove any color or tonal shift. If you have more than one valid monitor profile (such as one for daytime and another for night work, when the ambient light changes), you can select the one your want in your operating system's display settings.

It used to be that buying and using a monitor calibration device was both expensive and difficult. No more. Colorvision, GretagMacbeth, Monaco, and others make colorimeters that sell for less than $200. What's more, they require no special knowledge to use because everything is automated.

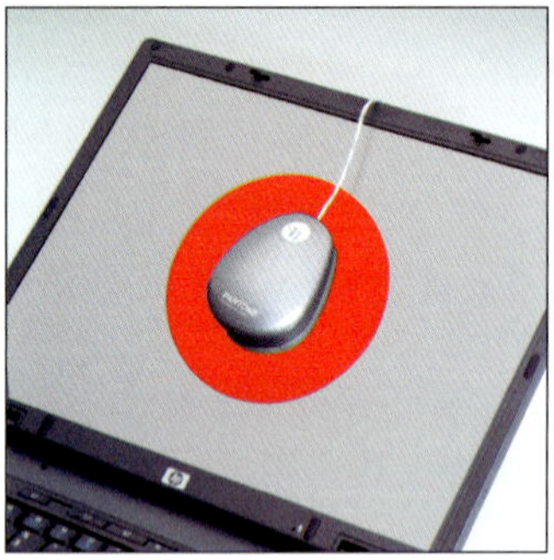

Figure 11-6: A Pantone/GretagMacbeth Eye-One colorimeter calibrator on an LCD screen. (The difference between a colorimeter and a spectrophotometer is that the latter is more expensive and uses more sampling points. We have had good results using a less pricey colorimeter for our monitor calibration.) (Photo courtesy of Pantone)

Tip

A properly calibrated monitor displays more muted colors and tones than you may be used to viewing. The punchy, artificially bright and oversaturated colors of typical computer screens are designed to be exciting. But they aren't natural or true to what are inherent in your photo files. What's more, they are irrelevant and quite misleading to what your printer can produce. If you want to edit your photos using your computer monitor, get used to working with the muted colors and tones, and you'll end up with much better pictures.

While monitor calibration is quite easy, you will get the best results if you follow these guidelines:

- Make no changes to your monitor's onboard color, saturation, and brightness settings after you have calibrated it.
- It's best to not have any light shining on your monitor during calibration.
- When editing a picture on your computer, make sure that the only lights around the monitor that are turned on are ones that were active during the calibration process.
- Because computer monitors tend to drift and change, we recommend setting the calibration software to remind you to recalibrate every few weeks. In addition, most pros will recalibrate just before an important project.

If You Don't Have a Monitor Calibrator . . .

We can't emphasize enough how much we recommend spending the little extra and getting a colorimeter or spectrophotometer to calibrate your monitor. But if you can't or don't want to, you can use a software utility, such as Adobe Gamma.

Software calibration involves eyeballing a series of targets and moving sliders until you can discern slight differences between blocks of colors and steps of greys in a greytone scale, or until nested colors fade into surrounding colors. (See Figure 11-7.)

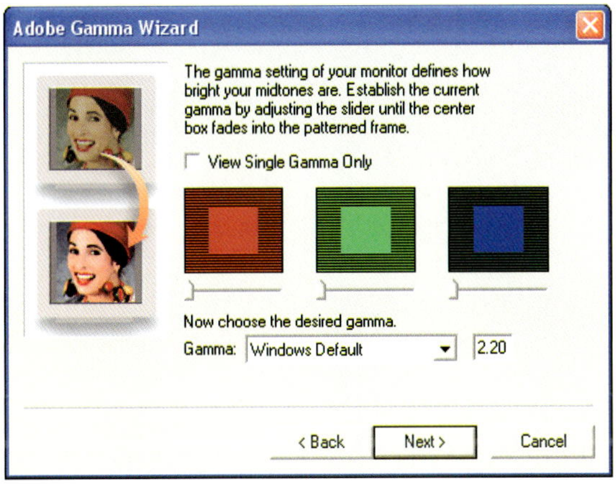

Figure 11-7: Monitor calibration utilities have you make visual choices that are then used to create a profile for the monitor. When using Adobe Gamma to calibrate your monitor, you move the sliders under each block until the inner solid square seems to disappear into the surrounding striped frame. The software uses your input, via the sliders, to develop a profile for your monitor. (Screen capture courtesy of Adobe Systems)

Obviously, you have to have a very discerning eye to do software monitor calibration correctly. Instrument calibration is much easier and more precise.

Tip

All the overhead lights in our studio are daylight (5000 K), color-corrected 4' tube-type fluorescents. We buy them at Home Depot. While more expensive than regular fluorescent tubes, they provide a better viewing environment for checking colors on our monitors and on prints. Besides, we're told that daylight corrected lighting is also good for us psychologically, especially in winter.

SETTING UP YOUR PRINTER

Once you have your monitor calibrated, the next step is getting your prints to match what you see on your computer screen.

Most contemporary photo-quality desktop printers come equipped with ICC profiles embedded in their software driver, which means they tend to produce significantly better, more predictable colors and tones than their predecessors. Use the driver provided (and periodically update it from the manufacturer's Web site), and you should be able to produce excellent-quality prints. However, it is important to set the driver correctly for the type of paper and ink you are using. (See Figures 11-8a and 11-8b.) That's because the brightness, reflectivity, and absorbent characteristics of paper directly affect the colors when they are printed. In addition, different inks have their own colors, as well as the way they interrelate to each other and to the paper.

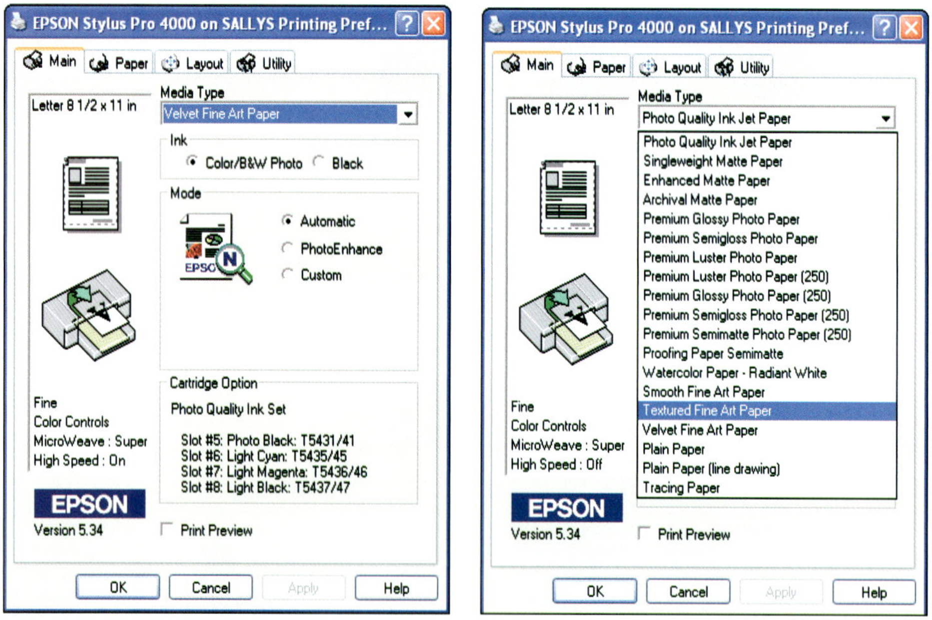

(A) (B)

Figure 11-8: In your printer's driver, select the correct profile by choosing the specific paper that you are using. (A) In this Epson Stylus Pro 4000 printer driver, notice that we have selected Velvet Art Paper, and that the driver automatically read the ink cartridges to determine what inks are installed. (B) You usually select your paper from a pull-down list in the driver. (Screen captures courtesy of Epson America)

As we have said previously, the profiles provided by your printer manufacturer are based on averages. If you want to be certain that the profile you are using is bang-on correct for your specific printer, and/or if you are using paper and inks that are not listed in the driver menus, you will want to do a custom calibration.

Until recently, custom printer calibration was out of our reach. In fact, the cost (which could range into thousands of dollars) was justified only if you had a service bureau, had a professional print shop, or were a very successful photographer with considerable disposable income who output lots and lots of prints. What's more, it often required specialized expertise to make it work.

Although printer calibration is still more time-consuming and more expensive than monitor calibration, it's come down considerably in price and is much less intimidating. Here's how it works:

1. Load the calibration software into your computer, select the target that you want, and output it to your printer, using the paper and inks that you plan to utilize.
2. Plug the printer calibration sensor into the USB port of your computer.
3. Following the instructions from the software, use the sensor to read the blocks of color on the printed target. (See Figure 11-9.)
4. The software will calculate the differences between the ideal colors in the original software target and those that were output by your printer. With that information, it can create a custom ICC profile for that printer, paper, and ink combination.

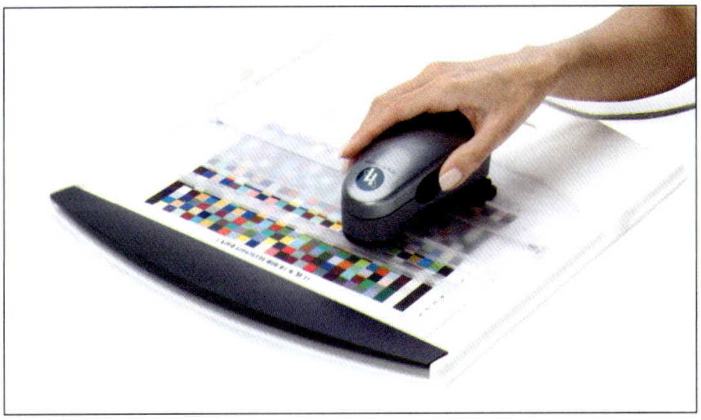

Figure 11-9: A GretagMacbeth Eye-One Pro spectrophotometer reading a target output by the printer being profiled. It comes with the shown plastic ruler, to help guide your hands in reading the small color squares of the target. Less expensive devices may not offer a similar guide, while even more expensive ones have an automated reading arm that takes all the guesswork (and handwork) out of the process. (Photo courtesy of GretagMacbeth)

Calibrate Your Camera (and Scanner)

We seldom calibrate any of our digital cameras. However, we do keep our firmware up to date. This we do by periodically going to the manufacturer's Web site to see if an update is available. If so, we download it to the computer and follow the instructions on how to upload it to our camera.

A Library of Sample Output

Before we had reliable color profiles from printer manufacturers, and before we had the ability to create our own custom printer profiles, we created and maintained a library of sample image files and matching prints of those files. It's a form of insurance that still makes sense. And for those photographers who choose to not create custom printer profiles, it's invaluable.

Here's how it works:

1. Select a group of photos that represent different types of pictures you typically shoot—daylight and nighttime landscapes, indoor and outdoor portraits, various still lifes, and so forth.
2. Save these files in a special folder on your computer that you can quickly access.
3. Output them to your desktop printer, creating as many prints of each photo file as you have different kinds of paper and ink that you typically use.
4. Holding a print up to the monitor where the original photo file is displayed gives you a concrete example how those displayed colors and tones will be output by that printer, using that paper and set of inks.
5. When you are working on a photo and getting ready to output it, bring up one of your sample library files that most closely resembles the working image. Look at the print related to that sample file. That will give you a sense of how the colors in your working photo will be output.

Having said that, calibration is useful and can even be necessary, especially if your pictures exhibit a certain color shift that you have to remove from all your pictures (such as a 10 percent reduction in blue), or if your photos are always over or underexposed by a certain amount. Similarly, you may find that certain lenses tend to vignette or distort in undesirable ways.

Your photo-editing software may allow you to save camera "calibrations," which are nothing more than visual corrections that you make to the colors, tones, or other characteristics of your photos. Such corrections are then automatically applied to all future photos taken with that camera (and/or lens). This can be done as a macro or action (see Chapter 10). Or, your software may have a utility for saving and using such camera settings.

Fortunately, instrument calibration of digital cameras is a relative simple matter, since you already own the instrument—your camera. Here are the steps we follow in LaserSoft's SilverFast DC Pro (`www.silverfast.com`). By the way, the following information also works for scanners.

1. Take a picture of the digital camera target developed by LaserSoft Imaging. Other targets may be used by some calibration software, but this is a standard trusted throughout the industry. (See Figure 11-10.)
2. Bring the captured photo into DC Pro software.
3. Overlay the provided reference image of the target onto your captured photo of the target.

4. The software reads the bar code on the captured photo, to identify which target you used.
5. The software automatically calculates the differences between the colors of the captured photo and those of the reference image. It then generates an ICC profile.
6. The ICC profile is automatically saved in the correct folder on your computer.

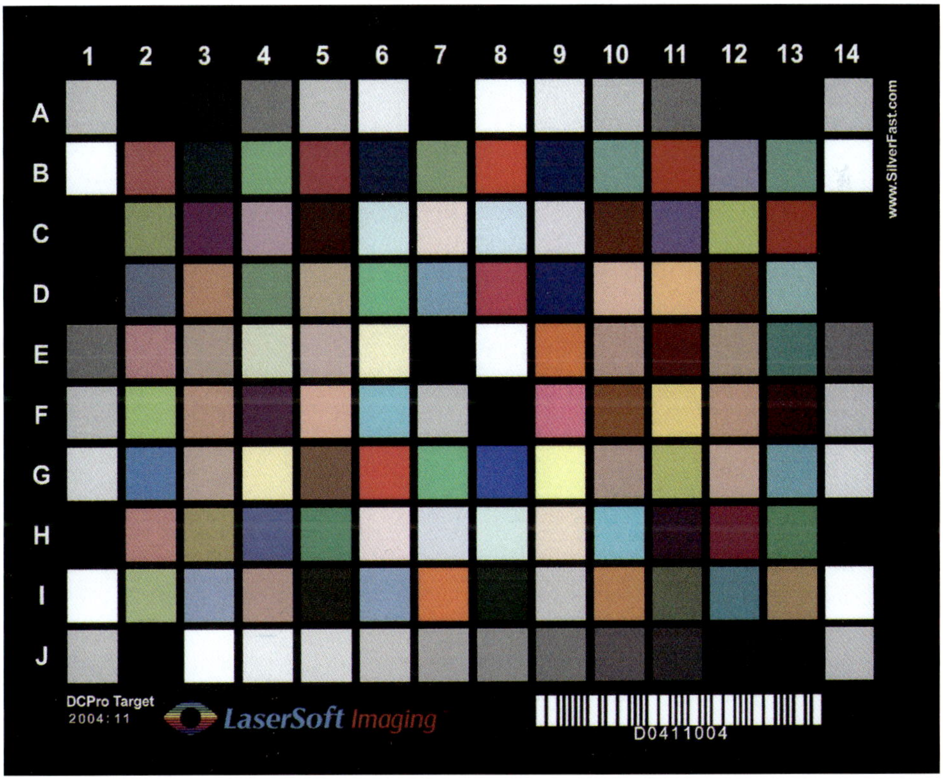

Figure 11-10: A digital camera target from LaserSoft Imaging, which can be used for calibrating cameras and scanners. (Scanned by an Epson Perfection 3200 Photo)

Summary

You have spent the money to outfit yourself with a great DSLR system, and spend your time, energy, and talent getting the best photos you possibly can. Maintaining a good color management system is the final step in the process that makes it all worthwhile. Otherwise, the colors and tones of your photos will be left to guesswork, and you will end up wasting lots of paper, inks, and time trying to get good prints.

Chapter 12

Preparing Your Photos for Output and Sharing

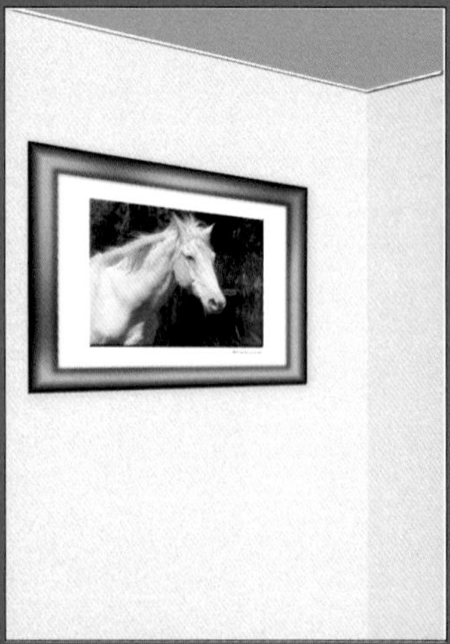

If you follow some basic guidelines when preparing your photos for printing, your DSLR can produce exhibition-quality images.

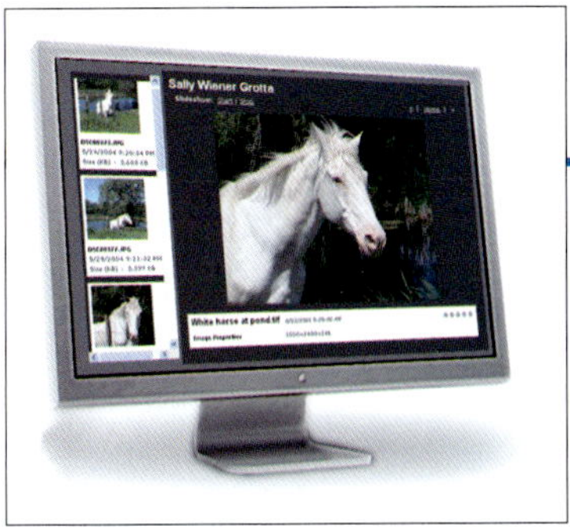

Photos are meant to be shared, as on this Web site.

Art for art's sake is all well and good. But, in the final analysis, the purpose of photography is to share it — with clients, associates, gallery goers, photo aficionados, friends, and/or family. That's when you want to be sure your photos look great, regardless of how you send, deliver or share them.

In this chapter, we discuss:

- Sizing your photos appropriate to your output purposes
- Optimizing JPEG and balancing compression with quality
- Selecting your desktop printer and using it effectively
- Trying different papers for various effects and results
- Letting others do the printing for you
- Delivering photos over the Web
- Burning CDs and DVDs for sharing
- Using slideshow software

Making the Picture Fit

DSLRs create remarkably large photo files, which is just the way we like them. But when it comes time to print them, upload them to the Web, or share them via email, all that image data is often way too much — or maybe, not enough (for very large prints).

If your photo has too little image data for your intended output, the computer and software will interpolate, or invent the pixels, based on what is already in the file. All that does is increase picture size without increasing definition within the photo. In fact, we have found that it often decreases image quality by blurring details. (See Figure 12-1.)

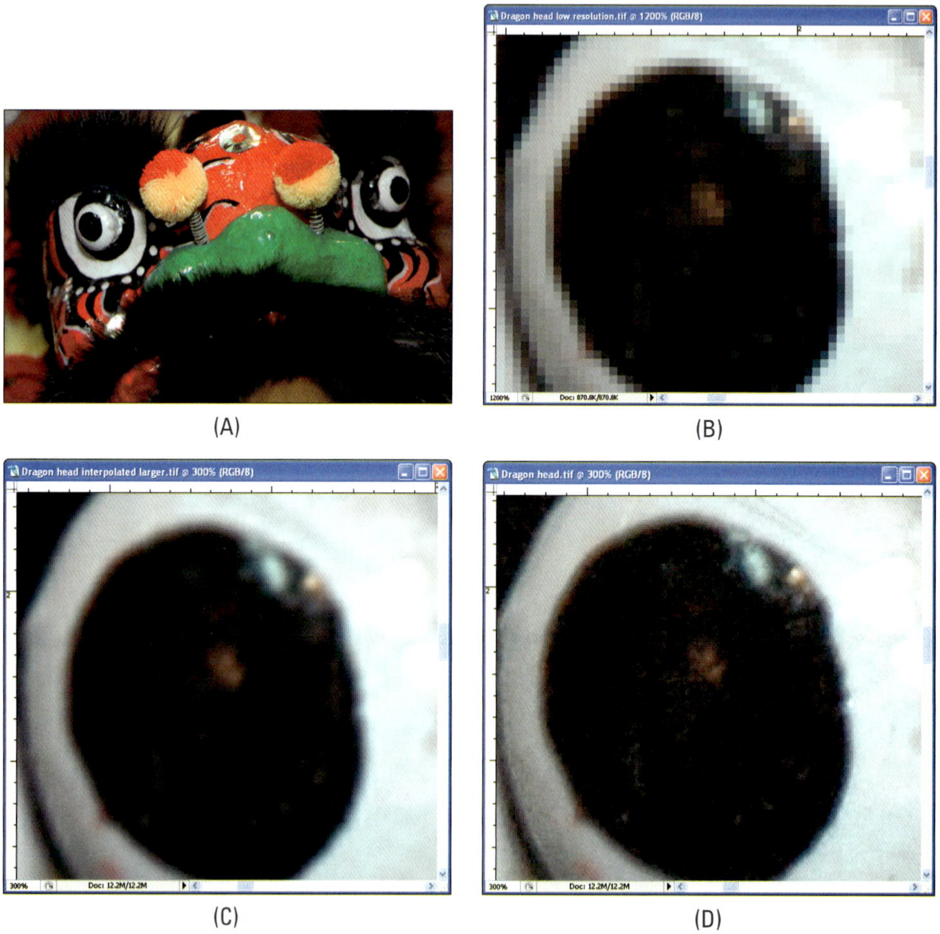

Figure 12-1: (A) We magnified the left eye detail from three different sized versions of this photo of a Chinese dragon. (B) In this low-resolution version (less than 871K in size), you can see the individual pixels that make up the eye, and the heart-shaped highlight to the right is broken up. (C) Interpolating (resizing) the low resolution picture in (A) up to 12.2MB filled in the step-like pixelization; however, it is soft and quite blurry. (D) Compare (C) to this 12.2MB version, which is made up of original captured image data, rather than data invented by software. Notice how clear the heart-shaped highlights are, and how well defined the transitions are. (Photo taken with a Nikon D70, 50–200mm set at 62mm, 1/60 at *f*5.6.)

If you have too much data for your intended output, one of three things will happen:

- When you post it on a Web site, it will take long minutes to transmit and download, even using broadband. Anyone trying to view it will likely become quite impatient and click away before the full picture is finally displayed. Or, if they do wait it out, the image can end up being too large to display on their monitor, which means they will have to use scroll bars to see it all.
- When you email it, the overly large image will bog down both your email system and the recipient's. They will probably not be able to receive any other email in their inbox until your enormous file finally downloads — that is, if it even gets it through to them. Many network servers have limits on the size of email-attached files and will reject any that exceed it. (See later in this chapter for information about how to deliver large image files over the Internet.)
- When you output it to a desktop printer, the printer driver will automatically throw away any image data that it deems as excess and unnecessary. That process adds to your print time. More importantly, it is leaving the decision of what pixels to keep and which ones to discard up to a machine. We prefer to do our own resampling (resizing downward), so we can preview the results on our monitor, before outputting to our printer.

Resizing Your Photos for Print

When printing your photos, you want the photo file to be the size of the output. In other words, it should be the optimum resolution for the printer, as well as the physical dimensions of the intended print. (See Figure 12-2.) The optimum resolution depends on the particular printer you are using, typically ranging from 200 to 400 dpi. Most devices do quite well at 300dpi.

We use the image size dialog in photo-editing software to resample our photos to smaller file sizes. But we try never to use it for interpolating them into larger pictures because, as we demonstrated in the zoomed photos in Figure 12-1, it can result in poor image quality. We have found one exception to this rule. If you must enlarge a photo, we have been generally pleased with the results we have achieved with a piece of software called Genuine Fractals (`www.ononesoftware.com`). It works well, as long as we don't try to push the picture too far. A number of years ago, Genuine Fractals was used to create an enormous Times Square billboard from a photo taken with a 3-megapixel camera, but then, it was displayed far above, where no one was looking too closely at the image quality.

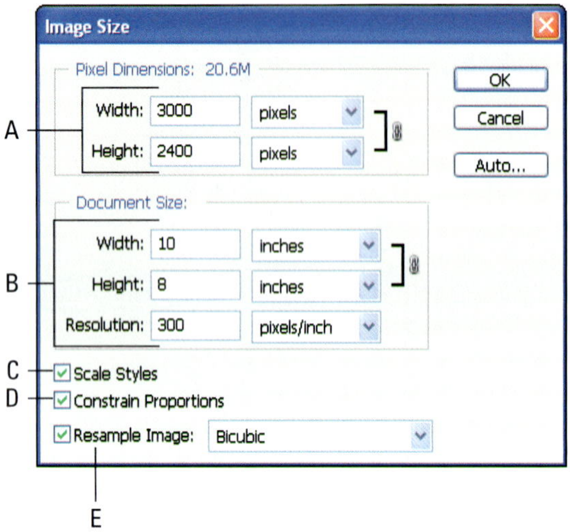

Figure 12-2: The Image Size dialog from Photoshop for a 20.6MB photo. (A) The top section describes the dimensions of the picture in terms of the number of pixels (3000×2400). Changing these numbers is one way you can resize your picture. (B) However, the middle section provides more intuitive information about your picture, describing it in terms of its physical dimensions (8×10") and what its resolution is when those 3000×2400 pixels are spread out on an 8×10" print (300 pixels per inch). This is the section we use to downsize (or resample) our photos. When you change the numbers here, it will automatically change the pixel dimensions in the upper area of the dialog, too. (C) If you have used styles on the image, such as a layer style to add a drop shadow, keeping this option checked will scale them so they maintain an accurate relationship to the resized photos. This is an option that may or may not be in other photo-editing programs. (D) Constrain proportions keeps the shape of your photo constant by linking the physical dimensions. Therefore, if you change the height of the picture, the software will automatically calculate the correct width. And vice versa. If you don't have constrain proportions checked, you can end up with a distorted picture. (This option may be called other names in other software.) (E) We generally keep our resampling option set to bicubic because it tends to yield the best quality. If resample isn't checked, every time you change one number (such as the height), the software will automatically alter the other numbers (such as resolution and width), to maintain the same file size. So, you'll want to keep it checked, to resize your photo. (The option may be called other names in other software.) (Screen capture courtesy of Adobe Systems)

Resizing Your Photos for Email and the Web

When preparing our photos for email and the Web, we tend to use a resolution of 100 ppi, because the resolution of a typical computer monitor is 72 ppi to 125 ppi. (Pixels per inch, or ppi, is how monitor resolution is expressed, although it's virtually the same thing as dpi.) If you take the same 3000×2400 pixel image from Figure 12-2 and output it at 100 ppi, it will be

Don't Be Fooled by High-Resolution Printers

Many desktop inkjet printers tout ultra-high resolutions like 1200 dpi, 1440 dpi, 2880 dpi, and even higher. And yet, typical printer driver resolutions are expressed in much smaller numbers, like 200 dpi or 300 dpi. What gives?

The large figures refer to the total number of dots that the printer's hundreds of tiny nozzles can spray onto paper in one inch. But each nozzle can paint only a single color, while every pixel (technically called a rosette when printing) may contain between four and eight colors, depending upon the number of different color inks or pigments your particular printer uses. Because it's really the number of pixels, and not dots, that counts, the real resolution of a six-color photo printer with a listed resolution of 1440 dpi is 240 dpi. Alas, most printer manufacturers are caught up in dpi inflation on the premise that more is better, but there's no reason why you, the photographer, have to buy into the hype.

displayed at 30×24 inches, which is way too large for any ordinary monitor. To display it without having to scroll, we would resize it down to the approximate size we would want on the monitor (say, about 4×5" for a picture that would be only part of a Web page), and at a resolution appropriate for the monitor rather than print. For instance, if we were preparing that 20.6MB photo for the Web, we could end up with a picture that is less than 600 kilobytes in size. That reduction throws away most of the image data.

In addition, you'll want to convert your photo to JPEG, since that is the most universal file format. And, yes, we do compress our pictures when we transmit via the Web, even though we recognize that compression can significantly degrade image quality. It's a question of recognizing the realities of the Web, in which speed can be just as imperative as image quality (if not more so).

It's important to understand how the resizing and compression will affect your image quality, so you can make informed decisions about your settings. That's why we prefer to use an optimizing dialog rather than do a straightforward image resize, when preparing our photos for the Web or email. (See Figure 12-3.)

Tip

Unless you know that a specific recipient for whom the picture is intended has a fast broadband connection to the Internet, we recommend assuming that the people viewing your pictures over the Web or receiving them via email have the slowest, dial-up connection. Many still do.

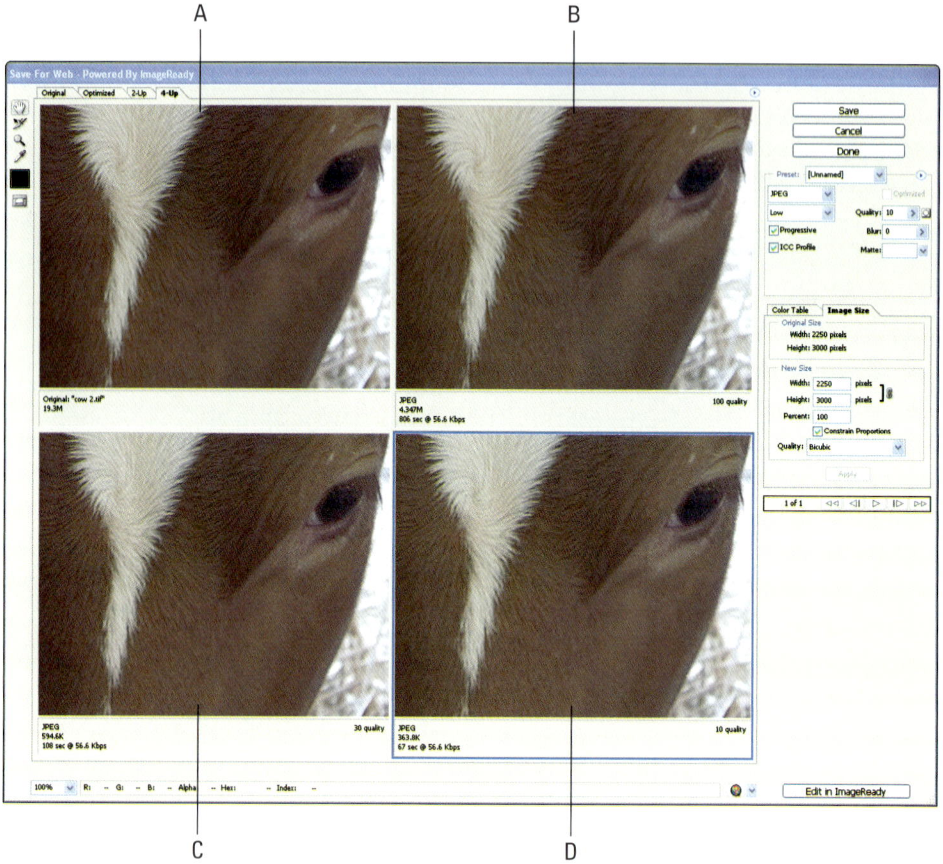

Figure 12-3: The Save for Web dialog from Photoshop, which we have set to show four different versions of the same photo, each at different quality settings for a 7.5×10" photo. These previews give you the necessary information to balance transmission speed against image quality loss when you compress an image to JPEG for the Web and email. (You can also use this dialog to resize the photo and preview how that affects the image quality.) (A) The original TIFF photo. (B) A preview of the quality we would get if we saved that photo to JPEG, using maximum quality settings. As you can see from the legend under this preview, that would yield a 4.347MB file, which would take more than 13 minutes to download on a slow, dial-up Internet connection. Looking closely at this preview, you can discern very slight image quality loss that might not be noticeable to most people. (C) Saving the same file to medium-quality JPEG, using a higher-level compression, would create a 594.6K file, which would take less than 2 minutes to download. However, image degradation is more pronounced. (D) At low-quality JPEG, the file would be compressed to 363.8K, which could download in about a minute, but the image quality is significantly impacted. (Screen capture courtesy of Adobe Systems)

Making Great Prints

One of the reasons we love DSLRs is the great prints we can get with them. The level of detail, tonality, and size we can output is remarkable, as good as or better than we used to get from film. But simply because DSLRs can capture and create great image files doesn't mean that they will unerringly translate into great prints. Fine printing is an art, just as photography is.

Even if you aren't interested in spending too much time or money on your printing, paying attention to details can help you end up with gorgeous prints:

- Maintain good color management. (See Chapter 11.)
- Prepare the image for optimum printing.
- Output to a true photo printer.
- Use the correct driver or RIP for the printer.
- Experiment with good paper that is rated for your printer, but use the correct ink.

Preparing Your Photos

As we discussed in the previous section, it is important that your image file be the correct size for your output. Other issues you will want to pay attention to are:

- Be careful not to overprocess your image.
- Inspect the histogram.
- Check your crop.
- Verify the photo's aspect ratio.

DON'T OVERPROCESS

As we have discussed, editing your pictures in the computer can destroy pixels. (The one exception is the editing in your RAW conversion utility. See Chapter 5.)

For instance, while a touch of sharpening may be useful for many photos, oversharpening destroys smooth transitions. You should always try to view your picture in your photo-editing software at 100 percent magnification to make certain that the details you need are still there. Then, zoom out to fit the entire picture on the screen, to verify that the overall image is what you want.

INSPECT THE HISTOGRAM

Depending on your printer, you may find that a histogram heavy in the shadows or highlights may lose details in those areas. If that is the case, try adjusting the exposure in your photo-editing software. Since every printer and paper/ink combination has a different exposure response curve, we can't tell you how the histograms should look for output to your printer. Look at the histograms of the files you have already successfully printed to learn the characteristics of your printer. It's a simple correlation that should become intuitive for you after just a few tries. (See Figure 12-4.)

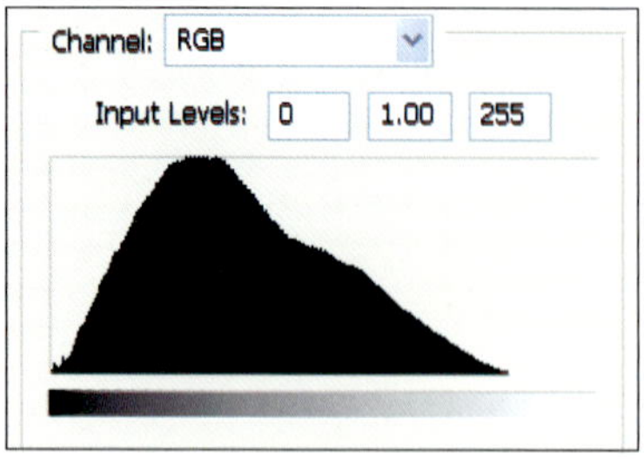

Figure 12-4: This histogram shows that the related picture has a good deal of image data in the shadows (the left of the graph). While the ideal reproduction of this photo would involve printing only the very far left data in the graph as black, some printers may apply black in place of the dark shadows (a bit in from the left). The question is, how much of the shadow detail will be reproduced by your printer, and how much of it will be obscured? Similar issues involve a print's highlights. These are questions you need to answer for yourself, by testing the ability of your printer, paper, and ink to reproduce shadow and highlight details. (Screen capture courtesy of Adobe Systems)

CROPPING AND ASPECT RATIO

When judging photo contests, we have been surprised at how many otherwise excellent pictures could have been great if only the photographers had cropped them more effectively. We have seen charming portraits marred by trash cans in the background, scenes whose center was a beautiful slice of life but surrounded by boring dark details and other disconcerting extraneous matter that pull the eye away without adding to the composition. In other pictures, keeping the entire frame completely changed the meaning of the picture. (See Figure 12-5.) Consider what it is you are trying to say with the picture and try to cut out anything that doesn't add to that purpose.

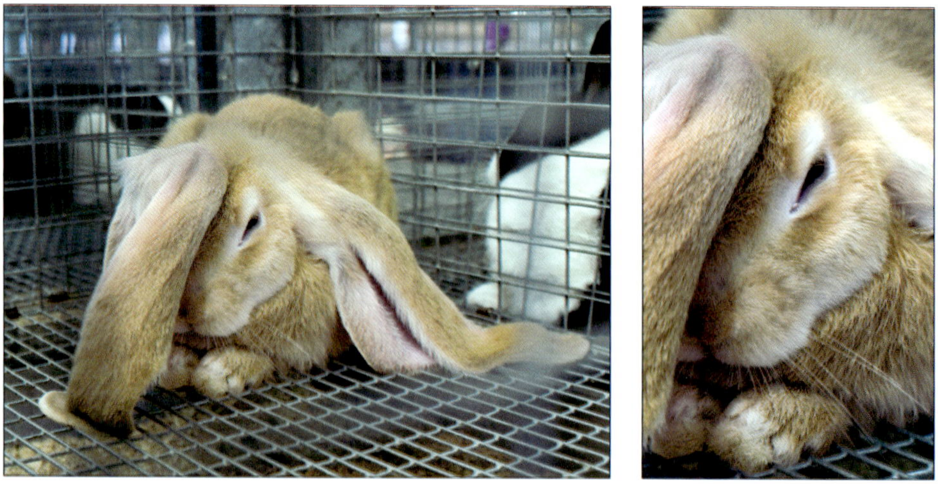

Figure 12-5: Cropping your photo can change the entire meaning and purpose of the picture. (A) This image is more about the cage and the plight of the rabbit than the animal itself. (B) This crop focuses the picture on the bunny rabbit. (Photos taken with an Olympus E-300, 14–54mm lens set at 35mm, 1/10 at *f*5.)

On the other hand, if you want to use standard matte sizes when framing the photo, then you'll want to also be sure that the cropped photo will fit into traditional spaces, such as 4×6", 5×7", 8×10", and so forth. We spend way too much money and time ordering custom-sized mattes because of our insistence in cropping for aesthetic and meaning. Alas, leaving your photos uncropped won't help reduce the need for custom mattes. That's because image sensors capture at a different aspect ratio (proportions) than standard mattes, so you'll end up cropping anyway. Therefore, if you want to save money and time on matting and framing your pictures, set your crop tool to specific sizes that match inexpensive precut matte sizes. (See Figure 12-6.)

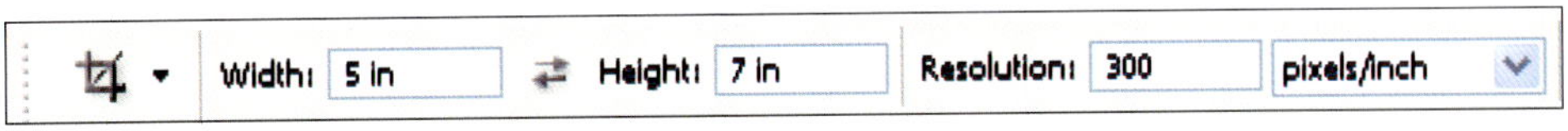

Figure 12-6: In your photo-editing software, you can usually set the crop tool to maintain a specific aspect ratio. When you use a crop tool whose aspect ratio is defined (as this one is to 5×7"), the program will automatically create a rectangle with the correct proportions, and your options are only the size of the cropping rectangle and where it is placed on the picture. This is useful if you want to use standard, off-the-shelf mattes and frames. (Screen capture from Photoshop, courtesy of Adobe Systems)

Choose Your Printer to Match Your Expectations

Fortunately, there are many different kinds, brands, and models of desktop printers, ranging in price from about 50 bucks to thousands of dollars. Unfortunately, choosing the right one for your needs, expectations, budget, and environment is all the more difficult because there are so many devices available. We're going to make it easy for you by eliminating most of them. After all, you have a DSLR because you want high-quality photos, right? We're not saying that you have to spend an arm and leg on a printer, but why use a fast food–type printer for gourmet-level photos? Your printer should be able to output quality on a par with the pictures your camera can capture.

The following technologies are not appropriate for high-quality photo prints:

- **Laser printers** — Great for documents, business graphics, and quick proofs, but not for photos.
- **Consumer inkjet printers** — These remarkably cheap devices often cost less than a round of replacement ink cartridges. Photo print quality never rises above fair to good.
- **AIOs, or all-in-ones** — Wonderful business devices for scanning, faxing, and general printing, but none can do photographs as well as a purpose-built photo printer.

We recommend the following:

- Photo-quality inkjet printers
- Snapshot printers
- A few specialty printers

Tip

To help you decide what size printer to buy, determine the largest size prints you output on a regular basis and purchase a device that will support that size paper. For the occasional or rare very large print, it is more cost-effective to use a professional service bureau. (Later in this chapter, we discuss service bureaus.)

PHOTO-QUALITY INKJET PRINTERS

The only inkjet printers that we recommend for printing DSLR-quality pictures are those that manufacturers designate and describe as photo printers. What's the difference? Photo printers are devices optimized to print images, not text, and that use at least six different inks. Why at least six inks? That number will give you more detail and better colors in your prints. What's more, manufacturers put higher-quality control and better technology into those printers that have more inks.

Canon, Epson, and HP make great photo-quality inkjet printers, but be cautious, because those manufacturers also sell consumer-level inkjets that can output photographs, though not highest-quality photos. That's why you must look for those printers that are specifically for photos, and not general purpose output, including photos.

Tip

A handful of consumer inkjet printers have the unique ability to print beautiful labels directly onto certain CDs and DVDs. If you plan on burning discs and want great-looking labels, consider purchasing one of these consumer-level devices. However, they won't do a very good job on your photos. (Later in this chapter, we discuss burning CDs and DVDs.) They're generally affordable enough that you might consider buying and using two printers, one for photos and the other for labels and everything else.

SNAPSHOT PRINTERS

We all grew up with 3.5×5" and 4×6" snapshots, the convenient-sized prints that we stuck on refrigerator doors or mailed to the grandparents on holidays. All you had to do was drop off a roll of film at your nearby photo shop or drug store, and a few days later, pick up a packet of small, beautiful prints. Because of this familiarity, many people consider 3.5×5" or 4×6" the ideal size of a good photo, which helps explain why today's snapshot digital printers are so popular.

Snapshot printers (see Figure 12-7) are great for outputting glossy photos that typically look great, fit nicely into family albums, and make wonderful gifts. Many are inkjets, though some use other technologies; regardless of the technology, these devices produce prints that look as good as or even better than those you get from a 1-hour photo lab. And while the cost per print is generally moderate ($0.33 to $0.50 per print, or 50 percent to 100 percent more than you would pay at the mall), the advantage is you can do it at home whenever you want and print only those pictures you wish. What's more, each print will only take between 90 and 120 seconds to output, depending upon the model.

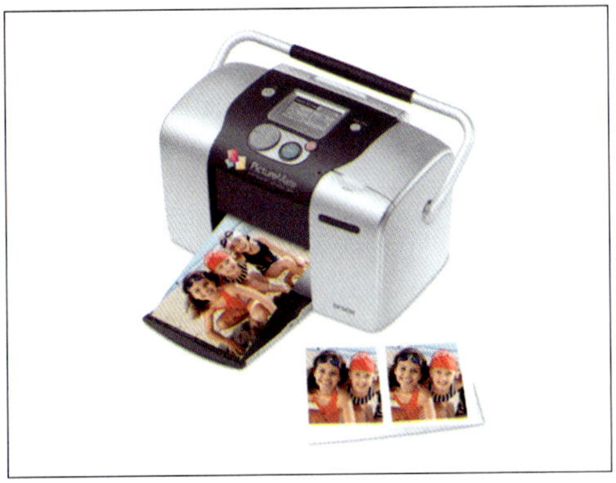

Figure 12-7: Snapshot printers, such as this Epson PictureMate, are great for family and fun pictures. (Photo courtesy of Epson America)

Of course, DSLRs produce photo files that are far too large for snapshot printers. So, be sure to resize before outputting, unless you want to wait a long time for the prints.

While they don't achieve the high quality of top-of-the-line photo inkjets (resolutions isn't as high, and most use only three or four different color inks or pigments), few printers enjoy such a high degree of viewer satisfaction as snapshot printers. They're especially good for quick, inexpensive proofs, prints you can give away without breaking the budget, and hard-copy that you may wish to keep in your files as reference to electronic photographs you delivered over the Web.

Snapshot printers typically sell between $125 and $350 and come equipped with a variety of special features, such as a built-in LCD screen, limited editing capabilities, a direct wired or wireless connection to a digital camera, memory card slots, and so forth. A good rule-of-thumb is the more expensive the printer, the less each print will cost. Any of the top brands, such as Epson, HP, and Kodak, are good.

SPECIALTY PRINTERS

If you like letter-sized glossy photos, you might want to look into two technologies: dye sublimation and thermo-autochrome. Both produce gorgeous prints, but both have significant drawbacks that keep them from becoming more popular.

- **Dye-sublimation** printers use heat to blend the pigments, creating a true photo-realistic picture with impeccably seamless smooth transitions and no dots. Some snapshot printers use this technology, but there are also full-size dye subs. Before inkjets became the superb printers they are today, dye subs were preferred by most photographers. Not any more, because of the cost difference, output limitations, and the question of permanence. A good dye sub sells between $400 and $4,000, and can output 8.5×11" to 8.5×14" prints, at roughly $1.50–$2.50 per print. (There are larger dye sub printers, but their cost is somewhat stratospheric.) Alas, for those who like to experiment with different surfaces and colors, there's only one choice of ribbon and at most two or three paper textures. The other drawback to dye sub is that the dyes are less stable than archival inks, and the colors will begin to fade within a couple years.

Many dye-sub printers, including all dye-sub-type snapshot printers, automatically apply an ultraviolet coating to the finished print, to help preserve it against dust, fingerprints, and the harmful effects of light. But this is really a stopgap — no dye-sub print is truly archival.

- **Thermo-autochrome** is Fuji's proprietary technology, similar in some aspects to dye sublimation, but with output that is supposedly more stable and therefore will last longer before fading. It's presently used only in Fuji's Pictography printers. Thermo-autochrome outputs highest-quality continuous-tone glossy photos at a maximum width of 8.5". The cost per print is about $1.25–$1.50. However, the printers are large and heavy — floor models, actually — cost several thousand dollars, and are suited for a high-volume photographic studio, and not for home or small studio use.

Tip

We all get spammed by those advertising emails offering really cheap ink and/or the ability to refill our ink cartridges, saving lots and lots of money. Without exception, they promise to be as good as, or even better, than the expensive brand-name cartridges. True, inks authorized by printer manufacturers are expensive, but these no-name, bargain basement options are not worth your time or the headaches they can create. Because they don't necessarily conform to any quality control standard, colors may not be consistent, may fade prematurely, and, if printer manufacturers are to be believed, may actually damage or destroy your inkjet heads (by lacking necessary lubricants or by drying and permanently clogging nozzles). DSLRs are high-quality cameras, so please, use only high-quality ink (and paper) to reproduce their photos.

Paper and Inks

The first thing to remember about the media (the paper and inks) you use is that it must match your printer. If they don't, you can end up with areas where the ink doesn't apply, smeary under- or oversaturated colors, or downright unappealing prints.

If you want to produce gallery-quality fine art prints, pay particular attention to your choice of paper. Different surfaces, textures, colors, and brightness will affect the entire feeling of your output. Sally particularly likes the depth of detail and colors she gets from Epson's Velvet Art paper and uses it often for her exhibition prints. She also likes Hahnemuehl photo rag (`www.hahnemuehle.com`). Artists/photographers Bruce Dorn and Maura Dutra (`www.idcphotography.com`) will often use a gloss waterproof canvas and then add a varnish or clear texture finish to make a crackling that looks like an old painting. However, since they usually work on their photos in Corel Painter, Maura told us, "We tend to choose our media by taking a cue from the media we used in Painter." In other words, if they use Painter's watercolor brushes on their pictures, they will output to watercolor paper. (For information on Painter, see Chapter 10.)

How Long Will My Prints Last?

Nothing lasts forever, and photographic prints last a lot less than that. While archivability doesn't really matter for the quick snapshot, it's an essential issue for preserving your family memory for generations or in selling a museum-quality print to an art lover.

Traditional black-and-white film prints have been known to last over a century with very little degradation. Color film prints, however, are as inherently unstable as the pigments and dyes that give us that beautiful color. Look at any color photo more than 10 years old, and you will see that it has already lost some or much of its reds and greens. Early computer generated prints were even worse. They'd last only 3 months to a year, before the colors leached out.

Fortunately, digital color printing has improved dramatically. Most color photos will last years without any special handling or treatment. But for those photos that you absolutely, positively want to preserve, some printer manufacturers and third-party vendors sell archival inks and paper that are guaranteed not to fade for up to 200 years. How long depends upon the material, how its stored or displayed, temperature and humidity, and other factors.

All other things being equal, we suggest paying extra to get and use archival papers and pigments. Also, when you frame them, use acid-free mattes and ultraviolet-absorbing glass.

For further information, check out Wilhelm Imaging's Web site, `www.wilhelm-research.com`.

Tip

Bruce Dorn and Maura Dutra create one-of-a-kind pictures, thereby increasing their intrinsic value. "We consider the print as the underpainting," Maura explains. "Then we add gel coats, impasto, and other media to the print." If the paper they use has a high rag content, such as watercolor paper, they will often tear the edges and mount it on a board. That gives it the feeling of handmade paper, as well as adding dimension.

Drivers and RIPs

A printer driver is software that controls the interpretation of your images and determines how they will be printed. As a rule, we recommend using the driver that came bundled with your printer. The manufacturer knows its printers better than anyone. In addition, check periodically for driver and ICC profile updates on their Web site. (See Chapter 11, regarding ICC profiles.)

The exception is if you are doing high-volume printing; proofing for a CMYK printing press; creating PostScript files in programs such as Quark XPress, Adobe InDesign, or Adobe Illustrator; or want more control over your black-and-white prints. That's when you might consider moving over to a RIP (Raster Image Processor). RIPs range from moderately priced to exorbitant, can be exclusively software or a software/hardware solution, and tend to be very specialized.

If you are shopping for a RIP:

- Look only at those RIPs marketed specifically to photographers. Others are more appropriate for graphic artists, signage, architectural blueprints, and so forth.
- Talk to other photographers about the RIPs they use, and whether they are satisfied with them. We find the discussions on ProRental to be particularly useful. (See Appendix A for information about ProRental.)
- Don't accept anyone's word for the quality of a RIP's output. Check the output, preferably using one of your own files, and compare it to what you are already getting from your printer.

In addition, before you buy any RIP, "Make a checklist of what you need," advises Robert Ozankan of Epson America. "Ask yourself: what does my current printer software not do that I need?" Also, he suggests, "Talk with folks who have been using the same printer in similar projects as you do."

Let Someone Else Do the Printing

There are several reasons why you may want someone else to do your printing:

- Printing takes time and effort.
- You might need larger prints than your printer can output.
- You might have a high-volume job that would be too slow and/or too wearing on your printer.
- You want specialty items, such as a photo book (which is one of the most popular items for weddings these days).
- The job requires a CMYK press.

Printing services are available at retail print shops, service bureaus, and Web sites, and the quality they produce varies widely from barely acceptable to fabulous. One of the yardsticks that some photographers use in trying to determine if a print shop or service bureau knows what it is doing is to ask, "How do you handle embedded ICC profiles?" Since so many shops have employees that are not familiar with the special needs of photography and high-quality imaging, some will simply not know how to answer that question, or they might say, "Oh, we just delete them." Those kinds of answers indicate a *laissez-faire* attitude toward color management.

If the print output is vitally important to you, and/or it is a job that will cost a lot of money, we suggest logging onto photography chat boards or talking with nearby pro photographers to find out which shop in your area is doing a good job lately. We can't make recommendations because employees of shops can change so quickly, and it's the person handling your job who will make the difference.

Delivering Digital Files

As we mentioned earlier, emailing photos has its limits. Not only is it difficult, if not impossible to send large, high-resolution images, but it can also be darned inconvenient and discourteous, given how it can bog down the recipient's email.

Much better methods for delivering digital files include:

- Burning CDs or DVDs
- Delivering via your Web site
- Using an Internet-based delivery service

Burning CDs and DVDs

Burning CDs and DVDs used to be much more complex, requiring you to decide among various types of formats. DVDs were especially problematic, because there were serious incompatibilities among various drives and the media itself. Today, if you use modern drives and software, everything should work pretty automatically.

One of the essential differences between CDs and DVDs is that CDs can hold up to 660 megabytes of data, while (current technology) DVDs can contain up to 4.7 gigabytes. CD drives will burn and display CDs only. While most DVD drives will burn DVDs, some can burn both DVDs and CDs, and all display both DVDs and CDs. But you don't need a computer drive to show a CD or DVD, since many standalone CD and DVD players can play discs on your television set or other types of viewers.

Burning a CD or DVD is quite easy if you are sharing photos with someone who wants nothing more than the ability to view and use the files on a computer. Simply use your computer's operating system to drag and drop the files into the CD/DVD drive folder and then invoke the burn command. For those discs that you want to play in other devices that aren't necessarily tethered to a computer, such as a DVD player attached to a TV, we suggest using any of the dozens of DVD authoring programs readily available. (See the following section.)

DVD SLIDESHOWS

One fabulous way of showing off your digital photographs is to create a slideshow, and burn it to a CD or DVD, or upload it to a Web site. However, while many different photo management, photo-editing, and other image programs allow you to create slideshows, they don't all create *shareable* slideshows. What you need to look for is the ability to export your slideshow to a universal file format, such as AVI, MPEG, or QuickTime. The best software for this purpose is DVD authoring software.

Unless you have a DV camcorder and want to do some sophisticated video editing, we recommend that still photographers should use relatively simple, consumer-type slideshow programs, such as ArcSoft DVD SlideShow, Microsoft Plus! Photo Story, or Ulead DVD Picture Show.

When choosing your DVD slideshow software, the guiding principle is try before you buy. Many companies offer free trial versions, downloadable from the Internet. The trial versions are either limited in output, imprint an undesirable legend onto your slideshow or have a time limit, unless you buy the permanent unlock key. Here are some of the things you should check out when testing the program:

- Does it provide interesting ways to present your photos? For instance, can you customize the slide durations and transitions, zoom in and out of areas of a picture, add music and/or narration?
- Do you like the templates? Are they attractive and professional looking? If you want to change a color, add your own icon, or alter other aspects of the way they look and work, are they customizable?
- Check out how the menus are created. (These are the splash screens that your viewers click on to get to specific parts of your slideshow.) Is there an easy-to-use wizard? Can you edit them after they have been created?
- Does it include the ability to create matching labels for the disc and the plastic jewel box? Can you print out a table of contents and thumbnails?
- Does the way things work in the software make sense to you, or are you jumping through hoops trying to understand what to do next?
- Compare a few programs, to see what features or functions one has over the others that might make your slideshows easier, more fun, and more representative of you as a photographer.

One advantage in sharing your photos via a slideshow is that it gives you an attractive way to display your pictures without giving the viewers high-resolution images that they could then print without your permission.

Delivering via Your Website

We often use our Web sites for delivering our photos to clients, associates, friends, and family. This we do by uploading the pictures to the Web site and emailing links to the people we want to access them.

In fact, we once created private folders on our business Web sites specifically for this purpose: `www.DigitalBenchmarks.com` and `www.TheWellConnectedWoman.com`. However, we found it easier to maintain a separate site on `www.Smugmug.com` dedicated to delivering photos. While we maintain a small public folder on the Smugmug site, the bulk of the photos we upload to it are viewable only by the specific people to whom we want to deliver those pictures. Smugmug limits the size photos we can upload, plus they have to be JPEGs. In most instances, that doesn't represent any undue restriction to us.

There are, of course, scores of photo sharing sites. Some are free, and some, like Smugmug, cost money. The free ones inundate our associates and clients with advertising, which we feel doesn't look professional.

Using an Internet-Based Delivery Service

When we need to deliver really high-quality, uncompressed pictures and other large files to clients, we use `www.YouSendIt.com` or `www.Dropload.com`. They are free services where you can upload pictures and send emails with links to download them. We have used both quite successfully, delivering files that were dozens of megabytes in size. You can use `www.Streamload.com` for even larger pictures — up to 10GB free.

Summary

The real reason you have a DSLR is to capture and create photographic images. Once it is secured, processed, and perfected, the final step is to present your work in some form that others can see and enjoy. Printing photographs and preparing files for the Web should be done with the same attention to detail as you applied in framing, shooting, and editing your images. This requires choosing how your pictures will be output, as well as considering many important details, such as cropping, suitable media, getting the colors right, archivability, and appropriate file format and size. After all, great photos deserve great output.

Appendix A

Internet Services and Web Sites

As befitting the world's most popular hobby, there probably are more Web sites devoted to digital photography than any other subject or technology. Many are arcane and technical, opinionated and parochial. We cannot vouch for any information provided by any of these sites, but the ones we list here do tend to be useful and interesting.

Note

This appendix and the ones that follow contain basic information and contacts about companies and organizations that may be useful to Digital Single Lens Reflex owners. The information is by no means exhaustive (nor was it ever intended to be encyclopedic). We thought that you might want to have the names and resources on hand for those times when you want to reach out and buy something, read a review about a particular piece of equipment, join a forum of fellow camera owners, or learn more about photography. Appendix E, the glossary, is a quick reference of words and terms related to photography in general and digital cameras in particular.

Cleaning Digital Cameras

One of the pesky problems inherent to DSLRs is the fact that the image sensor will need to be periodically cleaned. That's because, unlike consumer digital cameras, whose lenses are fixed and therefore the image sensor is never exposed to the elements, the fact that your camera uses interchangeable lenses means that you will inevitably accumulate dust on your image sensor. There are many ways to keep your image sensor clean, but the conundrum is that the most effective methods also involve the highest degree of risk of damaging your image sensor. Cleaning Digital Cameras (`www.cleaningdigitalcameras.com`) is dedicated to guiding you, carefully and cautiously, through the steps necessary to keep your camera in tip-top shape. It offers tips and tricks, where to buy cleaning products, and other necessary information and useful cleaning advice. However, do check your camera manual, first, to be sure not to do anything that the manufacturer warns against.

Digicam Help

For beginners, Digicam Help (www.digicamhelp.com/) offers all sorts of useful basic information on digital cameras and photography, written in an easily digestible, nontechnical language. While it doesn't focus exclusively or even primarily on DSLRs, each entry is short, succinct, and tells you no more than you really need to know to get into that subject. The user forums and blogs can be useful and interesting, and its newsletter is a welcome, regular shot of photo enthusiasm in the arm.

DPreview

This is the big one, encompassing just about everything you would ever want to know (plus a whole lot more!) on digital cameras. DPreview (www.dpreview.com) is a London-based photo site whose staff and contract writers produce some of the most authoritative, objective, opinionated, and detailed camera reviews anywhere. Most reviews run thousands of words and require something of a technical expertise to understand and appreciate. But they are always thorough and thoughtful, and if you ignore everything else, reading the conclusions, pro and con, will probably give you the essence of a particular camera. Of equal importance are the camera reviews and opinions posted by owners willing to share their observations with fellow readers, and the camera forums whose threads may cover problems and solutions that you have personally encountered.

Epson Academy

One of the foremost makers of photo printers and photo scanners, Epson runs a first-rate Internet-based series of eseminars, presented by some of the top photographers and graphic artists in the world. The multipart program is designed to teach you how to achieve the highest-quality photos possible. Don't worry if you think you're not ready for the big leagues because Epson has a two-tier program, one for advanced amateurs ($49.95) and the other for professionals ($99.95). You can learn more about Epson Academy by logging onto its Web site at www.EpsonPrintAcademy.com. And no, you don't have to own an Epson photo printer or scanner to take advantage of the eseminars.

PC Magazine

We would be remiss if we didn't mention our own imprint's online reviews and digital photography information Web pages. *PC Magazine* is less technical and more power user–oriented (readable and comprehensible) than many exclusive photo Web sites. Check out www.pcmag.com.

Photo Workshop

A comprehensive Web site for photographers at all levels of knowledge and sophistication, Photo Workshop (www.photoworkshop.com) consists of two parts. The first is a free public section, replete with prepared lessons, events calendars, forums, workshops, eseminars, user groups, newsletters, and white papers from advertisers regarding their products. There also is a subscription-only section, where users pay a small monthly fee to access even more services, including portfolio critiques, a private message board, digital camera shootouts, and more. We should note that we occasionally contribute lessons and profiles of professional photographers to Photo Workshop, so feel free to log on and read them.

ProRental

A highly informative, email-based discussion board dedicated to digital photography in which professional photographers exchange real-life ideas, questions, and solutions. Moderated by Mark Williford, it is free and freewheeling. Be warned: it may get very technical at times, but the information is absolutely cutting-edge stuff, relevant to real-world problems and concerns, and designed to help produce top-professional-quality images. To subscribe (there's no cost), go to lists.drizzle.com/mailman/listinfo/prorental, or send an email to prorental-request@prorental.com with "Subscribe" in the subject line. And say "hi" to Mark for us.

Appendix B

Support Organizations

ASMP

The American Society of Media Photographers—ASMP for short (www.asmp.org)—is one of the photographic industry's best-known and most important professional associations. Most of the cover shots and glossy ads you see in major magazines were probably shot by one of ASMP's 5,000 members. ASMP provides support, information, legal advice, contacts, and a place to meet and exchange ideas with fellow photographers. (Sally used to be a chapter president of ASMP.) The catch is this: ASMP is for full-time professionals only, and an invitation to join is extended only after a peer review of your portfolio. However, you may qualify for one of ASMP's associate memberships, such as those for students, photographic assistants, art buyers, industry contacts, and supporters. Even if you aren't eligible, the public portion of ASMP's Web site is a gold mine of information on the state of professional photography. In addition, non-members are often welcome to the local chapter meetings where information and advice is freeflowing, and you can rub elbows with some of the best photographers in the world.

Photographic Society of America

Unlike ASMP, which is strictly for pros, the Photographic Society of America, or PSA (http://www.psa-photo.org/) is open to advanced amateurs as well as those who make a living from photography. More a camera club than a professional organization, PSA's mission is to help its members understand more about photography, to provide a showcase for members to display their best images, to hold regional and national meetings where members get together to discuss common issues and listen to renowned experts, and to offer a variety of instructional programs designed to improve members' photographic skills. PSA is divided into regional chapters, each of which holds regular meetings that are open to the public as well as to members.

Appendix C

Warranties, Insurance, and Repair

Though DSLRs tend to have very rugged construction, because they have mechanical parts and large, complex optics, they are more prone to break down than other types of digital cameras. In addition, they are more likely to be damaged by impact (dropping the camera, accidentally hitting it against a wall, and so on) than consumer digital cameras. Therefore, your DSLR should be treated with a great deal of respect and careful handling. However, despite your best efforts, it may someday need servicing, either under warranty by the manufacturer or by one of the many third-party companies that repair photographic equipment. However, be forewarned: repairs can cost hundreds of dollars and, given the backlog, your DSLR can be in the shop for weeks or months before it's seen to. That's why warranties are so valuable.

But warranties won't help you if you are unlucky and you lose your camera or have it stolen. That's when you'll be thankful that you had the foresight to buy insurance.

Warranty Repair

The first place to check for repair is the vendor where you bought your camera, or the camera's manufacturer. If your camera is still under warranty and stopped working due to mechanical or electronic failure, it may be covered. But if the damage is the result of some sort of impact (which they call "willful negligence" or abuse), you're probably out of luck.

Most digital cameras carry a 1-year parts and labor warranty, which means that you must pay shipping and insurance to send it to the authorized repair center, and the manufacturer will repair and return it to you on their nickel. Incidentally, once you get a repair or replacement, the meter is still running on your warranty — it won't be extended a year beyond that date.

Repairing versus Replacing

Repairing state-of-the-art electronics is usually more trouble than it's worth. Rather than troubleshoot a bad circuit board, it's more cost-effective for the manufacturer to simply throw it away and send you a replacement. Chances are the replacement is a "refurbished" unit — a like-new item that cannot be sold as new because it was returned for whatever reason (didn't like the color, wasn't powerful enough for its intended purpose, or so on.). Refurbished units are always checked out to ensure that they are in perfect working condition. Your warranty probably states that the manufacturer can, at its discretion, repair or replace your unit with a refurb unit.

Buying Extended Warranties

Buy a camera, and the vendor usually asks if you wish to purchase a 1- to 3-year extended warranty that kicks in once your original factory warranty ends. The price may be steep, however — as much as 10 percent of the value of your camera every year. We're of two minds about whether or not it makes good economical sense to buy an extended warranty. On one hand, they're probably the most profitable item an electronics or camera store sells, since relatively few buyers ever have occasion to use them. On the other, we've had extended warranties for major appliances, such as our washer, dryer, and refrigerator, that have saved us hundreds when those items malfunctioned. So, while the wise consumer in us says no, pass up extended warranties, the experienced user says yes, you'll count your blessings if you ever have a problem and had the foresight to buy that extra insurance.

Of course, an extended warranty assumes that you intend to keep and use your DSLR for years to come. Today's DSLRs are definite keepers — cameras that will continue to capture great photos for years. But are you the kind of person who needs the hottest, newest model, or are you content when something works well for you? Factor your answer to that question into your decision about whether or not an extended warranty makes sense for you.

Out-of-Warranty Repair

If your camera is out of warranty, you're free to have anyone repair it. But the best place is probably the manufacturer. After all, they know the product best and getting spare parts won't be a problem. The other alternative is to take or send it to a company that repairs digital cameras, lenses, and other photographic items. Some are authorized repair stations, while others are not officially affiliated with a particular camera company. We have had good and not-so-good experiences with both types, so we won't offer any opinion as to which is better. You can start by searching the Internet for a local contact. We suggest checking out `www.acecam.com/srindex.html` for a state-by-state list of repair stations. Or you might want to send your camera to a national repair station, such as `www.keh.com`. There are scores listed on the Internet. Also, check the photography chat sites (you can find a partial list in Appendix A) for repairpeople that fellow photographers would recommend.

Tip

Don't throw away that original packing. We always keep the shipping material and boxes of our camera and computer purchases for at least as long as the warranty lasts. Should we find it necessary to return an item for any reason, it will have the same sort of protection that the manufacturer or vendor gave it when it was shipped or sold to you.

Insurance

Digital cameras are valuable items, and their loss or damage can represent a significant financial hit. So, like other major and important investment in your life — car, house, antiques, your continuing good health — they should be insured. Actually, if you have a homeowner's or apartment renter's policy and are *not* a professional photographer (that is, you don't make money from your shots), you may already be covered. Many policies include riders that cover electronic goodies and photographic equipment, not only in the home or apartment but also outside, in your car, while traveling, and so on. There are usually caveats and restrictions (such as not being covered in a parked car that isn't in an attended parking lot) and deductibles ($50–$250, depending upon your policy), so check with your agent before assuming that you are protected. And check whether your camera equipment is covered against breakage; alas, many policies insure against loss or theft only. If your policy specifically excludes photographic equipment, check with your agent anyway. For an extra premium, you may be able to buy what is known as an "all risk" floater from your regular insurance company.

Tip

Keep up-to-date records. To protect yourself if you should ever have to file a claim, keep detailed information about your equipment handy: the official name and model numbers of the items, date and place purchased, amount paid, serial numbers, and so on. Make certain that you put that information away someplace safe, not in your camera bag. So, if you ever have a loss, you'll be able to quickly provide the adjustor with that information.

For a non-pro, the cost of covering your equipment should range between $1.15 and $1.80 per $100 coverage, depending upon the company insuring you, the size of the deductible, if you live in the city or country, and what, if anything, is excluded.

If you are a pro or semi-pro, you'll need to purchase commercial camera insurance. Actually, it's known as a commercial inland marine policy, and besides covering your equipment, it adds liability insurance against claims due to your efforts or negligence. For instance, if someone trips over your light stand and breaks his leg, you'll be covered. Commercial inland marine insurance costs approximately $1.75 and $2.35 per $100 of coverage.

When buying camera insurance, make certain that you are covered for replacement value and not fair market value. Digital cameras have high depreciations (they very quickly become worth much less than you paid for them), so losing your $1,500 DSLR may yield a check for only $300 or $400, after the deductible and depreciation are factored in. Replacement insurance means that the company will replace your equipment with the same equipment or something comparable.

Tip

Register that camera. Going abroad, and taking your new DSLR and lots of accessories? You will need proof that you purchased your equipment within the United States to bring them back in without having to pay duty to U.S. Customs. A valid sales slip constitutes proof or you might want to obtain a copy of CBP Form 4457, U.S. Customs' Certificate of Registration. We keep our Certificates of Registration along with our passports (they're small, so you may need more than one for all your camera equipment, plus your laptop, iPod, and so on.), as well as photocopies in our camera case. That's just in case they got lost. Otherwise, you may end up paying mucho bucks to get them out of the airport and will have to jump through hoops to get the money refunded when you later provide proof of purchase in the United States.

Appendix D

Buying Tips

While this book is not a DSLR buyer's guide, you may find the following information valuable when considering what model to buy and where to buy it. We also discuss the pros and cons of renting equipment, as well as how to get on your manufacturer's "pro team" for preferential service and other advantages.

Rentals

Unless you are a pro, it doesn't make good economic sense to rent a digital camera, lens, or accessory. The price is quite steep; 2 week's rental usually costs as much as buying a new body or lens. You also must pick up and drop off the equipment, or pay to have it shipped both ways. A pro can always pass the cost onto the client, whereas the non-pro will have to pay it out of pocket.

However, there is a case that can be made for renting a piece of equipment before you buy: it could save you from a very expensive mistake. If, for instance, you are thinking of getting a Nikon D200 but have no experience with Nikon cameras, renting it for a day or two may make good economic and practical sense. That time will allow you to quickly learn the camera, take lots of test shots, and view or print out the results. You can't get that kind of experience handling a camera in a store or joining a photography chat room.

Many full-service photo stores that sell DSLRs also have a rental department. What's more, some firms will apply the rental against the sales price should you decide to purchase that model camera or lens from them after the rental period is up. Check the Web for companies that rent DSLRs in your area, or check out a national firm, such as Alkit (`www.alkit.com`) or Prorental (`www.prorental.com`).

Camera and Equipment Sales Leads

There are many thousands of stores, shops, and Internet sites that sell digital cameras and photographic equipment. Most are good, reliable establishments and Web sites, and most can deliver the items you want at competitive prices. A few minutes with Google or any other search engine can turn up links to companies that have the equipment you are seeking. Of course, there are many search engines that will automatically rank Web sites that sell what you want, according to price. While we're not about to tell you where to buy your equipment, we have briefly profiled a few companies we've been dealing with for some time.

B&H Photo

The largest photo store in the world, B&H Photo (www.bhphoto.com) is the photographic mecca for every serious photographer in or near the New York City area. Its Manhattan location is a huge, high volume, pressure cooker of a megastore, with lines at the checkout counter. More than likely, they'll have the item you're looking for in stock, new or used, and at a very competitive price. As large as their store is, it's only the tip of the iceberg, since most of their business is done via mail order, telephone, or the Internet. Only, because it's owned and operated by Hasidim — ultra-orthodox Jews — no business is conducted on the Sabbath (Saturday) or Jewish holidays.

eBay

Much of our studio equipment — strobelights, light stands, tripods, camera stands, soft boxes, copy stands, backdrop systems — were purchased on eBay (www.ebay.com). Some were bought new, from eBay stores at fixed prices, while others were used, won through offering the highest bid. eBay isn't for everyone; you have to know what you want, be willing to forego personal interaction, and accept the minor risk that what you bought wasn't exactly what you thought it would be. But it's a great way to get affordable equipment, especially hard-to-find items.

eCost

Yes, it's annoying getting those twice-daily email ads from eCost (www.ecost.com), offering a plethora of electronic goodies and other consumer items at closeout costs. But eCost happens to offer some of the best buys on memory cards we've seen on the Web, some even for free after rebate. And sometimes, even the shipping is free.

Samy's

The West Coast equivalent of B&H, Samy's (www.Samys.com) is a full-service retail and commercial outfit with five stores located in and around Los Angeles. Known the world over for its extremely knowledgeable staff and ability to cater to almost every professional photographer need and whim, Samy's sells and rents almost everything related to digital cameras and photography. It also sponsors regular in-store seminars and demonstrations, publishes several newsletters, and hosts a variety of forums and bulletin boards. If you're a photographer living in the area, Samy's is the first, best, and probably only place you'll want to go to for all your needs. If you live elsewhere, its online services are first rate and its prices reasonable.

TigerDirect

While you can buy digital cameras and peripherals from them, TigerDirect (www.tigerdirect.com) is the Internet company from which we buy much of our computer equipment — PCs, hard drives, memory chips, graphics boards, cables, and almost everything else to keep our computer network up to date and trouble-free. If you're a pro, open a business account and you'll not only get extra discounts and preferential service, but you'll also get a real live, technical-savvy sales rep to assist you over the phone.

Join Your Camera Manufacturer's "Pro" Team

Are you a pro, making money on your photography? If so, you may be eligible to join your camera manufacturer's program for professionals. Members get preferential treatment, such as fast turnaround on repairs and even free loaner units and other equipment. Nikon, Canon, and Olympus have had pro programs for many years, but they're unadvertised, and they don't go out of their way to even admit it exists — if you don't know about it, obviously, you're not qualified to join. (In fact, we have met employees of the camera companies who didn't even know about the service.) You can check those manufacturers' Web sites, and if you're lucky, you'll stumble onto the page that lists the eligibility requirements and provides a fill-in-the-blanks application. Or, you might simply call or email them to ask about their respective pro programs. Another source is to ask other pros who shoot the same cameras you do. We first learned of them at ASMP meetings. (See Appendix B, regarding ASMP.)

Of course, given the harsh realities of the economy, these programs may be among the services that may be discontinued by manufacturers.

Appendix E

Glossary

8-bit A measure of the amount of data used to define a color, a photo, or a photo file. Essentially, 8 bits consist of 256 different levels of information. Traditional greyscale photographs are 8-bit, which means they have 256 steps from pure black through the greys to white. If a color photo is 8-bit (as opposed to 24-bit), it will not be photo-realistic because it doesn't have enough information to produce photo-quality smooth transitions. Such a color photo is often referred to as posterized. However, in 24-bit RGB photo-realistic pictures, each color channel (red, green, and blue) has 8 bits of data. Therefore, such 24-bit photo files are sometimes referred to, in a confusing turn of phrase, as 8-bit files, when you are working in photo-editing programs and especially in RAW processors.

16-bit This refers to an enlarged TIFF file that contains extra color data, consisting of 16 bits per color channel. This provides a greater amount of picture information from which to edit a photo for potentially higher image quality. To use many image-editing commands, output to the Web, and print the picture, you will first have to convert it to an 8-bit file, consisting of 8 bits per channel

24-bit color Also called photo-realistic color, it's when an image has 8 bits of data, or 256 different shades, for each of the primary colors of red, green, and blue. That creates a palette of 16.7 million colors.

ADC Short for analog-to-digital converter, it's the chip(s) in every digital camera that translates the electronic analog signal from the image sensor to digital data that can be used to create a digital image.

Additive color A color model in which light is directly transmitted or emitted, and the primary colors red, green, and blue are used to make up all other colors. The absence of color is black.

Aperture Measured in *f*-stops, aperture is the size of the diaphragm opening in a lens that lets light pass through to the image sensor. The aperture is used to control the amount of light that passes through the lens to the image sensor, as well as to regulate depth-of-field.

Archivability A photographic print that will last at least 25 years without the colors shifting or fading is said to be of archival quality. How long it will last is called its archivability. Some paper-and-ink combinations can last (when stored and viewed under ideal conditions) for over a century.

Aspect ratio The relationship of the height of a photo and its length. A picture with a height of 4" and a length of 6" has an aspect ratio of 2:3. It's sometimes also used to describe the dimensions of an image sensor.

Batch processing By setting up a software macro or invoking a program command, batch processing enables multiple tasks to be performed automatically on any number of files or images. For instance, batch processing can automatically enable instant renaming of several or many files with a single mouse click.

Bitmapped All digital photographs are composed on hundreds of thousands or millions of computer bits, called pixels (picture elements), each of which is defined by its color and position. In other words, each bit is precisely positioned, or mapped, in such a way that collectively, they make up a recognizable image. The opposite of bitmapped is the vector image, which is defined by mathematical formula. In other words, all photos are bitmapped; all illustrations and drawings are vectors. However, each type of picture can have elements of the other type embedded into it.

CCD Short for charge-coupled device, a CCD is a type of image sensor used in most consumer digital cameras and many DSLRs.

Clipping When an image sensor is unable to record bright highlights, midtones, or dark shadows, the part that is not captured is said to be clipped. You can easily see whether an image exhibits clipping by looking at its histogram and seeing where the data ends on the scale.

CMOS Short for complementary metal-oxide semiconductor, CMOS is a type of image sensor used in some DSLRs at the high end and inexpensive consumer digital cameras at the low end.

CMYK Short for cyan/magenta/yellow/black (the *K* is used rather than the *B*, so it's not confused with blue), CMYK is the subtractive color model used for professional printers and printing presses. In it, the primary colors cyan, magenta, yellow, and black are combined to create all colors, including black. The absence of color is white. All digital cameras, computer monitors, and most desktop printers use the opposite color model — RGB (red, green, blue) — in which a combination of all colors is white, and the absence of color is black.

Color management Color management is a series of processes and procedures that ensure consistent, reliable, and accurate colors throughout the imaging chain, from camera or scanner to the computer monitor and printer.

Compression Image files can be large, sometimes too large, especially if they are to be posted or transmitted over the Web. To make file size more manageable — to squeeze those bits and bytes down in size — a software scheme called compression is applied to the file. The most commonly used compression type related to images is JPEG. Compression works well to reduce overall file size, but it also reduces overall image quality — the more an image is compressed, the more its quality degrades.

Constrain proportions This refers to maintaining the aspect ratio of a print. When you change either the width or height dimension, the other will automatically change as well, so the picture won't change proportions or aspect ratio.

Digital asset management system As relates to digital images, a digital asset management system, or DAMS for short, is software that keeps track of all image information and attributes, such as when and how a photograph was taken, the file format, who owns the copyright, where it is stored, how it was used, and so on. All this information is also searchable, making it easier to find specific pictures. A photo management program is a DAMS.

DNG Short for Digital Negative, DNG is Adobe's attempt to standardize the RAW file format. Camera manufacturers' RAW file formats can be converted into DNG, which retains all the unprocessed information taken by a digital camera, but in a file format that supposedly will be supported by major software for many years to come.

Down sampled The act of reducing the resolution or dynamic range of an image or video clip so that its file size and display are smaller, and thereby, manageable and practical for certain uses. Also called sampling.

dpi Short for dots per inch, dpi is the term used to describe print resolution.

EV *See* exposure compensation.

EXIF Short for Exchangeable Image File Format, EXIF is the hidden metadata file attached to digital photographs that lists when it was taken, *f*-stop, shutter speed, lens focal length, whether flash was used, color model used, and so forth.

Exposure compensation The act of adjusting the camera to lighten or darken every photograph taken, regardless of the *f*-stop or shutter speed. It's used when a photographer prefers the images to be intentionally under- or overexposed, for effect, or to compensate for a camera's propensity to capture images slightly lighter or darker than preferred. Also known as EV, for exposure value.

Focal length The distance from the center of the lens to the film or image sensor plane when focused at infinity, focal length determines how much of a scene a lens can capture. Telephoto lenses have long focal lengths, while wide angle lenses have short focal lengths.

***f*-stop** The universal measurement of the amount of light passing through a lens. A lens is said to be high speed if its maximum *f*-stop is *f*2.8 or less. The *f*-stop is also how much the diaphragm inside the lens (the aperture) is opened or closed (stopped down), either to regulate exposure or to control depth-of-field.

Full-size image sensor An image sensor that is the same size as a frame of 35mm film. That is, which measures 24×36mm and has a diagonal of 43.3mmn. When a DSLR uses a full-size sensor, there is no magnification factor in the effective coverage of a lens' focal length.

Gamut The range of every possible color that a digital camera, printer, computer monitor, scanner, or other device is capable of capturing or reproducing. If a color can't be reproduced, it's said to be out of gamut.

Gradient The transition from one color or shade to another. 24-bit, or photo-realistic color, should exhibit a smooth, seamless gradient.

Histogram A graphic representation of the statistical analysis of where the pixels in an image lie—how many are in the shadows, midtones, and highlights. All DSLRs can display a histogram of captured images in playback, to determine how good or bad the photographer's exposure and lighting were. Histograms are also useful software tools.

HSB Short for hue/saturation/brightness, HSB is a color model that is seldom used for digital photos. However, it is also the name of an adjustment tool in some image-editing programs, which gives you individual control over those three aspects of a picture.

Image sensor A photosensitive semiconductor chip that captures visual data. It's the heart of every digital camera and camcorder and is roughly the electronic equivalent of film.

Interpolate The opposite of down sampling, interpolation is the process of creating additional image data within a picture. It's used to pump up the amount of data in an image so that it can be printed or displayed larger. Though the file becomes larger, image quality is not improved by interpolation, and it can be degraded.

IPTC Metadata that conforms to standards set by the International Press Telecommunications Council. These can include headlines, captions, copyright notice, location, specific codes for subject and scene, and so forth. If you work with a newspaper, it may require that the IPTC fields be filled out in certain ways to make it easier to slot your pictures into their databases.

ISO equivalent ISO (International Organization for Standardization) is used in conventional photography to describe film speed, or sensitivity to light. In digital photography, an image sensor's sensitivity to light is measured using similar units, but they are properly called ISO equivalency. ISO equivalency is usually shortened to ISO in most discussions of digital cameras.

JPEG Short for Joint Photographic Experts Group, JPEG is a file format used in almost all digital cameras that compresses data as it saves it. It's a universal file format that can be read by almost every device and is used extensively for sending or posting pictures over the Internet.

Keyword In image databases and digital asset management system software, a keyword is a searchable identifier (such as a name, place, or characteristic of a photo) that the user can create and associate with the image, so the picture can be catalogued, archived, and retrieved more efficiently.

L*A*B Officially known as CIELAB (for Commission Internationale d'Eclairage), or simply LAB for short, it's a color model that most closely represents the wide gamut of colors that humans can perceive. *L* stands for luminance; *A* is a continuum of colors along the red-green axis; *B* covers the blue-yellow axis. It's much less used than RGB and CMYK in digital photography, except internally, within the hidden code of image-processing programs.

Landscape orientation Any picture shot or displayed that is wider than it is tall is said to be in the landscape mode or orientation.

Live histogram Because the image sensor is continuously exposed to the lens on non-DSLR digital cameras, it's possible to display a real-time histogram of the subject in the LCD viewfinder, while you are framing up your shot. This isn't possible on most DSLRs because the image sensor is exposed only at the instant of exposure. You won't see the histogram until the image is captured, on playback.

Lossy and lossless compression Compression in a file format reduces the size of the file, but usually, it also diminishes overall image quality. That's because some or much of the data is thrown away when the image is compressed and stored and recreated when the image is opened up. Any compression scheme that throws away data is said to be lossy compression. However, a few compression schemes shrink file size without throwing away data. When that occurs, it's said to be lossless compression. JPEG is the best-known type of lossy compression.

Metadata The data detailing information about the conditions under which any photograph was taken, such as the time and date, *f*-stop and shutter speed, lens focal length and flash setting, and so forth. Types of metadata include EXIF and IPTC. Metadata is permanently attached to every photo file. Portions of it can be read in playback on your DSLR. More extensive metadata is viewable in software, including photo management programs, RAW converters, and photo-editing software. In addition, you can add to the metadata, such as information about your copyright, descriptions of the image, the client for whom it was shot, and so forth.

Multiplication factor Most DSLR image sensors are physically smaller than a frame of 35mm film, so the lenses they need to cover the entire image sensor needs to be correspondingly smaller. Therefore, most image sensors have a diminished field of view when coupled with traditional 35mm lenses. In other words, a 50mm lens that was designed for a 35mm film camera may capture less than a true 50mm frame when put onto a Digital SLR. The diminished field of view that a lens covers on an image sensor is called the multiplication factor (sometimes referred to as the magnification factor) and is usually expressed as a multiple of the baseline of 1.0 (such as a multiplication factor of 1.3X).

Noise Also called gain, noise is the unwanted effect of increasing the photosensitivity of an image sensor (also known as boosting the ISO) or of electrical interference by any of a digital camera's components. It is manifested by random patterns of unwanted pixels that look like snow, dust, or the grain on a high-speed silver halide film negative.

Open up the lens Whenever a photographer enlarges the lens *f*-stop to affect exposure or decrease depth-of-field, she is said to be opening up the lens. The opposite is stopping down the lens.

Optical resolution The true resolution of an image sensor or image file, without interpolation. Many consumer digital cameras (and scanners) feature digital resolution, which is a scheme to enhance a portion of the image, to make it appear larger. Optical resolution typically yields superior image quality as compared to digital resolution.

Out of gamut Any colors that cannot be captured or reproduced by a digital camera, computer monitor, printer, or other display or output device are said to be out of gamut.

Oversharpening The act of applying too much sharpening to a picture so that it appears that the edges are too dramatic and pronounced, unreal and unappealing. Oversharpening also tends to increase image noise.

Pentaprism A pentagon-shaped glass prism inside most DSLRs that inverts and reverses the image sent through the lens and passed through to the optical mirror in front of the shutter. It's what allows eye-level through-the-lens viewing. It's what's under the hump on the top of most DSLRs.

Photo management program Software that allows users to import, view, organize, index, save, and retrieve images, sensibly and quickly. It's a type of digital asset management (DAM) program.

Polarizing filter Light has polarity, or direction. Light from any typical source is diffused, coming on different planes. A polarizing filter removes some or most of the diffuse rays, limiting the light that passes through it to a single or few planes. Polarizing filters consist of two pieces of polarized glass sandwiched together, and as one is manually rotated while the other remains stationary, the filter can reduce reflection and glare, as well as darken a blue sky or ocean.

Porro-mirror A configuration of several fixed mirrors inside a camera that inverts and reverses the image sent through the lens and passed through to the optical mirror in front of the shutter. It's what allows eye-level through-the-lens viewing. It serves the same function as a pentaprism, but the image seen may not be as bright. A DSLR camera with a porro-mirror does not need to have the hump on the top, but some manufacturers retain it for a traditional appearance.

Portrait orientation Any picture shot or displayed that is taller than it is wide is said to be in the portrait mode or orientation.

Posterized When color is displayed at less than photo-realistic, or 24-bit, the transitions or gradients between different colors or shades may not appear natural, but abrupt and unrealistic. When the transition from one color or shade to another is dramatically apparent with few or no transitional gradients, it is said to be posterized.

ppi Short for pixels per inch, ppi is the measurement used in describing computer monitor resolution. While not exactly accurate, it's also commonly used for printing and is virtually interchangeable with the more widely used dpi.

PSD Photoshop's proprietary file format, which saves all the editing data in an image file, including layers and adjustment layers.

RAW A type of proprietary file format in advanced digital cameras that saves all captured image data unprocessed. It must later be processed in the computer, using that camera manufacturer's software or a third-party software that reads that particular file format. It's the preferred file format for shooting highest-quality images. Unfortunately, each manufacturer has its own RAW file format, often different ones for different camera models.

Reflective color When the viewer looks at something that requires light to be shone on it, such as a photographic print, it is said to have reflected colors. The opposite is transmissive (or emissive) color, when light is sent directly to the viewer's eye, for example from a computer monitor.

Resize Resizing is changing the file size of a picture. It's a command that we often recommend using to ensure that the file contains the right amount of data for an optimum-quality print or for displaying on the Web.

RGB Short for red/blue/green, it's the additive color model used for defining digital images by digital cameras, scanners, computer monitors, and most desktop printers.

Sharpening In the camera or using image-editing software, sharpening is the process of enhancing and emphasizing the edges of the subject in your pictures so that it has the appearance of being sharper.

Stop down the lens Whenever a photographer reduces the lens *f*-stop, to affect exposure or increase depth-of-field, she is said to be stopping down the lens. The opposite is opening up the lens.

Subtractive color A reflective color model whose primary colors are cyan, magenta, yellow, and black (CMYK), which can be mixed together to make all other colors, including black. In this model, the absence of color is white. In photography, it is used principally for professional printing.

Tethered Tethering involves attaching a digital camera to a computer or power source. Usually, a tethered camera is positioned on a tripod and used in a studio situation. Any digital camera that is shot and handled independently of a power source or computer link is said to be untethered.

TIFF Short for Tagged Image File Format, TIFF is an uncompressed, high-quality image file that can be universally read, written to, or displayed by almost every device. Because it is slow and takes up an inordinate amount of file space, most DSLRs have replaced the ability to save images in a TIFF file format with that of the more efficient, high-quality RAW file format.

Transmissive color When light is conveyed directly to the viewer's eye, for example from a computer monitor or a video projector, it is said to have transmissive colors. The opposite is reflected colors, when the viewer looks at something that requires light to be shone on it, such as a photographic print. Purists say that monitors have emissive color.

TTL, or through-the-lens An ingenious combination of mechanical and optical components in DSLRs that allows the photographer to preview the subject through the same lens used to take the photograph. Similarly, a TTL strobe takes its readings of the scene through the lens for greater precision in controlling the length and the amount of the flash.

Unsharpen Although the definition may sound counterintuitive, unsharpening is really a software mask that attempts to sharpen soft or blurred edges.

Vector A vector image is a drawing or illustration defined by mathematical formulae. It's the opposite of a photographic image, which is defined by bitmapped pixels.

XMP Adobe's Extensible Metadata Platform, which is used to organize and store data in Adobe Bridge, Photoshop, and the rest of Creative Suite.

Index

B

C

continued

D

G

H

I

J

K

L

continued

N

O

P

Q

R

S

T

Your Subscription to PC Magazine *is Waiting...*

Congratulations! Your purchase of this book entitles you to a special introductory offer for a one-year subscription (25 issues) to *PC Magazine* — just $1 per issue! Starting your subscription is easy. Simply log on to **http://bookoffer.pcmag.com** or call **(800) 289-0429 x4CAN8**. Then we can start sending *PC Magazine* straight to your mailbox!*

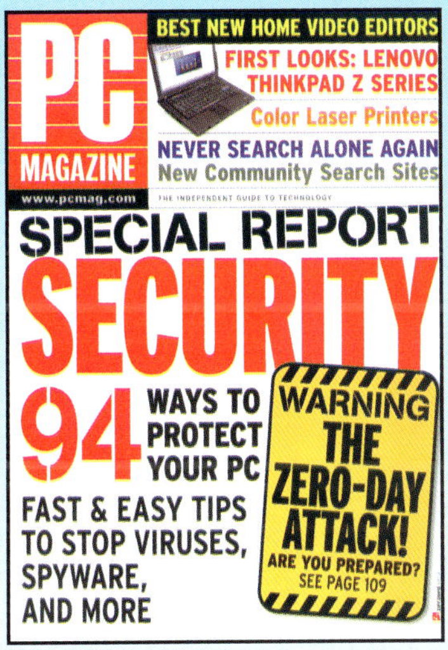

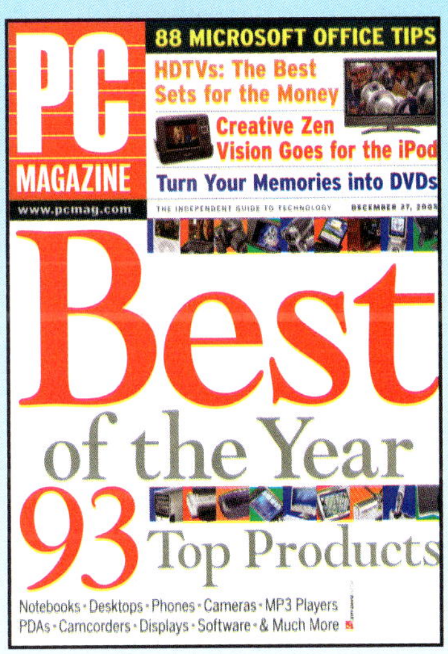

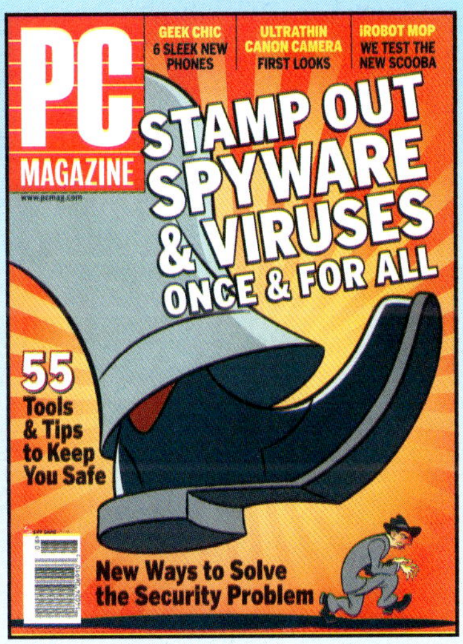

PC Magazine is the most reliable source for first-rate features and exclusive looks at the latest tech products and services, real world solutions and expert tips and insight. As "The Independent Guide to Technology", it consistently produces content relevant to the serious technology professional.

SUBSCRIBE TODAY!

Log on to **http://bookoffer.pcmag.com** or call **(800) 289-0429 x4CAN8.**

*Offer valid only in the United States

PC Magazine is published bi-weekly, except for occasional extra, special, combined or expanded issues. Allow 3-6 weeks for delivery. Satisfaction guaranteed — If you no longer wish to subscribe you may cancel your subscription at any time and receive a full refund for all un-mailed issues.